T0321315

WHEN THE WORLD CLOSED
ITS DOORS

A Council on Foreign Relations Book

The mission of the Council on Foreign Relations is to inform U.S. engagement with the world. Founded in 1921, CFR is a nonpartisan, independent national membership organization, think tank, educator, and publisher, including of *Foreign Affairs*. It generates policy-relevant ideas and analysis, convenes experts and policymakers, and promotes informed public discussion—all to have impact on the most consequential issues facing the United States and the world.

The Council on Foreign Relations takes no institutional positions on policy issues and has no affiliation with the U.S. government. All views expressed in its publications and on its website are the sole responsibility of the author or authors.

WHEN THE WORLD CLOSED ITS DOORS

THE COVID-19 TRAGEDY AND THE FUTURE OF BORDERS

EDWARD ALDEN

AND

LAURIE TRAUTMAN

A COUNCIL ON FOREIGN RELATIONS BOOK

OXFORD
UNIVERSITY PRESS

Oxford University Press is a department of the University of Oxford.
It furthers the University's objective of excellence in research, scholarship,
and education by publishing worldwide. Oxford is a registered trade mark of
Oxford University Press in the UK and certain other countries.

Published in the United States of America by Oxford University Press
198 Madison Avenue, New York, NY 10016, United States of America.

Library of Congress Cataloging-in-Publication Data
Names: Alden, Edward H. author. | Trautman, Laurie, author.
Title: When the world closed its doors : the covid-19 tragedy and the
future of borders / by Edward Alden, Laurie Trautman.
Description: New York, NY : Oxford University Press, 2025. |
Includes bibliographical references and index.
Identifiers: LCCN 2024028606 (print) | LCCN 2024028607 (ebook) |
ISBN 9780197697818 (hardback) | ISBN 9780197697825 (epub)
Subjects: LCSH: Border security. | Travel restrictions. | Travel—Health aspects. |
Covid-19 Pandemic, 2020—Political aspects.
Classification: LCC JV6035 .A498 2025 (print) | LCC JV6035 (ebook) |
DDC 325.09/052—dc23/eng/20240824
LC record available at https://lccn.loc.gov/2024028606
LC ebook record available at https://lccn.loc.gov/2024028607

DOI: 10.1093/oso/9780197697818.001.0001

Printed by Sheridan Books, Inc., United States of America

Contents

Acknowledgments

This book came out of two sets of experiences. One of the authors, Ted Alden, moved to Bellingham, Washington, in 2019 in part to be close to his family across the border in Vancouver, BC. The border closure between Canada and the United States in March 2020 cut both him and his Canadian wife, Fiona James, off from their parents, their siblings, their daughter, and other family members. Peace Arch Park became a lifeline—Ted would meet his Mum and stepdad there almost every month, and other family members would regularly join as well. A columnist for *Foreign Policy*, Ted wrote a series of pieces in the magazine and in Canadian media about the deleterious impacts of the closures, not just in North America but more broadly. Laurie Trautman, director of the Border Policy Research Institute (BPRI) at Western Washington University (WWU), was engaged in analyzing the economic and social impacts of the closed border, and working with local and national officials in both Canada and the United States, trying to minimize the negative impacts of the shutdown. As the border restrictions dragged on, she received countless emails from residents and business owners who shared their frustrations and their pain. She wrote and coordinated a series of BPRI publications that analyzed the economic, social, and personal impacts of the border closure.

The two of us would meet regularly to talk about the border, especially about the ways in which the concerns of those living cross-border lives—like the residents of tiny Point Roberts, Washington—were being ignored by national governments. It became increasingly clear to both of us that the border issues were not just local in our region, or even national, but truly global in their scale and impacts. In the fall of 2020, sipping coffee outside less than 30 miles from the border, we realized that someone needed to write a book capturing all of this. We nominated ourselves.

Living next to an international border, both authors of this book were personally and professionally impacted by the Covid border restrictions, and over the course of our research, travels, and interviews we became even more aware of the millions of people across the world facing similar separations. First and foremost, we would like to acknowledge all the people who shared their experiences, their expertise, and their knowledge with us during the research and writing of this book. In particular, thanks to Marty Cetron, Jean Peyrony, Martin Guillermo-Ramirez, Alberto Giacometti, Tudor Clee, David Edward Ooi-Poon, and all our interviewees. The Covid-19 pandemic was a stressful time for everyone, and we are grateful for those who were willing to share their time to speak with us about it. Our goal in writing this book is to carry these stories forward and put them in a larger context so the lessons we have learned are not lost, but rather can help to inform the ways in which such hardships may be avoided or alleviated in the future.

This book could not have been written without the efforts of a wonderfully talented group of research assistants at Western Washington University, Harvard University, and the Council on Foreign Relations. Thanks to Jennifer Bettis, Joyce Chen, Erin Dahlman-Oeth, Bryndis Danke, Skylar Magee, Cameron McKenzie, Dan Selden, and Tess Turner.

We were fortunate to have superb feedback from colleagues and friends who read portions of the manuscript. We are indebted to Thomas Bollyky, Max Boot, Esther Brimmer, Shi-Fen Chen, Steven Cook, Laura Dawson, Liana Fix, Wing Fok, Michelle Gavin, Alberto Giacometti, Yangzhong Huang, Miles Kahler, Stephen Kelly, Scott Klimo, Jiexun Li, Sebastian Mallaby, Stephen Olson, and Gideon Rose. Luciana Borio provided important insights and helped set up interviews with public health officials. We also appreciate the robust feedback on the original proposal from two anonymous reviewers for Oxford University Press. They provided many excellent insights that set the project off in a fruitful direction. We also benefited greatly from readings of the complete manuscript by Meghan Benton, Michael Froman, Lawrence Huang, James Lindsay, and Shannon O'Neil, as well as two other anonymous Oxford reviewers.

An extra thanks as well to Ms. Benton and the Migration Policy Institute for including us during the pandemic in a series of off-the-record discussions with policymakers from many countries who were involved in implementing and analyzing the impacts of travel restrictions during Covid. Ted Alden would also like to offer a special thanks to Stefan Thiel, deputy editor at *Foreign Policy*, whose early guidance was invaluable in shaping the ideas in this book. And a special note of appreciation for the generous support over fifteen years from Bernard Schwartz, who passed away in 2024 at the age of ninety-eight after a life of public-spirited engagement. Mr. Alden's work at CFR would not have been possible without his unflagging support and encouragement. This book was supported in part by funds from the Bernard and Irene Schwartz Foundation.

We'd also like to thank all of our colleagues and friends at WWU, including the mentorship and vision of Don Alper, who established the BPRI nearly twenty years ago, as well as those who continue to support that work. Ilhyung Kim generously organized a colloquium in the College of Business and Economics to discuss the book. In addition, this project benefited from a global network of border scholars and practitioners supported by the Association for Borderland Studies and the Borders in Globalization project at the University of Victoria. Laurie Trautman is grateful to her husband and daughter for accommodating her time away from them, and her mother Jean, who has led a cross-border life that continues to inspire her.

Finally, many thanks to Patricia Dorff, CFR's managing director of publications, to Oxford University Press, and to our editors David McBride and Emily Benitez for ushering this book to publication.

I

The "Summer of Love"

For the thousands who came to Peace Arch Park in the summer of 2020 as the Covid-19 virus was spreading across the world, it would come to be known as the "Summer of Love." Located roughly halfway between the Canadian city of Vancouver, British Columbia, and the US town of Bellingham, Washington, the Peace Arch was constructed in 1921 to celebrate the signing of the Treaty of Ghent, which ended the War of 1812, the last war between the United States and Great Britain. The white marble arch sits on the 49th parallel, agreed by the two nations in the 1846 Oregon Treaty as the dividing line between American and British possessions in North America. Canada and the United States proudly call this line "the world's longest un- defended border." Some sixty-seven feet high, the Peace Arch flies the flags of both nations. On the US side, a large inscription across the top of the arch reads: "Brethren Dwelling Together in Unity"; on the Canadian side, it reads "Children of a Common Mother," a reference to the settlers from Europe who populated both countries. On its interior wall is a boldly inked promise: "May These Gates Never Be Closed." Since the 1930s, both countries have maintained conjoining cross-border public parks, which allow visitors to mingle freely across the 49th parallel without formally crossing the border. On a typical sunny summer weekend before the pandemic, a smattering of families and picnickers would meet in the two parks, which were separated only by the normally long car lines of shoppers and vacationers moving back and forth across the border.

Then on March 21, 2020, for the first time in the history of the two coun- tries, the gates were closed. Faced with the worsening spread of the deadly virus, the governments of the United States and Canada issued a joint announce- ment: the land borders between the two countries would be shut to all "non- essential" travel. While trade and the movement of some essential personnel like hospital workers would be permitted to continue, for all other purposes the border would be closed.

Except, as it turned out, for Peace Arch Park. The ambiguous legal status of the park—physically straddling US and Canadian territory but long freely open to visitors from both sides—made it the sole breach along the entire 5,500 miles of the border. At first gradually, and then in ever larger numbers, families, couples, and friends separated by the border began to discover the park as a meeting place. Where a typical pre-pandemic day would see maybe fifty people scattered around both sides of the park, as the days warmed from spring to summer in 2020, as many as 1,000 people would meet there each day. Most were families and couples living in Washington State or British Columbia, in close driving distance of the border. But as word spread, people started to arrive from all across both countries. "I've had people drive from Montana, Texas, Arizona. I mean, all over," said Rick Blank, the Washington State park ranger who patrolled Peace Arch.[1] Christina Winkler, president of the nonprofit International Peace Arch Association, said she met people "from as far away from Florida who have flown in just to meet their family in the park" (Figure 1.1).[2]

Many of the visitors were couples separated by the border. Canada and the United States permitted married couples to reunite—with a two-week quarantine required for those entering Canada—but unmarried couples that summer enjoyed no special exemptions. For those who had built the most intimate parts of their lives across borders, confident they could always move back and forth freely, the shutdown was devastating. A young British Columbia woman discovered three months after the border closure that she was pregnant by her Washington State boyfriend; several months later she miscarried, and her boyfriend pleaded with Canadian border officials to be permitted to join her in Canada. He was told such a trip was not "essential" and warned he could be banned from Canada for a year if he returned to the border seeking admission. Another woman in Washington State had a partner of four years who lived across the border in Canada; when they were separated by the border closure, she says, it "killed my mental health in a way I never could have imagined."[3]

For those who could get there, the park was a lifeline. Chris Irlam and Dana Johnson met online in February 2020, hopeful they could make a relationship work even though one lived in northern Idaho and the other in Chilliwack, British Columbia. But with the border closed a month later, the only place they could meet was in the park. They spent three days there in June, mostly on

Figure 1.1 Christina Winkler, founder of the Peace Arch Park Association, in the "Summer of Love" shirt she designed. Photograph courtesy of the authors.

the Canadian side of the park, and from then on met every month on the US side, camping out for three or four days, weathering sunburns, wind and rain storms, long lines at the park's only bathroom, and ever colder temperatures as the summer of 2020 ebbed to fall and winter.[4] On top of this was what

Irlam says was the shaming from close friends for "circumventing" BC health rules that discouraged nonessential travel, even though by May 2020 the provincial government had reopened parks and was permitting small gatherings to resume within the province. The US rangers allowed couples like Chris and Dana to set up tents on the US side of Peace Arch Park, prompting quips that the park had been separated into "adult" and "family" sections. The tents had to come down at dark, though, and couples would return to their respective sides of the border, staying in nearby campgrounds, motels, or Airbnbs. Ranger Rick roamed the park throughout the year, encouraging families to maintain a safe distance and to wear masks in the bathrooms. On a sunny summer weekend, the park was filled with happy families, children playing, and other bits of normal life.

Canada closed its side of the park in June 2020, citing concerns over the high number of US Covid cases and traffic congestion at the Canadian entrance to the Peace Arch parking lot that was spilling out onto land controlled by the Semiahmoo First Nation. Some Canadian officials urged the United States to do the same, but Washington governor Jay Inslee kept his side of the park open throughout the remainder of the pandemic.[5] Over time, Canadian police who patrolled the shallow ditch that separated the southernmost homes along Zero Avenue in Surrey, BC, from the US side of the park became stricter, demanding passports or other official documents from Canadians returning home and checking bags for any US goods that might have been passed along by friends or family in the park. But except for a brief period in late March and April 2020 when Washington shut all its state parks, Peace Arch Park was never blocked off, and since there were no formal border crossing procedures, Canadians who walked across the ditch to meet with friends, family, or lovers on the other side did not have to endure the country's mandatory two-week quarantine when they returned home.

Chris and Dana married in November 2020, with Chris hoping she could finally bring her wife back to Canada for the first time in their relationship. They were far from alone—on a typical weekend in the summer of 2020, the park would host a dozen or more weddings a day; in the entire year of 2019, just seven couples had chosen to marry in the park. "It wasn't my ideal wedding," said Christina Kelly, a Vancouver legal assistant who had been crossing easily for two years to spend time with her boyfriend in Washington when the border was closed. The day of their wedding was cold, wet, and muddy, and just a few family members and friends were able to join them in the park.[6] But in some ways, she said, it was the perfect place. "The park has been my life for the past year, the only place where I can see my husband." Len Saunders, an immigration attorney in the border town of Blaine, Washington, would meet almost daily with clients in the park. "What a lot of people did when they only allowed spouses entry to Canada was, they would literally get married in the park, get in the car, drive down to Bellingham, file the marriage certificate and then drive back into Canada," he said.

Why the World Closed Its Doors

In the months that followed the first Covid outbreaks in China in December 2019, governments across the world responded with a bewildering array of different policies to deal with what was appropriately called a "novel" virus. In the absence of effective medical treatments, they faced three broad choices—try to stay one step ahead of the virus by identifying and isolating affected individuals and their close contacts; try to slow the spread of the virus through lockdowns that closed shops, workplaces, and schools; or continue life more or less as normal, hoping the illness would not prove too serious and the population would build natural immunities. Few countries chose the third strategy. Sweden left most schools, restaurants, and ski resorts open and opted for reduced capacity to avoid mandatory lockdowns. Some tourist-dependent economies like the Caribbean islands locked down for several months in 2020, but then opened up when the economic costs became unsustainable.[7] Several countries in Asia such as Taiwan and South Korea were able to use quarantine and contact tracing to successfully isolate infected individuals without completely locking down their economies; Taiwan largely reopened businesses and schools by May 2020.[8] Some countries pursued stringent lockdowns—the Australian city of Melbourne faced no fewer than six lockdowns, a cumulative 262 days. Buenos Aires in Argentina had the longest continuous lockdown of 234 days. For nearly three years, China would continue to lock down its major cities every time there was a new outbreak. The financial capital of Shanghai was shuttered for three months in early 2022, with residents locked in their homes or apartments and dependent on unreliable food deliveries. Some countries, like the United States under President Donald Trump and Brazil under President Jair Bolsonaro, cobbled together what historian Peter Baldwin called "chaotic, almost deliberately inept, responses," with some uncoordinated lockdowns by state and local governments but little in the way of national plans.[9] Most European nations lurched between short lockdowns and reopenings that often allowed for a resurgence of infections.

But amid all this variation, there was one constant—nearly every country in the world shut its borders. North Korea was the first, on January 22, 2020.[10] By April 2020, more than 90% of the world's population was living in countries that had imposed some sort of border restrictions, and 40% were in countries that had completely closed their borders to non-citizens and non-residents.[11] By August 2020 every one of the World Health Organization's (WHO) 194 member states had imposed travel restrictions; in comparison, just 127 countries had implemented domestic social distancing or other preventive measures.[12] Some countries even closed their borders to their own citizens. When effective vaccines were rolled out early in 2021, most countries eased their domestic restrictions, but most borders remained restricted until late that year, and in some countries well into 2022 or even 2023.[13]

Why did every country restrict its borders during Covid? The WHO had long argued that travel restrictions were ineffective, at best briefly delaying the spread of diseases, while harming economies and violating human rights.[14] Yet when Covid-19 began spreading in early 2020, nearly every government imposed significant travel restrictions. In some countries, state or provincial-level governments even closed internal borders, blocking people who wished to travel from one region of the country to another. Part of the reason was fear and uncertainty. Governments knew little about the severity of the disease, who the most vulnerable populations were, details about how the virus was spread, or the prevalence of asymptomatic transmission. Traditional border health screening tools such as fever checks quickly proved ineffective because many of those infected did not show symptoms. The few studies available on the efficacy of border restrictions in reducing disease spread strongly suggested they were effective only if imposed early, before the disease had embedded itself in the community.[15] Governments were therefore faced with a stark choice in which the scale of the threat was unknown, and the speed of the response was vital. In the face of such uncertainty, many governments felt they had no choice but to shutter their borders quickly and sort out the consequences later.

But uncertainty was not the only driver. For governments, border controls were both popular and relatively easy to enforce. As Baldwin puts it: "In the zero-sum situation where no medical solution allows an escape, some unfortunates must pay the price for sparing the majority."[16] Writing in the early stages of the pandemic, Baldwin had assumed the "unfortunates" would be those who were exposed to Covid; they would be forced into isolation and their close contacts would be traced and monitored to stop the spread of the disease. But few countries—South Korea was one of the standout exceptions—had the capacity to test and trace cases effectively enough to staunch outbreaks. Others—China is the most obvious example—were willing to use the full powers of the state against their own citizens to require mandatory daily testing, enforce lockdowns, and remove the infected and exposed to government-run quarantine facilities. But few governments were willing to act in such a heavy-handed fashion.

Instead, the easiest population to target was foreigners. Most borders—at least at the official ports of entry—were hard lines that could be closed relatively easily; they were a controlled environment in which government agents decided who would be permitted to enter. In the two decades following the terrorist attacks of September 11, 2001, most governments had become much better at controlling their borders. Secure passports, biometric scans, advanced passenger information—and big increases in the number of border agents using those tools to screen arrivals—had made national borders more robust than at any previous time in modern history. Policing mobility restrictions domestically was, in contrast, extremely difficult—authorities outside of China, which committed the vast resources of the state to its "zero-Covid" approach, mostly lacked the will and capacity to stop everyone who was outside their homes to determine if their reason for being in public fell under one of the "essential" exceptions. In the early stages of the pandemic, most who could do so voluntarily stayed at home, but few countries could maintain these lockdowns beyond a period of several months.[17]

Border controls were also widely supported by the public. In an Ipsos poll of 21,000 people in twenty-eight countries in late 2020, two-thirds of respondents said their countries should "not allow anyone in or out" until the virus was contained.[18] Border measures were especially popular in Malaysia, Australia, Canada, Chile, and Peru, with 80% or more in favor. Support was lowest in Europe, where national borders had been largely dismantled in the 1990s and many people live in regions where they cross national borders daily for work, shopping, and even medical treatment. Even as vaccines were rolled out and domestic restrictions eased, border closures remained popular; the same Ipsos poll in November 2021 found 56% of the public still wanted the borders to remain shut.[19] Governments that resisted closing their borders to outsiders—as

South Korea had done in staying largely open to Chinese travelers in the early stages of the pandemic—faced vocal public opposition.

In most countries, the costs of travel restrictions were small and fell on others. As political scientists Michael Kenwick and Beth Simmons argue: "Policies can focus on externalizing the costs of pandemic control (by restricting travel and closing borders, for example) and/or they can internalize these costs (by regulating social distance, contact tracing, and regulating where and how many people gather)."[20] The choice was obvious for most political leaders. In many countries there was public resistance to domestic control measures such as school and business closures, and to masking and testing requirements. Border controls had few opponents; most of those separated from their families or stranded outside their own countries could do little but complain on social media. Border restrictions, therefore, are "a good political bet for most leaders," Simmons and Kenwick argue.

For political leaders, border closures have much to admire—they are quick, visible, and popular. In the face of complex external threats, restricting borders is an easy way for governments to signal that they are taking the security of their citizens seriously.[21] Throughout the pandemic, US president Donald Trump repeatedly reminded Americans that he had "cut off China"—the United States blocked travel by non-citizens who had visited China on February 2, 2020—as evidence that he was leading the Covid response, even as his administration was actively undermining less popular domestic measures to reduce the spread of the disease such as lockdowns and masking.[22] Governments that closed borders during Covid were widely lauded by their own citizens, and sometimes even abroad. New Zealand's prime minister Jacinda Ardern became an international star for her country's success in keeping the virus contained by using some of the world's most stringent border measures, including restrictions that even kept many citizens from returning home.[23]

Governments, of course, have shut their borders before. The Soviet Union and the People's Republic of China for several decades maintained an "Iron Curtain" that severely limited the ability of foreigners to visit and prevented their own citizens from leaving. More than 100,000 East Germans tried to flee across the fortified border to the West between 1961 and 1989; over 600 died in the attempt.[24] Wars have repeatedly closed borders across the world. Many countries—in Africa, the Middle East, Europe, and North America— have shut their borders temporarily to refugees and asylum seekers from neighboring states seeking to escape conflict and violence.[25] The United States went to the highest security level at its land borders and closed its airspace after the 9/11 terrorist attacks, though the measures were lifted within days. Border restrictions had also been used in the past to slow the spread of disease, from cholera outbreaks in the nineteenth century to the first appearance of Severe Acute Respiratory Syndrome, or SARS, in 2003.

But the world had never seen anything like the Covid border shutdowns. The United Nations World Tourism Organization stated that "never before in history has international travel been restricted in such an extreme manner."[26] The measures varied—from modest screening, testing, and later vaccination requirements to complete bans on foreign citizens to restrictions that excluded citizens as well. Immigrant workers were especially vulnerable, often blocked from returning home even as domestic lockdowns shuttered their places of employment. Even after vaccines had been widely distributed in 2021 and deaths from Covid were down sharply, many countries still maintained significant border restrictions. Taiwan and Japan did not fully reopen to foreign tourists until the end of September 2022. China would keep its borders closed until January 2023, nearly three years after first closing them.[27]

The Covid border restrictions stand out for another reason—for all the claims that governments had "lost control" of their borders, most proved extremely effective at controlling their borders during the pandemic. The restrictions permitted trade and small numbers of "essential" travelers to continue crossing borders while keeping everyone else out. For many decades, and especially since 9/11, wealthier countries in particular had worked to develop "smart borders" that would permit governments to control entry without disrupting lawful trade and travel.[28] The Covid-19 pandemic was the proof of concept—governments showed themselves remarkably adept at facilitating trade and the movement of some essential personnel while closing their borders to the vast majority of travelers. By permitting commercial rail and truck crossings without impediments, and container ships to continue crossing the oceans—even as the ship workers themselves were unable to return home to their families—governments ensured that store shelves remained stocked and public discontent was minimal. Covid border restrictions did lead to some product shortages and supply chain challenges, but overall trade proved remarkably resilient—indeed, the supply problems were caused largely by surging demand for electronics and other consumer goods from shut-in populations.[29]

This meant that, despite growing desperation as the months rolled by from tourist-dependent industries and their workers, from separated cross-border families and couples, from container ship workers stranded on the high seas, from universities losing foreign students, and from businesses struggling to hire or keep foreign workers, there was minimal pressure on governments to ease the restrictions. In the United States, the border restrictions under Title 42—a provision of US public health law that permits emergency actions at the borders to keep out communicable diseases—remained in place more than three years after the initial outbreak of Covid-19, and long after the United States had abandoned all domestic measures to control the spread of the virus. The Trump and Biden administrations used Title 42 to expel more than 2.5 million people attempting to cross the southern border from Mexico. Many US Republicans wanted the measure to remain in place permanently as a tool of border control.

Covid taught governments—in a way that had been far from certain beforehand—that borders could be closed or heavily restricted for extended periods with strong public support and minimal disruption to the everyday lives of *most* of their people. The temptation to do so in future crises—from pandemics to terrorist attacks to flows of desperate asylum seekers—will be irresistible. Even as borders reopened in the aftermath of the pandemic, pressures were growing across the political spectrum in the United States to seal the Mexican border against a rising surge of migrants from South and Central America and shipments of deadly fentanyl. Populist parties running on platforms calling for tighter borders and immigration restrictions gained ground not just in Hungary and Poland, but in Italy, Austria, Germany, Sweden, and Finland. In September, 2024, following election victories by the anti-immigration party Alternative for Germany, the country reintroduced border checks in an effort to keep out asylum seekers and unauthorized migrants. Climate change is creating more opportunities for deadly viral mutations; few health experts believe we will wait another century for a major global pandemic. In the face of such external threats, governments will be more willing than ever before to close their borders.

There is therefore an urgent need for an in-depth assessment of the harms caused by the unprecedented closure of borders during the pandemic and the implications for the future. Unfortunately, few countries are doing the sort of in-depth independent reviews—the kind that the United States did after the 9/11 attacks—that would allow for considered judgments about the effectiveness of border restrictions during Covid, and would also assess the enormous costs paid by the millions of people whose lives were upended. Publics, understandably traumatized by their experiences during the pandemic, are reluctant to look back, but failing to do so makes it likelier that governments will feel free to impose the same restrictions in future crises. This book is an effort to examine the lessons learned from this historic experiment in closing borders, and the implications for the future of borders and those whose lives straddle them.

The Future of Borders

The Covid border shutdowns accomplished something that would have once seemed inconceivable; billions of people were locked in or out of their countries, but goods largely kept moving around the world. For the past two centuries, the risks of disruptions to trade and the economic costs that would follow had been one of the strongest arguments for keeping borders open, even during crises. But Covid showed that governments could do both—they could restrict the movement of people while minimizing the harm to trade and the larger economy. Border scholars have debated for decades whether governments have become more effective in controlling their borders or have been ceding control in the face of global trade and capital flows, rising population movements, and international agreements that protect the rights of some migrants. Covid-19 ended that debate.

The Covid shutdowns showcased the enormous authority and capacity that modern governments have acquired; they have gone much further than was previously recognized in developing and implementing systems to control who comes and goes across their borders. During the pandemic, governments demonstrated virtually unlimited authority—and in many countries' capacities to match—to restrict or close borders in the face of declared emergencies, and to keep them closed for long periods of time.[30]

This raises fundamental, and in many ways novel, questions about how states should be using these powers. If governments are going to use border restrictions as a regular tool of governance, then difficult issues arise over how expansive those powers should be. Should states have effectively unlimited ability to declare emergencies that close their borders, even sometimes keeping out their own citizens? If there are reasonable limitations to such powers, where should those lines be drawn? Should national courts—which have a long history of deferring to governments both on public health and border control measures—play any role in protecting the rights of those whose lives straddle borders? These questions need clearer answers, and the constraints on government powers need to be more clearly defined, understood, and accepted. Unconstrained authority will tempt governments to use those powers more often and more broadly, especially when, like border closures, such measures are popular with voters.

Or consider another set of issues that was novel during the pandemic but will surely arise again. If borders are to be closed temporarily, what should the exceptions be—in other words, what sorts of cross-border travel should be regarded as "essential"? Most would probably agree that optional travel like tourism can be reasonably restricted in emergencies, though for many countries this has severe economic costs. Those fleeing persecution or torture, on the other hand, should never be barred from seeking refuge in safer countries; international law is clear on the obligation that governments have to refugees and asylum seekers. Nonetheless many countries, including the United States, blocked the entry of refugees and asylum seekers during the pandemic. In between those two extremes is a large gray area. Foreign students for whom border restrictions would disrupt their education? Cross-border workers who could lose their jobs? Other business travelers who need to cross borders for work? Those with family or lovers or other close relationships across borders? In its border measures, for example, the Canadian government said it was restricting "optional and discretionary international travel." But are education, work, and love optional and discretionary? Under Canada's formulation, the answer was largely yes, though some sorts of work and education were declared "essential," some travelers could petition for exceptions, and the exemptions became broader as the pandemic progressed. Other countries drew the lines in different places.

Finally, for decades the march of economic globalization and the growing ease of travel have encouraged people to develop professional and personal ties that required them to cross borders regularly. With the growth of remote work, the number of people who live across borders is likely to grow further as memory of the pandemic fades. Do those relationships enjoy no protections at all? Most states have for decades now—even while hardening their borders against asylum seekers and unauthorized migrants—encouraged millions of people to travel for vacations, for work, and for schooling. Should governments then be free to bar those same people from their jobs, their property, their education, their friends, their spouses, and their children if they happen to live on the wrong side of a national border when an emergency is declared? These are fundamental questions that have yet to be properly engaged in the wake of the Covid-19 border shutdowns.

The stakes are especially high for those who live in border communities, and whose professional and/or personal lives are based on moving relatively freely across national boundaries. Coming out of the pandemic, many governments are again opening their doors to migrants, tourists, and foreign students, eager for the economic gains that come from openness. Foreign student numbers had fully rebounded to pre-Covid levels by the middle of 2023 and are set to keep growing.[31] International tourism had reached 88% of pre-pandemic levels by the end of 2023, and the United Nations World Tourism Organization predicted a full recovery by the end of 2024.[32] That means that millions more people will build lives that straddle borders, leaving them vulnerable to the next time that governments—for reasons from pandemics to terrorism to other sorts of national emergencies—decide to restrict their borders. The pandemic showed that, if governments are willing to visit a high cost on some of their people—those with strong ties across national frontiers—restricting borders can be done with minimal economic or political cost. As a consequence, border closures have become just another tool in the toolkit for governments, one they are likely to turn to quickly in future crises. The defense of openness is going to require a much stronger voice from those who, whether from choice or necessity, have built their lives across national borders—including the authors of this book. Even as memories of the Covid-19 pandemic fade, we cannot afford to be quiet.

At Peace Arch Park along the US-Canadian border, where families and couples found a unique place to unite across borders during the pandemic, the two governments are already working to ensure they don't lose control again in the future. On the Canadian side of the park, the government has built a low wooden fence blocking off access from the US side. There is a small opening in the fence, and it would be easy to jump, but signs clearly warn in capital letters "NO ACCESS TO PARK" and state that entry is only permitted from the Canadian side. At the US end of the park, officials have erected signs across the ditch that mark the border with Canada stating that all entrants "must be inspected by Customs officers." The signs warn that failure to do so "may result in criminal and civil penalties, including imprisonment." In May 2024, for the first time in nearly a century, US Border Patrol officials began blocking Canadians entering the park from Zero Avenue in Surrey—the entry point for thousands during the pandemic—citing a rising number of illegal crossings. The park remains open, but the common meeting space across the border has been shrunk dramatically. The intention of officials on both sides of the border to assert greater control in future crises could not be any clearer.

2

The World Shuts Down

The virus that led to the most comprehensive, enduring border closures the world has ever known originated near Wuhan, China, sometime between November and December 2019. The first confirmed cases of human infection were reported in Wuhan in late December.[1] On January 9, the World Health Organization (WHO), which is responsible for global monitoring of diseases with pandemic potential, reported that Chinese authorities had made a preliminary determination of a patient displaying pneumonia-like symptoms who had likely been infected with a novel coronavirus. The last reported novel coronavirus—known as Middle East Respiratory Syndrome (MERS-CoV)—had surfaced in 2012, likely from human contact with infected camels. MERS, which is still circulating, has so far produced 2,500 known cases in twenty-seven countries and 858 known deaths.[2] The respiratory virus known as Severe Acute Respiratory Syndrome (SARS)—the closest precursor to Covid—likely originated from close human contact with bats or other infected wild animals. The largest outbreak in 2002–2003, known as SARS-CoV2, infected over 8,000 people in thirty-seven countries and killed 774, mostly in China and Southeast Asia, though there was also a significant outbreak in Toronto, Canada.[3] The WHO's January 9, 2020, statement on the new coronavirus noted that over the previous week, passengers with pneumonia-like symptoms who had been in Wuhan were identified at several international airports. Nonetheless, the WHO did not recommend any responses targeting travelers and advised "against the application of any travel or trade restrictions on China based on the information currently available."[4]

Such advice was standard for the WHO, the outcome partly of decades of experience dealing with previous pandemics and partly of its own weaknesses as an international organization in a world of sovereign states. Quarantine measures, including travel restrictions, have a long history dating back at least to the Italian city-states of the fourteenth century. The first recorded border closures to prevent the spread of disease were imposed by the Adriatic port city of Ragusa (modern-day Dubrovnik in Croatia) to combat bubonic plague. The plague likely originated in Sicily, and beginning in 1347 was transmitted across Europe by sailors, rats, and cargo. It wasn't until late in the pandemic that authorities, still knowing little of the science about the vectors of infection, began restricting human movement in an effort to slow the spread.[5] On July 27, 1377, Ragusa's Major Council passed a law stipulating "that those who come from plague-infested areas shall not enter [Ragusa] or its district unless they spend a month on the islet of Mrkan or in the town of Cavtat, for the purpose of disinfection."[6] Other city-states established blockades along transit routes, using force to keep out merchants and others attempting to enter the cities. Venice was the first to establish a screening system for arriving ships, requiring those suspected of carrying disease to quarantine for forty days before entering the city.[7] (The word "quarantine" comes from the Italian words for forty days, "quaranta giorni.")[8]

In the intervening 650 years, techniques for preventing the spread of infectious diseases across borders had not advanced very much. Absent effective vaccines or treatments, quarantine and restrictions on people traveling and assembling remain the only proven way of slowing the spread of deadly pathogens. Travel restrictions were used, though sparingly, to fight cholera outbreaks in the nineteenth century. Border restrictions were used in some countries during the Spanish Flu of 1918–1919, particularly in Australia and several South Pacific islands that had greater control over their borders.[9] Australia imposed a strict maritime quarantine in October 1918 that helped it avoid the worst wave of the Spanish Flu, though it suffered about 15,000 deaths when the virus broke through the quarantine in 1919. Neighboring and still more isolated Tasmania escaped with one of the lowest recorded death rates in the world.[10] New Zealand, in contrast, did not impose a similar quarantine and was among the countries hardest hit during 1918, with death rates especially high among its indigenous Maori population. The Spanish Flu would kill at least 50 million people worldwide.[11]

During the SARS outbreak, quarantine and contact tracing were used with considerable effectiveness. Some countries instituted airport screening checks to identify passengers with fevers or other potential symptoms, though subsequent research suggested those measures had little impact in reducing the spread of SARS.[12] The WHO for the first time issued recommendations against travel to infected areas, drawing a rebuke from Canada and other countries affected by the SARS outbreak.[13]

Since its formation in 1948 as part of the United Nations system, the WHO had largely deferred to national governments on epidemic control measures. As public health expert David Fidler has argued, this "Westphalian" approach to disease control recognized the primacy of sovereign states in implementing health measures. The WHO did not intervene in domestic health policies for controlling diseases such as cholera or yellow fever, even though measures like improved sanitation were critical to reducing infections. Instead, the WHO confined its mandate to preventing the international spread of infections. The WHO's International Health Regulations (IHR), first codified in 1969, reflected that paradigm; the objective was, Fidler writes, "to ensure the maximum security against the international spread of disease with minimal interference with world traffic."[14] States were required to notify the WHO of disease outbreaks, to maintain screening and monitoring capacities at ports and airports, and to minimize the use of travel restrictions consistent with public health. The framework largely served the interests of the wealthy countries, which sought to insulate themselves from imported diseases but do so in a way that limited disruptions to commerce.

The experience of SARS, which jumped borders with particular speed from its origin point in southern China, led to significant changes in the WHO's approach. In the 2005 revisions to the IHR, which came into effect in 2007, the WHO began actively promoting the idea of "global health security" premised on the need for greater international cooperation to tackle common threats.[15] China's lack of transparency in reporting the initial SARS outbreak was of particular concern. At the heart of the new approach was a move away from national measures such as border controls intended to interrupt the spread of disease to early surveillance and containment at the source.

While the WHO would at times endorse temporary travel restrictions, the 2005 regulations reinforced the organization's suspicion of borders as a tool of pandemic control. First, the WHO saw such controls as ineffective, at most delaying cross-border spread of diseases for a few days. The best research available prior to the Covid outbreak suggested that travel restrictions would do little to contain the new virus and that governments should focus on domestic control measures.[16] Second, reliant as it is on national reporting, the WHO also feared that the threat of travel bans would make countries reluctant to share what they knew about emerging pathogens. Peru had suffered losses of more than

$700 million from trade restrictions when it reported a cholera outbreak in 1991; in 1994 a plague outbreak in Surat, India, led to flight cancellations and travel restrictions that cost India more than $2 billion.[17] Indeed, when South Africa reported its discovery of the fast-spreading Omicron variant of Covid-19 in November 2021—giving the rest of the world a valuable head start in developing countermeasures—the country and its close neighbors immediately faced new travel bans from the United States, Japan, the EU, the UK, and Australia, even though the new strain had already been detected in other countries. As Benjamin Wallace-Wells put it in the *New Yorker*, South Africa "seemed to be getting punished for good global citizenship."[18] The 2005 regulations were supposed to prevent this—countries were incentivized to be forthcoming by the promise they would not face travel and trade sanctions. The WHO also feared that border restrictions could block the movement of critical health personnel and material, though during Covid the bigger problem turned out to be export restrictions—countries hoarding masks, ventilators, and other critical medical supplies.[19] And the organization had long worried that such restrictions could endanger human rights and civil liberties, opening the door for discriminatory measures against groups of individuals that were not justified by public health concerns.[20] Finally, the WHO feared that border measures would mistakenly be seen as a panacea, giving a "false impression of control" when serious domestic preventive measures were needed.[21]

Covid-19 would require the WHO to reconsider many of these assumptions. But in the early stages of the pandemic, the organization stuck to its playbook, reiterating its opposition to border restrictions. On February 29, 2020, nearly a month after declaring the new virus a "public health emergency of international concern"—its highest level of warning—the WHO updated its "recommendations for international traffic in relation to Covid-19 outbreak." In general, the statement said, "evidence shows that restricting the movement of people and goods during public health emergencies is ineffective in most situations and may divert resources from other interventions." It acknowledged that restrictions could prove "temporarily useful" but "may only be justified at the beginning of an outbreak." Such measures, the agency said, "must be based on a careful risk assessment, be proportionate to the public health risk, be short in duration, and be reconsidered regularly as the situation evolves." With such limited exceptions, the WHO concluded, travel bans "are usually not effective in preventing the importation of cases but may have a significant economic and social impact."[22] By mid-February 2020, however, most countries had stopped paying attention to the WHO. Dozens of nations had already implemented travel bans, largely focused on blocking travelers from China. Within another month, most of the world would be closed down.

A Golden Age of Mobility

As Covid was quietly spreading in Wuhan in late 2019, more people were traveling more often to more places in the world than ever before in human history. During the Spanish Flu outbreak, the disease was initially carried mostly by conscripted troops moving to and from the war fronts in Europe, and by sailors moving cargo. International travel for work, study, or pleasure was rare, and World War I had shut off most of the immigrant flow from Europe to North America. When Covid hit, in contrast, the virus had hundreds of millions of volunteer super spreaders who were accustomed to traveling the globe for work, education, and fun. In 2019, there were more than 1.5 billion overseas travel and tourist trips worldwide, a number that had been rising steadily, and then sharply, since 1950, when just 25 million travelers flew or sailed beyond their own shores.[23] The first non-stop transatlantic commercial flight was in 1958, a Pan American 707 flying from New York to Brussels. Even that small number of international travelers in the 1950s had been sufficient to seed deadly pandemics; when a new strain of influenza appeared in Singapore in 1957, it spread broadly enough to kill more than a million people globally and 116,000 in the United States. A similar flu in 1968 was even more deadly, killing between 1 million and 4 million people.[24] But these were just tiny demonstrations of how disease could spread in a more mobile world. After decades of improvements in airline technology, "open skies" agreements that reduced air travel costs, and the lowering of border restrictions with the end of the Cold War, international travel had exploded. Before 1990, more than 60% of tourist visits had been concentrated in a few Western European nations like Great Britain, France, and Italy; since then, travelers had increasingly flocked to Asia, Latin America, Africa, and other destinations.[25]

Within regions, cross-border mobility had flourished as nations eased or lifted their border inspections. In June 1985, foreign ministry officials from France, Germany, Belgium, the Netherlands, and Luxembourg met in the village of Schengen in southern Luxembourg and agreed on the "gradual abolition of checks" for people crossing their common borders.[26] By the time the Schengen

Convention was ratified a decade later, it included Spain, Italy, and Portugal as well. Today, the so-called Schengen Zone includes most of Western and Central Europe except for Great Britain and Ireland, twenty-nine countries in all. Two generations of Europeans and visitors to Europe have lived in a world in which traveling from Paris to Budapest across three countries was nearly as hassle-free as driving from Paris to Strasbourg within France. The end of the Cold War in 1989 and the opening up of Russia and Eastern Europe created dozens of new travel destinations and millions of new travelers. Like the Soviet Union, China had been largely closed to foreign visitors until the mid-1970s; in 1978 just 230,000 international tourists visited the country. But China began easing its border restrictions as part of the economic and trade opening launched by Deng Xiaoping that same year. By 2010, China had become one of the largest tourist destinations in the world, with over 133 million foreign arrivals, and Chinese were the single largest group of international tourists.[27]

In North America, the borders had long been little or no impediment to travel. Before the 9/11 terrorist attacks led to a significant tightening, Canadians and Americans could cross quickly by flashing a state or provincial driver's license. Mexicans faced more scrutiny, but millions who lived near the border were able to cross freely into the US border regions using a Border Crossing Card issued by the US government that permitted Mexicans to visit, study, or shop in a narrow border region on the US side. Car and bus crossings to and from Canada and Mexico reached record levels in the 1990s before declining in the 2000s as US document requirements tightened after 9/11. Still, in 2019 there were nearly 200 million car and bus passenger crossings from the two countries into the United States.[28]

Growth in global air travel had also slowed briefly at times, during the 1981 and 2008 global recessions, and had even shrunk slightly after the 9/11 attacks and during the SARS outbreak. But those proved to be blips in a steeply rising curve.[29] For those living in wealthier countries and holding the right passports, the several decades prior to Covid were a golden age of international mobility, facilitated by technology and by governments eager to win their share of travel dollars and convinced that such mixing of people would contribute to global peace and prosperity.[30] The real costs of air travel had fallen by more than half since the late 1970s, a consequence largely of US deregulation of the airline industry, similar liberalization in Europe, and the resulting explosion of competition.[31] In the decade from 2009 to 2019, the number of air passengers doubled from 2.25 billion to more than 4.5 billion.[32]

Cross-border travel, once the pleasure of a wealthy few, became increasingly democratized. The average British citizen today has visited a dozen countries; Australians have on average visited ten different countries.[33] Americans are among the world's more reluctant travelers, but even so seven out of ten say they have gone abroad at least once in their lives. A January 2020 survey of a dozen countries, including China, Vietnam, Thailand, and Saudi Arabia, found that 68% had traveled abroad at least once, with most traveling multiple times.[34] While Americans are much less likely than Europeans to hold a passport, the number of passport-carrying Americans nonetheless grew from just 4% in 1990 to 42% by 2017. Much of this was driven by new document requirements for travel to Mexico and Canada, the two most popular destinations for Americans.[35] But it also reflected a growing expectation among many Americans that foreign travel would be a regular part of their lives.

As cross-border mobility became easier, people found more and more reasons to cross borders—for recreation, for work, for religious pilgrimages, and for love. International tourism became sufficiently popular, and sufficiently reliable, for countries to build their economies around foreign visitors. The tourism industry is roughly the size of the oil industry, and one in every ten jobs across the world prior to the pandemic was tied to tourism.[36] Most tourism is domestic—people traveling for holidays in their own countries—but international tourism alone contributed some $1.7 trillion to the global economy in 2019, about 2% of the world's GDP, and nearly 7% of total global exports (international tourism is considered a "service export").[37] The most tourism-dependent countries are the small island nations in the Caribbean, Indian, and Pacific Oceans and the Mediterranean Sea, but many larger economies also rely heavily on travelers. Fifteen percent of Croatia's GDP depends on foreign visitors, as does 8% in Thailand, 7% in Greece, and 5% in Portugal.[38] Even in places where tourism is less important to the overall economy, it is still a big employer. In 2019, inbound international tourism supported 1.2 million jobs in the United States and $155 billion in spending.[39] Hawaii in 2019 welcomed a record 10.4 million visitors, netting the island more than $2 billion in tax revenues.[40]

International education—from study abroad to exchange programs to full-time study—also encouraged many young people to leave home. In the United States, the number of international students rose from just a few thousand in the early 1950s to more than 1 million by 2019, a record. The growth was especially rapid in the 1990s and again beginning in the mid-2000s.[41] Globally, more than 5 million college and university students were studying in other countries in 2018, twice the number of the late 1990s.[42] After the United States, the next most popular countries for foreign students were the UK, China, Canada, and Australia. Japan, which had increased its efforts to attract foreign students, had more than 200,000 in 2019. China was sending more students to study abroad than any other country, followed by India, South Korea, and Saudi Arabia.[43] As with tourism and travel, international education is a multibillion-dollar business. In the United States, foreign students contributed nearly $41 billion to the US economy in 2018–2019.[44]

When the pandemic hit, foreign guest workers and other international workers were especially vulnerable. For many countries, encouraging their citizens to work overseas is a crucial source of revenue. There were an estimated 169 million foreign workers in 2019, about 5% of the global labor force.[45] Those foreign workers labored under a variety of legal work programs, ranging from temporary "guest worker" programs that offered no path for permanent immigration to labor recruitment programs like the US H-1B program that could lead to citizenship. Remittances from migrant workers sent to their families in low- and middle-income countries had grown slowly in the 1990s and then exploded; remittance inflows totaled US$75 billion in 2001 but then grew to nearly US$550 billion by 2019.[46] India, China, Mexico, and the Philippines were the four largest recipients of remittances.[47] More than two-thirds of migrants were working in wealthier countries in Europe, North America, or the Middle East; in the Arab Gulf States, more than 40% of the workforce was made up of migrant workers, most on temporary guest visas.[48]

In the early months of the pandemic, the International Organization for Migration estimated that roughly 2.7 million workers were stranded abroad and prevented from returning home by travel restrictions.[49] Migrant workers were especially likely to be in temporary or insecure employment, subject to Covid-related layoffs or forced to keep working in dangerous conditions, and ineligible for the government support programs that shielded many workers in wealthier countries. Some 1.2 million of those foreign workers were in the Middle East and North Africa.[50] When the pandemic hit, roughly 400,000 seafarers were working on container and cruise ships across the world. Many would be unable to return home for months. In the cruise ship industry, which suffered some of the earliest and most visible outbreaks and was forced to shut down in March 2020, some 300,000 crew members from across the world remained stranded six months later in various ports, unable to work or to return home.[51] Those less vulnerable still found themselves in difficult situations after the border closures. Foreign workers residing in the United States on temporary work visas can, under normal circumstances, travel back and forth to their home countries. But with US travel restrictions against many countries and the shutdown of US consular processing, many found themselves stuck on expired visas, unable to leave the United States because they would be barred from returning.

As more and more people were moving across borders, those travels shaped not just economies and politics but the most intimate parts of personal lives. As *The Economist* reported in 2011: "International marriages matter partly because they reflect—and result from—globalization. As people holiday or study abroad, or migrate to live and work, the visitors meet and marry locals. Their unions are symbols of cultural integration, and battlefields for conflicts over integration."[52] The growth in cross-border marriages and other personal relationships introduced a vast new dimension of regulation. Relationships across borders have long been affected by visas and other restrictions on both temporary visits and long-term immigration; even before Covid, couples could face significant obstacles, including long periods of separation. But in some regions—the US-Canada border, the Schengen Zone in Europe, Hong Kong and mainland China—crossing borders had become so routine that individuals felt secure in building their families across national boundaries. Data on cross-border marriages is difficult to find, but regional examples suggest it grew enormously as travel became cheaper and easier. In Hong Kong, for example, cross-border marriages were just 2% of those registered in 1986, but 43% of all marriages by 2006, facilitated by the easing of restrictions on mainland travel to Hong Kong following the handover to China in 1997.[53] In Taiwan, the number of cross-border marriages rose from just a few thousand annually in the early 1990s to more than 50,000 each year in the early 2000s; in most cases these involved Taiwanese men marrying women from Vietnam and China.[54]

As the pandemic spread, the variety of border measures posed an often-insurmountable obstacle for many couples. Japan, for example, permitted Japanese nationals to return home, but blocked all entry of foreigners, including foreign spouses, and those who already held visas and had permission to live in Japan.[55] Those restrictions remained in place for more than two years. The United States permitted immediate family and married couples to reunite but did not offer automatic exemptions for those who were engaged or in long-term relationships. As the Covid measures dragged on for many months, more and more of those stories began to be shared on social media. Online groups such as #LoveisNotTourism, a Facebook group that attracted more than 45,000 members, most of them separated from spouses or partners, emerged to share stories and lobby governments for exemptions. Australian citizens barred from returning home similarly established support groups like #StrandedAussies. Those barred from Japan banded together in the group "Students, workers, spouses stranded outside Japan." And in North America, couples and families separated by the border closures formed groups like "Faces of Advocacy" and "Let Us Reunite" to lobby their governments for eased border restrictions and expanded exemptions. Many couples would be separated for as long as two years until travel restrictions began to ease.

Those who could afford to do so found workarounds. Wealthy Canadians hired helicopters or chartered flights to jump the land border and travel to the United States.[56] Jasmine Jasper, an Italian-German dancer, was able to come to New York in February 2021 to reunite with her boyfriend Anthony Pototski, but only by spending two weeks first in Serbia, which was not then on the list of countries where travel to the United States was forbidden.[57] Indian tour companies offered their clients the "fifteen-day quarantine package"—flights from Mumbai to Mexico City, fifteen nights in a four-star hotel, after which they would be permitted to fly to the United States.[58] Those who preferred could do the same journey via Cairo or the Maldive Islands.[59] Tour operators promised specially prepared Indian meals throughout the journey.[60]

The World Closes Down

US president Donald Trump had nothing but the deepest contempt for the WHO, and indeed for all international organizations. On April 14, 2020, when the Covid pandemic had spread across the world, he announced that the US government would withhold all funding for the health agency, and a month later announced it would pull out entirely. "One of the most dangerous and costly decisions from the WHO was its disastrous decision to oppose travel restrictions from China and other nations," he said. "The WHO's attack on travel restrictions put political correctness above life-saving measures."[61] It was classic Trump. Anti-internationalism had been the core of his beliefs since the 1980s; he had no interest in the "post-Westphalian" international order.

Trump had campaigned in the 2016 election on restoring US sovereignty and control over its borders. He denounced "a leadership class that worships globalism," calling for a great wall to be built on the border with Mexico, a "Muslim ban" that would halt travel to the United States from certain Muslim-majority countries, and new tariffs on imported goods to protect US manufacturers.[62] Closing US borders in response to Covid fit naturally with his beliefs that the world was a dangerous place, and other countries were taking advantage of a feckless United States.

On Sunday, January 31, Trump's Health and Human Services Secretary Alex Azar walked into the White House Briefing Room, forty minutes behind schedule, to announce that the United States would block all entry by noncitizens who had recently been in China, making exceptions only for immediate family members of US citizens and permanent residents.[63] Those family members, as well as returning Americans, were expected to quarantine for two weeks after they came home, though enforcement would be minimal. The announcement came following a contentious internal debate among Trump's top officials. Deputy National Security Advisor Matthew Pottinger, who had worked as a newspaper reporter in China and spoke fluent Mandarin, was persuaded that the United States needed to move immediately to block travel from China. Covid, he had learned from medical contacts there, produced no symptoms in many of those testing positive for the virus, making it impossible to slow the spread through temperature checks and other screening at airports. Trump's economic team opposed the move, calling it an overreaction that would hurt the economy and financial markets. Health officials like Anthony Fauci, director of the National Institute of Allergy and Infectious Diseases, and Robert Redfield, director of the Centers for Disease Control, echoed the WHO's concerns, fearing that a travel ban would jeopardize cooperation with China.

Trump himself was ambivalent; his administration had just negotiated its "Phase 1" trade deal with China. Trump portrayed the deal as a great victory, arguing that his actions in slapping new tariffs on Chinese imports had forced China to make concessions, promising a big increase in exports of US-made products. Over the course of that month, he had several times lauded China for its early response to Covid. In a January 24 tweet he wrote that "China has been working very hard to contain the Coronavirus. The United States greatly appreciates their efforts and transparency. It will all work out well. In particular, on behalf of the American People, I want to thank President Xi!"[64] But the urgency of the moment was on Pottinger's side; it was clear that infected people had almost certainly flown from China to the United States already, and the government had no reliable means to identify and stop those who had been exposed to the virus.[65]

Azar announced that the new ban on travel from China would begin at 5 P.M. on February 2.[66] Trump let his officials take the lead, waiting to see the reaction from the American public and from the Chinese government. He would later brag that his travel ban was an "early" decision that had "saved thousands of lives" by barring travelers arriving from "heavily infected China."[67] But the United States was at best keeping up with the global pack. Some forty-five other countries had already restricted travel from China before the US ban came into effect, including Russia, Taiwan, Singapore, Italy, and Australia. By the time the administration imposed the new measures, more than 40,000 travelers from China had already entered the United States since the virus was first identified, and over the next month several million more would arrive from other countries experiencing their own outbreaks.[68] Before the first plane from China was halted, Covid had been thoroughly seeded in Seattle, Washington, and in several other western states.

A month later, Trump announced a ban on visitors from Iran, where cases were surging. And then on March 11, he barred travelers from Europe, where Covid was spreading quickly in Italy, France, and Spain. Again, there was a heated fight within the administration. Treasury Secretary Steven Mnuchin and White House National Economic Council director Larry Kudlow warned that cutting off travel from Europe would "cause a Great Depression."[69] This time, Trump took ownership of the decision, announcing in a rare prime time television address that the United States would block air travel in forty-eight hours, starting Friday, March 13, at 11:59 P.M. But his staff mangled the speech, and Trump stumbled over some of the lines, making it sound as though the United States was cutting off trade with Europe as well, and leaving unclear whether American citizens would be permitted to return. The address triggered a panic, with Americans desperately trying to jump on flights home before the travel ban was implemented. Thousands arriving back in the United States were crammed, very few wearing masks to inhibit viral spread, into the customs and immigration corridors at US airports. The order further restricted returning Americans to arriving at one of just thirteen US airports, where they would face additional health screening measures.[70] This led to similar overcrowding for several days. The chaos almost certainly contributed to the further spread of Covid in the United States. But it also likely didn't matter much; later studies would show that travelers from Europe had already brought the virus to New York City, which would become the first US epicenter of the infection, as early as late January.[71] European leaders, who were given no warnings in advance that the United States would shut down flights, were furious. "The coronavirus is a global crisis and requires cooperation," EU leaders said in a joint statement.[72]

Five days later, the United States and Canada announced they would close their land border for thirty days starting at 12:01 A.M. March 21, restricting border crossing to "essential" travelers, including medical workers as well as truckers and others needed for cross-border trade. Canadian prime minister Justin Trudeau said the exceptions were aimed at ensuring that "food, fuel and life-saving medicines reach people on both sides of the border." Similar exceptions were put in place at the land border with Mexico, which was also closed. In contrast with the US ban on European travelers, this one at least was discussed by the governments involved. Trudeau lauded the new measures as "collaborative and reciprocal"; Trump wrote on Twitter that "We will be, by mutual consent, closing our Northern Border with Canada to non-essential traffic."[73] But the significant differences suggested the plan had been hastily stitched together. Canada would require all "non-essential" border crossers, including returning Canadian citizens, to quarantine for a minimum of fourteen days; the United States had no such requirement. Canadians were blocked from driving south across the land border but still permitted to fly into the United States; Canada, in contrast, barred all non-essential Americans regardless of the mode of travel. Further differences would emerge as the pandemic continued. While Mexico partly cooperated with the land border closures, it did nothing to discourage air travel into Mexico from the United States or anywhere else, requiring only minimal health screening.[74]

While the US measures were far from the earliest, the US travel restrictions sparked a wave of similar actions across the world. By the end of March 2020, according to a database compiled by the International Organization for Migration, there were no fewer than 43,000 separate restrictions on international travel.[75] As with the United States and Canada, the travel measures formed a bewildering patchwork, with rules differing dramatically from country to country. Some 60% of the world's nations had by then restricted entry, with another 8% requiring conditions such as advanced testing or quarantine upon arrival. At one extreme, countries like Australia, New Zealand,

and Japan all but shut their borders. Australia in late March banned all entry by non-citizens and required returning Australian citizens to isolate for fourteen days at government-sanctioned quarantine hotels; the country would later establish a metering system that effectively barred many of its own citizens from returning. New Zealand followed Australia's playbook. China closed its borders to all foreigners, including those with valid visas and resident permits, on March 28. Japan, while it had faced one of the earliest crises when the cruise ship *Diamond Princess* docked in Yokohama in early February filled with nearly 700 Covid patients, was slower to move. But on April 1 it announced a ban on travel from seventy-three different countries, including the United States, Canada, Britain, and most of Europe. Unlike New Zealand and Australia, Japanese citizens were free to come home if they quarantined for fourteen days, but the ban excluded all non-Japanese, including permanent residents of the country, if they had visited any of the proscribed countries.[76]

By the end of March, most of the world's borders were closed to all but essential travel. Even in the European Union (EU), where freedom of movement is considered a "cornerstone of EU citizenship," many member states blocked travel from their neighbors as the epidemic surged in Italy and Spain. On March 16, nine countries—Cyprus, Czech Republic, Denmark, Hungary, Latvia, Lithuania, Poland, Slovakia, and Spain—closed their borders to all foreign travel, including other EU member states. Several others—including Germany, Austria, and Hungary—imposed partial restrictions.[77] At the German border with Poland, trucks backed up for twenty-five miles as Polish border officials checked to see if truckers might be infected with the virus. Estonia, Latvia, and Lithuania—which found themselves cut off from the rest of Europe by the Polish blockade—chartered ferries and ordered their national airlines to help bring their citizens back home from the rest of the continent.[78] By the middle of March, nineteen of the twenty-six members of the EU had moved unilaterally to restrict travel. The next day, the European Commission, trying desperately to catch up with the actions of its member states, announced it would block most travelers entering the EU entirely, exempting only European citizens and residents.

Norway and Sweden had not had a border dispute since the Treaty of Strömstad was signed in 1751, making it the oldest unchanged border in Europe. They had agreed not to impede cross-border movement of their citizens for any reason under a treaty dating back to the 1950s. Since 1952, Norwegians and Swedes had been permitted to travel across the border without passports, and to live and work without special permits in either country.[79] But in March 2020, dismayed by Sweden's policy of permitting the virus to spread to encourage "herd immunity," Norway placed barriers, police patrols, and other obstacles at all crossings along the 1,000-mile border. As at the US-Canada land border, couples, families, and friends suddenly found themselves on opposite sides of an uncrossable divide, forced to meet over concrete barriers at road crossings.[80] Many Swedes and Norwegians who had traversed the border freely for work lost their jobs. The town of Strömstad, ninety minutes by car from Oslo but six hours away from Stockholm, lost most of its business overnight as Norwegians could no longer cross the border to purchase cheaper goods in Sweden and then return home. The Nordby Center—110 shops near the border offering a mostly Norwegian clientele lower prices on meat, cheese, sweets, and alcohol than in heavily taxed Norway—did some $500 million in business in 2019, making it the largest shopping mall in Scandinavia. But with the border closure, business plummeted by 95% overnight. "The whole idea of Nordby is to sell to people on the other side of the border," Stale Lovheim, the head of the shopping center, told the *Financial Times*. "Without any customers, our idea isn't functional."[81]

At the height of the restrictions in the middle of 2020, there were few places in the world that were not affected by some sort of travel ban. Some 220 countries and territories had imposed more than 70,000 different restrictions, according to the IOM.[82] In April and May 2020, international air travel fell by 92% from the previous year's levels.[83] Even Antarctica—which is jointly administered under treaty by nearly thirty countries—canceled all its tourist visits. It managed to avoid even a single Covid case until December 2020, when a breakout occurred at a Chilean army base on the northern tip of the continent.[84]

3

Borders, State Authority, and the Right to Travel

In January 2022, two years after the initial outbreak of the pandemic and with more than 90% of its population vaccinated against Covid, New Zealand was still rationing the return of its own citizens as a Covid preventive measure. The government required all returning nationals to quarantine for two weeks in one of the scarce hotel rooms allotted by the government, known as "Managed Isolation and Quarantine," or MIQ for short.[1] Charlotte Bellis, a thirty-five-year-old Kiwi journalist working for Al-Jazeera in Doha, Qatar, unexpectedly found herself pregnant in the fall of 2021 and applied to the New Zealand government for permission to come home. But she kept failing to secure a place in the MIQ lottery. In Doha, it is illegal for a woman to be pregnant and unmarried; she was warned by a friendly doctor that "you need to get married or get out of the country as soon as possible." Her options were desperately few, so she decided to return to Afghanistan, where she had previously worked as a reporter and where her boyfriend, a *New York Times* photographer, was based. She made inquiries with the Taliban government, and was promised that, as a foreigner, they would ignore her unmarried status and permit her to deliver the baby in Kabul. She would later write: "When the Taliban offers you—a pregnant, unmarried woman—safe haven, you know your situation is messed up."[2] After arriving in Kabul, she pursued her final option, applying to the New Zealand government for an emergency medical exemption to allow her to return to deliver her baby at home. Despite peppering her application with evidence on the dangers of childbirth in Afghanistan—the United Nations says Afghanistan is among the worst countries in the world for pregnant women, with a woman dying in childbirth every two hours—her request was denied (Figure 3.1).[3] It was only after she told her story publicly in the *New Zealand Herald* that the embarrassed government relented and

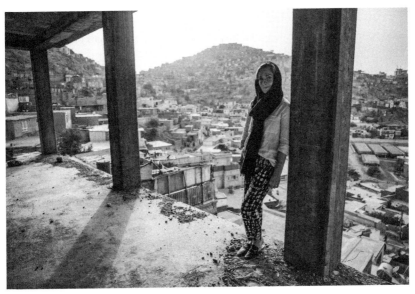

Figure 3.1 Charlotte Bellis in Kabul, Afghanistan, January 2022, following the New Zealand government's rejection of her emergency appeal to return. Photograph courtesy of Charlotte Bellis.

granted her the exemption to return home.[4] Many other citizens wishing to return to New Zealand were not so fortunate.

Such cases were far from rare during the Covid border closures. A group of Australian citizens unable to come home complained to the United Nations Human Rights Committee, arguing that the restrictions violated their fundamental rights as citizens. When the petition was filed in June 2021, Australia's Department of Foreign Affairs and Trade estimated that 40,000 citizens who wanted to return had been barred from doing so, including 5,000 listed as "vulnerable."[5] In New Zealand, about 1 million of the country's 5 million citizens were living abroad when the borders were closed in March 2020. Nearly 200,000 citizens were able to secure a place to return through the MIQ system, though many were left out. As of September 2021, more than half of those still registered in the system—232,000 out of nearly 400,000—had failed to secure permission. The opposition National Party dubbed it "a Hunger Games–style lottery."[6]

Even in places where the border restrictions were less severe or of shorter duration, decisions over who could come and go were often arbitrary. Bolivia closed its border with Chile on March 26, 2020, and did not make exceptions for its own nationals, most of whom had been seasonal agricultural workers forced to leave when Chile locked down; some 1,300 Bolivian nationals ended up stranded on the Chilean side of the border, in freezing temperatures and with little food and water.[7] Trinidad and Tobago, the Caribbean island, closed its border entirely for fifteen months; citizens wishing to return had to seek a special exemption from the Minister of National Security.[8] Nicaragua never fully closed its borders, but it blocked repatriation flights by many of its own citizens and halted others at its land border with El Salvador for several months.[9] Aschchaye Mohitram, a citizen of the African island nation of Mauritius, was working on a cruise ship along with more than 100 other Mauritians who were blocked from returning home when the government shut its borders to both foreigners and citizens. He was one of tens of thousands of cruise ship workers who were stranded on their ships during the early months of the pandemic, barred from returning home by travel restrictions or lack of flights, and confined to windowless cabins for much of the day. The mental health of the crews deteriorated badly.[10] In September 2020, six months after the outbreak of the pandemic, Mohitram was still marooned on his ship off the coast of Brazil, with minimal food and the cruise company no longer paying his salary. "We feel like hostages here, being far away from our family and not being on land for so long," he said.[11]

Such actions prompted the United Nations High Commissioner for Human Rights, former Chilean president Michelle Bachelet, to issue a strongly worded statement calling on all countries to permit repatriation of their citizens. "Under international law, everyone has the right to return to their home country—even during a pandemic," she said. "When migrants wish to return home voluntarily, governments have an obligation to receive their own nationals, and to ensure that they have access to health care and other rights."[12]

Japan allowed its citizens to leave the country and return if they were willing to quarantine for two weeks upon arrival, but barred foreign residents from coming back to the country—forcing thousands of people to leave behind jobs, apartments, friends, and family.[13] In the early months of the pandemic, this restriction included permanent resident spouses married to Japanese citizens, who were kept out of Japan if they had been abroad when the borders closed.[14] Some countries recognized exceptions for foreign students, especially as schools transitioned from remote learning back to in-person instruction; Japan did not permit foreign students to return until March 2022, two years after the borders were closed.[15] In China, in Europe, and in North America, there were significant carve-outs for "essential" border crossers. But the definition of "essential" was neither consistent across countries nor consistently enforced. The United States chose to restrict land border crossings from Canada and Mexico while freely permitting air travel, a piece of epidemiological nonsense for which the government never offered an explanation. It was not until November 2021 that the US government imposed a vaccination requirement on air travelers, and then it kept the restriction in place well after Canada removed its own vaccination requirement for travelers in October 2022. When Norway closed its border in March 2020, it made exceptions for the thousands of Swedish workers who crossed regularly for jobs. But then in January 2021, amid fears over the spread of the deadlier UK and Delta variants, Norway shut the border entirely, making exceptions only for "socially critical personnel" like healthcare workers.[16]

In most countries, the rules were never precise enough to cover all contingencies. Border officials could offer exemptions, for example, for those who wanted to visit dying relatives or attend funerals, or they could refuse. Crossing for work could be deemed "essential," but much was up to the discretion of border officials. Ron Rouse, who headed a construction company in Ontario, had been able to cross freely into Michigan throughout the pandemic to check on a new grocery store his company was building in the state. But in February 2021, he was pulled aside on return by Canadian border agents and fined C$3,755 for failing to present a negative Covid test or a quarantine plan; the agents on duty deemed that because he only crossed occasionally for work, he was "non-essential."[17] In December 2021—long after Canada had lifted quarantine requirements for returning travelers but still required testing—the Wright family of Sarnia, Ontario, arrived at the Bluewater Bridge on the way back from a vacation in Mexico. The family all had negative PCR tests taken before they left Mexico but were informed by border agents that the tests had to be given in the United States; they were told they could stay in the United States for the two days or more it would take to get the test results, or pay a C$10,000 fine. But friends who had traveled with them to Mexico, and arrived at the bridge an hour earlier, were let back into Canada without incident.[18]

Such random, arbitrary application of border restrictions—long familiar to asylum seekers trying to enter wealthy countries or to would-be immigrants holding temporary working permits—became commonplace during the pandemic. Even citizens from wealthier countries who had long assumed they could freely cross borders for work, vacation, or love suddenly found those doors closed.[19] The pandemic showed that governments today exert greater authority than ever before over those who wish to cross borders, in an environment that is largely beyond the reach of the courts or other constraints on that authority. In most Western liberal democracies, the public assumption is that borders are out of control, and voters are calling for tougher measures to control who crosses their national frontiers. The Covid border closures showed instead that governments have enormous powers to close or restrict borders, and that under certain circumstances they are quite prepared to use those powers. That raises difficult questions about how such powers are, and should be, wielded.

The Power to Filter

Setting aside the relatively small—if highly visible and controversial—number of unauthorized migrants, borders can be crossed only with the explicit permission of national governments. Modern nation-states, as John Torpey has argued, have established a monopoly over the "legitimate means of movement."[20] For most of the nineteenth and twentieth centuries, governments rarely attempted to assert that monopoly, and when they tried, they lacked the capacity to enforce it. As roads, rail, ships, and commercial airplanes brought travel within the reach of ordinary citizens, the ability of individuals to cross borders exceeded the capabilities of governments to control them. With the exception of wartime, or authoritarian regimes willing to use troops and military fortifications to seal their borders, most governments until recently lacked real authority over their borders. As Alan Dowty wrote in his history of Cold War–era border restrictions: "Few governments actually had comprehensive physical control of their borders; nor did they have bureaucracies sophisticated enough to pick out legal from illegal migrants as they passed through border posts."[21] The Soviet Union was a rare exception—it was one of the few countries where, as Andrea Chandler argues, "the right to travel or cross the border was an isolated privilege available to a fortunate few, not a right of society as a whole."[22] In the United States, in contrast, as Jeffrey Kahn writes: "Outside of wartime, early American border controls were extremely lax." International travel was no more constrained by law or practice than travel from one state to another within the country.[23] That began to change in the late nineteenth century as the United States sought to restrict immigration from Asia. After

World War I, most governments began requiring foreign citizens to produce passports upon entry. But the US government did not force its own citizens to carry passports for overseas travel until after World War II. The United States and Canada only instituted passport requirements for cross-border travel by their citizens in 2009.[24]

Today, even liberal democratic states exercise significant control over their borders. Over the past several decades, governments in many parts of the world—worried over crime or terrorism or illegal migration or large flows of asylum seekers—have invested heavily in the infrastructure and personnel necessary to control their borders. Effective border control has two core elements—secure identification documents that allow border inspectors to determine who should be admitted, and the enforcement capacity to prevent people without acceptable documents from entering. Such capabilities are quite recent. When the so-called Millennium bomber, Ahmed Ressam, tried to cross from Canada in December 1999 on a mission to detonate a bomb at the Los Angeles airport, he used a Canadian passport under a false name he had obtained through a document vendor who had stolen blank baptismal certificates from a Catholic church.[25] He was only stopped thanks to an alert US Customs agent. But the 9/11 terrorist attacks focused governments on the risk of such fraudulent identification; today, most new passports and other travel documents have been linked to biometric identifiers like fingerprints, iris, and facial recognition that make them extremely difficult to forge. Over 140 countries are now issuing such ePassports.[26]

Secure identification is only half the challenge of border control, however, and the easier half. The bigger hurdle for governments is developing the capacity to enforce border restrictions—to admit those with the proper sorts of permissions and exclude those who lack them. Simmons and Kenwick refer to this capacity as "the authority to filter." Border controls permit states to "determine who and what enters, and on what terms." The state, they argue, seeks "to publicly and visibly display its ability to permit entry of goods and people on its own terms."[27] Such filtering primarily takes place at the physical borders of nations, and requires significant investments in infrastructure and personnel, ports of entry at highway and rail crossings, passport controls at airports, and surveillance and physical barriers that discourage crossing between the legal ports of entry. Many states have increasingly cooperated with others to push their borders out, performing screening at foreign airports or other sites far away from national borders.[28] Filtering requires significant amounts of data on cross-border travelers and putting that information in the hands of front-line agents who make entry decisions. In addition to secure travel documents, filtering tools include advance screening for red flags, such as the US Advanced Passenger Information System, and trusted traveler programs such as the Nexus and Sentri programs in North America for which travelers submit to detailed security background checks in exchange for expedited border crossing. At the borders, travelers can be subject to more intrusive screenings such as searches of cell phone or computer data. Health screening tools like temperature checks or vaccination requirements may also be imposed.

The Covid-19 pandemic struck a world in which many governments had for decades been increasing their capacities to enforce these filtering decisions in an effort to ensure that only those with proper legal permission are able to enter the country. In the United States, the number of armed agents patrolling the land borders between the legal ports of entry grew from just 4,000 in the early 1990s to more than 20,000 two decades later.[29] The country built some 700 miles of fencing and other barriers along its border with Mexico and uses surveillance technology along the entire border. In Europe, while border controls were lifted among members of the EU, the bloc stepped up enforcement at its external borders. The agency Frontex was established in 2004 to assist national governments in patrolling the external borders of the Schengen Area; today it directly employs more than 900 border guards.[30] Many European states have built fencing and barriers to block asylum seekers.[31]

The human consequences for those seeking refuge have been devastating, but that has not discouraged Western governments from expanding their deterrent efforts. More than 1,200 people died in the Mediterranean Sea in 2022 alone trying to reach the shores of Europe; more than 25,000 have been killed since 2014.[32] The same number—1,200—died or disappeared in 2022 trying to cross the border from Mexico into the United States despite US Covid restrictions that barred most from requesting asylum. In Australia, governments for the past decade have taken extreme measures to deter those trying to reach the island by boat, forcing them into offshore detention camps on the islands of Nauru and Papua, New Guinea. Once there, many remain for years in inhumane detention camps with no chance of being admitted to Australia except for serious medical needs.[33] Since August 2012 more than 4,000 people have been sent to the offshore processing facilities.[34]

Despite such brutal measures, political demands for still harsher border controls have increased in many countries. Control over borders has become a key measure of public confidence in governments; support for populist parties in Sweden, Italy, and Denmark, and for Brexit in the UK, was driven in large measure by the sense that Europe had lost control over who is permitted to cross its external borders. Breakdowns in border control are readily exploited by nationalist political forces. Securing borders is a top political concern of right-wing populist parties including the Trump Republicans in the United States, the Brothers of Italy, the Alternative for Germany, and the Sweden Democrats.[35]

Control over borders is seen as a core mission of governments, visible evidence of their capacity to govern effectively. As Gabriel Popescu puts it: "[S]tate borders throughout the world have been entrusted with a new long-term rationale of being the guarantors of our security in a globalizing world characterized by increased cross-border mobility of people, capital, goods, diseases and ideas."[36] Governments face a dilemma in trying to promise their citizens the economic benefits and personal freedoms that come from a more open global economy, while protecting them from the unwanted consequences of openness. As former Coast Guard commander Stephen Flynn put it two decades ago: "The global economy's movement towards more open societies and liberalized economies does not just facilitate the movement of products and workers—it also expedites passage for terrorists, small arms, drugs, illegal immigrants and disease."[37] Many governments believe an essential part of their mission is to use borders to keep out unwanted intrusions—in the case of Covid, a deadly contagious virus—while maintaining the open trade and limited cross-border travel that are critical to support the economic needs of their citizens.

Shutting borders in the face of perceived emergencies can certainly demonstrate control, but even during Covid the world's borders were never shut entirely. In the modern global economy, countries are simply too dependent on trade to retreat into hermetic isolation. The growth of a truly global economy by the end of the twentieth century makes it vital that borders function efficiently for trade despite the restrictions. In North America, the 9/11 experience had left an indelible impression on officials making the Covid border closure decisions. In the immediate aftermath of the terrorist attacks, the United States had gone to a "Level 1" alert at its land borders with Canada and Mexico, subjecting all crossers to intensive inspections and scrutiny. Within hours, backups of trucks and cars had soared at heavily used commercial crossings like Detroit-Windsor and Laredo–Nuevo Laredo on the border with Mexico. Within days, US auto companies were complaining of parts shortages and began shutting down production, leading Washington to quickly ease the restrictions.[38] Chastened by the experience, the US and Canadian governments sat down and hammered out new rules and procedures to help segregate commercial from passenger traffic at the busy border crossings, and to separate "low-risk" from higher risk travelers and shipments of goods. These "smart border" tools revolutionized border control, not just in North America but in much of the world.[39] Covid was the first big test since 9/11 of how effective such measures could be in a crisis.

The ability to keep trade flowing and to discriminate between essential and non-essential crossings—however arbitrary those distinctions were at times—made the Covid border restrictions acceptable in most countries.[40] The restrictions affected only a subset of the population, those whose working or personal lives had been built around the expectation of crossing borders easily. Outside of the EU and a handful of other places with multiple national borders in proximity, the border restrictions left most people's lives untouched; they were far more inconvenienced by the domestic lockdowns that closed businesses like gyms and restaurants, and the switch to remote work and schooling. It is hard to imagine the borders having worked so smoothly in a pre-9/11 world. Dan Ujzco, a Columbus, Ohio–based lawyer who specializes in US-Canada trade, said that if Covid-19 had hit two decades ago, the borders in North America would have been locked tight, with harmful consequences for cross-border trade. "I guarantee you," he said. "There's not a doubt they would have shut the border completely—had we not had this painful lesson from history."[41]

Is There a "Right to Travel"?

Governments showed during Covid that they can control their borders. But are there any limits to how they should exercise those increased capabilities? The people whose lives were upended by the Covid border closures certainly had reason to believe they should be permitted—with appropriate health safeguards—to reunite with families or loved ones. This was especially true for those who sought to return to the countries of their citizenship. As British human rights advocate Geoffrey Robertson, who represented Australian citizens barred from returning home during the pandemic, put it: "International law recognises the strong bond between individuals and their homeland and no respectable government would impose travel caps to prevent, for over a year, its citizens from returning if they are prepared to do quarantine." But successful claims protecting a right to cross borders have rarely been made, and the few legal challenges during the pandemic mostly failed. While the number of court decisions on mobility rights is small, border controls enjoy special protections that have made successful challenges by aggrieved parties all but impossible. Throughout the pandemic, those whose lives were upended by the border closures had no legal recourse. They could do nothing but voice their displeasure—often via the press or social media—and hope governments would change their minds and lift border restrictions or expand exemptions.

Normally, national courts could be expected to play some role in constraining such sweeping state authorities, balancing the security or health emergency claims of governments with the rights of those wishing to enter or exit the country. But in practice, courts have rarely intervened to protect cross-border mobility rights. Plaintiffs in such cases face many hurdles. The legal norm, even in liberal democracies with expansive notions of individual rights, has been for courts to defer to national authorities whenever governments declare emergencies. Given its highly transmissible nature and the risk of serious disease and death, Covid would easily fit any reasonable definition of an emergency. But governments have frequently used "emergency" border restrictions for threats that are much less obvious. The post-9/11 US restrictions on travelers from Muslim-majority countries, Donald Trump's broader "Muslim ban," Australia's policy of mandatory offshore detention for asylum seekers, and the bans on asylum seekers trying to enter the United States during the pandemic all survived review by the courts.

Courts have also deferred to national governments on matters of foreign policy. While borders are the line that divide domestic from foreign, those crossing borders do not possess the same range of legal protections available within countries. Once admitted to the United States, for example, even temporary visitors enjoy the normal constitutional protections against unlawful search and seizure by police or other authorities. But US borders have been rightly called "a constitution-free zone."[42] Border officials can conduct routine searches of any border crosser without a warrant or probable cause. Even US citizens may face warrantless searches of their computers, phones, and belongings when they arrive at a border or an interior border checkpoint.[43] Customs and Border Protection (CBP) carried out more than 45,000 electronic device searches in 2022, and much of the data gathered is retained in a searchable database that CBP officials can access in future investigations without a warrant.[44] The Supreme Court has found that the government's security interest in monitoring cross-border entry outweighs the privacy rights of individuals, including citizens.[45]

Such deference opens the door to discriminatory measures that target certain travelers based on race or religion or other personal characteristics. The post-9/11 period was rife with travel restrictions imposed on national security grounds but aimed almost exclusively at nationals of Muslim-majority countries. The National Security Entry-Exit Registration System (NSEERS), launched in 2002 by the US Justice Department, required citizens of two dozen Muslim and Arab countries to undergo detailed advanced scrutiny before being permitted to enter the United States, and then to re-register with the US government thirty days after arriving. Initially, the program also required "special registration" by nationals of those countries already living in the United States. NSEERS resulted in many people with no connection to terrorism being arrested or barred from the country.[46] The government gradually scaled back its intrusiveness, but NSEERS remained in force until the program was suspended by the Barack Obama administration in 2011.[47] Such measures explicitly targeting foreign nationals on the grounds of religious belief would have appeared vulnerable to successful court challenges given US constitutional protections for religious freedom, but the program was consistently upheld by US courts. Eight federal appellate courts examined the NSEERS program, and all of them found that the government had acted within its authority to discriminate on the basis of nationality for immigration purposes (though many of those affected by NSEERS were students, business travelers, tourists, and other non-immigrants).[48]

The Supreme Court similarly upheld on a 5–4 vote in 2018 President Trump's authority to ban travel to the United States by citizens from seven countries—six with majority-Muslim populations.[49] The actions followed Trump's campaign promises to block all entry by foreign Muslims until the United States could improve security at its borders. The travel ban should have been vulnerable to court challenge given the president's own repeated public statements that he intended to discriminate against Muslim travelers. During the campaign Trump had called for "a total and complete shutdown of Muslims entering the United States." But the Supreme Court still upheld Trump's order, with the majority writing that the president had expansive authority to control entry based on his national security judgments.[50] Writing for the majority, Chief Justice John Roberts concluded that the relevant statute—Code §1182(f) of the Immigration and Nationality Act—"exudes deference to the President in every clause. It entrusts to the President the decisions whether and when to suspend entry, whose entry to suspend, for how long, and on what conditions." He added that the president was free to block non-citizens if he determined their entry "would be detrimental to the interests of the United States."[51] The same statute gives the president clear authority to bar any foreign travelers determined "to have a communicable disease of public health significance."[52]

Border restrictions raise the greatest legal concerns when it comes to a nation's own citizens. If citizenship means anything, it is the right to reside in one's own country. It is a right that cannot be abrogated by the government, even for the most heinous of crimes. Legal exile has largely been abolished in the modern world, though since 9/11 there has been a significant increase in laws that empower governments to strip citizenship from naturalized citizens for "disloyalty, treason, nationality security or involvement in terrorism."[53] Outside of a handful of authoritarian countries, citizens have long enjoyed the right to travel abroad and return freely. The Magna Carta in 1215 included in its listing of freedoms that could not be restricted by the King of England the right, outside of wartime, for "any man to leave and return to our kingdom unharmed and without fear, by land or water, preserving his allegiance to us."[54] The revolutionary French Constitution of 1791 similarly recognized "the freedom of everyone to go, to stay, or to leave, without being halted or arrested unless in accordance with procedures established by the Constitution."[55] Article 13 of the Universal Declaration on Human Rights, adopted by the United Nations General Assembly in 1948, states: "Everyone has a right to leave any country, including his own, and return to his country." Many countries, including Canada, France, and Germany, have explicit constitutional guarantees of the rights of citizens to return.[56] In the United States, there are no explicit guarantees of a right to travel outside the country, but it wasn't until well into the twentieth century that US governments outside of wartime restricted the ability of their citizens to leave or re-enter.

US courts have recognized—based on a variety of constitutional provisions—a right to interstate travel, though it too can be restricted under narrow circumstances.[57] But the protections are weaker for citizens traveling internationally. The few cases to make their way to the Supreme Court involved the US government withholding passports on national security grounds, which made it impossible for some citizens to leave the country. One of the highest-profile cases involved Paul Robeson, the singer and civil rights activist, and Peace Arch Park again played a starring role. In July 1950 the State Department had revoked Robeson's passport on the grounds that his strident criticisms of American foreign policy could harm US interests if he were permitted to deliver them abroad. He was one of dozens in the 1950s denied the right to travel by the US government based on their political beliefs. The State Department tried to compel Robeson not to speak publicly in other countries in exchange for a new passport, and to sign an affidavit stating he was not a member of the Communist Party; he refused both. In January 1952 Robeson was invited to speak and perform at a labor union convention in Vancouver, Canada, a trip for which he did not require a US passport. But he was blocked at the border north of Seattle by US officials, who refused to let him leave the country, citing legislation passed during World War I to prevent the entry or departure of citizens "during the existence of the national emergency."[58] In response, the Canadian labor unions brought him back in May before a huge crowd in Peace Arch Park, where he spoke from the flatbed of a truck backed up to the US edge of the border with Canada. More than 25,000 people crowded the park on the Canadian side and another 5,000 on the US side; Border Patrol and FBI agents were left with little to do but jot down the license plate numbers of those attending.

Robeson challenged the government's actions unsuccessfully in the lower courts, and the State Department refused until 1958 to issue him a passport, relenting only after the Supreme Court ruled in a separate case that the department could not deny passports to Americans based on their political beliefs. The court, in a 5–4 decision, wrote: "Travel abroad, like travel within the country, may be necessary for a livelihood. It may be as close to the heart of the individual as the choice of what he eats, or wears, or reads. Freedom of movement is basic in our scheme of values."[59] Despite such strong language, the court did not find a constitutional right to international travel, ruling instead that mobility could only be restricted by the government with appropriate due process protections.

Those protections have proved weak in practice. In the aftermath of 9/11, the US government added thousands of names to watch lists restricting travel by people suspected of ties to terrorism; the names of more than 4,600 US citizens and permanent residents are on those lists.[60] In several high-profile cases in the wake of 9/11, US citizens were prevented from returning home on vague national security grounds. Muhammed Ismael and his son Jaber, both US citizens, were left stranded during a visit to Pakistan in 2006 because the FBI had placed their names on the "No Fly List," which blocked them from boarding their flight home. They remained in Pakistan against their will for six months. It was only after the American Civil Liberties Union took up their case, filing administrative complaints and bringing public attention, that the Department of Homeland Security permitted them to return home.[61] The US government still imposes travel restrictions on its own citizens on national security grounds, and these actions have been upheld by the courts.[62] A federal judge ruled in 2019 that such "watchlisting" of US citizens violated their constitutional rights, but the decision was overturned in 2021 by a US Appeals Court.[63] The appellate court majority wrote: "What history suggests, precedent confirms: the right to travel is qualified, not absolute."[64]

On top of the reluctance of the courts to act in matters of border control, the Covid pandemic involved public health measures, which have also enjoyed wide deference from court challenges. As Noah Smith-Drelich writes: "Courts have been quick to bend constitutional rights and liberties in service of controlling the spread of contagious diseases."[65] Pandemics create a utilitarian logic that trumps concerns over civil rights; restrictions on ordinary freedoms are justified in the name of preventing the spread of disease. Severe restrictions on a few, in the form of mandatory quarantines or onerous travel restrictions, are accepted as necessary constraints for the greater public good. Adam Klein and Benjamin Wittes argue that involuntary measures to restrict public movement on health grounds have a long history.[66] US states enjoy inherent police powers to protect public health, including mandatory quarantine and isolation of those infected; the federal government has similar powers to prevent the transmission of disease from one state to another. The Supreme Court has confirmed such powers, most explicitly in *Jacobson v. Massachusetts*, a 1905 case that upheld the state's authority to mandate compulsory vaccination during a smallpox outbreak. Smith-Drelich argues that "contemporary courts have repeatedly used Jacobson as a license to adopt a standard of near-absolute deference toward legislatures responding to a perceived public health emergency."[67]

There has been no significant change in the courts' approach to public health issues in over a century. The *Jacobson* decision was used to uphold involuntary quarantines of travelers returning from West Africa during the 2014–2016 Ebola outbreak. The rare cases in which the courts have determined that such measures were discriminatory or went beyond what was reasonably required to protect the public are many years in the past. In 1900, San Francisco cordoned off 10,000 residents of Chinese origin during an outbreak of bubonic plague; in *Jew Ho v. Williamson*, the Supreme Court ruled the measure discriminated against residents and citizens of Chinese heritage and struck it down. The prohibition on Chinese residents traveling out of the city, the court ruled, "deprives them of their liberty, causing them great and irreparable loss and injury."[68]

Outside the United States, most national courts have been similarly deferential. In Australia, the courts sided with the government on the full range of Covid-19 travel restrictions. Australia's chief medical officer, Brendan Murphy, told the Senate Select Committee investigating the Covid-19 response that the government "cannot stop Australian citizens from coming home" and suggested that doing so was "not constitutional or legal in any way."[69] But Australia's courts did not agree. The Federal Court considered a challenge to the government's ban on Australian citizens returning home from India during the height of the Delta variant outbreak in India in early 2021—a measure more explicit than the de facto restrictions on citizen returnees created by limited flight and quarantine capacity. The court upheld those restrictions as a reasonable measure under Australia's Biosecurity Act, which was passed by Parliament in 2015 and replaced the century-old Quarantine Act. The government's judgment on what was necessary to protect public health, the court found, effectively overrode whatever rights Australian citizens enjoyed to return home. The court said that citizens should enjoy no special treatment in a biosecurity emergency, since they could just as easily return with the virus as non-citizens, thereby weakening protection for public health.[70] In a separate case, Australian citizens challenged the government's restrictions on outbound travel, which prevented most Australians from traveling abroad unless they could demonstrate a "compelling need" to the satisfaction of the government. The Federal Court ruled that Parliament had properly considered such restrictions when it approved the Biosecurity Act. "It may be accepted that the travel restrictions are harsh," the court found. "It may also be accepted that they intrude upon individual rights. But Parliament was aware of that."[71]

India has the largest diaspora population in the world, many of them migrant workers in the Persian Gulf region. In the early stages of the pandemic the government made significant efforts to repatriate its overseas citizens from the hardest-hit countries, including China, Italy, and Iran. But despite pleas from the state of Kerala where many Indian migrants originate, India did not make similar efforts to repatriate the much larger number of migrants—some 9 million before the pandemic—who were working in the Gulf region.[72] On March 24, 2020, the Indian government announced a twenty-one-day border closure to all incoming travelers, including citizens, as well as a ban on domestic travel intended to reduce the spread of Covid from the cities to rural areas. The international travel ban, which was extended to May 3, 2020, was challenged at the Indian Supreme Court. Plaintiffs included Indian students stuck in the UK, pilgrims stranded in Iran, and migrant workers in the Gulf countries. But the Indian Supreme Court ruled that the government was not required to assist the return of its citizens given the challenges of fighting Covid at home. The chief justice of the court pleaded with expatriate citizens to "stay where they are."[73] The Indian government eventually followed up, however, with one of the more ambitious airlifts of the pandemic, repatriating nearly 4 million of its citizens, most from the Gulf region.[74]

The biggest exception to governments asserting unchecked freedom to restrict their borders was the European Union (EU), the only jurisdiction in the world that formally recognizes a right to cross national borders. Cross-border mobility is one of the fundamental freedoms guaranteed by Community law, and the European Commission calls the guarantee of free movement "perhaps the most important right under Community law for individuals, and an essential element of European citizenship."[75] The right extends to the full Schengen Area, which includes Norway, Iceland, Switzerland, and Liechtenstein. Member governments retain authority to restrict travel during outbreaks of diseases with epidemic potential (as defined by the WHO), but with a series of checks, balances, and procedural safeguards designed to keep those measures as limited as possible to achieve public health goals.[76] From the early days of the pandemic, the Commission fought with member states to reverse the unilateral border restrictions most had put in place in March 2020 and re-establish cross-border mobility. The Commission also pressed EU members to coordinate their restrictions on travel from outside the EU, and to ease those measures as quickly as possible. "International travel is key for tourism and business, and for family and friends reconnecting," EU Commissioner for Home Affairs

Ylva Johansson said in June 2020.[77] At the least, the Commission insisted that states reopen for international students and essential non-EU workers. Unlike in many countries, where public health officials defended border restrictions on precautionary grounds, European health authorities argued that the restrictions had been costly and ineffective. The European Center for Disease Prevention and Control concluded in May 2020 that the border closures had at best slowed the initial spread of Covid, but at very high cost to the economy. "Available evidence does not support recommending border closures, which will cause significant secondary effects and societal and economic disruption in the EU," the agency said.[78]

In some countries, internal travel was restricted as well. State and municipal jurisdictions imposed their own measures, with varying levels of restrictiveness and enforcement. In the United States, the islands of the Florida Keys for several months set up roadblocks on the two access roads, permitting only "residents, property owners and those actively involved in work in the Florida Keys"; the state of Florida announced a fourteen-day quarantine requirement aimed specifically at residents of New York State following the March 2020 Covid outbreak in New York City.[79] Several other states similarly imposed a self-isolation requirement on incoming travelers. Many tribal governments set up internal border controls that kept out non-residents.[80] In Canada, the provinces of Nova Scotia, New Brunswick, Newfoundland, and Prince Edward Island established an "Atlantic bubble" from July 3 to November 26, 2020, permitting free travel within those provinces but restricting entry from the rest of Canada to essential workers or those prepared to quarantine for fourteen days.[81] In Australia, the state of Western Australia closed its borders to all but a small number of exempt travelers in April 2020 and kept the closure in place for nearly two years.

Few of these measures faced legal challenges, and with the notable exception of Argentina, where courts limited the travel ban imposed by the northern province of Formosa, courts upheld the public health powers of the governments invoking the measures. In Canada, an inter-provincial travel restriction imposed by the province of Newfoundland in May 2020 was challenged by a woman who was barred from coming to the province to attend her mother's funeral. The Supreme Court of Newfoundland and Labrador found that the action violated her rights under Section 6 (1) of Canada's Charter of Rights and Freedoms, which explicitly protects the mobility rights of Canadians.[82] But the court ruled the restriction on her constitutional freedoms was still justified by the legitimate public health objectives of the measure.[83] The restrictions in Western Australia were challenged by the mining magnate Clive Palmer, who owns an iron ore mine in the state. He argued that the border closures violated Section 92 of the Commonwealth Constitution, which guarantees that "trade, commerce and intercourse among the States, whether by means of internal carriage or ocean navigation, shall be absolutely free."[84] But the High Court ruled that state border closures were lawful and justified under Australia's emergency powers.[85] Palmer was ordered to pay the government's legal costs for the case.[86] In the United States, the few inter-state border restrictions imposed during the pandemic did not face court challenges, but legal experts suggest they probably would have been upheld by the courts.[87]

What Is an "Essential" Traveler?

The absence of legal constraints on the Covid-19 border restrictions meant that governments were free to decide who could come and go from their countries. If there is no right to cross borders, in some cases even for citizens of those countries, then the constraints on governments are utilitarian and political rather than legal. They could close borders based on judgments about the greatest good for the greatest number, ignoring the impacts on the affected individuals, and continuing as long as the economic costs or political backlash were not too large. It is not surprising that border restrictions in most countries lasted far longer than domestic lockdown measures. From a public health perspective, mobility restrictions likely had some positive effects in slowing the spread of Covid.[88] And restrictions on international borders were the easiest to enforce and politically the most popular. While most people accepted the need to stay home early in the pandemic, such restrictions became increasingly less popular as months passed, particularly after vaccines were rolled out.[89] Prolonged masking and social distancing might have been justifiable on public health grounds even after vaccines were introduced, but they were unsustainable politically in most countries. Border controls lasted much longer because they had strong advocates within governments and few opponents.

For governments, the biggest decision they had to make at the borders was who would be admitted and who would be excluded. Complete border closures would be economically disastrous, so governments needed to decide which border crossers were "essential." They described these choices in different ways. New Zealand referred to "people with a critical purpose for travel." China barred entry to non-residents except those conducting crucial "economic, trade, scientific, or technological activities" or fulfilling "emergency humanitarian needs."[90] The European Commission responded to growing national border closures by directing member states to continue permitting cross-border movement for "workers exercising critical occupations." These included health professionals, childcare workers, medical and pharmaceutical scientists, engineers, firefighters, transport workers, and those involved in maintaining supply chains.[91]

The concept of an "essential service" is borrowed from labor laws. Countries that permit workers to organize into labor unions and withhold their services by striking for better pay or working conditions nonetheless circumscribe that right. Many governments prohibit or restrict the right to strike by public employees, especially in such critical sectors as health care, police and fire services, and rail and air transportation.[92] The International Labour Organization (ILO) has recognized that limitations on the right to strike are permitted in essential services, defined as those where interruption "would endanger the life, personal safety or health of the whole or part of the population." The ILO acknowledges that "the determination of which services are to be considered essential in each case is a delicate matter."[93] The main impact of essential worker designations during the pandemic was to require those in jobs considered necessary for the functioning of society to remain on their jobs despite the high risks of face-to-face work.

During the pandemic, the idea was adapted by governments to make determinations both on which workers would be required to stay on the job at home, and who would be permitted to enter the country from abroad. The distinction turned out to be one with enormous human, legal, and moral consequences. Domestically, many of those required to remain on the job were low-wage workers in hospitals, nursing homes, agricultural work, food processing and meatpacking, grocery stores, and transportation and warehousing services.[94] Many were immigrants or migrant workers, and the requirement to continue in-person work placed them at a much higher risk of contracting Covid.[95]

At the border, being declared an "essential worker" meant that one was relatively free to cross back and forth despite the travel restrictions. The Canadian government, for example, defined essential services as "services and functions [that] are considered essential to preserving life, health and basic societal functioning."[96] Some of the travel purposes considered essential included economic services and supply chains, critical infrastructure support, health and medical work, and "any other activities that are deemed 'non-optional' or 'non-discretionary' by the Canadian government."[97] Truckers crossing the border from the United States, for example, were considered essential and not required to quarantine after arriving in Canada; the same rules held for Canadian nurses living in Windsor, Ontario, and crossing the border to work in Detroit-area hospitals.[98] The US government published a list of those who would be permitted to enter during the pandemic, and the exceptions were comparatively broad, including foreign students, those traveling for medical treatment, those working in the United States, and workers engaged in cross-border trade. The only specific exclusion was for "Individuals traveling for tourism purposes, such as sightseeing, recreation, gambling, or attending cultural events in the United States."[99] Both Canada and the United States made exceptions throughout the pandemic for seasonal agricultural workers, fearing that crops would be left to rot otherwise.[100]

Canada went much further in making fine distinctions. The Canada Border Services Agency developed a lengthy memo for its agents filled with scenarios laying out what sorts of travel would be considered "discretionary and optional" rather than "essential." Crossing the border to have dinner with a spouse, or to spend time on days off from work? Such travel would be "recreational/leisure in nature" and the request should be denied. Attending the funeral of a family member? That was "discretionary/optional," and therefore "non-essential." Shared custody agreements between parents separated by the border were considered "essential," however, and such travel was permitted provided the parent isolated for fourteen days upon arrival in Canada. The status of immediate family members was one of the most contentious distinctions. Family members of Canadians or permanent residents were permitted, subject to a fourteen-day quarantine if they were being admitted for an "essential purpose." What if a foreign national wished to come to Canada to ride out the pandemic with a spouse or immediate family? If the foreign national's purpose was to "minimize his own risk to the pandemic in the U.S. and access Canada's health care system, it would arguably be reasonable to deny," the memo said. But if the purpose was to "help to ensure each other's health, safety and well-being during the pandemic period," then "it arguably would be reasonable to authorize entry."[101] The scope for case-by-case discretion by Canadian border agents was enormous.

The "essential" designation would prove to be the most controversial element of the otherwise popular border restrictions. The broad scope for discretion opened the door to political influence by those with wealth or connections. Even as thousands of Australian citizens were stranded abroad, for example, the Australian government permitted a who's who of Hollywood stars to enter the country for film productions that had been lured by generous tax breaks. Matt Damon, Zac Efron, Natalie Portman, and Mark Wahlberg were among the A-listers given such permission. Australian stars like actress Nicole Kidman and her country musician husband Keith Urban were permitted to fly home from the United States on a private jet and isolate in their own home rather than in the mandatory quarantine hotels.[102] In a December 2021 poll, 80% of Australians believed the government was permitting celebrities and wealthy people to evade the travel restrictions.[103] Kylie Jenner and Brad Pitt flew to France in the summer of 2020 when the country was off-limits to Americans; the loophole appears to have been an exception for "highly qualified third-country workers if their employment is necessary from an economic perspective and the work cannot be postponed or performed abroad."[104] American models Bella Hadid and Hailey Bieber released photos from the island of Sardinia, where they were permitted to travel for a Versace advertising campaign.[105] Canada permitted foreign hockey players to enter and created protected "bubbles" for the 2020 National Hockey league playoffs.[106] The president of UPS, the US-based shipping giant, was granted a special exemption in October 2020 to come into Canada quarantine-free to lobby the company's employees to accept a new labor contract.[107]

By far the largest "essential services" loophole was trade and commerce. A big reason the 2005 revisions to International Health Regulations had strongly discouraged border closures for pandemic control was the potential for disruption of commerce.[108] Governments decided early on that exceptions needed to be made to permit cross-border trade and commerce to continue. Fearing public panic if grocery store shelves started to empty, governments were determined to keep goods moving across borders. On one level, of course, the difference in treatment of people and goods was obvious and necessary; Covid was being carried and transmitted by people, not by shipments of food or clothing or Pelotons. But the distinction falls apart on closer inspection.

Trade was hardly risk-free—throughout the pandemic, even countries with quite restrictive border regimes like Canada permitted millions of truckers, airline pilots, and others involved in the movement of goods to enter without even taking a Covid test or being required to quarantine upon arrival. Such transport workers invariably interacted with others at rest stops, airports, refueling stations, or during the loading and unloading of goods, and many had personal ties in the communities where they were traveling. Trucking routes were vectors for the spread of the virus. In South America, which was harder hit by Covid than any region in the world, 80% of trade in the continent moves by truck. A study of Colombia, the region's fourth largest economy, found that the five cities with the highest levels of trucking activity also had the highest rates of infection.[109] Colombia had enforced a domestic lockdown and restricted its borders early in the pandemic, but trucking was declared essential, and truckers continued to operate freely within Colombia and across its borders. In Africa, cross-national trucking was a large source of early infections; in Uganda, more than 70% of the positive Covid tests in the first three months of the pandemic were among truck drivers.[110]

The decisions made by governments to preserve cross-border trade and commerce as essential also had enormous human consequences for those required to keep the goods moving. Truckers traveling long distances through diverse communities faced higher risks of becoming infected and spreading it to their families or other close contacts; in North America, truckers would often travel from US states with few pandemic restrictions into Canada, where despite the tougher restrictions they were not required to quarantine.[111] Many countries required truckers to work longer hours given the surge in goods trade and a shortage of truck drivers.[112] Many of the necessary amenities for drivers like rest stops, restaurants, and hotels were shuttered.[113] In the United States and the UK, rates of Covid infection among transportation workers—which includes bus and taxi drivers—were as much as forty times that of the general population.[114]

Perhaps the biggest cost was paid by the workers who kept trade flowing across the oceans. More than 80% of trade is carried on huge, oceangoing container ships. Even though the movement of goods was treated by most countries as an essential service, many countries refused to declare "essential" the hundreds of thousands of seafarers who staff those vessels. As a consequence, they found themselves stranded at sea for months and months, barred from disembarking at ports and returning to their families. International maritime law prohibits seafarers from working more than eleven months in a row at sea, but by September 2020 some 400,000 were stuck at sea, some having served as long as seventeen months of seven-days-a-week, twelve-hour shifts.[115] United

Nations Secretary-General António Guterres pleaded for countries to declare the seafarers as key workers, enabling them to leave their ships and return home and for crew members stuck on land to return to work. The Consumer Goods Forum, a consortium of giant importers like Unilever, Carrefour, and Tesco, warned that the border restrictions that barred crews from disembarking had "inadvertently created a modern form of forced labor."[116] By December 2020, some forty-five countries had declared the ship workers as "essential," but the list did not include major shipping nations like China, India, South Korea, Italy, and Australia. Six months later, in July 2021, there were still 250,000 crew members stuck at sea and forced to work beyond their contracts.[117]

It was also striking—though little noted during the pandemic—that governments made virtually no effort to distinguish between essential and non-essential trade. There are many trade items—food, energy, medicine, medical equipment, and some household items—that are obviously vital to the safe functioning of a society. But a great deal of trade—electronic entertainment, exercise equipment, new cars, even many clothing items—could quite reasonably be described as discretionary and non-essential. But governments did not make such fine distinctions—in practice, all trade was declared essential. Government emergency declarations during the pandemic were in many respects the equivalent of wartime; governments assumed virtually unrestrained powers in the name of protecting lives and public health. But during the emergencies of the two world wars, many products were rationed in the United States, Britain, and elsewhere in order to turn the country's full economic capacity to the war effort. Sugar, tires, meat, cheese, butter, and other commodities were all rationed.[118] No similar sacrifices were expected during Covid, despite the risks that unrestricted trade posed to the workers who kept goods flowing, and the risks that transportation workers could introduce new infections into the general population.

A truly serious effort to control the spread of Covid would have restricted trade to further reduce the risk of contagion and protect the well-being of the workforce. Reducing both international and domestic commerce would have limited the human movement needed to keep goods flowing, lowering risks for the workers themselves and for the broader public. But no government implemented, or even seriously considered, such measures. By the early twenty-first century, such broad restrictions on trade had become unthinkable.

Can International Law Protect Those Crossing Borders?

International law is never less binding than in situations deemed to be national emergencies. International commitments made to safeguard the movement of people or goods, with rare exceptions, contain opt-out clauses that allow governments to bypass their international obligations if they fear that national security or public health could be jeopardized. International trade rules under the World Trade Organization, for example, contain a broad carve-out that allows countries to block trade for "national security" purposes.[119] What was striking during the pandemic, however, was that one body of those laws—those meant to preserve and expand the movement of goods—was largely upheld by nations. Another body of international laws—those intended to protect human mobility, and especially the rights of refugees and asylum seekers—was largely ignored.

Governments on paper have made international commitments and set up international institutions to encourage and protect people moving across national borders. But in practice those same governments have jealously guarded their prerogative to decide who may come and go from their territories. There is, as Vincent Chetail has put it, "a non-negligible set of international norms regulating admission of non-citizens," but enforcement has long been weak to non-existent.[120] The 1948 Universal Declaration of Human Rights, for example, states that: "Everyone has the right to leave any country, including his own, and to return to his country."[121] Other treaties and conventions have built on that language. Those provisions primarily apply to the rights of citizens to leave and return to their own countries, not to the rights of non-citizens to enter foreign countries. But even citizenship rights are not absolute. The UN Covenant on Civil and Political Rights, for example, says that the right of departure and re-entry can be impeded if such restrictions "are necessary to protect national security, public order (order public), public health or morals or the rights and freedoms of others."[122] The treaties suggest that such travel restrictions should be proportional, equitable, and non-discriminatory, though in practice those judgments have been left to the governments that implemented the measures. International treaties also exist to protect the rights of refugees and migrant workers, as well as those being trafficked across borders, though very few countries have ratified the treaties protecting migrant workers.[123]

The strongest international prohibitions on closing borders during public health emergencies are contained in the 2005 revisions to the International Health Regulations discussed in the previous chapter. While those norms were agreed to by most world governments, they have no binding legal force and, in practice, little moral force. The WHO has no authority to monitor compliance with the regulations, no enforcement mechanisms, and has been unwilling to use its power to "name and shame" countries for lack of compliance.[124] There are effectively no consequences for countries that breach their obligations under the IHR.[125] Health law scholars lamented the widespread breaches of the IHR norms early in the pandemic. "Effective global governance is not possible when countries cannot depend on each other to comply with international agreements," a prominent group wrote in *The Lancet*, a leading medical journal.[126] But such pleas were widely ignored as countries forged their own paths on border and travel restrictions.

The vague, non-binding nature of mobility commitments contrasts with the harder law governing international trade. Through the WTO and various regional and bilateral trade agreements, most governments have made binding commitments to remove impediments to international trade. Many of these agreements have enforcement mechanisms, so that states face economic consequences in the form of higher tariffs on their exports for violating their commitments. Unlike the IHR or other treaty commitments on mobility, the commitments to protect international trade were taken seriously at the highest levels of government during the pandemic. In early March 2020, for example, even as some countries were taking steps to hoard and restrict trade in vital medical equipment like ventilators and protective gear for doctors and nurses, the leaders of the G20 nations pledged to "facilitate international trade and coordinate responses in ways that avoid unnecessary interference with international traffic and trade." Any emergency restrictions on trade, they promised, would be "targeted, proportionate, transparent, and temporary."[127]

These were not hollow promises. By the middle of 2020, the disruptions to trade in medical and protective equipment were largely resolved; indeed, a WTO survey of forty-one countries found that international trade in medical goods grew by nearly 40% during the first half of 2020.[128] Governments also made a variety of efforts to facilitate trade, creating special "trade corridors" and delaying or even removing customs duties on imported goods. China and the EU set up "green lanes" that allowed for rapid inspection and release of goods. Other countries lowered barriers to trade by removing tariffs and customs fees and streamlining border procedures for goods. The WTO and other organizations helped countries to speed up trade facilitation measures such as the digitization of entry forms, which made it possible to process clearances and duty payments through a single online portal and to update shippers on changing entry restrictions.[129]

If any persons should have enjoyed the same high-level attention as the movement of goods, it was those fleeing violence or persecution and seeking asylum. International laws on the treatment of refugees are strong, unambiguous, and widely ratified. The principle of *non-refoulement*, codified in international agreements starting with the 1951 Geneva Convention Relating to the Convention against Torture, forbids states from expelling non-citizens "when there are substantial grounds for believing that the person would be at risk of irreparable harm upon return, including persecution, torture, ill treatment or other serious human rights violations."[130] Unlike many of the other international commitments states have made to protect mobility, there are no "national security" or "public emergency" or "public health" exceptions that permit asylum seekers to be turned away. According to the United Nations Human Rights Commission, "the principle of *non-refoulement* is characterized by its absolute nature without any exception." Such protection covers all persons, regardless of their citizenship or migration status.[131]

Yet during the pandemic, there was no international obligation more widely and egregiously violated than the commitment to protect refugees and asylum seekers. At the height of the pandemic in early 2020, more than 100 countries blocked asylum seekers from making claims.[132] Australia had already barred asylum seekers arriving by boat before Covid hit, but the ban on entry by non-citizens shut down the air route as well. New Zealand halted refugee admissions for more than a year.[133] Canada stopped the processing of asylum applications at its land borders under its Quarantine Act. Asylum seekers traveling via the United States had previously been able to seek refuge in Canada, but the government of Justin Trudeau determined "there were no reasonable alternatives to prevent the introduction or spread" of Covid-19.[134] The United States suspended refugee admission on March 19, 2020, and while the program was formally restarted at the end of July, very few refugees were admitted.[135] On its land borders, the Trump administration invoked Title 42, a World War II–era provision that gives the government power "to prohibit, in whole or in part, the introduction of persons and property" from countries facing epidemics. It was the first time the provision had ever been used in the United States.

The closest the world came to a cooperative response on human mobility during the pandemic was a statement in April 2020 by the tourism ministers for the G20—hardly an influential group—calling for "relevant authorities to minimize undue restrictions for essential travel such as for medical workers and stranded individuals" and pledging to "work with these authorities to ensure that the introduction and removal of travel restrictions are coordinated and proportionate to the national and international situation."[136] The recommendation was widely ignored.

Cross-Border Rights

Existing domestic and international legal regimes provide little recognition of mobility rights for those who live across borders. And the pandemic showed that in a crisis, governments will do little to protect their interests. That should be a warning signal for the millions of people who, as memories of Covid-19 fade, are again resuming lives built around the expectation that they will be able to work, study, or love across borders with reasonable security. Governments around the world are actively encouraging just that; Australia, which was locked tight during the pandemic, took in nearly 500,000 immigrants in the year after its borders reopened in 2022, far above pre-Covid trends. Countries from Japan to Canada to the UK are again vigorously competing for international students. When the next crisis hits, these people will enjoy no assurances that their lives will not be torn in half again, as they were during Covid.

We will return in Chapter 8 to the question of whether there should be a limited set of rights—or at the least governmental norms of greater protection—for those living across borders. During Covid, there were countries that, even as they were restricting travel to discourage the spread of the virus, took the needs of cross-border populations seriously—much of Europe stands out, and there were other isolated exceptions like South Korea. But most of the world turned inward and protected their own resident citizens at the expense of those who were abroad, including in some cases their own nationals, when the borders were closed. In North America, borders were not as tightly shut as some parts of the world, but well-established norms of border cooperation collapsed, leaving many cut off from work, from friends, and from relatives and other loved ones. In the Asia-Pacific, islands from Japan to Australia and New Zealand closed their borders in historically unprecedented ways. China's pursuit of "zero-Covid" led not only to draconian lockdowns at home, but to unprecedented extremes in border control.

In each of these regions, there are lessons that could lead to more effective, less disruptive approaches in future crises. But most of the story is a cautionary tale. From the siege of Point Roberts in the state of Washington to China's "Great Anti-Covid Wall," countries closed their doors to their neighbors, and to the world, in ways that would once have been unimaginable.

4

The Siege of Point Roberts

How Border Cooperation Broke Down in North America

The border separating Canada from the United States traverses a meandering 5,525 miles from its easternmost point in Lubec, Maine, to its western tip along the 141st meridian between Alaska and the Yukon territories. In some areas, it runs through vast stretches of wilderness, while in others it is adjacent to densely populated cities. The lines were first drawn in the late 1700s based on the cartography of the time—little of which involved geographical knowledge beyond the Great Lakes. Treaty negotiators tasked with resolving disputes between the United States and the UK drew the border running from the Eastern seaboard west along the St. Lawrence River and the Great Lakes, following rivers from Lake Superior to the Lake of the Woods in current-day Minnesota. It was agreed that the boundary line would then go straight west until it met the Mississippi River.

What negotiators didn't know at the time was that the source of the mighty Mississippi was too far south to be intersected by that line. It wasn't until the Treaty of 1818 that the two countries continued drawing the border westward to the Rocky Mountains along the 49th parallel, and eventually in 1846 all the way to the Pacific Coast. In the spirit of what one observer has called "the wisdom of Solomon," the line was a compromise that neatly split the British and American claims, but with scant attention to geography. Treaty negotiators made an exception for Vancouver Island, which dips below the 49th parallel and was given to Great Britain rather than being divided up between the two nations. But along the far west coast of the continental United States and modern Canada, the line cut through a more obscure outcropping known as the Tsawwassen Peninsula. It was only after the deal was done that the British noticed that the bottom of the peninsula had been lopped off, and suggested the Americans may want to return it to Great Britain to avoid the inconvenience. But nothing was done.[1] And for the next 174 years no one paid much attention to the tiny community that grew up on the American side of the border, known as Point Roberts. All of that would change in the spring of 2020.

A town of roughly 1,200 residents, Point Roberts can only be reached by land from the rest of the United States by traveling 25 miles through the Canadian province of British Columbia (Figure 4.1). Many of its residents are dual Canadian-US citizens, who take advantage of the cheaper real estate on the US side of the border, with some of the homes literally just across the street from Canada. Because of its location, Point Roberts depends on its neighbors to the north for utilities, health care, and many basic commodities. The economy relies on Canadians, who take advantage of lower fuel prices—Point Roberts has five gas stations and is the only US town with gas prices in liters— and who own second homes with beachfront locations. As the Chamber of Commerce president and vocal Point Roberts advocate Brian Calder describes

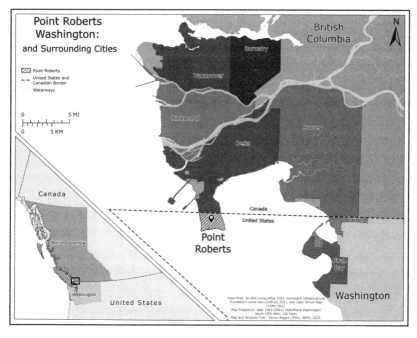

Figure 4.1 Map of Point Roberts, Washington, and surrounding area. Courtesy of Skylar Magee, Border Policy Research Institute.

it, "basically, British Columbia, in a sense, owns us—we just didn't give them the keys."[2]

On a typical weekday, Point Roberts residents Louise Mugar and Pat Grubb, co-publishers of the *All Point Bulletin* newspaper in Point Roberts and *The Northern Light* in Blaine, would cross the border four times on the roundtrip commute to Blaine, Washington. To leave Point Roberts, they drove north into Canada, then southeast roughly 25 miles to the Peace Arch border crossing; returning home from Blaine was the same commute in reverse. Point Roberts only has a primary school—"home of the Borderites"—so after the third grade, schoolchildren faced a similar commute, with the school bus crossing the Canada-US border twice to attend classes in Blaine and then crossing it twice to return home. Many families opt instead to pay out of pocket to send their kids to schools in British Columbia or to participate in sports teams based just across the road in Canada. Daily cross-border travel has always been an epicenter of life for residents of Point Roberts—whether students who transit through Canada, residents who visit their dentists in Vancouver, or Canadians who own over half of all residences in Point Roberts. Attached to Canada and cut off from the United States, for Point Roberts an open international border is the lifeblood of the community.

And then the border closed. When the pandemic restrictions were implemented in March 2020, normal life for most in Point Roberts ended. The local newspaper publishers, for example, were still able to undertake their daily commute through Canada because the trip was deemed "essential." But residents who tried to enter Canada for medical or dental appointments were questioned about the urgency of their conditions so that Canadian border officials could determine if their trips were actually essential. Calder, an eighty-year-old with dual citizenship, tried to enter Canada from Point Roberts to see his optometrist to have surgery on his eye, which had been damaged by glaucoma. But when he arrived at the border he was turned away. His only options were to quarantine for two weeks in Canada, risk the hefty $3,000 fine for violating quarantine, or to return home. He went home.[3] Even in situations where a medical appointment was deemed necessary by Canadian border officials, the person driving the patient, or accompanying them for a procedure, might be refused entry.

Sandra Procter and her husband had chosen to send their sixteen-year-old son to school in Canada rather than face the bus ride to Blaine. When schools in B.C., which had been shut in the initial lockdowns, briefly reopened in June

2020, he was permitted to return with the rest of students. Canada's Border Services Agency said at the time that "healthy, non-symptomatic" students would be allowed across the border. But then in July 2020 in advance of the fall school year, Canada's Public Health Agency suddenly changed the rules— cross-border students would no longer be exempted from the fourteen-day quarantine requirement. "Since they could not reasonably comply with this on a daily basis for the purposes of attending school, such students would be denied entry," said the agency's spokeswoman.[4] The Procters reluctantly decided to send their son to live with friends on the Canadian side of the border so he could continue his schooling. "We're not asking for the border to be opened up," she told Reuters." We're just asking that our kids' education is considered essential."[5]

Before the pandemic, Jennifer Smith[6] crossed the border regularly from Point Roberts to care for her ninety-year-old mother and disabled sister, who live together just across the border in Canada. They relied on her to drive them to medical appointments, shop, clean, and take care of paperwork. Once the border restrictions were enacted, she was still allowed to enter Canada as a Canadian citizen, but because her trip was not considered essential, she was required to quarantine for two weeks. "I have asked CBSA agents if I can drive across the border to help my family," said Jennifer. The answer has always been "no—not without the quarantine." As the border restrictions dragged on, Jennifer had to make a decision on whether to leave her partner in Point Roberts so she could live with her sister and mother, where she would have no medical care and could potentially lose her US permanent residency. Jennifer's decision to stay in Point Roberts is one she "has to live with every day. Without my help in Canada, my sister and I have begun the process of institutionalizing our mother. My sister really cannot cope with both her own medical condition and our elderly mother without assistance. The expense and guilt of having my mother placed in a care facility because her daughters cannot (or will not) care for her in her own home is a terrible burden."[7]

Uncertainty and unpredictability plagued virtually every aspect of life in Point Roberts. Homeowners who needed to buy building supplies or tools were denied entry to Canada, those bringing their pets to the veterinarian for vaccinations were turned away, and even elderly people who needed to visit their banks in Canada were told that "banking is not considered essential."[8] This scenario played out regardless of whether or not Point Roberts residents were traveling *to* Canada or simply *through* Canada to reach the rest of the

United States. Given the unique nature of the geography, some residents were granted an exemption and allowed to transit through Canada, but only for certain purposes deemed essential. The interpretation rested with the Canadian officer in the booth. And a different officer often meant a different interpretation on any given day, leaving residents with the feeling that "the rules seem arbitrary at best."[9]

There are several isolated communities along the Canada-US border that are cut off from their own countries, such as Hyder, Alaska; Northwest Angle, Minnesota; and Campobello Island, New Brunswick. All of these suffered disproportionately during the border restrictions, but none on the scale of Point Roberts. Canada made exceptions six months into the pandemic for the sixty residents of Hyder, including allowing them to shop for groceries and return their kids to Canadian schools.[10] Northwest Angle is home to about 100 people and depends almost solely on summer tourism; its economy was devastated by the border closures that cut off American visitors who needed to drive through the Canadian province of Manitoba to reach the peninsula that juts into the Lake of the Woods.[11] Campobello Island fared somewhat better—American authorities granted the 800 residents permits to drive through Maine to the rest of New Brunswick, and a seasonal summer ferry connected the island to the province. But the loss of Canadian tourists similarly hammered the local economy.[12] Point Roberts, however, was the place that consistently captured national and international media attention. Calder kept a tally that reached over 400 news articles—a testament to the absurd rigidity of the border restrictions and their devastating effects on the town. Point Roberts did not have a single recorded Covid infection until February 2021, nearly a full year after the border was shut.[13] Yet Canadian officials resisted over many months while residents of the community begged governments to find a more rational compromise that responded to their unique situation.

The failure was not from lack of effort. In an August 2020 letter to Canadian Prime Minister Justin Trudeau, Washington State governor Jay Inslee pleaded for Ottawa to recognize "the tradition of cooperation between Canada and the state of Washington" and the "unique hardships" to Point Roberts from the border restrictions. In February 2021, Washington State's congressional delegation wrote to President Joe Biden, lamenting that "Point Roberts has seen businesses shutter, school children fall behind, an emerging food scarcity crisis, and deteriorating community mental health, while not contracting a single case of COVID-19."[14] They urged the administration to "push for further flexibility in border crossing for our constituents that live in severely isolated geographies." The US and Canadian consulates in Vancouver and Seattle were engaged, pilot projects easing restrictions were proposed to US Customs and Border Protection and Canada's Border Services Agency, and negotiations were pursued through the Department of Homeland Security's attaché in Ottawa. But still, nothing happened.

It was not until a full year into the border closures that some small exceptions were made for Point Roberts, as the border restrictions shifted away from a focus on trip purpose and toward vaccination and testing. Vaccinated Point Roberts residents were exempted from the land border testing requirement implemented by Canada in February 2021 and were allowed to enter Canada within a certain travel radius for shopping and other activities.[15] Residents achieved a vaccination rate of over 70% by April 2021—several months ahead of the rest of the state.[16] But the easing of border controls was too little and came too late for a town that had already lost 80% of its economic activity. In the absence of a solution at the federal level, in August 2020 the nearby City of Bellingham funded an emergency, twice-weekly passenger ferry service to enable residents to reach the US mainland. At a cost of $3,500 per trip, the service was unpredictable during winter weather and did little to alleviate the economic hardship that resulted from the inability of Canadians to travel to Point Roberts.[17] By the summer of 2021, the town's only grocery store was on the brink of closing its doors; only an emergency $100,000 subsidy from the State of Washington kept it alive. By then the sole marina was already up for sale and the golf course had been closed for over a year.[18]

Point Roberts, while an outlier, exemplifies the struggle of many people living in communities that could only exist because of a functioning border. The social and economic health of such communities depends completely on efficient cross-border travel. When governments throw up barriers, those communities cease to thrive. That story has played out for many decades along the border between Mexico and the United States, where US fears of unauthorized migration have separated once closely connected communities like Juárez, Mexico, and El Paso in Texas, and Laredo and Nuevo Laredo. During Covid, the US government went still further, invoking never-used epidemic control powers—known as Title 42—to bar entry by most Mexicans. The story of Point Roberts casts an especially harsh light, however, because it shows how two nations that are trusted allies and close trading partners, and whose citizens rely on each other, tossed these communities aside by failing to cooperate in the most basic and sensible ways to mitigate the harms of the pandemic border restrictions. The two governments had a long history of collaboration on border measures—most significantly following the terrorist attacks of September 11, 2001. But those norms of mobility broke down utterly during Covid; it seems unlikely they can be rebuilt anytime soon.

Why Border Cooperation Broke Down

Canada, Mexico, and the United States established models for border cooperation in a crisis in the aftermath of the 9/11 attacks. But during the Covid crisis, they acted largely independently, controlling border crossings with little concern for the effects on residents of the other two countries. Initial agreements enacted hastily in March 2020 kept freight flowing; other than an initial dip in trade that occurred early on and was largely the result of domestic workplace closures, goods continued to move freely across borders. However, when it came to the movement of people, the situation was much more varied and complex. Each country treated "non-essential" travel differently and prioritized politically popular restrictions in the name of public health, despite the seemingly robust frameworks for border cooperation that were in place when Covid appeared. Combined with bureaucratic dysfunction, the result was an arbitrary system that allowed millions of people to cross borders with no health precautions at all, while others were unable to visit dying relatives. Despite the deep integration and dependencies across North American borders, governments rejected the long-standing precedent of keeping borders operating, save for the movement of goods. The consequence was an extended period of severely restricted borders, which inflicted continual harm on border communities and those dependent on cross-border mobility, even as the Covid virus was nonetheless spreading across the continent.

In a typical year, roughly 240 million passengers and pedestrians, along with 12 million trucks, enter the United States across its land borders.[19] Another 128 million people arrive from Canada and Mexico on airplanes.[20] The US-Mexico border is the most frequently crossed border in the world.[21] The ability of goods, people, and services to flow between the United States and its northern and southern neighbors depends largely on how well the borders function.[22] Those borders had only been shut once before—for six hours following the assassination of President John F. Kennedy in Texas in

1963. After the 9/11 terrorist attacks in Washington and New York in 2001, the US Customs Service declared a "Level 1" alert at the borders with Mexico and Canada, the most stringent level short of a complete closure. Within a day, US auto companies were forced to shut down assembly plants as the flow of "just-in-time" parts across the border dried up.[23] US-Mexico trade fell by 15% over the following month. The debacle was a wake-up call to officials in Washington, Ottawa, and Mexico City. "There was a degree of panic on both sides of the border," said Anne McLellan, who was Canada's justice minister during the events. "The visual of 9/11 was powerful . . . miles of trucks on both sides of the border backed up for seventy-two hours, not moving. That visual was so powerful in terms of . . . helping Canadians and Americans understand . . . somebody had to fix it."[24]

The 9/11 attacks ushered in a new era of border management, with Canada and the United States especially collaborating to develop "smart borders" that would dovetail security and efficiency. Agreements hastily negotiated in the fall of 2001 increased information sharing between the governments, expanded joint screening of travelers and cargo, set up "filtering" systems to separate high- and low-risk traffic, and formalized collaborative mechanisms. The goal was to strengthen defenses against infiltration by terrorists and criminals without slowing vital cross-border trade and travel. By 2011, both countries took a further step, signing the Beyond the Border Accord "to pursue a perimeter approach to security, working together within, at, and away from the borders of our two countries to enhance our security and accelerate the legitimate flow of people, goods, and services between our two countries."[25] This included highly integrated "trusted" traveler and trader programs that allowed frequent border crossers to speed through checkpoints, as well as expanded preclearance operations, whereby US Customs and Border Protection officers located in Canada processed shippers and travelers before they departed for the United States. The larger goal was to weed out suspicious travelers before they could enter North America instead of relying primarily on inspections at the border itself; the two countries agreed to share, for example, intelligence on incoming airline passengers so that those raising concerns could be blocked before boarding flights to the continent.[26] For Canada and the United States, this perimeter strategy deepened a long-standing approach to security, initially formalized by the North American Aerospace Defense program in the 1950s and later by multiple border-focused security agreements.[27]

The United States and Mexico made less progress after 9/11 but still managed to deepen their border cooperation. New arrangements helped to speed the shipment of goods while enhancing security, vital to both economies. The two governments signed the US-Mexico Border Partnership Agreement in 2002, which mirrored many of the Canadian border arrangements in trying to separate low-risk from high-risk flows.[28] But 9/11 also accelerated the militarization of the border that had begun in the 1990s when the Clinton administration built border barriers and massed Border Patrol agents in California and Texas in an effort to slow illegal migration.[29] The terrorist attacks created an opportunity for immigration opponents in the United States to conflate undocumented immigrants and terrorists—despite the fact that all the 9/11 hijackers entered the United States through legal channels.[30] In 2005, Congress passed the "Secure Fence Act" authorizing the construction of 700 miles of physical barriers along the southern border.[31] While there are many elements of collaboration, especially on trade, the US-Mexico border has been plagued by politicization and mistrust. Unlike the Canada-US trusted traveler program NEXUS, for example, its equivalent on the southern border, known as SENTRI, is for US entry only and lacks any bilateral integration. Controlling the movement of people, especially between ports of entry, has been the defining and unresolved challenge of US policy toward Mexico.

Despite these strains, North America should still have been ready for the challenge of Covid. The three countries had even planned together for just such an event. In the 2012 North American Plan for Animal and Pandemic Influenza (NAPAPI), they agreed that "emphasizing a North American approach, rather than individualized approaches among the three countries, could provide a means of slowing the spread of a novel strain of human influenza into our respective countries."[32] The plan incorporated lessons learned from the North American response to H1N1 in 2009, which was the first Public Health Emergency of International Concern declared under the International Health Regulations of 2005. The NAPAPI called for a collective response to pandemic management given the depth and breadth of supply chain connections and travel volumes. It focused largely on public health screening, recommending "disease surveillance systems coupled with appropriate public health measures at North American airports, seaports and regional perimeters."[33] While acknowledging the sovereign right of each country to shut its borders, the plan cautioned that highly restrictive measures "might initially delay but would not stop the eventual spread of a novel strain of human influenza within North America, and could have significant negative social, economic and foreign policy consequences. Less restrictive measures could potentially slow the spread of disease to/within North America with fewer significant negative consequences."[34] The governments concluded that during the H1N1 pandemic, the decision "to keep the borders open and minimize travel restrictions limited disruptions of travel and trade, avoided panic, and saved resources."

Yet when the Covid pandemic hit less than a decade later, each country went its own way in closing borders and restricting travel. While they worked together to keep cross-border trade flowing—largely by exempting truckers, rail, and air freight workers from most of the public health restrictions—the rules for other border crossers were a study in incoherence. In March 2020, the three countries agreed to restrict non-essential travel at their land borders, but in practice they behaved in radically different ways. Canada required two weeks' quarantine for all but essential incoming travelers like truckers, while those who were not Canadian citizens or residents were largely prohibited from entering; the United States and Mexico had little or nothing in the way of quarantine requirements. Canada barred most air and land travelers from its neighbors. The United States blocked its land borders but continued to allow incoming flights from both Canada and Mexico. "Non-essential" Canadians, including tourists who could not drive to the United States, were permitted to fly. In theory, Mexico cooperated on the land border closures, though its regime was far less restrictive than in the north, and actively encouraged tourists to fly in from the United States and Canada.[35] The result was an extended, misaligned, and uncoordinated approach among the three countries—a patchwork of policies that enabled some travelers to cross borders for tourism and recreation, while others were blocked from seeing family and loved ones, or even from fleeing life-threatening violence. It was anything but a North American approach.

Why did border cooperation break down? The simplest answer is Donald Trump—his administration's chaotic response to the pandemic undermined the trust needed for closer cooperation on border measures. Public messaging from his administration in the early days downplayed the potential severity of the virus, with Trump tweeting on February 24, 2020, that "the Coronavirus is very much under control in the USA." At a press conference two days later, he stated that "because of all we've done, the risk to the American people remains very low." In the course of the next two years, nearly 1 million people in the United States would lose their lives to Covid-19.

But the pandemic also revealed deeper differences in national cultures that, even with more stable leadership in the United States, could have swept aside the ethos of cooperation that had developed after 9/11. Canadians, for example, have long been proud of their national public health system, and are appalled by the largely private American system that leaves many millions without access to proper medical care. Canadians were determined to protect their system, in part by limiting the number of Covid cases that might spill across the border and potentially increase demands on the already overburdened hospitals. And Canadian trust in government officials, while weaker than some decades ago, is far deeper than in the United States.[36] Canadian health officials who gave regular updates to the public during Covid never became lightning rod figures in the way that Anthony Fauci did in the United States. From early in the pandemic, Canadians showed themselves far more willing than Americans to support government-imposed lockdowns, masking, and other restrictive measures to slow the spread of Covid. Canada's death rate during the pandemic would be less than half that of its neighbor to the south.

Mexicans too had their issues with Donald Trump; he had run his successful 2016 presidential campaign warning that Mexico was sending drugs, criminals, and rapists across the border, and then after taking office he had threatened tariffs on Mexican goods if the government did not halt the flow of migrants.[37] But in practice Mexico was even more allergic to lockdowns and other Covid restrictions than it was to Trump. In part to reject its history of authoritarian rule and in part to try to boost the economy, the Mexican government refused to impose any coercive public health measures.[38] Mexico had also been burned by health-related travel restrictions in the past. In 2009, Mexican epidemiologists had isolated the first outbreak of the H1N1 virus and following WHO norms had quickly reported their findings to the world. The response was a rash of flight cancellations to and from Mexico that cut travel by 40%.[39] During Covid, Mexico would reject all but the most cursory travel restrictions. Its eventual death toll was among the highest in the world.

In striking contrast to the post-9/11 reaction, North American cooperation on border management gave way to nationalistic responses. With the exception of a swiftly implemented policy enabling the movement of trade, the pandemic border restrictions between the United States and its northern and southern neighbors are largely a story of missed opportunities and national retrenchment. Border communities were hit especially hard; border rules formulated in distant capitals divided communities that had long been intimately connected.[40] And the measures lasted a long time—the final pandemic-era border measures were not lifted by the United States until May 2023, even after China had finally reopened its doors. "[O]nce the restrictions were imposed," wrote a US-Canadian task force organized by the Woodrow Wilson Center, "the governments failed to respond to public concerns, health conditions, or the concerns of citizens and elected representatives who sought to mitigate the damage done to local communities, families, and the economy by those restrictions."[41]

The Half-Closed US-Mexico Border

On March 21, 2020, the "US-Mexico Joint Initiative" was announced; the two governments would temporarily restrict all non-essential travel across their shared land borders in a "collaborative and reciprocal" initiative.[42] Essential commerce, trade, and travel would remain unaffected. But the Mexican government did little beyond its initial head nod, and travel continued relatively unrestricted both from the United States and from abroad. From the outset, Mexico's handling of its borders stood in stark contrast to its continental neighbors. Passengers arriving in or departing from airports in Mexico were subject to minimal health screenings; flights continued between the United States and Mexico, and between Mexico and other countries where outbreaks were ongoing.[43] The only Covid-19 related requirement implemented by the Mexican government on foreign nationals was the completion of a health declaration form to be processed upon entering Mexico.[44] International tourism slumped in 2020, but American tourists quickly returned to popular beach destinations like Los Cabos, where 25% more people visited in July 2021 than in 2019 before the pandemic.[45]

While travel into Mexico flowed relatively freely, those going the other way were subject to the Joint Initiative suspending all land and ferry arrivals related to tourism and recreation. The result was that US citizens and permanent residents were able to cross the land border into Mexico with relative ease, and readily return to the United States—which, unlike Canada, had no quarantine requirement for returning travelers. Mexican citizens, however, could only enter the United States for essential reasons. The loophole was still a big one—those considered "essential" included the large number of Mexican workers holding border crossing cards who continued to commute to work in the United States, as well as those traveling for educational or medical reasons. However, Mexicans who previously crossed the border to shop in the United States, or to visit friends and family, were not permitted. There are also many dual-citizen children who live in Mexico and attend schools in the United States. While they were able to resume attending school in the fall of 2020, in many cases their parents were unable to drive them if they did not also have US citizenship or an essential reason to cross.[46]

This asymmetry resulted in very different economic impacts on either side, where roughly 19 million people live near the border on the US side and an estimated 11 million more on the Mexican side.[47] For some Mexican border towns like Juárez and Tijuana, the pandemic was a small windfall; they continued to welcome American shoppers and tourists, while at the same time serving more Mexican customers who were no longer able to shop in the United States.[48] But the restrictions hammered US border cities, like El Paso and Laredo, Texas, that suddenly lost what had been a steady stream of cross-border Mexican shoppers.[49] Prior to the pandemic, Mexican shoppers had accounted for nearly 45% of retail sales in Laredo, and some 35% in McAllen and Brownsville.[50] But the costs went far beyond shopping. Residents of communities like El Paso–Juárez and San Diego–Tijuana were accustomed to frequent travel across the border, where they could receive medical care and visit family with ease.[51]

Even for people with permission to cross, unpredictable wait times due to reduced hours and a funneling of traffic at crossing points created major impediments. After nighttime operations were temporarily suspended at Otay Mesa, California, in May 2020, dozens of workers took to sleeping in their cars while waiting for the border to open so they could avoid delays in the morning.[52] Prior to the restrictions, families with mixed legal status with only some members possessing legal permission to enter the United States— a common scenario in the borderlands—would rely on those with status to cross the border, bringing goods and medical supplies back with them. Sandra Rojel, a dual citizen living in San Diego, found it nearly impossible to bring medicine to her mother in Tijuana, despite her ability to cross in both directions. "Before the restrictions went into effect, I would come at least once or twice a week," she said in July 2020. "The lines were very short and very fast. But now, it takes the whole day just to cross."[53] As a result, Sandra's trips to bring her mother medicines only available in the United States were reduced to once a month.

Title 42 and the Abuse of Emergency Powers

The pandemic also provided a rationale for imposing border restrictions that would have been inconceivable absent the health emergency. The most striking example was Title 42 of the Public Health Service Act of 1944, which permitted the US government to turn back border crossers on health grounds. The law was intended to prevent the spread of a communicable disease by prohibiting the entry of people from countries where the disease existed. While the United States had imposed similar restrictions in the past—including an effort in 1929 to bar people coming from China and the Philippines during a meningitis outbreak—Title 42 had never been used before. One day prior to the launch of the US-Mexico Joint Initiative on March 21, the director of the US Centers for Disease Control (CDC), Robert Redfield, signed the order.

The official explanation for Title 42 was to protect public health at the holding centers used for migrants who had crossed illegally, as well as "the serious danger of the introduction of COVID-19 into the interior of the country . . . when certain persons are processed . . . and move into the interior of the United States."[54] These centers were viewed as potential sites for spreading the virus, providing a rationale for immediately turning migrants back to Mexico upon arrival rather than following the normal procedure of detaining them in the United States and processing their asylum or other claims. The deportations were a blatant violation of long-standing US commitments, under both domestic and international laws, not to return asylum seekers to potentially dangerous situations. But the pressure came directly from the Trump White House. Stephen Miller, the president's top advisor on immigration policy who had been pushing to stop the flow of asylum seekers at the border, chaired the inter-governmental meetings that led to the order.[55] Miller had been the driving force behind the "Remain in Mexico" program that forced asylum seekers, mostly from Central and South America, to wait on the Mexican side of the border until their asylum claims were heard in US immigration courts. Title 42 doubled down. "It was closing the border more formally than we could by building the wall," said Theresa Cardinal-Brown, director of immigration and cross-border policy at the Bipartisan Policy Center. The use of Title 42 was opposed by top CDC officials, including Martin Cetron, the veteran director of Global Migration and Quarantine at the agency, who refused to sign the order.[56] Anthony Fauci, the nation's leading scientist during the pandemic, explicitly stated that Covid-19 transmission "is not driven by immigrants" and "expelling [migrants] is not the solution to an outbreak."[57]

The order was particularly hollow given the absence of other serious US federal measures to contain the spread of the disease, such as mandatory quarantine for returning travelers. Leading epidemiologists argued that Title 42 was never about public health, but rather "a cynical manipulation of public health arguments to advance political policies of immigration control."[58] Implementing and maintaining Title 42 allowed the Trump administration to bypass immigration laws in order to harden US borders—a goal Trump himself had championed during his election campaign. When he announced the border restrictions, Trump described them as being necessary to stop "the grave public health consequences of mass uncontrolled cross-border movement."[59]

But Title 42 failed both at both public health and migration control. Unlike standard immigration laws related to asylum claims, Title 42 allowed for the immediate expulsion of migrants at the border. Migrants were not subject to formal processing and therefore faced no consequences, including expedited removal and criminal prosecution, which often dissuaded repeated efforts by those crossing the border illegally. Under Title 42, migrants were simply returned to the Mexican side of the border, and many just kept trying.[60] The result was that, after an initial drop in crossings between the ports of entry, the number of arrests by the Border Patrol surged to record levels.[61] During the first six months of Title 42's enactment, nearly half of all single adults encountered by the Border Patrol had attempted to cross in the previous year.[62] Title 42 did little to reassure the American public that the border was under control.

The human consequences were enormous as well. Migrants returned to Mexico faced significant dangers at the hands of criminal gangs and the Mexican police. Human Rights First, a US-based group, compiled reports of more than 13,000 incidents of violence against those removed to Mexico, including murder, rape, torture, and kidnapping.[63] Amanda Maribel-Sanchez, who fled Honduras with her two young children to escape a violent husband, spent more than a year in Mexico after they were expelled under Title 42, moving between shelters and an abandoned home in Piedras Negras along the border with Texas. "It's been very hard because my daughter is very thin, my son is always dirty, and I am, too," she said. "They are without school, without medicine, because they close their doors on us and don't want to help. We are very hungry."[64] Others desperate to reach the United States risked dangerous crossings to try to evade the Border Patrol; more than fifty migrants from Mexico, Guatemala, and Honduras were found dead in 2022 in a locked tractor-trailer north of San Antonio in the heat of summer.[65]

Both the Trump and Biden administrations continually renewed the March 2020 order. Even after the US border restrictions were modified in November 2021 to allow the entry of vaccinated travelers at land and ferry crossings, top officials continued to assert that the public health crisis necessitated the enforcement of Title 42. The result was a situation in which millions of travelers were allowed to cross the border, yet those seeking asylum were still being turned away without due process. By spring of 2022, when effective vaccines had been widely available in the United States for over a year, Biden faced mounting pressure from his own Democratic Party to lift the order, even as Republicans warned of a new rush of migrants. The CDC announced its intention to lift Title 42 in April 2022, saying it was "no longer necessary" given increased access to vaccines and other tools to fight the spread of Covid-19.[66] But a series of lawsuits from state Republican attorneys general prevented its removal.[67] The case made its way to the Supreme Court in December 2022, which also kept the order temporarily in place but stated that "the current border crisis is not a COVID crisis. And courts should not be in the business of perpetuating administrative edicts designed for one emergency only because elected officials have failed to address a different emergency."[68] A year after announcing its intention to end Title 42, the United States finally rescinded the policy in May 2023 alongside its declaration that the public health emergency had ended.[69] During the three years Title 42 was enforced, it served as the legal basis for more than 2 million expulsions.

The Canada-US Illusion of Cooperation

The Canada-US border is often described more as a relationship than as a boundary line. The value of merchandise trade between the two countries was the second highest on earth in the year leading up to the pandemic, and nearly three quarters of Canada's exports go to the United States.[70] This US$611 billion bilateral trade relationship, supported in part by the half a million trucks that cross the border monthly, is defined not just by imports and exports but by integrated supply chains that both countries rely on to make everything from cars to airplanes to hamburgers. Early on in the pandemic, Canada's official stance was aligned with the prevailing science of the WHO International

Health Regulations, which discouraged the use of travel restrictions during public health emergencies. As late as March 13, 2020, Canada's health minister Patty Hajdu argued that "what we see is a global pandemic, which means that border measures are highly ineffective and, in some cases, can create harm."[71] When Canada first announced restrictions on the entry of foreign travelers on March 16, 2020, Americans were exempted.[72] Canada's Deputy Prime Minister Chrystia Freeland said the decision to keep the border open to Americans was based on the deep level of integration between the two countries. "That border is absolutely vital to the daily lives of the people who live on both sides," stated Freeland.[73] But nonetheless it was Freeland who first proposed closing the land borders on a call the next day with US Vice President Mike Pence.[74] Trudeau and Trump then spoke by telephone the morning of March 18 and announced they had agreed to temporarily restrict all non-essential travel. The decision reversed decades in which Canada had consistently been the champion of a fluid border, staunchly resisting US measures to "thicken" the border in ways that could harm trade and travel.

In the summer of 2019, Kirsten Hillman became acting ambassador to the United States amid the final stages of the NAFTA renegotiations. She played a central role in negotiating with US officials over the details of the border restrictions in the hectic week leading up to their implementation on March 21. The cooperation between the two countries was in stark contrast to the US ban on travel from Europe, implemented with no forewarning or consultation with the EU. But the collaboration proved to be short-lived. Just days after announcing the joint restrictions, President Trump raised the idea of sending troops to the border.[75] "We had had such success with orderly and quick and coordinated restrictions on the border to nonessential travel," Hillman said. "To then somehow suggest that something wasn't going well at the border, and therefore there needed to be troops deployed potentially to assist at the border, just was taking that incredibly positive tone and potentially undermining it."[76]

Each country established different rules and interpretations of the restrictions, and cooperation quickly gave way to minimal coordination. Month after month, Washington and Ottawa would extend the restrictions for another thirty days, with no hint of any consultations on when and how they might be eased. Border region politicians, cross-border industries, and families separated by the border closures complained in any way they could. Hastily formed groups like Let Us Reunite and Faces of Advocacy spoke to the Canadian Parliament and submitted letters to the elected officials in their jurisdiction, advocating for better avenues for families and loved ones to cross the border. The co-chairs of the Canada-US Interparliamentary Group lamented in June 2021 that "the lack of transparency surrounding these negotiations is a disservice to our constituents and the millions of residents on both sides of the border waiting to see their loved ones, visit their property, and renew business ties."[77]

The border restrictions varied considerably between the United States and Canada, with each country defining "essential" and "non-essential" trip purposes differently.[78] The United States, for example, considered all work as essential, while Canada initially defined only certain types of work as essential. As travel reopened with restrictions in 2021, each country recognized different vaccines and test types, and even the timing for the validity of test results varied. The United States accepted rapid antigen tests and only required them for air arrivals, while Canada required the more expensive and time-intensive PCR tests and required them for both land and air arrivals.[79] Both countries allowed entry for particular family members, yet categories and approaches differed significantly. Canada implemented exemptions for immediate family members as early as June 2020 (subject to a fourteen-day quarantine and other requirements), and by fall of 2020 allowed entry for extended family members, later creating an application process for those seeking entry for compassionate reasons. The US Federal Register notice omitted family need or other compassionate grounds, instead granting border officers full discretionary authority upon arrival.

Indeed, both Canada Border Services Agency and US Customs and Border Protection jealously guard their sovereign discretionary authority and their power to refuse entry upon arrival. This had been a problem in the past, particularly for those seeking entry related to business or work.[80] The pandemic border restrictions, however, ushered in a new period of confusion and inconsistency, as both the traveling public and border officers themselves lacked clarity. There were numerous accounts of the same trip purpose being allowed at one port of entry and denied at another, or of different officers at the same port adjudicating trip purposes differently from day to day.[81] For example, if a Canadian grandmother wanted to visit her grandchildren in the United States she might be denied entry if the purpose of her trip was simply to spend time with her grandchildren. However, if her daughter was ill and needed help taking care of the children, she might be allowed to cross. That decision would be completely up to the officer she encountered upon arrival at the border, leaving no ability to plan ahead. The inconsistencies, in combination with the discretionary authority of border officers in both countries, were almost impossible for those living in border communities to navigate and only contributed to the anxiety and uncertainty that millions of people impacted by the restrictions were already facing during the pandemic.[82]

The miscoordination continued right to the end. Canada began easing border restrictions for vaccinated Americans in July 2021, and then fully by September 2021. The United States did not reciprocate for another two months.

The Randomness of Border Restrictions

In March 2020, Aimee Beauchamp returned to Canada after one of her weekly visits to see her partner in the United States A few weeks later, the border restrictions were announced, and shortly afterward, she discovered she was pregnant. Aimee and her partner Cody celebrated via Skype and started planning for the arrival of the baby. But at the end of May, she suffered a painful miscarriage, and Cody planned to cross the border so he could pick her up from the hospital. Both of them believed he would be granted entry for compassionate reasons and would quarantine upon arrival with her if necessary. But he was turned away at the border on his first attempt and later returned with a letter from Aimee's healthcare provider, which included her discharge papers and a recommendation that she have mental and emotional support during her grieving process. However, as Aimee recounts, "he was told that caring for me and grieving the loss of our child was not essential. We were both devastated, and I was forced to be alone at home while I grieved. This was one of the most painful experiences of my life. I wasn't able to seek comfort or provide comfort to my partner." Even after Canada carved out exemptions for extended families and compassionate reasons months later, uncertainty and quarantine requirements made it difficult for the two to be together, leaving Aimee with what she called "deep anxiety and fear."[83]

Aimee and Cody's experience was not an isolated one. With towns and cities abutting each side and the historic ease of crossing, thousands of couples have built their lives on opposite sides of the border. After Canada and the United States jointly launched the NEXUS trusted traveler program in 2002, frequent crossers could speed across the border with waits that rarely exceeded five minutes. Many Vancouverites have second homes in the rural golf communities just south of the border in western Washington State, while New Yorkers enjoy their summer cottages on lakefront property in Ontario and Quebec. Distinct borderland economies have formed to draw cross-border tourists and shoppers. The town of Bellingham, Washington, for example, has hosted an "at par" day at the local mall to entice Canadian shoppers, with businesses valuing the Canadian dollar—typically worth about eighty US cents—at par with the US dollar.

Those who needed to continue crossing the border during the pandemic found themselves in a Kafka novel, with the fate of each trip in the hands of border bureaucrats. As one Canadian woman separated from her spouse put it, "you couldn't do the right thing, because the goalposts were constantly moving, and it almost started to feel intentional."[84] Or, as Canadian Annie Hall recounted, her US colleague "flew from Atlanta to Detroit and drove into Windsor unhindered, *unhindered* and people that live in this border community could not go see their dying relatives, could not see grandparents, grandchildren, parents."[85]

During the twenty months that the United States restricted land border travel to essential reasons only, cross-border travel fell by 83%. However, there were still over 17 million trips taken across the border from Canada to the United States (compared to over 100 million the previous twenty months), few of which required any testing, vaccination, or other health precautions for entry.[86] Air travelers were required to have a negative Covid test starting January 2021, but the US government never required tests to cross the land border. While the virus and its multiple variants continued to spread in both countries, the United States and Canada remained wedded to border restrictions that had questionable efficacy in protecting public health, while producing substantial social and economic disruptions.[87] The reality on the ground was much as it had been predicted in the North American Plan for Animal and Pandemic Influenza—border restrictions had high costs with little public health benefit. An evaluation from the Auditor General of Canada found numerous gaps and failures in Canada's border measures, leading to the conclusion that the Public Health Agency of Canada "did not adequately enforce additional border control measures imposed to limit the introduction of the virus that causes COVID-19 and its variants into Canada" and that "the agency cannot determine how effective the imposed border measures are for protecting public health."[88] Leading public health experts argue that policymakers have "two key challenges: how to use travel measures to mitigate public-health risks most effectively while limiting secondary harms to individuals and societies; and how to communicate in ways that foster public trust."[89] The United States and Canada failed in both regards.

Despite government claims that the countries were in "constant communication," the disparities in coordinating the easing of border restrictions point to the superficial extent of that communication.[90] After nearly two decades of developing integrated border management policies, there was a gaping absence of joint innovation and problem solving during the pandemic. There were numerous reasons for this: bureaucratic inertia, inadequate administrative capacity, different infection rates, and a novel virus that mutated rapidly. Undergirding all these challenges was the toxic relationship between Prime Minister Trudeau and President Trump. The Trump administration had launched a trade war by imposing tariffs on Canadian aluminum and steel in 2018, leading Canada to retaliate. The mutual dislike broke into public view following the summit of G7 leaders in Ottawa in 2018. Trump's trade advisor, Peter Navarro, slammed Trudeau after the meeting, saying there was "a special place in hell for any foreign leader that engages in bad-faith diplomacy with President Donald J. Trump and then tries to stab him in the back on the way out the door."[91] The collapse of good will at the highest level explains in part why Canada was ready to abandon its long-standing position that a seamless and efficient border was a matter of the highest national interest, and that coordination with the United States to maintain that openness was vital.

But even after Joe Biden became president in 2021 and relations improved, little changed at the border. By this point, Canada was fully entrenched in its unilateral approach to border management, and the United States faced bigger problems, particularly given the anticipated challenges of revoking Title 42. It would take much more than improved relations to untangle the politics of the border restrictions enacted in the name of public health. In a reflection of national clichés, the US approach, on the whole, embraced liberty over mandates, while Canada opted for order and enforcement. In the United States, for example, quarantine requirements were the exception (applied only by Alaska and Hawaii for certain air arrivals and cruise repatriations). In contrast, Canada imposed a complex system of interprovincial travel restrictions, mandatory quarantine requirements for returning travelers, and a layered testing regime. The US Federal Register, in which the federal government's regulatory guidance for the border restrictions was published, was only modified a few times during the pandemic; Canada modified its policy guidance, known as Orders in Council, eighty times.[92]

Beyond Border Restrictions: Canada's Complex Covid Regime

One of Canada's most powerful policy tools during the pandemic was the Federal Quarantine Act. First invoked in April 2020, the Act required anyone entering Canada by air, land, or sea to quarantine for 14 days.[93] The quarantine requirements were burdensome for many travelers, often keeping people apart who were allowed to cross but could not afford a two-week isolation period. But given the potentially lengthy incubation period of the virus, it was one of the few effective measures available to governments before vaccines were widely available. Canada also briefly experimented with the Asian model of mandatory hotel quarantine in response to the spread of new variants, despite the fact that less than 2% of cases in the country were connected to international air travel when the measures were implemented.[94] Starting in February 2021, as variants began to spread, the government required all air travelers returning from non-essential trips abroad (with limited exceptions) to quarantine at a government-approved hotel for three nights at the traveler's expense before returning home to isolate for the remaining eleven days. In addition, a series of negative Covid tests were required before travelers could be released from the hotel. Violating any entry instructions could result in a fine of up to $750,000, up to six months in prison, or both. Passengers were required to cover the costs of the hotel stay, which sometimes amounted to $2,000. The measure was unpopular—numerous instances arose of travelers being fined for refusing to quarantine in hotels, whether to save money or because they believed returning home would be a safer alternative.[95] Frustrated travelers described crowded and congested waiting areas, which further contributed to the sense that the program was "to punish people who travel. It's not about safety."[96] What did such an expensive and problematic program achieve? "The multiple layers of what was essentially pandemic theatre, unsurprisingly, did not prove effective against seeding the variant," write authors Van Geyn and Baron.[97] For many, the hotel quarantine program served to undermine public trust in the government approach, prompting multiple legal challenges against the Canadian government, all of which have been unsuccessful to date.[98]

Overall, Canada's quarantine requirements were not only expensive, but also difficult to enforce and monitor. From March 2020 to August 2021, the cost of administering quarantine facilities, testing requirements, and government authorized hotels reached CAD$614 million.[99] A 2021 report from the Auditor General found that the Public Health Agency of Canada (PHAC) could not verify quarantine requirements for 37% of incoming travelers and that 30% of Covid test results could not be matched to. Despite the severity of the mandatory hotel quarantine requirement, which lasted roughly five months, there was no automated system for tracking compliance. As a result, PHAC could only verify hotel stays for 25% of air arrivals.[100]

As in many countries, there were special exceptions to the rules for some visitors. The same month the mandatory hotel quarantine requirement was implemented, the federal government exempted 750 Olympic and Paralympic athletes from a number of quarantine-related travel restrictions. In a letter to Health Minister Hajdu, Conservative Member of Parliament Michelle Rempel Garner wrote: "Those travelling to reunite with a spouse, an ailing relative or to access medical treatment should not be faced with what is an insurmountable barrier for many in these situations. Your government recognized this principle when you made an exemption for athletes, citing affordability concerns."[101]

After the border with the United States was reopened to non-essential travel in mid-2021, Canada's testing regime for entry was complex, costly, and confusing.[102] A family of four could expect testing costs up to $600, and if results did not come back within the required seventy-two hours, they risked forfeiting their test results or potentially receiving hefty fines at the border. Business travelers complained about the uncertainty and time commitment of test requirements and random sampling upon arrival. Canadians living in borderland communities who wanted to make same-day trips to the United States navigated the test requirement by taking a test in Canada prior to leaving, so they could get results back in time to present them at the border upon returning to Canada. This was all further complicated by Canada's introduction of a mobile application known as ArriveCAN, which was used to collect contract tracing information and other Covid-related entry requirements. But the platform had no way to actually verify the handwritten vaccination records of Americans and was plagued by glitches, user difficulty, and its inability to incorporate changes made to the border restrictions. For example, when Canada eased restrictions for American travelers at the land border, people who took same day trips were still required to list an address where they would quarantine if symptoms arose. Unable to provide one, many travelers simply made one up.

Despite grumbling from business and those separated from friends and family, Canadian public opinion overwhelmingly supported the border restrictions. Surveys conducted by Nanos Research from June 2020 to April 2021 showed that a strong majority of Canadians felt the border should "stay closed for the foreseeable future."[103] Opinions started to shift in early summer of 2021 and by July, when nearly half of eligible Canadians were vaccinated, 63% supported ending pandemic-related border restrictions with the United States.[104] It was at this same time that Canada began to ease restrictions, starting with vaccinated Canadians, and a few months later, opening up to vaccinated Americans, all with Covid test requirements. Pushback from local leaders and the business community eventually brought an end to the use of the ArriveCAN requirement, which became embroiled in controversy and was removed alongside all other border-related measures in late 2022.

A Whole of Government Failure

Border policy in Canada and the United States involves multiple players. While both countries have agencies with primary jurisdiction over the border (Public Safety Canada and the US Department of Homeland Security), there is a patchwork of responsibilities for border management. Prior to the pandemic, public health authorities had little role in controlling the who, why, and where of cross-border flows. So when the US CDC and Department of Health and Human Services and Canada's PHAC became involved in border policy decisions, public health goals butted up against long-standing border practices, multiplying the confusion. Professionals from agencies that rarely talked with each other were suddenly making decisions in combination with top elected officials in a very politically charged environment. Decisions were made by both countries with little transparency and a muddling of science and politics.

With the benefit of hindsight, it is apparent that Canada, like much of the rest of the world, did not have the institutional capacity in place to respond to the pandemic. Despite the experience with SARS in the early 2000s, and later with H1N1 in 2009, PHAC "was not adequately prepared to respond to the pandemic, and it underestimated the potential impact of the virus at the onset of the pandemic," according to the Auditor General.[105] By the time Canada implemented travel bans—one of the last countries in the world to do so—Covid was already present within its borders and spreading rapidly. And the competing political pressures to maintain trade flows resulted in numerous exemptions. As health researchers at Canada's Simon Fraser University put it: rather than a strict adherence to science, Canada's border restrictions "reflected policy choices based on agreed trade-offs among political and economic interests" and were heavily shaped by an "unclear relationship between science and politics."[106]

The United States looked better prepared. An October 2019 report from Johns Hopkins University had rated the country top in the world in readiness, though it noted that "no country is fully prepared."[107] Much like in Canada, the United States had been preparing for a global pandemic for decades. After the avian influenza outbreak in 1997, and its re-emergence in 2003, pandemic preparedness planning accelerated, though it would be periodically defunded and refunded.[108] During much of the George W. Bush administration, and throughout the Obama years, monthly meetings were held on pandemic response planning. Not only were there plans in place to respond to a global pandemic, there were also relationships and channels of communication established, both domestically and with counterparts in Mexico and Canada. But in the chaos of the Trump administration, carefully prepared plans were tossed aside. Administrative responsibility for the pandemic was handed from Cabinet leaders to a newly established White House COVID-19 Task Force headed by Vice President Pence. The Task Force quickly began writing Executive Orders in place of traditional CDC public health authorities, allowing political goals to override professional judgments. Bradley Dickerson, former senior biodefense officer at DHS from 2007 to 2018, said, "the administration was caught wholly unprepared, not because there hadn't been work done, but because they ripped it up. We had plans in place that were completely ignored."[109]

But even the best-laid plans remain only ideas that still have to be put into practice. A detailed investigation by the Covid Crisis Group—set up by former 9/11 Commission executive director Philip Zelikow when the US government refused to launch a similar national investigation into Covid—spread the blame far beyond Trump officials. "Experts both outside and inside of the government knew that the system, from top to bottom, was unready for a pandemic."[110] The failure, they argue, was part of a broader erosion of operational capabilities in the US government that had been decades in the making—Covid, the experts argued, "revealed a collective national incompetence in governance." This incompetence, combined with the woefully inadequate response and engagement by the Trump administration as the pandemic took shape, set the stage for the botched US response.

Both governments had gone into the pandemic with plans that recommended only a modest role for border measures. The 2006 US plan had envisioned limited international travel restrictions and concluded that "For practical purposes it will be impossible to prevent completely the migration of disease across land borders."[111] Canada's 2018 plan similarly concluded on border and travel measures that "evidence for their effectiveness is limited and their implementation would depend on the risk assessment and resultant risk/benefit analysis of the actions being considered."[112] Yet both countries defaulted to border restrictions with no risk assessment. "This is always something that came up," said Luciana Borio, former director for Medical and Biodefense Preparedness at the National Security Council from 2017 to 2019. "The first question was always borders, borders, borders, do we close the borders. There's always a point when this issue comes up. The border is no place to stop it [a virus]."[113]

But neither country was prepared to implement a fully stringent border regime. The United States was even less prepared than Canada. The Crisis Group report makes clear that the government had no capacity to implement and monitor a large-scale quarantine program for arriving travelers, for example, and lacked the technology to track cases. So, it resorted to half-measures that imposed enormous costs with questionable public health benefits. "American leaders faced a seemingly binary choice between either doing a travel ban—for instance on travelers coming from Europe—or doing nothing," the report argued.[114] And the measures—as ineffective as they were with Covid spreading domestically throughout the country—stayed in place for a long time. It was not until November 2021 that the United States eased restrictions for vaccinated travelers from much of the rest of the world,[115] lagging months behind both Europe and Canada. The United States continued to require test results for air arrivals until June 2022, reinstating them for arrivals from China as late as January 2023 in response to a spike in Covid infections after China relaxed its border measures. The final pandemic border measures, including all testing, vaccination requirements, and the Title 42 provisions, would last until May 2023, over three years after Covid was first declared a pandemic by the World Health Organization.

The Legacy of Border Closures

Point Roberts recovered slowly after the border restrictions started to ease in the summer and fall of 2021. Covid testing requirements—and Canada's requirement that border crossers fill out the balky ArriveCAN app—continued to dissuade the casual visitors who came in the past to buy gas, pick up packages in the United States, or visit the beaches.[116] US requirements that Canadians be vaccinated also hampered the ability of some to enter Point Roberts, a requirement that didn't end until May 2023. Following another sluggish summer in 2022, Chamber of Commerce president Calder feared that "the lengthy border lockdown has changed people's patterns and habits regarding Point Roberts, and I do not know if we will ever get it back. Our summer season economic boom has fizzled, yet again." Nearly three years of shifting pandemic border measures also impacted service providers' willingness to transit through Canada to reach Point Roberts. As a result, construction that required electricians or concrete pourers remained stagnant. Border crossings in July 2023 were still down 30% from their levels in 2019.[117] The border closures came suddenly, but reopening did not.

By the summer of 2023, when all Covid-related border measures had been eliminated by both Canada and the United States, the population in Point Roberts had dropped by 25%, leaving it desperately short of workers when the Canadians finally came back. Westward Marine, a boat repair yard, sought skilled boat technicians for months without receiving a single application; the owners took to offering classes in boat repair and renting out tools to their customers. The golf course reopened, but the superintendent had no option but to take over the maintenance responsibilities of what had once been a twelve-to-fifteen-person crew. In an effort to fix the problem, Point Roberts found itself in a familiar position—pleading with the US government to ease restrictions on immigrant workers so Canadians could more easily fill open jobs on the peninsula.[118]

Along the Canada-US border as a whole, by the summer of 2023 cross-border traffic had recovered to about 80% of its 2019 levels—a figure that has remained surprisingly stagnant since most border measures were eased.[119]

Borderland communities welcomed back many of the visitors, homeowners, shoppers, and recreationists from the other side of the border. Yet a tentative and speculative feeling remains in places that were shell-shocked both economically and socially from an extended period of a highly restricted border. The knowledge that the Canada-US border could be similarly restricted in the future looms over decisions to engage in cross-border business, to retire or purchase real estate across the border, and even whether or not to start dating someone who might live twenty minutes away on the other side. This feeling has spread well beyond those who live next to the border, to all those in North America who may have taken their freedom of cross-border mobility as a right, rather than a vulnerable privilege.

5

The Return of European National Borders

For nearly seventy years, it has been hard to tell where Norway ends and Sweden begins. The Norwegian municipality of Eidskog, for example, sits adjacent to the Swedish border some two hours north of Oslo. The town relies overwhelmingly on workers from Sweden to provide medical care and education to its residents. Nearly 75% of caregivers who work in Eidskog's schools come from Sweden, in addition to many government workers. While many places along the Norway-Sweden border are intertwined, in Eidskog crossing borders is like breathing—an integral part of everyday life for families, friends, and workers. But in the fall of 2020, the oxygen was cut off. Fearing the growing number of Covid cases in neighboring Sweden, which had limited its own lockdown and social distancing measures, Norway slammed the border shut. Those who crossed and failed to quarantine for fourteen days suddenly faced fines as much as $2,000 or a fifteen-day jail sentence.[1] As Norway implemented increasingly restrictive border measures in response to the emergence of new Covid variants, "everybody was worried what it would mean if they [Swedes] couldn't come to work," said Kamilla Thue, a member of the municipal council of Eidskog. "If we can't have our Swedish workforce coming, our community can't function."[2]

The impacts were much broader than just labor shortages. The region's borderless ethos, which predates the creation of the European Union (EU), was shoved aside in the crisis. Businesses that depended on cross-border shoppers lost their customers, friends could no longer meet, and parents with children across the border faced a complex and changing set of rules just to see their children. The deeply felt belief that it is "against our DNA to divide people," as an official from a nearby county government in Norway said, was shattered.[3] Thue said, "it felt for at least the older people that the border was more

closed now than during the Second World War. It caused great harm and sad-
ness among a lot of families, for both young and old . . . great heartache."[4]
Those who lived within sight of the border, which was nearly invisible, found
themselves in an unimaginable scenario. "Where I live . . . they patrolled with
guns," she commented. "You don't see that in Norway. It's very strange. I
would never ever ever think this would happen."

Across Europe, similar scenarios would play out in different ways and at different times during the pandemic, but with the same effect: communities that
had been built based on the commitment to free movement between countries
found themselves divided by border controls and travel measures that were unpredictable, discriminatory, and often contradictory. Unfettered movement of
goods, people, services, and money was the founding principle of the creation
of the EU in the 1990s.[5] For over thirty years, border-free travel expanded and
increasingly became an integral part of the European way of life. "People have
built their lives around the freedoms offered by the Schengen Area, with 3.5
million people crossing between Schengen States every day," the European
Commission says. "The free flow of people, goods and services is at the heart
of the European Union."[6] While the core principle of free movement has been
tested repeatedly in the past, no other region of the world is a stronger champion for integration and cross-border cooperation than Europe. Yet in March
and April 2020, country after country imposed travel restrictions and closed
border crossings. These controls were implemented despite a recognition of
their harmful impacts and their rejection by EU authorities. In May 2020,
after many EU member states had imposed border restrictions, the European
Centre for Disease Prevention and Control stated unequivocally that "available evidence does not support recommending border closures, which will
cause significant secondary effects and societal and economic disruption in
the EU."[7]

The story of pandemic border restrictions in Europe is especially compelling for two reasons. The first is the fundamental conundrum they presented
to the core principle of a borderless Europe and associated European identity, as member states actively undermined their commitments to coordinate
responses in times of crisis. The pandemic border controls followed not long
after many European states reimposed checks at national borders to block
asylum seekers during the "migrant crisis" of 2015–2016.[8] In a relatively
short period, European states resurrected national border controls to combat
vastly different problems portrayed as external threats, from mass migration

of asylum seekers to terrorism and then a pandemic. Between November 2020 and May 2021, amid ongoing battles with new variants of Covid-19, six member states introduced temporary border controls for reasons other than the pandemic, most claiming risks related to terrorism.[9] The other reason border controls were such a shock in Europe is the tangible disruption they caused to the European way of life, which for decades had been premised on cross-border integration. Forty percent of EU citizens live in border regions and nearly 2 million people commute across a border for work every day.[10] Yet during the early months of the pandemic, border controls were erected in many locations where previously no border infrastructure even existed, severing many cross-border ties that had been actively fostered by the EU.[11]

Europe stands out not just for the systemic shock that border controls created for the region, but also for the ability of European leaders to eventually overcome those barriers and forge common approaches despite ongoing threats from the virus. In most countries across the world where national border controls were imposed, they were popular with the public and politicians alike, and they stayed in place long after their original public health utility had been exhausted. But the deep level of cross-border integration in Europe, and the sophisticated network of local and regional authorities across borders, drove a widespread recognition of the harm they caused, which prompted a stronger reaction against border closures. As a consequence, most European countries eased their border restrictions more quickly than in the United States, Canada, and Asia, and worked to negotiate common European-wide approaches to controlling travel. By October 2020—several months before the rollout of effective vaccines—many European states had come together on a common set of coordinated travel restrictions. The result was not uniquely successful on public health grounds—most of Europe experienced infection and death rates somewhere between the very high levels in countries like the United States, Brazil, and Mexico and the much lower numbers in most of the Asia-Pacific. Despite the sporadic reintroduction of border controls by some EU countries, Europe nonetheless stands out as the only place in the world where the forces of cross-border collaboration successfully pushed back against the demands for ever-tighter border restrictions. "The discussion is much deeper than it used to be before the pandemic, and all these new challenges, and everybody now takes more seriously the EU framework" said Martin Guillermo-Ramirez, the secretary general of the Association of European Border Regions.[12] If it is possible to rebuild the norms of freer international mobility in the wake of the pandemic, Europe will lead the way.

The Right to Freedom of Movement

Europe is one of the few regions in the world that has codified the freedom of movement as a right for its citizens, granting the right to move and reside freely between member states. This right applies to twenty-five of the twenty-seven EU member states (excluding Cyprus and Ireland) and encompasses the entire Schengen Area, which currently consists of twenty-nine member states (Iceland, Norway, Switzerland, and Liechtenstein are members of the Schengen Area of free movement but not members of the EU). At times, there are also countries that sit outside of the EU and Schengen Zone but are part of the European Economic Area (EEA).[13] Citizens of Schengen and EEA countries are able to freely cross the internal borders of all member states.

The right of free movement is codified in several treaties, first established by the Lisbon Treaty in 2007. Since its passage, two pieces of secondary legislation, the Free Movement Directive 2004/28 and the Schengen Borders Code, have further built upon the right to freedom of movement. Free cross-border movement is part of the daily lives of millions of Europeans; border regions comprise over 40% of EU territory and are home to more than 150 million people.[14] Yet there are limits to this freedom. States are permitted to reintroduce internal border controls temporarily in the face of threats to the public policy, public health, or the internal security of one or more member states. But that power is circumscribed; according to the Schengen Borders Code, the reintroduction of border controls should not exceed what is strictly necessary to respond to a serious threat.

The Code also includes exceptions based on public health grounds, but these are not *carte blanche*. National governments and their ministries of the interior are supposed to justify the suitability, necessity, and proportionality of any policy restrictions in relation to both their effectiveness in meeting the proposed public goal and the impacts on fundamental rights and EU standards.[15] The burden of proof is on member states to re-examine and re-assess the necessity and effectiveness of border controls. In the context of the Covid-19 pandemic, the onus was on those states to justify their use of border controls over other, less intrusive measures. Ultimately, while there is a legal basis for European countries to close their internal borders, doing so is not in the spirit of the legislation and goes against the level of coordination and alignment that is central to the EU project. Those norms would function, to varying degrees, throughout the pandemic to limit the scope and duration of the national border closures.

The Allure of National Borders: From Migrant Flows to Covid-19

The Covid-19 pandemic brought about the longest and most restrictive border measures in Europe since World War II. But 2020 was not the first time that European states had turned their backs on the commitment to free movement. There have been many isolated instances of border controls between Schengen states,[16] to the extent that some have argued that they are "a constant feature of the area since the abolition of those controls in 1995."[17] But until 2015, such controls tended to be limited in nature, temporary in duration, and justified according to specific events, such as NATO summits. This changed with the influx of migrants and asylum seekers from Syria, Afghanistan, and Africa in 2015 and 2016, which prompted some countries within the Schengen Area to introduce internal border controls in response to perceived threats.[18] This paved the way for a similar reaction during the pandemic. France introduced internal border controls in 2015 for reasons associated with the migrant crisis, closing some remote crossing points, and checking documents at others. While these controls ebbed and flowed, in some locations they were kept in place for years, with France later citing the Covid threat as a reason to maintain them.[19] In both 2015–2016 and again in 2020, a number of European countries reverted to nationalist approaches, and the embrace of border restrictions became a mainstream rather than a fringe position in many places.[20] During the Brexit referendum in 2016, nearly one-third of voters said their main reason for supporting the "leave" campaign was for the UK to "regain control over immigration and its own borders."[21] Nigel Farage of the UK Independence Party, an architect of Brexit and the first British politician to meet US president-elect Donald Trump, seized upon immigration as one of the central arguments for leaving the EU, despite the UK never having been part of the Schengen Zone of free movement. In June 2016, the campaign distributed a poster titled "Breaking Point," with an image of a long line of migrants and refugees accompanied by the slogan "we must break free of the EU and take back control of our borders."[22]

In 2015, an unprecedented number of asylum seekers arrived in Europe, driving 2 million asylum applications over the next two years. Many of these migrants initially arrived in Turkey and Greece after departing Syria and Afghanistan, or other war-torn countries in Africa, braving perilous sea or land journeys to try to reach the borders of Europe. Much has been written about the refugee crisis in Europe and the degree to which this humanitarian situation was exacerbated by a failure of European institutions to adequately recognize and respond to the reality of increased migrant flows.[23] In place of a strategy to manage migratory influxes, Europe was accused of relying on a "questionable practice of outsourcing boundaries" in which European nations paid countries like Turkey and Libya to stop migrants from continuing on to Europe; United Nations investigators argue that Europe's actions "aided and abetted" crimes and human rights violations.[24] Wrote Italian researcher Laura Zanfrini after a two-year-old Kurdish boy drowned on the shores of Turkey: "It took the shocking image of the dead body of a small child washed up on the beach to remind Europe that over time it had forgotten the principles of justice, equity and freedom upon which the very delicate issue of border management should be based."[25] The human consequences of those failures were appalling: in 2015–2016 alone, nearly 10,000 migrant deaths were recorded in the Mediterranean Sea, with more to follow in the years to come.[26]

As the number of migrants and asylum seekers continued to rise in 2015, Germany announced in August that it would stop the deportation of Syrian asylum seekers.[27] The move was hailed as an act of European solidarity. "For the commission, this constitutes a recognition of the fact that we cannot leave the member states at the external borders alone in dealing with a large number of asylum seekers seeking refuge in Europe," said Natasha Bertaud, spokeswoman for the EU Commission.[28] But less than a month later, Germany reversed course. After receiving over 40,000 migrants in one weekend, Germany became the first country to implement intra-Schengen border controls. Traffic from Austria was halted, with only EU citizens and those with valid documents allowed to enter.[29] In what *The Economist* described as "the greatest blow to Schengen" in its twenty-year existence, Germany's border measures set off a domino effect soon followed by Hungary, Austria, Slovenia, Sweden, Norway, France, and Malta.[30] In the Nordic region, where free mobility dates back to 1954, Sweden imposed passport controls on Denmark in 2015, citing concerns about the increasing flow of migrants (several years later, Denmark reciprocated based on concerns about criminal gangs in Sweden).[31] Border controls varied, with some countries building fences, and most requiring identification checks at selected crossing points.[32] While such actions were clearly against the spirit of Schengen, states justified them within the exceptions related to public policy or national security concerns in the Schengen Borders Code. While debate remains on the legality of some of those justifications, the Code allows for the reintroduction of borders immediately for up to ten days in response to exceptional circumstances and emergencies.[33]

The use of border controls in 2015–2016 shattered agreements on Europe's asylum policy, as laid out in the Dublin Regulation. The regulation states that migrants must remain in the first European country they enter, and that that country bears responsibility for their asylum applications. Migrants who travel to a different EU country face deportation back to the first EU country they entered.[34] However, countries like Greece and Italy, overwhelmed by the volume of migrants, permitted them to continue on into the rest of Europe. Some countries, like Slovenia, lifted their border restrictions relatively shortly after implementing them. France renewed its controls repeatedly for more than two years, continually changing both their justification and the extent to which they were actually enforced.[35] The majority of countries used border controls to essentially sort migrants and asylum seekers from people with proper documentation, who were allowed to cross borders freely. Many member states, however, chose not to reintroduce border controls. Some that did receive larger numbers of asylum applications responded by either beefing up their external border control measures or increasing patrols at internal borders. Hungary, for example, constructed a barbed wire fence at its external border with Serbia and Croatia. Belgium, Denmark, Finland, Luxembourg, the Netherlands, and Switzerland all accepted relatively large numbers of asylum requests in 2015. Belgium and the Netherlands intensified police controls in the zones behind their internal borders rather than introduce controls at the border itself. Even countries that had strong anti-immigrant sentiments did not necessarily close their national borders but opted for different tactics. For example, Denmark, which received 21,000 asylum claims in 2015, triple the level of two years prior, did not restrict its borders; instead, it passed one of the harshest anti-migrant laws in Europe, stripping new asylum seekers of cash and assets exceeding $1,450 in order to offset the costs of their settlement, hoping that those measures would drive asylum seekers elsewhere.[36]

The movement of asylum seekers into Europe prompted the European Commission to declare that "the system has been shaken to its core by the scale of the challenge."[37] It developed a "Back to Schengen" roadmap in March 2016 in response to the internal border controls that were set up by some member states. The roadmap recommended that all internal border controls be lifted as soon as possible, and in the future be implemented only as a last resort. "Schengen is one of the most cherished achievements of European integration," stated EU Commission vice-president Frans Timmermans. "The costs of losing it would be huge."[38] However, five member states (Denmark, France, Germany, Sweden, and Austria) were able to keep some border controls in place either by changing the legal grounds used to justify them or by claiming that a new notification to the Commission represented a new border control, as opposed to the extension of an existing one.[39] For example, France first justified its continuation of border controls in preparation for the 2015 Paris Conference on Climate Change and later as a response to the Paris terrorist attacks earlier that year.[40]

The Covid Border Shutdowns

On February 20, 2020, the first case of Covid-19 in Europe was confirmed in the Lombardy Region of Italy. Italian authorities moved quickly to respond, closing schools and canceling events in the following weeks, and imposing a nationwide lockdown by March 9.[41] Just a few days later, the World Health Organization finally declared Covid-19 a global pandemic and by week's end identified Europe as the epicenter. In Italy, nearly 60,000 cases had been detected before the end of March, and the death toll had exceeded China's.[42] Images of bodies piled up in churches for lack of appropriate funeral services stood as a warning not just to Europe, but to the rest of the world.[43] It was only a few more days before every country in Europe had a confirmed Covid case. By mid-March, ten of the twenty-six member states had reintroduced a combination of border controls such as checkpoints and travel restrictions that limited or precluded crossing altogether, ranging from bans on non-essential travel to complete border closures. On March 16, after a coordinated response between member states and the European Council, the Commission announced restrictions on non-essential travel from outside the Schengen Area. This restriction did not apply to EU citizens, their family members, and essential workers and included additional exceptions.[44] To the Commission, the common external measures were not just a health measure; they "would also enable the lifting of internal border control measures, which several Member States have recently reintroduced in an effort to limit the spread of the virus." The internal controls "risk having a serious impact on the functioning of the Single Market as the EU and the Schengen area is characterized by a high degree of integration, with millions of people crossing internal borders every day."[45] While the European Commission supported travel restrictions at Europe's external perimeter, it continued to urge against internal travel bans, pointing to the potential for large negative impacts and emphasizing the need to "promote European solidarity."[46] But European solidarity was already on life support. Over the next two months, and as new Covid variants emerged throughout the following year, member states would continue to unilaterally impose travel restrictions to varying degrees.[47]

Although the European Commission repeatedly emphasized alternatives to travel restrictions, such as targeted police checks or health screening, measures remained uncoordinated and varied widely among member states.[48] In many instances, travelers were able to circumvent border controls by transiting through countries that had not imposed them. Few countries complied with the obligation to justify their decision-making, which required them to provide sufficient evidence that border controls were being employed as a last resort.[49] French authorities essentially re-enacted border controls that had been justified on the basis of protecting internal security and tackling terrorism, repackaging them for the purposes of mitigating the risks related to Covid. The French notification to the Commission was justified on the grounds of a "continuing threat of terrorism and the risk that terrorists would use the health situation to carry out attacks."[50] When Germany reinstated border controls in February 2021, refusing travelers from areas of Austria and the Czech Republic without proof of a negative Covid test, it was heavily criticized by the European Commission for not following the Commission's recommendations for a common approach to travel restrictions and avoiding blanket travel bans. The German interior minister pushed back: "We are fighting the mutated virus on the border with the Czech Republic and Austria," he said. "The EU Commission should support us and not put spokes in our wheels with cheap advice."[51]

Despite the commitments under the Schengen Borders Code, many member states introduced unilateral and ad hoc border measures, resulting in

an incoherent and overlapping set of mobility restrictions with little mean-
ingful coordination between states and EU institutions.[52] Each country decided on its own who was permitted to enter, which travelers were considered
essential, and what documents were required.[53] Countries hastily rebuilt
abandoned border barriers; Slovenia and Belgium resorted to using rocks and
containers to serve as border closures, while others relied on police screening
or health checkpoints. At the border between Lithuania and Poland, a line of
cars and trucks backed up for nearly 40 miles when Poland closed its borders
to foreigners.[54] In response, Lithuania sent military airplanes to evacuate its
stranded citizens.[55] As member states modified restrictions with neighboring
countries based on the emergence of new variants, travelers were able to exploit
inconsistencies. For example, when Germany reintroduced border controls
with the Czech Republic in February 2021, it kept its border with Poland
open. With no border controls between Poland and the Czech Republic,
people could simply travel through Poland to reach Germany.[56]

While their initial responses varied, nearly all the Schengen states adopted
some form of border control or travel restrictions along with other public
health measures like quarantine requirements.[57] Some national leaders fretted
over the new mobility restrictions. In an address to the nation in March,
Germany's chancellor Angela Merkel defended the importance of freedom of
movement while also justifying Germany's border closures. "For someone like
me, for whom the freedom of travel and the freedom of movement were a
hard-fought right, such restrictions can only be justified if they are absolutely
imperative," she said. "These should never be put in place lightly in a democracy and should only be temporary."[58] She went on to cite the overwhelmed
healthcare system and the need to protect communities as justifications for
closing borders and implementing lockdowns. French president Emmanuel
Macron argued for European solidarity while simultaneously imposing border
controls, claiming their reintroduction was "a measure of last resort and the
French authorities wish to reaffirm their commitment to the principle of free
movement, one of the founding principles of the European Union."[59]

As in North America, Europe made broad exceptions to keep goods
flowing. By the end of March 2020, the European Commission had set out
a framework to ensure the free flow of cargo and commercial vehicles known
as "Green Lanes." Such lanes were open to all freight vehicles, and checks
or health screenings were to be limited to a delay of no more than fifteen
minutes.[60] The vast majority, some 90%, of crossing points were compliant

with the Green Lanes initiative. Solidarity around protecting the single market for goods proved much stronger than protecting the freedom of movement for Europeans.[61] Similar to North America, truckers crossing borders did not face quarantine requirements or other restrictions imposed on ordinary travelers.

The Impact on Border Regions

Very few countries considered the integrated nature of cross-border regions, or the regional infection rates, as they began shutting borders.[62] Rather, the decisions were made by national governments in capital cities with little understanding about the economic, social, and cultural integration in a Europe in which "borders are not only lines, but also regions," said Jean Peyrony, the director general of the Transfrontier Operational Mission, an association established in France to support dialogue across borders.[63]

On the border between Germany and France lies Strasbourg-Kehl/Ortenau, which has been designated as a "Eurodistrict" for nearly twenty years, with funding and administrative support from the EU dedicated to building four bridges crossing the Rhine River to connect the two countries. The border in this region is normally as invisible as the border between Sweden and Norway."[64] Yet on March 16, the German government—with no prior coordination with France—closed the border overnight, including all four bridges connecting Strasbourg with Kehl/Ortenau (Figure 5.1). It was a "saddening and almost spooky experience," said Birte Wassenberg, a resident and border studies professor.[65] On the French side in Alsace, hospital beds reached capacity and began transporting patients by helicopter to other parts of France. In Strasbourg, Covid patients were transported by jet to Marseille, over 600 miles away, while "in neighboring German communities across the river, there are empty beds in hospitals and German partners willing to welcome French patients," she wrote.[66] A cross-border worker, and a parent of children with both French and German nationality, Birte became "a Franco-German captured on the German side of the border. . . . When the border closes, mobility ends, and, as a borderlander, my life as a European citizen, navigating daily between France and Germany, also ends."[67]

Similar divisions and chaotic disruptions occurred in cross-border regions throughout Europe. On March 13, 2020, the Danish foreign minister announced that Denmark would not close its borders; a few hours later, his

Figure 5.1 Temporary fence at the tram bridge connecting Strasbourg and Kiehl, April 2020. Courtesy of Birte Wassenberg.

own government reversed course. The year 2020 happened to be the 100-year anniversary of the drawing of Denmark's border with Germany, and planning had been underway for a major celebration of how the border had vanished in daily life.[68] With the announcement of border closures, the anniversary celebrations not only came to a halt but instantly lost their meaning. Local and regional German authorities denounced the closures, only to see their own national government take similar actions just two days later.[69]

Unlike many neighboring countries, Portugal and Spain cooperated in restricting their land border travel. They agreed to allow only eight heavily controlled and monitored "authorized crossing points," which remained in place until July 1, 2020. As a result, many workers had to travel an additional 60 miles daily. On the Galicia-Norte border area in the north, for example, there were more than 12,000 cross-border commuters who suddenly had only two crossing points in the region to choose from, compared to the normal twenty-seven.[70] During the three months of border restrictions, mayors from seven borderland communities composed a joint petition urging their governments to restart the free movement of people in regions affected by the border controls and to decree free movement of citizens within these areas.[71] A resident of Galicia remarked, "nobody thinks of closing our border as a solution because it is as absurd as closing one of the main streets of Madrid and separating one side of the street from the other."[72]

Even in places where cross-border movement of commuters and immediate families was allowed, there were prohibitive barriers. Roads that crossed the border were often closed in an effort to funnel travelers through checkpoints, resulting in lengthy and challenging journeys. Border controls between the Czech Republic and Germany resulted in detours that sometimes took an hour and half for trips that previously took about five minutes. Those who were able to use their typical cross-border commuting routes often faced congestion and unpredictable wait times as traffic was funneled through chokepoints. Additional quarantine and testing requirements greatly inhibited daily cross-border commutes. In response, some Czech and German employers offered paid accommodations to commuters from Poland, allowing them to avoid the hassle of daily checks at the border.[73] In many instances, cross-border workers were initially unable to collect social security from their employers when they started working from home in their own countries. For example, the Spanish employment agency did not allow online payments to foreign bank accounts. Cross-border workers who were unable to open a Spanish account could not receive unemployment benefits.[74]

Beyond the employment and economic repercussions of the border controls in highly integrated communities, residents also faced severe social impacts as many couples and families were separated. Workers who faced quarantine requirements found themselves unable to return home to see their families. One Polish bus driver who worked in the Czech Republic rented an apartment a stone's throw from the border so that he could see his wife and children on the other side while continuing to work.[75] In the borderlands of Italy and Austria, over fifty complaints were recorded by families who were unable to see each other without quarantine, because the countries had different definitions of what constituted a family. Austria considered extended relatives as part of a family, while Italy only included people residing within a common household.[76] In many instances, "it was often not really clear what the rules were, both for people affected and for the police," investigators concluded in a report to the European Commission. "At every crossing point, at every shift, different decisions were made due to the lack of clear indications. The unpredictable situation was very uncomfortable for people who wanted to cross the border."[77] Such circumstances led to a feeling by many that border measures were enacted with little appreciation for the people they impacted the most.[78] Watching the situation unfold along the German-French border, Franco-German Birte Wassenberg remarked that the "management of the border appears to me more and more absurd . . . these inconsistencies undermine public trust not only in national governments, but also in the broader commitment to free mobility."[79]

In the place of free movement, smaller travel bubbles emerged throughout the pandemic. These enabled mobility among a defined set of countries. These bubbles were often formed between countries who had similar Covid-19 responses as well as close relationships prior to the pandemic, due to regional proximity, economic integration, or cultural ties. Examples include a bubble among the Baltic States,[80] and another between Hungary and Slovenia.[81] The European Commission came out strongly against travel bubbles, arguing that they were discriminatory and therefore against the Schengen codes as well as the spirit of the region.

Throughout the pandemic, the European Commission pushed hard for states to lift their unilateral border measures and coordinate their responses.[82] Just one month after states began restricting their borders, the Commission issued a "Roadmap towards Lifting COVID-19 Containment Measures," which outlined a phased approach to "restoring the normal functioning of the Schengen area."[83] This was followed one month later, in May 2020, with a report specifically tailored to a coordinated approach for lifting border controls.[84] The insistence of the European Commission on better cooperation was aided by a gradual reduction in Covid infections as well as the anticipation of summer holidays.[85] Coordination among European countries increased, largely driven by Germany, Austria, Switzerland, and France, and by July 1, 2020, most member states had eased their most restrictive border measures.[86] However, border controls and restrictions were reimposed when infections spiked. In the fall of 2020, Hungary closed its border to virtually all foreigners without notifying the European Commission.[87] Hungarian prime minister Viktor Orbán justified the decision in a speech, saying "Solidarity means common success . . . [but] you cannot be successful together if you are not successful one-by-one."[88] However, the majority of member states opted for a system that allowed mobility within a broader regime that varied between testing and quarantine requirements—still relying on the border as a mechanism for screening.

In October 2020—still months before the widespread rollout of vaccines—member states came together on a common set of standards to assess Covid-19 prevention measures, allowing for the launch of the EU's "traffic light" system. The system was intended to provide clarity for travelers and to overcome the patchwork of intra-Schengen mobility restrictions. It designated regions as green, orange, or red, based on infection rates (and gray if data was insufficient). The European Centre for Disease Prevention and Control published a weekly color-coded map with updated risk levels. All countries were expected to grant access to visitors from green zones, while those coming from an orange, red, or gray zone could be required to undergo quarantine or screening, but not refused entry. While not mandated, EU countries were highly encouraged to have consistent measures with the same entry requirements for each color. Upon announcing the framework, the European Commission stated, "we have learned our lessons: we will not surmount the crisis by unilaterally closing borders, but by working together."[89] Most EU countries agreed to adopt this system, though a few dissented based on the metrics used to designate colors.

The new system was not seamless. It helped to bring member states into greater alignment, but countries generally used the EU system as a guide, with each country ultimately setting its own requirements. Similar to the early days of the pandemic border restrictions, quarantine and testing requirements varied and could be challenging to navigate, particularly for families or multistage journeys.[90] In response to a new wave of cases in early 2021, nine member states (Austria, Belgium, Denmark, Finland, Germany, Hungary, Norway, Portugal, and Spain) reintroduced border controls, primarily imposing new testing requirements. Germany's controls on the Czech Republic were particularly stringent, with no exemptions for cross-border families, truckers, or government officials. This prompted the EU Commission to send a letter "to remind them of their commitments," arguing that protecting public health can be achieved by less restrictive measures.[91]

It was not until the summer of 2021 that intra-Schengen mobility was shifted from one based on regional infection rates under the traffic light system, to one based on the actual health risk of an individual traveler. In July 2021, the EU Digital Green Certificate program was launched to facilitate free movement and to help ensure that "restrictions currently in place can be lifted in a coordinated manner."[92] All member states accepted the certificate, and any movement restrictions placed on a certificate holder would have to be justified to the Commission. The program enabled travelers to show they had been fully vaccinated, recovered from a previous infection, or tested negative for Covid-19. Throughout 2021, there was a continual ebb and flow in quarantine and testing requirements based on variants of concern and infection rates. In February 2022, the European Council recommended that all EU countries allow entry of all non-essential travelers who had been vaccinated with approved vaccines, in addition to accompanying children with negative tests.[93] This was the final hurdle to the reopening of Europe's borders. By summer of 2022, all internal and external border restrictions related to Covid had been lifted in Europe.[94]

There were a few stark outliers from the European approach, especially the UK and Sweden.[95] Neither embraced locking down their borders like their European neighbors, though Sweden did impose border restrictions for several months at the end of 2021. The UK opted for a combination of quarantine, testing, and travel guidance based on its own "traffic light" system for entry requirements for arrivals from other countries.[96] For a time, non-resident arrivals from red-list countries with high infection rates were banned, but as vaccination rates increased in mid-2021, this was replaced by a requirement to quarantine in government mandated hotels.[97] Unlike Sweden, the UK was already outside of the Schengen Area when member states started imposing border controls. The UK officially left the EU as a result of the Brexit referendum in January 2020, less than two months before Covid-19 was declared a pandemic by the WHO. With the UK no longer part of the EU, it faced the same restrictions as other non-EU countries.[98] As a result, citizens of the UK were in many cases denied entrance to the EU, even as Schengen countries began to ease their internal border restrictions.

Sweden opted for a containment strategy based on recommendations and voluntary behavior rather than lockdowns or mandates. This strategy had severe repercussions for mobility across Sweden's borders. A full member of the EU and the Schengen Area, Sweden was essentially cut off from the rest of the Schengen countries and shunned by its Nordic neighbors for well over a year.

Norway and Sweden: The Unlikeliest Border Closure

Straddling the border between Norway and Sweden is a place called Morokulien—a combination of the Norwegian and Swedish words for "fun." Morokulien is the site of a peace monument, built in 1914 to commemorate 100 years of peace between the two countries (Figure 5.2). It is also the location of the Grensetjänsten, an information service that exists to foster cross-border

Figure 5.2 Photo of Peace Monument between Norway and Sweden. Courtesy of the authors.

cooperation and reduce border obstacles for businesses, travelers, and workers. The border between Norway and Sweden literally runs through the middle of the Morokulien InfoCenter. The line itself is internally marked and adorned with flags, symbolizing unity, rather than division. But when Norway imposed border restrictions in March 2020, what had once been a symbolic line was transformed overnight into a hardened, impassable, policed international border. Norwegians and Swedes who worked at the InfoCenter were expected to enter and exit the building from their respective sides and have no physical interaction inside the building. At the peace monument just a few hundred yards away, families and friends would set up chairs to chat across the divide. Swedes were prohibited from stepping across the line, and Norwegians who crossed the parking lot to use the only bathroom, located in a gas station on the Swedish side, faced a hefty fine if caught—more than $1,000—upon their return for violating quarantine rules.

Norway's border restrictions during the pandemic were some of the most enduring and stringent in Europe.[99] They also changed frequently, with cross-border workers facing continued uncertainty as to whether they would be able to travel to work from week to week. Much like border restrictions in other parts of the EU, essential travel was allowed to continue, and exemptions were made for families. But cross-border travel remained very difficult and was complicated by mandatory quarantines, constantly changing requirements, and increased congestion at crossing points.

The length and extent of the border shutdown between Norway and Sweden would have been unfathomable before the pandemic. The two countries had embraced passport-free travel in 1952, well before the establishment of the EU and the Schengen Zone (Sweden is a member state of the EU, while Norway is a member of the separate European Economic Area and the Schengen Zone). The border between the two countries is the longest in Europe, spanning over 1,000 miles. Norwegians and Swedes in borderland communities are linguistically intertwined, with some communities even speaking a form of both languages interchangeably. "The border is hardly a barrier at all," says the regional Nordregio research institute.[100] But in March 2020 the Norwegian government set up police blockades on the dozens of small roads crisscrossing the border, many of which had been previously unmarked. Norwegians and Swedes who had freely crossed the border for jobs over the past sixty years were suddenly unemployed, and families and friends who straddled the border were separated. In an extreme example of Norway's treatment of Swedish workers who were allowed to enter the country for work, Swedish workers were required to wear yellow vests identifying them in order to ensure their physical distance from Norwegians.[101]

Trust is often cited as "the glue that holds Nordic countries, institutions, and people together," so it is not surprising that a lack of trust led to the breakdown. Sweden's unique approach to the pandemic was viewed with skepticism by all its Nordic neighbors, and by the rest of the EU.[102] Though Sweden never openly defined its strategy as one of pursuing "herd immunity" by letting the virus spread, it looked that way to the rest of Europe. Sweden avoided strict lockdowns and regulations, instead relying largely on guidelines and recommendations. Most institutions and training facilities were left open, including elementary and kindergarten schools and children's sports programs; high schools and universities were closed, but businesses remained open.[103] The only explicit prohibition Sweden passed in the early days of the pandemic was a March 11 ban on public gatherings of more than 500 people, which was then lowered to 50 two weeks later.[104] However, this ban did not apply to private parties—baptisms, weddings, and funerals were only subject to voluntary recommendations. Sweden also prohibited visits to homes for the elderly in an effort to protect the most vulnerable populations.

Norway's response was similar to other European and North American countries but considerably more effective. The country had three goals: controlling the spread of the virus domestically, mitigating the impact on the economy, and addressing the social costs of the policy response.[105] Its public health outcomes were among the best in the world—deaths from Covid were similar to the Asia-Pacific islands that imposed lengthy border closures and far below the rest of the Nordic region except for another island, Iceland.[106] Norwegian officials were extremely transparent about the uncertainty of the pandemic as they passed initial restrictions, which generated high levels of trust in their public health institutions.[107] In March 2020, Norway closed schools, but officials acknowledged considerable uncertainty about the benefits; by late spring they were open again and mostly stayed that way.[108] Norway also banned organized sporting events and cultural activities and closed most discretionary services like restaurants and hair salons.[109] In addition to shutting the border with Sweden, Norway imposed a mandatory ten-day hotel quarantine for the few international travelers still permitted to come. Case counts remained low enough that Norway managed to trace most of the outbreaks successfully.[110]

The different responses between two otherwise similar countries were shaped by political structures and institutions. In Sweden, executive authorities for public health are separated from elected political officials. The Agency for Public Health—run by scientists—presented and explained the government response to Covid-19, while cabinet ministers and the prime minister stayed largely in the background. As a result, Sweden's approach was to avoid measures that lacked a scientific basis, and at the outset of the pandemic there was little evidence favoring border closures. During the pandemic, the prime minister and elected officials rarely made statements. The Swedish constitution also prohibits the use of lockdowns and codifies that "all Swedish citizens shall ... be guaranteed freedom of movement within the Realm," with no explicit exemptions for the case of a pandemic.[111]

In Norway, by contrast, the prime minister and other politicians were actively involved in making decisions about lockdowns and border restrictions. Lockdowns were formally enacted by the Directorate of Health, but unlike in Sweden, the Directorate isn't exempt from government instructions. The role of political influence on public health matters is in part why the Norwegian response was more similar to that of other European countries.[112]

Government and public health officials in Sweden and Norway also had different priorities at the outset of the pandemic.[113] The Swedish government focused on limiting the virus enough to keep hospitals from being overwhelmed and to protect high-risk groups such as the elderly. This kept officials from supporting sweeping lockdowns, arguing there was little evidence to justify such drastic measures. The Swedish government also issued guidelines, rather than restrictions, believing that the Swedish population could be trusted to follow them. Norway, on the other hand, prioritized limiting the number of deaths resulting from the pandemic over all other concerns. The government's stated goal was to "break" the wave, followed by a strategy of "suppression"—both of which demanded tough restrictions. The Norwegian government defended travel restrictions and other control measures at the border as undesirable, but necessary.

Both countries maintained different approaches to their national borders throughout the pandemic. Norway eased and tightened border restrictions, largely in response to the emergence of new Covid variants. At different points, mandatory quarantines and testing were implemented, and exceptions for essential travel and other non-work-related travel were expanded and contracted. Norway, along with Finland and Denmark, introduced some of the most stringent restrictions in Europe on their borders with Sweden. Sweden, on the other hand, did little to restrict cross-border travel with other countries within the European Economic Area (EEA).[114] Anders Tegnell, an epidemiologist at Sweden's independent Public Health Agency who led Sweden's approach, said in April 2020 that "closing borders is ridiculous in my opinion, because COVID-19 is in every European country now."[115] It wasn't until December 2021, in response to the Omicron variant, that Sweden instituted its first travel restrictions from within the EEA, banning entry from Denmark and the UK, and requiring Covid tests from its Nordic neighbors, who had previously been exempt from that requirement.[116]

In the context of the Nordic countries, Sweden's excess mortality rate in 2020 was an outlier, suggesting that Covid deaths were significant.[117] While its Nordic neighbors all had excess mortality rates less than 2% above pre-pandemic trends, Sweden's was four times as high, reaching nearly 8%. However, when compared to Europe overall, Sweden fared better than over twenty other countries. Spain and Belgium, for example, saw excess mortality rates of 18% and 16% respectively.[118] And by 2023, when the pandemic had more or less run its course, and access to vaccinations was widespread, Sweden's excess mortality rate of 5% was lower than the majority of European countries.[119]

Decisions Made in the Capitals, Impacts in the Borderlands

Cooperation among the Nordic countries is a defining feature of a shared Nordic identity. One of the key pillars of this cooperation is rooted in freedom of movement and open borders, which the Finnish Institute of International Affairs calls "one of the most appreciated aspects of Nordic cooperation among the regions' citizens."[120] In this respect, the Nordic region exhibited on a smaller scale the free cross-border mobility that is at the heart of the Schengen project in Europe. Yet, during the pandemic, there was no collective Nordic approach to managing borders. As researchers at the Finnish Institute described, "national security solutions gained primacy, similarly to what was happening around the globe."[121] While the Baltic States managed to create a travel bubble in mid-May 2020, on the basis of similarly low infection rates, the Nordic countries never did so.[122] Decisions were made at high levels of government in capital cities, yet they had the greatest impacts on border communities, which were largely overlooked. In March 2020, the Norwegian police established operations on the land border with Sweden for the first time since 1905. The decision to close the border to all foreign nationals who lacked a residency permit in Norway came with virtually no advance consultation or guidance, prompting confusion and concern by Swedes whose families, friends, and places of employment were just across the border in Norway. The impacts were especially acute in Svinesund, one of the busiest border crossings in the entire Nordic Region.

The quintessential icon of the Svinesund region is the arched Svinesund Bridge connecting the southern areas of Norway and Sweden. During the border restrictions, the bridge was often used as a meeting place for people unable to cross. The Swedish twins Ola and Pontus Berglund met weekly on the bridge, each sitting in camp chairs less than 10 feet apart on their respective sides of the border. Residents of this highly integrated region said that erecting border restrictions was "shocking" and "unthinkable."[123] The nearby seaside tourist town of Strömstad, Sweden, depends on seasonal Norwegian tourists, while Swedish workers in need of year-round employment traveled across the bridge to Norway, providing businesses with a steady labor force. The huge Nordby shopping center on the Swedish side caters almost exclusively to Norwegian shoppers taking advantage of lower Swedish taxes on sweets, alcohol, tobacco, and other retail goods. This dynamic is duplicated in other areas along the Norway-Sweden border, such as Storlien, with shopping centers on the Swedish side designed for a much larger customer base than what exists domestically.

In Stromstad, unemployment rose to 9.2% by September 2020, while unemployment nationwide was a full percentage point lower.[124] In a similar pattern, other Swedish communities adjacent to the Norwegian border saw higher increases in unemployment compared to those in other areas.[125] The Nordby shopping center, the biggest mall in Scandinavia and one almost entirely dependent on shoppers from nearby Oslo, saw sales plummet by 95%.[126] Cross-border labor markets were severed, creating a complex situation in which Swedish residents with employers in Norway were unable to go to work, yet also unable to receive social benefits from the Swedish government. Norwegian workers were technically able to go to Sweden for work but many would face two weeks of quarantine upon returning to Norway—an impossible situation that prohibited the pattern of daily commuting and isolated them from family and friends.

In remote and rural communities in the north, the situation was particularly bleak. On the border between Finland and Sweden, the small cities of Tornio (Finland) and Haparanda (Sweden) are completely codependent. They share a binational school and many essential services that only exist on one side of the border yet are constructed to serve residents from the other side. The IKEA store, for example, is located in Haparanda, and the swimming pool, the shopping mall, and only photo-shops in the area are in Tornio. When Finland closed its border to Sweden, Finnish border guards patrolled the newly built temporary fences, splitting the city and creating an atmosphere that one resident called "scary, like we were in a war."[127] While Finns were allowed to enter the Swedish side of town, Swedes could not enter the Finnish side. A person living in Haparanda had to drive 80 miles in order to get a professional photo taken, for example, when there were three photo-shops in Tornio within walking distance.[128]

Quarantine rules also greatly affected families divided by the border restrictions, which was particularly difficult for split families. It is not uncommon for divorced parents to live on either side of the border, with children dividing their time between one home on the Norwegian side and the other on the Swedish side. This was the case with many families in Svinesund, due to the high level of integration between Swedes and Norwegians in the area. When the border was restricted, a father in Norway who wanted to visit his children in Sweden would have to quarantine for two weeks upon returning home. This made such visits prohibitive for many and only added to the emotional burden many people faced during the pandemic. It was a jarring departure; as one resident in Svinesund remarked, "we haven't had any border for seventy years, our societies are based on open borders, that's how people here live. It's our social fabric."[129]

The decisions about border restrictions were made in the capital cities of Oslo and Stockholm, both hours away from places where most people's daily lives relied on cross-border mobility. As the Schengen countries adopted the "traffic light system" in October 2020, little consideration was given to border communities. The European Centre for Disease Prevention and Control published a weekly map of infection rates based on regions, which lumped together urban communities, where rates tended to be higher, with rural ones, where rates were often lower. The color-coded system was used by Norway to inform border restrictions, which considered rural areas located hours from Stockholm as part of the same region. If infection rates in the capital were high but those in communities adjacent to the border were low, border communities would nonetheless be restricted from cross-border travel.

There are many examples of how decision makers in the capital cities lacked a sufficient understanding of how life in the border regions functions.[130] This was by no means unique to the Nordics; it was also very evident in North America and in parts of Asia, Latin America, and Africa. But it should never have happened in the Nordic countries given the governance structure in place to support cross-border collaboration, as well as the historical commitment to cross-border mobility. "We have so many structures, but they were completely bypassed . . . the national governments have the legitimate power of action and soft governance was completely disregarded," described Alberto Giacometti, a researcher of Nordic cooperation.[131] This includes the Nordic Council of Ministers, which consists of a representative from each country and serves as the official body for intergovernmental cooperation in the broader Nordic Region. But in most cases, these ministers were not consulted on matters related to cross-border mobility and border restrictions. In addition to a top-down governance structure, there are also border information services, which function as networks of connection between border communities and their respective capitals. Cross-border committees, information services, and associations of border municipalities not only support Nordic cooperation from the ground up, but they are also supported financially by the Nordic Council of Ministers in addition to supranational sources of support like the EU's Interreg program.[132] These sub-national, regional entities were heavily involved in advocating for better Nordic cooperation, yet "Oslo and Stockholm were too far, they didn't feel the pain. They didn't listen," said Linda Engsmyr, an elected official from the Norwegian side of the border engaged in cross-border cooperation.[133]

As the pandemic began to abate and border restrictions were eased, there was a lingering sense that relations between Swedes and Norwegians had been scarred. While this may prove to be short-term, feelings were injured, and relationships of trust weakened.[134] In the autumn of 2022, after the restrictions had been lifted for nearly seven months, residents living adjacent to the border described ways in which their cross-border relations felt different. "I'm most worried about the people that are working here, it scarred their soul, they were looked down on, they felt that they were second degree citizens," said a municipal official from Norway. "It's harder to get people to work here in Norway now, and in Eidskog we are totally dependent on our

Swedish friends."[135] Many emerged from the restrictions feeling an "us" versus "them" dynamic that had not previously existed in borderland communities. This fear of neighbors, and of each other more generally, highlights how the difference between national policies eroded trust on the ground, even between communities that were intimately connected. Even as relations resumed their pre-pandemic patterns, people in the region say, "there is definitely a scar."[136] At the same time, there is new attention to overcoming these wounds, and demanding more coordinated crisis management among the Nordic countries the next time around. Regional leaders say they remain committed to achieving the goal of the Nordic countries to be "the most integrated region in the world" by 2030.[137]

Can the European Project Recover?

Norway shut the border to its Nordic neighbor and kept its doors largely closed for 562 days. The surprising surge in nationalism left bruised feelings on both sides. "We thought we had moved past all that, that we were so civilized, and that the Nordics were just like a family," said Anna Hallberg, Sweden's minister for Nordic Affairs. "That turned out to not be the case." Rather than serving as a model for cross-border cooperation, "in many ways, Covid-19 has shown us how fragile Nordic cooperation can be."[138] Despite the collaborative governance framework of the Nordic Council of Ministers, and the commitment to the freedom of movement, during the crisis countries retreated into their own shells. "The notable absence of Nordic collaboration in developing policy responses to the pandemic has also raised broader ideological questions about the role of Nordic co-operation in times of crisis," warned the Nordregio research group.[139] And as a representative from the Freedom of Movement Council remarked, "the national interests will dominate, but when the crisis comes, people should be confident that they will be able to cross borders. There is an absolute trust among people in this ideal. How long will that trust last, that Nordic identity, if we can't design policies to accommodate it?"[140]

The breakdown in cooperation on cross-border mobility during the pandemic tested the potential for the Nordic countries to be the most integrated region in the world. Yet it has also raised awareness about the depth of economic and social integration in border regions, and the importance of maintaining an open border among countries that are so interdependent. There is a sense that mobility can no longer be taken for granted but must be actively nurtured. "We depend on each other in different ways . . . it's been hard to get the national government authorities to see what effect the border has on us who live here. It makes it difficult for people to live on one side and work on another," said a Norwegian border resident. "It's much more at the forefront of the discussion now. Don't let anyone forget what we've been through. We have to learn from the pandemic, but we also have to talk to the people that decide things . . . they have to learn from this too."[141] Entities such as the Freedom of Movement Council, which reports to the Nordic Council of Ministers, were very critical about border management during the pandemic.[142] These criticisms were largely ignored early on, "because the governments didn't want to see the consequences of their actions." But the costs of not having a common Nordic strategy were enormous and did not go unnoticed. In June 2022, the Freedom of Movement Council was given a new mandate to have a role in times of crisis when mobility is impacted. Despite the nationalist retrenchment experienced during the pandemic, there is cautious optimism that the Nordic countries will do better during the next crisis.

A similar trajectory is apparent for the EU as a whole. There is optimism that the collateral damage of border controls during the pandemic was indeed a wakeup call for Europe. In restricting the mobility of EU citizens and residents, member states went too far—severing labor markets, separating families, and undermining the foundations of the European project. As European Commission president Ursula von der Leyen stated: "Different crises and challenges have shown us that we cannot take Schengen for granted."[143] Glimmers of this recognition appeared in revisions to the Schengen Borders Code, proposed in 2022, which established a safeguard mechanism to provide a common response to threats at internal borders in addition to further restricting the use of border controls.[144] Upon announcing the proposed revision, von der Leyen said: "Today, we are presenting a way forward that makes sure that Schengen can bear the test of time, one that will ensure the free flow of people, goods and services whatever the circumstances to rebuild our economies and for us to emerge stronger together."[145] Jean Peyrony, director general of the Transfrontier Operational Mission in France whose work influenced the Commission's proposed revisions, said: "What this crisis has revealed, many people seemed to ignore . . . that cross-border integration is not only about economics or legislation. . . . People in the border region are also a culture. This has been a discovery for the Commission."[146]

In Europe, there are sophisticated and structured cross-border networks that have been able to influence policymaking at both national levels and throughout the EU. Local and regional authorities, where a decrease in the freedom of movement is most acutely felt, have pushed national authorities to reopen borders, not just during Covid but at other times when free movement has been suspended (mass gatherings, terrorism fears, migration). Sometimes these subnational entities have formed alliances across countries and with EU institutions, bypassing national governments to identify—and try to alleviate—the impact of border restrictions in their regions, whether economically, socially, or culturally.[147] One example is the Nordic region. The information service Grensetjänsten that exists to support cross-border integration between Sweden and Norway serves as the conduit to share "border obstacles" encountered on the ground with the Nordic Council of Ministers. As a result of the Covid border restrictions, there are now stronger connections between the two entities. "Now, this is very high up in the political discussions," said Kikki Lindset from the Grensetjänsten. "As a border information [service], they really know what we are doing now."[148]

Detailed analyses undertaken for the European Commission by the French organization Transfrontier Operational Mission illustrated similar examples of the role and value of regional cross-border entities throughout Europe.[149] The Benelux Union, established over sixty years ago among Belgium, Luxembourg, and the Netherlands, developed a coordinated system of cooperation during times of crisis back in 2006. Throughout Covid, the crisis centers in each country were in continual contact. While each country still imposed some border obstacles unilaterally, the coordinated exchange of information among the three countries enabled local authorities and citizens to be prepared as border restrictions evolved. Given their successes, in 2022 the Benelux Union Secretariat advanced an initiative to set up a network across European crisis centers to increase preparedness in future crises. Even when "their impact on softening national level restrictions was rather low," the report states, such networks "were useful in . . . raising awareness at the national level of the issues identified locally related to border restrictions."[150]

It is clear that both member states and the European Commission failed to account for the integrated nature of border regions. The impact to these regions extends far beyond economic costs and will be experienced for some time; as one resident remarked, the "real long term effect won't be measured in effects on shopping or tourism but on the breaking of the cross-border psychology."[151] Personal choices that were once taken for granted, like commuting across borders for work, now seem riskier. In future crises, narrow national interests may again trump European solidarity, undermining "the proper functioning of the Schengen area of free movement and its benefits to European citizens."[152] The extent to which member states can resist the temptation to fortify their borders will shape the lives and livelihoods of millions of Europeans.

The Covid pandemic was the second great border disruption of the past decade in Europe, and the larger of the two. In 2015 during the migrant crisis, nearly 40% of land borders in Schengen were temporarily impacted; in 2020 nearly 70% of borders were restricted.[153] The 2015–2016 border controls were largely confined to specific crossing points, not the broad shutdowns that occurred during the pandemic. The most significant difference, however, is *whom and what* the border controls intended to keep out. Those implemented in 2015–2016 were largely about restricting the movement of non-EU citizens and residents. Emphasis was placed on securing Europe's external border in order to preserve its internal mobility. The deterrent strategies at the external borders of the EU existed in part to enable internal free movement.[154] The European Commission and many European countries advocated for the tightening of the external Schengen borders, with the Commission voting to allocate resources to the external borders to help countries manage them. The EU response—a very controversial one—was thus largely one of externalization, increasing border security at the edges of the EU through the expansion of FRONTEX, the European Border and Coast Guard Agency, in order to maintain the openness of internal (intra-Schengen) borders.

During Covid, however, EU institutions were unable for many months to turn the pandemic into a wholly external border control issue. Member states used border controls and travel measures to prevent the movement of other EU citizens and residents, even when the virus was already present within their own countries. In the early months of the pandemic, the response of a "borderless Europe" closely resembled that of other sovereign states around the world. The tools and levers used by national leaders were very much the same, and the impacts on communities were equally—if not more—disruptive. For some politicians, border controls were "a way of scoring easy political points," said a representative of the Freedom of Movement Council.[155] "International crises that cannot be addressed nationally . . . are still addressed nationally . . . because people want that." But many European leaders pushed back against these nationalist reactions, with the Commission urging countries to keep internal borders open and to coordinate among themselves on external travel controls—an insistence that eventually succeeded. There remains, of course, an inconsistency between the larger European vision and the reality of national identities and national policy priorities. The pandemic showed again that, in times of crisis, the latter tends to take precedence. As one Swedish resident living near the Norwegian border put it: "It's alarming how quickly nationalism came back."[156]

Freedom of movement is both a right guaranteed to Europeans, and a condition that serves as the scaffolding for the European way of life. It is a right that shapes where millions of Europeans work, where they live, and even whom they develop relationships with. The resurgence, and progression, of border controls in the Schengen Area raises doubts about their use as purely temporary measures that "shall only be made as a last resort."[157] The Covid pandemic exposed the vulnerability of cross-border mobility and how, during times of crisis, this binding feature of the European way of life was treated more as an ideal than a right. Even as the revisions to the Schengen Borders Code place limits and stricter parameters on invoking internal border controls, they simultaneously legitimize their existence by outlining their use. Requirements to notify the Commission and limit the duration of border controls existed prior to the onset of Covid, yet many member states ignored them. The right of cross-border travel remains subject to the mercy of sovereign countries. If member states do not trust each other, then the durability of the freedom of movement will continue to be chipped away at. "What lessons can we learn from this?" asked Emil Wannheden, formerly with Sweden's Ministry of Foreign Affairs. "One is the importance of creating trust and predictability for those who live close to the border. What I hope is that people working in the governments, in the capitals, don't fall back into complacency . . . but that we keep these lessons in mind. The danger is that we forget what happened."[158]

6

No Man Is an Island (But Some Countries Are)

The Asia-Pacific

By the standards of public health—lives saved, infections avoided—the Asia-Pacific region was the great success story of the Covid-19 pandemic.[1] The United States lost more than a million lives to Covid, and its fatality rate of nearly 340 per 100,000 people was shockingly high for a country with a modern public health system. Germany, France, Spain, and the UK all had high fatality rates of roughly 200 per 100,000. Covid deaths in the Asia-Pacific region were a fraction of those numbers. Australia lost just 76 out of 100,000 citizens. In Taiwan and South Korea, it was 74 and 76. In New Zealand it was just over 50. In Vietnam, Japan, and Singapore, the rate was well under 50.[2] Using the alternative measure of "excess deaths"—the difference between the expected number of deaths and what occurred during the pandemic— the Asia-Pacific did far better than North America, Europe, Latin America, and most of Africa; New Zealand actually saw fewer excess deaths than prior to the pandemic, with social distancing likely preventing the spread of other diseases.[3] Infection rates tell a similar story. During the worst periods of the pandemic, from early 2020 through September 2021, the region consistently had the lowest infection rates in the world; standout performers included South Korea, China, Taiwan, Singapore, Australia, and New Zealand.[4] While infections soared and deaths in the Asia-Pacific climbed with the emergence of the Omicron variant, it hit at a time when vaccines had been rolled out to much of the population and proved less lethal than the earlier strains.

Many Asia-Pacific countries did many things well during the pandemic. But there are two sets of lessons that could be drawn from the Asian experience— one that leads in the direction of greater national capacity building and international cooperation to respond to collective public health problems, and the other that leads to a further retreat behind national borders. The first lesson is about the importance of robust public health infrastructure, a clear coordinated government strategy, and effective communication to win public buy-in. Having learned in part from the experience of the SARS virus, which hit the Asia-Pacific hard in 2003, and the Middle East Respiratory Virus (MERS) in 2015, countries in the region were ahead of most in bolstering their public health capacities and winning public cooperation for preventive measures from masking to contact tracing to quarantine.[5] Richard Horton, editor in chief of *The Lancet*, argues: "The long history of epidemics in the region— Asian influenza in 1957, the Hong Kong influenza pandemic in 1968, a series of avian flu influenza outbreaks in the 1990s and early 2000s, and finally SARS and MERS—had acted as a kind of 'sociological imprinting' on the Asian mind. They were ready for COVID-19."[6] Countries that had been hit hard by SARS or MERS—including South Korea, Vietnam, Singapore, and Taiwan—had built robust institutions to coordinate such a massive disease-control effort. Governments moved in quickly rolling out Covid testing, distributing masks, tracing, and containing outbreaks, setting up quarantine facilities, and communicating clearly with the public.[7] As the world prepares for future pandemics, there should be a great deal of attention to what can be learned from Asia's successes and how other countries can build similarly strong public health capacities.

There was another feature of the responses in most of Asia; countries closed their borders early and kept them largely closed even after most of the rest of the world had eased up.[8] For some Asia-Pacific nations—China is a more complicated case and the subject of the next chapter—"zero-Covid" was a strategy that offered significant benefits, not only keeping fatalities low but allowing citizens in many of those countries to lead more normal lives than those in countries facing repeated domestic lockdowns, and causing less short-term harm to the economy. Taiwan's economy was the strongest in Asia in 2020, growing by 3.1%, while Vietnam grew by 2.9%.[9] Other Asian economies suffered slight GDP declines, but far less than the sharp downturns in Europe, the UK, Latin America, and North America.[10] Border restrictions were an integral part of such strategies, keeping to a minimum the introduction of new Covid cases from outside and allowing quick responses to stamp out outbreaks when they did occur.

Border controls to contain Covid made far more geographic sense here than in any other part of the world. Many countries and territories—Japan, Taiwan, Singapore, Indonesia, the Philippines, Australia, and New Zealand—are island nations that can be sealed relatively easily. Others like South Korea—bordered on the north by isolated North Korea—are effectively islands. Travel had exploded in the region—between 2010 and 2019 international arrivals had nearly doubled from 208 million visitors to 360 million.[11] But it was easier for governments to turn the taps off than in Europe, North America, Latin America, or Africa, where many people live in border regions and most travel takes place over land borders. Travelers could be stopped before they got on flights, and cargo—coming and going by plane or ship rather than by rail or truck—could be handled with fewer risky personal interactions. A year after the pandemic hit, in the January to July 2021 period, international travel in the region was still down 95% from pre-pandemic levels, the steepest decline in the world.[12] This geographic advantage made the pursuit of zero-Covid—as opposed to mitigation strategies to slow the spread of the virus—potentially achievable in many of these countries.

Even given its unique circumstances, Asia's border controls offer lessons for the world. The region's success has already prompted discussion over whether the International Health Regulations (IHR) should be revised to reflect the utility of travel restrictions under some circumstances.[13] While still calling for states to adopt "proportionate" and "evidence-based" restrictions during pandemics, the World Health Organization has become more supportive of temporary travel restrictions, even quite stringent ones.[14] Many public health experts now argue that Asia's experience showed that travel restrictions that are imposed early in an outbreak, as well as ongoing testing and quarantine requirements for international arrivals, are a key part of successful pandemic response.[15] When the more-contagious "Alpha" variant was first identified in the UK, for example, Hong Kong immediately banned incoming flights from Great Britain; it took nearly six months before the first Alpha case was recorded in Hong Kong. The United States, in contrast, took eight days before it banned flights from the UK, giving the new variant time to seed in the local community.[16] The success of Asia's Covid measures is certain to inspire future emulators; the region makes the strongest case for the argument that border and travel restrictions are an important part of the pandemic toolbox for government.

But there is another potential lesson that has more troubling implications—that border restrictions are not just a necessary strategy for pandemic control but a sufficient one. Australia and New Zealand, for example, relied primarily on border and mobility restrictions, maintaining long, tight travel bans that locked citizens in and kept foreigners and even some citizens out. In Australia, there were additional inter-state travel restrictions that separated friends and families who happened to live on opposite sides of state borders. Such tough border measures were popular at home and abroad, offering a response that was simple to understand and that asked relatively little of most of those living in the country. As long as the virus could be kept out, life could go on more or less as normal—though breaches in Australia's border walls resulted in several punishing lockdowns, especially in Melbourne. Jacinda Ardern, New Zealand's prime minister, became what the *New York Times* called "a global emblem of anti-Trump liberalism" for her unflagging efforts to stamp out the Covid virus by using some of the toughest border restrictions in the world.[17] Australia, which had faced international opprobrium for refusing since 2013 to admit asylum seekers and housing them in jail-like facilities on distant islands, suddenly found itself lauded for imposing rigid border restrictions to prevent the introduction of Covid.[18]

In the aftermath of the pandemic, there is a real danger that nations whose borders are geographically far more porous than the Asian island-states will nonetheless see border controls as the easiest and most popular way to respond to dangers like diseases that originate beyond national borders. The idea that border control alone can keep external threats at bay is what one of the authors of this book has called "the meaningless mantra of border security."[19] Critics of "open borders" imagine that ever tougher, more expensive, and more violent measures imposed on those trying to cross national borders can hold back dangers from abroad at minimal cost to the nation. The success of some Asian nations in combating Covid through border controls will reinforce the hope that perfectly secure borders are a legitimate, achievable goal of public policy.[20] Instead, what the most successful Asian countries showed during the pandemic is that border restrictions can help to ameliorate threats from abroad, but only as part of a broader strategy of effective governance. While there are valuable lessons for the world to learn from Asia's Covid-19 successes, there is a great danger that many countries will learn the wrong lesson and when the next threat surfaces, countries will simply close their borders and keep them closed.

Was There an "Asian Approach" to Covid?

Generalizing across a region as large and varied as the Asia-Pacific risks oversimplifying aspects of the pandemic response. There were innovations and challenges across the region. But what the successful Asian countries generally showed was the ability to combine flexible mobility controls—ones that changed as circumstances changed—along with the domestic public health capacity to quickly identify and control Covid breakouts. Strong governments with efficient health bureaucracies were able to work more directly in their communities than was the case in Europe or North America, rolling out widespread testing, requiring masking, mandating quarantine for the infected, supporting those in quarantine or isolation, and tracing contacts to try to stamp out the spread of infections. In some countries, the measures were intrusive on personal privacy in ways that would not have been tolerated in Western democracies. Those countries also relied on border controls, but only as one of many tools. South Korea and Taiwan stand out here. In other countries, domestic public health capacities were more stunted, and political pressures helped push those governments to a near exclusive reliance on border measures, Japan, Australia, and New Zealand are the three stand-out examples.

Singapore began screening travelers from China in early January and did a broader shutdown to travel in March 2020.[21] Throughout the pandemic, it showed the broadest range of flexibility at both extremes. It was among the first countries to experiment with reduced quarantine for travelers in September and October 2020. Tourists from New Zealand, Australia, and Vietnam were permitted to arrive with pre- and post-arrival PCR tests and forty-eight hours of isolation to await results.[22] Singapore entered into reciprocal "green lane" agreements with similar restrictions for countries that included China, South Korea, New Zealand, Japan, and Germany.[23] But the nation also lurched in the opposite direction in the face of new variants or breakouts; in May 2021 as the Delta variant was spreading, it instituted a twenty-one-day quarantine for arrivals from all countries except China, Hong Kong, Macao, Taiwan, New Zealand, and Australia.[24] And the restrictions were far more onerous for the country's large migrant workforce, who risked being blocked from return or facing the expense of long quarantines if they left the country.[25] Dale Fisher, a professor in infectious diseases at the National University of Singapore, credited the country's more "nimble" approach to its strong health system.

"We think that even if a traveler brought it in, we think there's a good chance it wouldn't spread anyway," Dr. Fisher said. "If you've got no faith in your system, then that would make you keep the borders harder."[26]

Vietnam's border measures were among the most restrictive in the region, but they came in the context of a domestic public health response that produced remarkable success for a lower-middle-income country.[27] Vietnam was one of the first countries to restrict incoming travel from China, and it maintained hard border closures for much of the pandemic.[28] But Vietnam had also invested heavily in its health infrastructure; from 2000 to 2016 its public health spending increased by an average of 9% annually.[29] While its hospitals could not have managed a large outbreak, the country's contact tracing system rivaled those in South Korea and Taiwan. It had also built a centralized system of health surveillance that encouraged rapid reporting and response to new Covid outbreaks. Through the end of 2020, Vietnam reported just 35 deaths from Covid.[30] And while tourism, which brought in 18 million visitors and $32 billion in revenue in 2019, was devastated, Vietnam's manufacturing sector thrived as export demand grew for electronics and other items.[31] Vietnam's economy grew by nearly 3% in 2020, one of the strongest performances in the world.

Thailand, which in 2019 was the eighth largest recipient of international tourists with some 40 million visitors, canceled all international commercial flights into the country on April 3, 2020, making an exception only for repatriation flights for Thai citizens. The travel restrictions—along with a brief, hard domestic lockdown—were helpful in containing the first wave of Covid.[32] But they were devastating for the economy, which shrunk by more than 6% in 2020, the biggest drop since the global financial crisis more than a decade earlier; tourism made up one-fifth of Thai GDP before the pandemic.[33] As a consequence, Thailand was more aggressive than most countries in the region in trying to find creative ways to welcome back international travelers. In December 2020, Thailand reopened to travelers from fifty-six countries, including France, and the United States, though a mandatory fourteen-day quarantine requirement continued to discourage most visitors. In July 2021, with most Thais already vaccinated, the government created what became known as the "Phuket sandbox" for the popular island tourist destination; fully vaccinated international travelers were exempted from quarantine provided they stayed in a certified hotel in the region for at least fourteen days before traveling to other parts of the country.[34] The easing came even though the country was in the midst of a major Covid wave associated with the Delta variant, which would cause Thailand's cases to surge ahead of many countries in the region. And in November 2021, a full year before some Asian countries reopened, Thailand began permitting vaccinated travelers from sixty-three countries with just a negative Covid test and a single day of quarantine and expanded the regions of the country open to international visitors.[35]

Any of these is an interesting case study in its own right, but in searching for lessons, five countries especially stand out—on one side, South Korea and Taiwan for the ways in which they integrated border control with domestic public health measures, and on the other, Japan, Australia, and New Zealand for their heavy reliance on border measures to control the virus (Figure 6.1).

Taiwan and South Korea: A Borders-Plus Approach

South Korea

Outside of China where the virus originated, no other country faced a bigger initial Covid outbreak than South Korea. The rest of the world quickly took notice. On February 22, 2020, a KAL flight from Korea arrived at Ben Gurion International Airport in Israel. The previous day, Israel had recorded its first Covid case, a returning passenger from the *Diamond Princess* cruise ship that had been moored off Japan amid a massive outbreak among passengers.[36] Israeli authorities held the KAL plane on the tarmac while the twelve Israeli citizens on board were allowed to disembark and rushed by ambulance to quarantine facilities. The plane was then refueled, and the rest of the passengers forced to fly back to South Korea; Israel immediately banned all future flights from the country.[37] Bahrain and Jordan also barred flights from South Korea, as did the US island territory of Samoa, while the UK and Ethiopia required two weeks of quarantine for arriving Korean travelers. *Fortune* magazine dubbed the country a "pariah" along with Italy, which was also seeing a surge of cases.[38] Critics said the South Korean government, fearful of Beijing's reaction, had erred in not blocking travelers from China more quickly.[39]

Yet within a month, Korea had brought the virus under control, reducing the daily number of cases to fewer than 100 by early March. In early May South Korea briefly reported no new Covid cases at all—despite holding parliamentary elections April 15 in which 29 million people had gone to the polls.

OVERVIEW OF TRAVEL RESTRICTIONS DURING COVID

	South Korea	Taiwan	Japan	Australia	New Zealand
Non-Citizens Restricted	No, except for Chinese arrivals in January and February 2023. Some countries faced new visa requirements.	Yes. Chinese nationals from China on February 11, 2020. Most foreign nationals from March 19, 2020. Re-opening began July 2022.	Yes. From most countries starting April 3, 2020. Re-opening began September 2022.	Yes. For travelers from China starting February 1, 2020. For most foreign nationals on March 1, 2020. Re-opening began February 2022.	Yes. Foreign travelers from China on February 3, 2020. Most other foreign nationals were barred from March 2020. Re-opening began April 30, 2022.
Citizens Restricted	No.	No.	No.	Yes. Australians needed government permission to travel. Returning citizens faced limited hotel quarantine space. Australians in India were barred for two weeks in May 2021, under penalty of fines/imprisonment. Phase-out began in November 2021.	Yes, from April 9, 2020 returning citizens were required to apply for limited hotel spaces under the MIQ system. Phase-out began in March 2022.
Permanent Residents Restricted	No.	No.	Yes, Treated same as non-citizens until September 2020 and then gradually eased.	Yes, but subject to the same restrictions as citizens.	Yes, but subject to the same restrictions as citizens.
Quarantine Requirements	Yes, hotel or at-home self-isolation depending on circumstances.	Yes, hotel or at-home self-isolation depending on circumstances.	Yes, hotel or at-home self-isolation depending on circumstances.	Yes, mandatory quarantine hotels required from March 28, 2020. Phase-out began in November 2021 for vaccinated returning citizens.	Yes, mandatory quarantine hotels required beginning April 9, 2020. Phase-out began March 2022.

Figure 6.1 Overview of travel restrictions during COVID. Courtesy of Jennifer Bettis, Border Policy Research Institute.

And it did so without imposing any significant travel bans. Korea was among the few countries in the world that largely adhered to its commitments under the International Health Regulations by not closing its borders to travelers from affected countries. It also largely avoided the domestic lockdowns that were imposed in China and many other countries. "We never considered a full lockdown as part of our policy response," said Park Neung-hoo, South Korea's health and welfare minister.[40] Instead, South Korea became the best example of how targeted public health measures, combined with sensible mobility restrictions like quarantine requirements for incoming travelers and restrictions on large gatherings, could contain even a highly contagious virus like Covid-19.

In the early days of the pandemic, South Korea seemed unlikely to emerge as a global role model. It experienced one of the first documented "superspreader" events, in which a single patient leaves behind a trail of contagion. The source was a sixty-one-year-old woman—"Patient 31" for the thirty-first case recorded in the country—who attended services at the Shincheonji Church of Jesus in Daegu, the country's fourth largest city. The Shincheonji Church is a secretive sect, founded by then eighty-eight-year-old Lee Man-hee, who is believed to be immortal by many of his followers. In the nine-story church in Dageu, Patient 31 would have been one of roughly 1,000 people packed into a windowless basement worship hall.[41] "Shincheonji followers hold services sitting on the floor, without any chairs, [packed together] like bean sprouts," said Shin Hyun-uk, director of the Guri Cult Counseling Center, a former church member.[42] The worshippers would "shout out 'amen' after every sentence the pastor utters, pretty much every few seconds. And they do that at the top of their lungs."

By the end of February, more than 900 new cases were being recorded daily in Korea, most clustered in the Daegu region; some two-thirds, more than 5,000 cases in total, were thought to be connected to Patient 31.[43] Tracking and containing those cases was enormously challenging given the church's history of secrecy. Public health officials had to hunt down and test the church's 210,000 known followers, who had long been taught to conceal their membership in the church, even from their own family and friends.[44] But fearful of a rising public backlash, church officials agreed to cooperate with the government, releasing the addresses of all its affiliates around the country, temporarily shutting church services, and agreeing that all 9,000 members of the

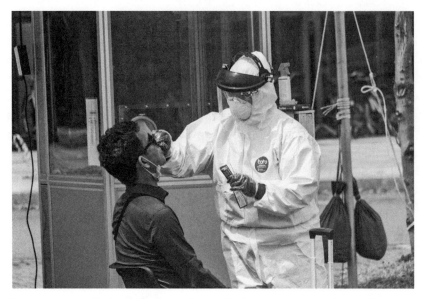

Figure 6.2 A walk-through testing clinic in Incheon, April 2020. South Korea rolled out testing more widely than any country, helping to contain the virus. Rapture 700/Shutterstock.

Daegu church would go into self-isolation.[45] After a peak on February 29, new case numbers had begun to fall sharply.

The extraordinary response showed that it was possible through public health measures to contain even large and difficult-to-trace outbreaks. For South Korea, the key elements apart from public mask-wearing—which was widespread—were mass testing, contact tracing, and isolation and treatment of those infected (Figure 6.2). South Korea was the first country to roll out accurate Covid tests on a national scale. In the aftermath of the 2015 MERS outbreak, which infected and killed more people in South Korea than any country other than Saudi Arabia where it was first identified, the Korean Center for Disease Control and Prevention (KCDC) and other health agencies had greatly bolstered the country's pandemic preparedness. Research on a Covid test had begun in mid-January, as soon as China shared the genetic sequences of the virus.[46] On January 27, government health officials met with representatives of more than twenty medical companies urging the immediate development of effective diagnostic tests. Funding for infectious diseases had tripled since the MERS outbreak, and by February 4 the government had authorized emergency use of new tests and began setting up drive-through and walk-through testing clinics. The US Food and Drug Administration issued emergency approval for a Covid test the same day, but the US test proved unreliable, allowing the virus to continue spreading unnoticed. In Korea, within a week of the Patient 31 outbreak the country was doing more Covid tests than any other in the world—some 10,000 tests a day by March 1, when the United States was still performing fewer than 100.[47] In an effort to contain the Daegu outbreak, an additional 2,400 nurses and other public health workers quickly descended on the region, isolating and treating most patients in special facilities and reserving hospitals for the sickest few. Korea's hospital system was also well prepared for the early surge of cases; the number of hospital beds per resident was the second highest among OECD countries.[48]

Most ambitiously, the government set about tracing all the public contacts of Patient 31 and others infected with Covid. Much of it was old-fashioned and labor-intensive—officials tracked down church members and their contacts and forced infected members into quarantine or treatment. Those suspected of contact with an infected individual were required to self-isolate at home or in a government facility, and to be monitored through a "Self-Quarantine Safety Protection" app. Case officers would check in twice daily with food and toiletries as well as psychological counseling. Those found violating quarantine were further required to wear an electronic wristband that allowed for precise location tracking. The fine for violations could be as high as US$8,000.[49] But the government also took advantage of technology, creating a "virus patient travel log" that used interviews, GPS phone tracking, credit card records, and camera surveillance to track the previous movements of confirmed Covid patients.[50] Emergency texts were sent to the phones of those who may have been exposed, allowing anyone who may have crossed tracks with an infected individual to take precautions.

Such intrusive surveillance had been embedded in Korea's public health laws following the MERS failure, giving the government authority to ignore usual privacy concerns and gather and distribute such information without warrants.[51] The patients' names were not used, though the public log still raised privacy concerns given that friends and family may have been able to identify specific individuals by their movements.[52] The intensive surveillance touched off difficult national debates over privacy rights in a pandemic. In one instance, relatives accused a man of having an affair with his sister-in-law after the tracing showed they had dined in a restaurant together.[53] A May 2020 outbreak in a Seoul neighborhood of nightclubs frequented by LGBTQ individuals sparked a surge in homophobia in a country where most gay people are not public about their sexuality. After a case was recorded by one of the club's clients, authorities set about tracking down more than 5,500 people who had visited the clubs.[54] By June 2020 the task became a bit simpler—high-risk businesses such as bars, gyms, and restaurants set up QR codes to record all entries, making outbreaks easier to track. To address privacy concerns, the government deleted such data after fourteen days.

The benefit of such intensive testing and tracing, apart from suppressing the virus, was to limit domestic lockdowns and other mobility restrictions. South Korea never issued stay-at-home orders, and daily life continued much as normal aside from ubiquitous mask-wearing. A new school term had been set to begin March 2, but schools were initially forced to stay closed, and other institutions with large gatherings like churches and community centers were advised to close.[55] Pop concerts were banned for most of the pandemic. But as the virus came under control, schools began to reopen by early May, one of the first countries to do so (a handful, including Sweden and Taiwan, did not close schools early in the pandemic).[56] The limited lockdowns helped the Korean economy avoid serious damage, with GDP contracting by just 0.7% in 2020. It also allowed life to continue much as it had before the pandemic, without the huge disruption in daily routines that occurred in most countries. Domestic travel, for example, hardly slowed. The air route from Seoul to the holiday island of Jeju off the southern coast of South Korea was the world's busiest route in 2020, with more passengers than the top ten international routes combined.[57]

While border restrictions were part of the country's successful mix, South Korea remained surprisingly open, imposing only what have been called "the most passive entry regulations in the world."[58] Acutely aware of its trade dependence and worried about the early travel restrictions aimed at Koreans, the country never implemented a hard border closure. The closest was a February 4, 2020, ban on travelers coming directly from China's Hubei province, which was lifted in August.[59] Even as the virus was spreading in China, the government resisted stringent travel bans; Korea sent special charter flights to Wuhan to repatriate not just citizens but their Chinese spouses and families. "It is the basic national duty to take care of our people isolated in a far foreign land while facing fears of disease," said Health Minister Park Neung-hoo. "The Chinese family members transported together are wives, husbands, sons and daughters of our citizens, after all."[60] Such openness in the face of a crisis was not popular—an online petition by Koreans calling for a ban on Chinese nationals garnered 700,000 signatures, and 1.4 million people signed a separate petition to impeach President Moon Jae-in. The president's "response to the new coronavirus shows that he is more likely the president of China and not the president of the Republic of Korea," the petition said.[61]

At its most extensive, beginning on April 1, 2020, Korea required "Special Entry Procedures" for all incoming travelers. That meant new arrivals would be checked for fevers, provide contact information and a mobile number, and be required to quarantine for fourteen days at government-designated facilities at a subsidized rate of about US$80 per day.[62] But for much of the pandemic, most arrivals were free to self-quarantine for two weeks with close government oversight; between February 19 and June 10, 2020, only 0.16% of people were reported to have violated quarantine.[63] Travelers from high-risk countries, including the United States initially, were also required to have a negative PCR test. The quarantine requirement discouraged most travelers; international arrivals to South Korea, which had surged in 2018 and 2019, fell by 96% between December 2019 and July 2020.[64] But by October 2020, Korea had set up "fast-track" quarantine-free entry for business travelers from China, Singapore, Japan, the UAE, and Indonesia.[65] The small number of actual travel bans Korea imposed were motivated by geopolitics rather than health; Korea retaliated against Japan in early March 2020, for example, when Tokyo blocked travelers from Korea, saying the move was "based on the principle of reciprocity."[66] There were other infrequent exceptions. In late 2021, Korea joined many other countries in banning travel from South Africa and other African nations following the outbreak of the Omicron variant.[67] And then in January 2023, Korea briefly suspended short-term visas for Chinese travelers following the surge in Chinese cases after the lifting of domestic lockdowns in China.[68]

Like almost every country, South Korea continually modified its restrictions to respond to the waxing and waning of case numbers. A spike in cases in late May 2020 slowed school reopenings and led to renewed restrictions on public gatherings; similar spikes occurred in August and November 2020, and again in April 2021. But in July 2021, South Korea abolished the two-week quarantine requirement for vaccinated travelers coming for purposes other than tourism (family, academic, business) provided they had not recently visited a high-risk country.[69] That reopening came more than a year before most other Asian countries began to ease their travel restrictions. South Korea's relatively open approach meant that public health authorities were frequently tracing and stamping out new outbreaks. South Korea never pursued a "zero-Covid" strategy and did not enjoy long periods where the country was free from the virus, as New Zealand and Taiwan were both able to do. But its modest number of deaths was similar to both countries. The largest spike in case numbers occurred in February 2022 following outbreaks of the Omicron variant. But by then more than 90% of the population was vaccinated with Western-made vaccines, and Korea had begun to lift the remaining restrictions and shifting to a policy of "Living with Covid-19."[70]

South Korea's performance has been hailed as a model for the world in responding to future pandemics. A Rand Corporation study argued that the country should export its public health model as part of a "soft power" initiative.[71] There are concerns to be sure—the government struggled to find a balance between the intrusive surveillance needed for testing and tracing and legitimate privacy concerns. By any reasonable measure, though, the harm done to personal freedom by such measures was far less than the draconian lockdowns implemented by China, and by many other countries across the world in more limited ways. And South Korea kept Covid at bay without resorting to travel bans and other harsh border restrictions. It was an impressive accomplishment.

Taiwan

Shih-Fen Chen, a Taiwanese-born professor of international business at Western Washington University in Washington State and a political commentator in Taiwan, traveled back to his home country four times during the pandemic, beginning in the summer of 2021. Before Covid, he had returned to Taiwan three or four times each year, but with the outbreak he had been out of the country for nearly two years, waiting to be vaccinated even though he was permitted to return earlier. During that time, his mother's health had begun to deteriorate, and by 2021 he was desperate to get back and spend time with her while he still could; she would pass away in early 2023. His experiences show a country that was relentlessly focused on keeping out Covid infections but able to do so in a way that allowed citizens, foreign residents, and some businesspeople to continue traveling if necessary. While the border measures were more severe than those in South Korea, and remained in place longer, Taiwan was closed to non-citizens only during the worst outbreaks, and the stringency of quarantine measures was constantly adjusted to the severity of the situation.

For most of 2020, border controls and a strict domestic testing and tracing program kept the virus in check; Taiwan went eight months in 2020 without a single domestically transmitted case of Covid, and had just seven deaths attributed to Covid infections that year; the United States in 2020 lost more than 350,000 people from Covid.[72] Taiwan had been among the first countries to impose travel restrictions and enforced several hard border closures during the year. On December 31, 2019, Taiwanese authorities began doing onboard inspections of passengers arriving from Wuhan, one of the earliest travel restrictions of the pandemic.[73] On January 26, Taiwan blocked all incoming flights from China's Hubei province ahead of the Lunar New Year holiday when thousands would normally have traveled between Taiwan and China.[74] Over the next month, Taiwan would temporarily ban travel from China, and from countries with rising infections, including Iran and Italy.[75] On March 19, the country implemented a broad travel ban barring most non-citizens and non-residents, though some exceptions were made for business travelers or diplomats with special visas.[76] Foreigners present in Taiwan were permitted to extend their visas.[77] Those border restrictions were as severe as any country in the world early in the pandemic.

But just over three months later, in an effort "to accelerate Taiwan's economic momentum and restore normal living conditions," Taiwan lifted travel restrictions for reasons other than tourism or social visits as long as visitors showed a negative Covid test.[78] New arrivals were required to quarantine for fourteen days, however, which as in South Korea discouraged most visits. The cycle would repeat several times. Taiwan barred most foreign nationals again in December 2020 after the emergence of the more contagious Alpha variant in the UK.[79] The restrictions were eased at the beginning of March 2021, only to be reinstated just two months later.[80] The May 2021 travel restrictions came after a cluster of new cases associated with the more contagious Delta variants were introduced by foreign pilots who had been permitted shorter quarantines—just three days followed by a period of self-monitoring. That outbreak even led to a soft lockdown with some business and school closures.[81] Taiwan would not lift all of its travel and quarantine restrictions on foreign visitors until October 2022, after most of the rest of the world had reopened.[82]

The first time Professor Chen returned to Taiwan was in June 2021; he had been twice vaccinated by this time. Before boarding the flight, he and his wife were required to show proof of vaccination and a negative Covid test, and to provide his travel itinerary, Taiwanese address, and a Taiwanese cellphone number to the government. As soon as his plane landed in Taipei, he got a text message from Taiwan's Ministry of Health informing him to start the process of entering the country. They were required to take an arrival PCR test, and were then guided to a station where the government provided a taxi—at a subsidized flat rate of about US$100—to take them to their home in southern Taiwan. Once there, they found a care package of food on the doorstep left by government officials; for the rest of the required two-week quarantine, they relied on groceries dropped on the doorstep by relatives or on deliveries from UberEats. Chen received a daily text message from the Ministry of Health and was warned to keep his cellphone charged and on to allow his location to be tracked. The phones were closely monitored. The wife of one of Chen's colleagues who was also quarantining turned off her phone briefly; the police arrived twenty minutes later. A local government official also called daily to check they were remaining in quarantine. At the end of the two-week period, they had to take one more PCR test before they were released from home.[83]

The protocols for incoming travelers were accompanied by a domestic testing and tracing system that rivaled South Korea's. In June 2021, during Taiwan's worst Covid outbreak, a cluster of Delta cases was discovered in Fangshan, a rural southern village with a large elderly population and still extremely low vaccination rates. But the outbreak was contained in just nineteen days, with only a single fatality. The first patient identified was a sixty-three-year-old taxi driver, just one of four in the community; the case appeared to be linked to a woman and her grandson who had recently returned from Peru. Within days, some 667 people were identified as known contacts of those infected and taken for treatment or into quarantine; 14,000 tests were conducted in the community, and vaccinations rolled out quickly for those who tested negative. The county's residents were not pleased, however. They were forced into a brief lockdown that interfered with the annual mango harvest, and the government paid little compensation. Some complained that the home quarantine permitted to returning Taiwanese citizens—as opposed to the mandatory hotel quarantine for foreign travelers—was to blame for the outbreak. "The CECC (Taiwan's central epidemic command) owes the people here a big apology," said the head of the local development association.[84]

Chen's next trip to Taiwan was on December 21, 2021. This time, Taiwan was facing the first outbreak of the Omicron variant, apparently brought back from southern Africa by a Taiwanese traveler.[85] This time the Chens were required to stay at a government-approved quarantine hotel in Kaohsiung in southern Taiwan, with the same daily texts and calls from government officials, and takeout food left outside the door. They paid for the hotel, but at a subsidized rate of about US$120 per night. If all had gone well, they would have been able to move from the hotel and do their final week of quarantine at home. But a passenger on their flight from Vancouver, Canada, by then reopened to US border crossers, had tested positive on arrival; the passengers in that section of the plane were forced to remain in the hotels for the full two weeks. Hotel quarantine was harder, Chen admits; for the first few days, their room had no view, but they were later moved to an upper floor. "I spent a lot of time right next to the window," he says. They were released after another negative PCR test. The following summer, 2022, he was again allowed to quarantine at home, and this time for just one week; antigen tests could now be substituted for the more reliable but slower PCR tests. And on his final pandemic visit, in December 2022, they were allowed to take public transport home—with masks on—and "self-manage" their care; they could travel outside their home as long as they carried a recent negative antigen test. But government officials still checked in daily to ensure they were following the protocols.[86]

Chen was lucky—as a citizen living abroad, he enjoyed the same rights as Taiwanese citizen residents. Taiwan did not block entry by foreigners throughout the pandemic the way countries like Japan, Vietnam, Australia, and New Zealand all did, with only narrow exceptions for essential travelers. But there was still significant discrimination based on citizenship. Lower-skilled migrant workers such as the many Filipina caretakers in the country, for example, were not given the option the Chens enjoyed of home quarantine or subsidized hotel quarantine. While migrant workers number nearly 700,000 in Taiwan, when returning from abroad they had to isolate in one of just 600 beds set up at a centralized quarantine facility.[87] Those requirements were eased later in the pandemic but were not fully lifted until March 2023 following protests by groups representing the migrant workers.[88] Foreign workers also faced large risks if they returned home; unlike high-skilled foreigners holding resident cards, migrant workers needed to seek permission to re-enter every time they left the country. If they were caught outside the country during periods of tighter border restrictions, they could not return. Indonesians, for example, who are the largest group of migrant workers in Taiwan, were barred from returning if they were out of the country from December 4, 2020, to November 11, 2021.[89]

Foreigners holding resident cards were generally able to leave and re-enter Taiwan for most of the pandemic. But there could be unpredictable obstacles that locked out those who had the misfortune of trying to enter Taiwan during periods where the restrictions were tighter. Those switching visa categories—from foreign student to a work permit, for example—are required to leave the country and re-enter. But if they were out of Taiwan when the government barred entry by foreigners, which happened repeatedly during the pandemic, they could end up stranded abroad. Wai Lok Tsing, a Hong Kong and New Zealand citizen who had done two internships in Taiwan, was offered a full-time job at a Taiwanese NGO in December 2020. She returned to Hong Kong to get her Covid-19 vaccine and to await approval of her new visa. But when it came through in May 2021, Taiwan was in its Delta-related lockdown, and she could not return.[90]

The periodic closures left many families separated. Yunus Aydin, a Turkish national, originally came to Taiwan to learn Mandarin, but stayed and graduated with an engineering degree. His high school sweetheart, a doctor, was able to find a postdoctoral research fellowship in Taiwan. He flew back to Turkey, and they were married in May 2021, just as the new restrictions hit. Aydin was forced to return to Taiwan on his own. In September 2021 the Taiwanese government eased the restrictions to permit spouses and children to return to Taiwan—but only the spouses and children of Taiwanese citizens.[91] Clément Potier, a French research engineer working for a Taipei electronics firm, was married in France, and returned to Taiwan in May 2021 hoping to bring his new wife with him. But she too was barred by the travel restrictions. "Five months after my arrival, I am considering returning to Europe," he wrote in a letter to the *Taipei Times*. "Not because of my job, not because of this beautiful island, but because some politicians decided that my wife cannot come because I am a foreigner. . . . This is clearly a bad message sent to all foreigners here: We do not count as much as others."

Japan, Australia, and New Zealand: A Borders-First Approach

Saanvi Naveen was just two and a half years old when her Australian parents took her to Bangalore, India, in November 2019 to meet her extended family. When the parents had to return home to Australia, the girl's grandparents begged them to leave her for a bit longer, promising to bring Saanvi back home in March 2020 using visas that allowed them to visit Australia. Their flight was scheduled for March 25; on March 20, the government of Australia closed the nation's borders. Sixteen months later, in July 2021, the girl was still stranded in Bangalore with her grandparents, unable to return home. "She is showing signs of depression that she can't communicate," her father Naveen Krishnamurthy told NPR. "Her growth is stunted." Naveen applied to the Australian government for special permission to allow the grandparents to bring his daughter home; it was denied. He and his wife sought permission to fly to India to bring her home; that too was denied. The only route offered by the government was that Saanvi could come home accompanied by another passenger—a stranger—who had permission to return to Australia. A Facebook group called Australians Stuck in India—with nearly 25,000 members—was helping to coordinate such trips. Some other parents of the roughly 400 Australian children stranded in India had tried to do that, but Krishnamurthy and his wife were too scared. "It's totally ridiculous to expect someone to accept this," he said. "She's not a parcel, she's a person."[92]

Such stories spilled out again and again over the months of the pandemic. More than any other country in the world, Australia—along with its island neighbor New Zealand—relied on closed borders as its primary tool of pandemic control. Japan did not impose the same restrictions on its own citizens but was all but closed to foreigners throughout the pandemic, separating many families including Japanese citizens with non-Japanese spouses and children. By many measures, those travel restrictions were a success. At times, the virus was almost entirely stamped out in these countries, allowing life to go on more or less as normal; New Zealand was Covid-free for extended periods in 2020 and 2021. When the pandemic hit, approximately 1 million Australians and a similar number of New Zealanders were living abroad; most did what their governments asked and stayed in place rather than rushing home, only to find later that they were barred from returning.[93] Experts at the University of Sydney, while praising the success of border closures as part of an initial containment strategy, found they "generated a multitude of adverse health, social and economic impacts."[94] Australia, by relying heavily on border and internal travel controls to prevent infections, was slow in vaccinating its population and tolerated enormous social and economic costs by "cutting Australian citizens off from our shores and preventing people from visiting relatives and friends overseas and taking advantage of international business opportunities."[95]

Even with late infection surges as restrictions were eased amid the spread of the Omicron variant, all three countries can rightly claim success in keeping down the number of deaths from Covid. But the social and human costs paid by those locked outside these countries—and their families within—were extraordinary.

Japan

Japan's early Covid experience mirrored that of South Korea—it suffered one of the largest early outbreaks, driven in part by incoming travelers from China. By mid-February 2020 it was reporting 750 positive cases.[96] But many of the known cases were aboard the *Diamond Princess*, the 3,700-person cruise ship that was being held in quarantine in Yokohama harbor. That suggested there was still time to contain the spread of the virus. And like South Korea, Japan was reluctant to shut its borders. "Introducing an entry ban has long been considered a prohibited strategy, out of concern that such a move could be considered discriminatory," said Yoshiyuki Sagara, a member of the Asia Pacific Initiative, a Japanese think tank that examined government countermeasures to the pandemic.[97] The government's initial actions included only modest travel restrictions, such as banning the arrival of foreign nationals who had recently visited China's Hubei or Zhejiang provinces, the two regions hardest hit by the initial outbreak. A broader travel ban on Chinese citizens—who made up about 30% of visitors to Japan—was initially rejected, in part because Prime Minister Shinzo Abe was preparing to host a state visit with Chinese leader Xi Jinping.[98] Over the course of March the government gradually extended travel restrictions, barring travelers from Italy and Iran and imposing quarantine requirements on arriving Europeans.

Then on April 3, 2020—much later than most countries in the region—Japan imposed one of the most rigid border lockdowns in the Asia-Pacific and kept it in place for much of the pandemic. Prime Minister Abe's measures barred all incoming flights from seventy-three countries; most controversially, it blocked return by Japanese foreign residents, including longtime residents without citizenship who were outside the country when the measures were imposed.[99] David Kvein, a twenty-nine-year-old graphic artist living in Tokyo on a valid working visa, was in Denmark making funeral arrangements for his father when the ban hit, stranding him in Copenhagen.[100] He would become one of hundreds of thousands of non-Japanese with valid residency permits or relatives in Japan who were trapped outside the country by the Covid restrictions; in October 2021 there were some 370,000 residents locked out of the country. Japan was the only member of the G7 leading economies that refused to permit the repatriation of permanent residents. "The government will continue to make decisions and implement necessary measures without hesitation, as our highest priority is to protect Japanese citizens' lives and health," said Abe.[101]

The measures were driven initially by concerns that the Covid testing capacity at Japan's airports and the ability to quarantine new arrivals would be overwhelmed if the number of incoming travelers was not sharply curtailed. "Quarantine measures would have gotten out of control if thousands of non-Japanese residents sought re-entry at once," Sagara said. "The testing capacity allowed for only several thousand tests per day at that time."[102] Japan never rolled out the sort of robust testing capacity that characterized the Korean and Taiwanese responses.[103] Unlike Korea, Taiwan, Vietnam, and Singapore, Japan had done little to bolster its pandemic preparedness in the wake of the SARS and MERS outbreaks, leaving it with few options other than border restrictions.[104] The government's response was to keep out not just foreign tourists, but also many longtime residents—including for a time the non-Japanese spouses and children of Japanese citizens.[105] Japan's border measures were the most overtly discriminatory of any country in the world. Australia barred not just foreigners but many of its own citizens from returning, and also locked its own citizens in to restrict demand for quarantine space by returning travelers. Japan imposed no such limits on its own citizens, who unlike Australians enjoy a clear constitutional right to enter Japan.[106] Despite the restrictions on foreign nationals, more than 500,000 Japanese citizens traveled abroad during 2021, with the government footing the bill for the fourteen days in government quarantine hotels on their return.[107]

Japan maintained its tight border restrictions throughout the pandemic, with some of the most rigid coming in late 2021 with the outbreak of the Omicron variant, even though Japan by then had some of the highest vaccination rates in the world.[108] Pablo Ortez, a thirty-three-year-old Argentinian, quit his job, sold his possessions, and was preparing to join his new wife in Japan in the fall of 2021 after the Japanese government finally eased restrictions on foreign spouses. But three days before he was set to board a flight for Tokyo, the government reimposed a complete travel ban. Vilhelm, a Lithuanian student, had been getting up at 4:30 A.M. for more than a year to continue her studies in international business at a university in Tokyo and was hoping to return when the new restrictions were imposed. "The most frustrating part is that I can see no end to this," she told *The Guardian*. "I've invested in studying in Japan and I feel like it is treating me very unfairly. I still love Japan, but sometimes I forget why."[109]

Japan's actions provoked intense controversy at home and abroad. Kochio Nakano, a political science professor at Sophia University in Tokyo, said in late 2021 that, while Japan was far from the only country in the world where the pandemic fanned xenophobic sentiments, "since last year, there has been an excessive, unscientific, and inhumane focus on 'offshore measures,' such as the entry ban, by the Japanese government."[110] The *East Asia Forum* wrote in a February 2022 editorial: "The core of the international condemnation of Japan's border policies is not its strictness, but the differential treatment of Japanese and non-Japanese nationals."[111] Harsher critics called it a "neo-sakoku" policy—a reference to Japan's strict isolation from the world from the seventeenth through the nineteenth centuries.[112] Aside from foreign residents and non-Japanese spouses and children, foreign students were the group most affected by the Covid restrictions. Japan had more than 300,000 foreign students studying in the country in 2019—double the number of a decade prior—making it one of the more popular international destinations for foreign students. By late 2021, more than 150,000 foreign students who were enrolled in Japanese universities were still locked outside the country.[113] A January 2022 letter to Japanese prime minister Fumio Kishida (Abe's successor), signed by more than 100 leading scholars and foreign experts on Japan, warned that the strict border closure for non-citizens "is harming Japan's national interests and international relationships." The authors argued that the prolonged closure "undercuts Japan's diplomatic objectives and status as an international leader."[114] Kishida's government responded, sort of—it agreed to admit eighty-seven students in February 2022.

Despite such criticisms, the border measures were extremely popular among Japanese citizens. A December 2021 poll by the Yomiuri newspaper found that nearly 90% of Japanese approved of the government's decision to reimpose a ban on entry of all foreign nationals when the Omicron strain broke out and led to a surge in Japanese cases.[115] Complaints at home focused largely on the exceptions granted by the government, such as the decision to allow foreign athletes to come for a spectator-less version of the Summer Olympics in 2021, which also occurred amid a rise in new cases.[116] Japan never did the sort of hard domestic lockdowns that were commonplace in many countries, with schools largely remaining open and businesses closing on a voluntary basis.[117] Even under an emergency declaration, the Japanese government believed it lacked the legal authority to impose the sorts of severe lockdowns, with financial or other penalties for violations, that other countries enacted.[118] Japan did not re-open fully to foreign travelers until October 2022 and did not lift all its border restrictions until May 2023.[119]

Australia

Australia adopted its closed border strategy almost by accident. For the first month of the pandemic, Australia, like many countries, used targeted border restrictions aimed at keeping out travelers from regions with severe outbreaks. It was not an especially early mover.[120] Foreign nationals traveling from China were barred on February 1 and returning citizens were required to self-isolate, the same day the United States imposed similar restrictions, and well after countries like Taiwan and Singapore had begun restricting arrivals from China.[121] Further travel bans against Iran, South Korea, and Italy came more than a month later. It wasn't until March 16 that the national government imposed broader measures against all incoming travelers, both citizens and non-citizens; arrivals would be required to self-isolate at home or in a hotel for fourteen days after landing in Australia, similar to measures being rolled out in Canada, Europe, and elsewhere. Australians were strongly encouraged not to travel abroad.[122] Then just four days later, on March 20, Australia closed its borders to all foreigners, permitting return only by citizens, permanent residents, and their families, with limited exceptions for flight crews.[123]

Two incidents launched Australia in a different direction from the rest of the world. First, on March 8 and again on March 19, some 2,700 passengers arriving in Sydney on the cruise ship *Ruby Princess* were permitted to return to their homes, despite significant evidence of flu-like infections on both cruises. Many took public transit or even boarded airplanes to get to their destinations (on its sister ship, the *Diamond Princess*, passengers and crew in February had been held in quarantine for up to a month in Japan's Yokohama Harbor before the passengers could disembark).[124] Some 900 of the *Ruby Princess* passengers would test positive for Covid-19, and 28 would later die.[125] Within days, many of Australia's states closed their own borders, with the Northern Territory, South Australia, Western Australia, and Queensland invoking their own public health emergency powers in an effort to keep the infections confined to New South Wales and Victoria, where the largest cities of Sydney and Melbourne are located.[126] Throughout the pandemic, Australia's states maintained the most rigid internal travel restrictions of any country, making it almost as hard to cross state borders as it was to cross the national border—separating many Australians from family, doctors, work, and schooling.[127] As case numbers in Australia soared following the *Ruby Princess* incident, the Australian Health Protection Principal Committee—which included the top national and state-level medical and public health officials—recommended enforced quarantine for "high-risk" cases. But the government of Prime Minister Scott Morrison and the state government in Victoria went further, deciding that all returning citizens would be required to quarantine for fourteen days at government-approved hotel facilities rather than returning home.[128] At the same time, Melbourne and several other cities went into lockdowns, closing businesses and schools and asking residents to stay at home. The measures, which lasted forty-one days, cost the economy billions of dollars but succeeded in bringing the first wave of infections under control.

The mismanagement of the quarantine regime was the second failure that impelled Australia into its hermit-like isolation during the pandemic. In late May and early June 2020, security guards and other workers at two Melbourne hotels—the Rydges and the Stamford—contracted Covid from returning travelers quarantined at the hotels and began spreading it to the city. The breach led to Australia's largest single outbreak early in the pandemic, with more than 90% of the cases traced directly to the Rydges, and the rest to the Stamford.[129] The outbreak led to a spike in Melbourne, with more than 700 new cases and 25 deaths per day occurring by August 2020.[130] Genetic tracing found that a single case of Covid-19 originating in the Stamford Hotel had sparked more than 19,000 cases in total, with widespread community transmission.[131] The outbreak led the state government to impose "Stage 4" restrictions in Melbourne—a hard lockdown that lasted for 111 days in which residents faced curfew restrictions from 8 P.M. to 5 A.M. Outside of curfew hours, residents could only leave home for necessary shopping (within 5 km, and only one resident per household), a single hour of exercise, or medical appointments.[132] In nine public housing complexes in Melbourne where cases were spreading rapidly, some 3,000 residents—many of them recently arrived refugees—were blocked by police from leaving their units for five days for any reason, an action the state's ombudsman later said was a violation of Australian human rights laws.[133]

Unlike South Korea and Taiwan, Australia's system for testing and tracing could not contain a large-scale outbreak. In contrast to South Korea, Vietnam, Singapore, and other countries in the region that were hit hard by SARS and/ or MERS, Australia had not developed a sophisticated capacity for contact tracing. Indeed, the Commonwealth Pandemic Plan in place before Covid had recommended against quarantining contacts in an outbreak of pandemic influenza. Such measures, the plan said, would be "highly complex to arrange," would pose onerous burdens on travelers, and were likely to be ineffective.[134] State governments had the responsibility for testing and contact tracing but lacked the capacity.[135] When Covid began spreading, cases were often reported to state governments by fax; in Victoria, it could take as long as two weeks for those who had been in contact with an infected individual to be notified of their exposure.[136] "Contact tracing is a difficult, laborious and really challenging task no matter how many close contacts you have, even a small number," said Daniel Andrews, Victoria's premier.[137] The state would not fully replace fax notification with electronic notification until the end of August 2020. The national government rolled out a Covid-tracing smartphone app in April 2020, but later studies found it to be almost wholly ineffective, identifying only 15% of close contacts.[138] All of this left Australia highly vulnerable to rapidly spreading outbreaks if new cases escaped the border and quarantine restrictions. A new outbreak in June 2021—this time of the more deadly Delta virus—occurred when a taxi driver was infected by an arriving FedEx airport crew he was transporting to quarantine, evidence of the risks posed from remaining fully open to international trade. The resulting lockdown would largely shutter the largest cities of Sydney and Melbourne for another three months, though the restrictions were eased slightly by mid-October.

As public agitation over the lockdowns grew, in July 2020 the Morrison government responded by imposing a weekly cap of just 4,000 citizen and resident returnees from overseas, about half the number that had been arriving previously. State governments, led by the largest, New South Wales, said that new arrivals would now pay out of pocket for the two-week cost of mandatory hotel quarantine.[139] The caps on returning Australians remained in place for the next eighteen months, though the weekly numbers would gradually be increased. The government cited limited space in quarantine facilities as the main obstacle to increased repatriation.[140] And the actual spots available were far fewer than the headline numbers. "Essential" travelers of various sorts, from business officials to oil and gas workers, were counted in the weekly cap;

so were returning Australians who had compelling reasons to travel abroad. And the government cleared space for athletes and other celebrities, though some were able to use their wealth to arrange special private quarantines outside the government system.[141] The Australian Open tennis tournament was held in February 2021 under what the state government of Victoria, where Melbourne is located, called "the strictest rules for tennis" in the world. Players were required to test negative for Covid before flying to Australia, and then faced fourteen days of mandatory hotel quarantine in which they could leave their hotel rooms only for training at a quarantined tennis facility. The tournament returned in 2022, though the previous year's champion Novak Djokovic was forced out of the country after a legal battle when it became public that he was not vaccinated against Covid and had received a special exemption from the government.[142]

Australians are some of the world's great travelers, with young Australians working in ski and hotel resorts around the world and many others living and working across the globe. With the new restrictions in place, thousands of Australians who wanted to return home suddenly found themselves unable to do so. James Turbitt was able to fly home from Belgium in June 2021 with the hope of seeing his sick mother before she died. He could not get a direct flight to Perth, where she lived, and flew instead to Melbourne, but he could not secure government permission to leave quarantine to go on to Perth. His mother died while he was confined to a hotel room at the Stamford. "I really deserved to be there when she passed," he said. "She was the most beautiful, caring woman. . . . I get that they're trying to keep COVID out, but they've completely lost their way."[143] While precise numbers are hard to come by, there were likely hundreds of thousands of Australians separated from family by the border closures. Half of Australians were born overseas or have at least one parent born abroad. In a survey of nearly 4,000 Australians affected by the travel restrictions, two-thirds in Australia and the rest overseas, more than 80% reported high or very high levels of psychological distress; separated couples and partners experienced the highest levels of distress.[144]

The wait for a spot in the queue to return stretched out for months. For those with the means, the few airlines still flying to Australia sold mostly business class tickets to recoup the costs with so few passengers; some passengers paid as much as US$16,000 for a one-way ticket from Europe. And the cost of the mandatory hotel quarantine added another AUS$3,000, about US$2,000, with an extra AUS$1,000 per person. Amelia Seeto spent AUS$28,500 bringing back her family of four from the UK; she and her husband and two toddlers were forced to share a small room with no opening windows or balcony in Sydney's Mantra Hotel.[145] As late as March 2021, Australia's Department of Foreign Affairs and Trade reported that some 40,000 Australian citizens were still stranded abroad trying to return home.[146] The government also banned its own citizens from leaving Australia for eighteen months during the pandemic, regardless of family emergencies or other urgent concerns, without explicit prior approval from the government. Senate committee investigators charged that "the government's efforts to support Australians overseas during COVID-19 have been woefully inadequate."[147] Olivera Simic, who fled Bosnia as a refugee during the Balkan Wars and finally settled in Australia, wrote that Australia's restrictions that barred her from leaving the country for more than two years to visit her parents brought back all the trauma of the war. "I would never have expected that Australia could become a country that would not allow me to cross its borders and reunite with my family for an indefinite time. If I had known, I would never have built my life here."[148]

During the outbreak of the virulent Delta variant in India in May 2021, as discussed in Chapter 3, the Australian government went still further by closing the country's borders entirely to anyone who had spent time in India, including Australian citizens and foreign residents; some 9,000 Australians—including young Sanvi Naveen—were forced to remain in India even as cases in that country were skyrocketing and hospitals were overwhelmed and facing shortages of oxygen and intensive care beds. The ban was accompanied with threats of up to five years in jail and fines up to AUS$60,000, making it a criminal act for Australians to attempt to re-enter their own country.[149] It was the first time in its history that Australia had legally barred its own citizens from the country. The Senate report concluded: "Legalities aside, that the government reached a point where it refused citizens entry to Australia is an extraordinary breach of its responsibility and deeply inconsistent with community expectations."[150]

The border closure was highly effective at keeping out those targeted by the government. In February 2020, just under 1 million non-Australians had arrived in the country as tourists, workers, or students; a year later, in February 2021, just 14,000 were permitted, almost all essential workers.[151] The government was not wholly indifferent to the plight of its own citizens trapped abroad; some 430,000 Australians were repatriated during 2020 (a count that includes those leaving the country and returning), and the government subsidized a limited number of lower-cost flights from the UK, India, and South Africa by the national airline, Qantas.[152]

Australia had more reasons than most nations to ignore the World Health Organization's arguments against travel bans during pandemics. During the Spanish Flu, Australia had implemented a strict maritime quarantine before the deadly second wave had hit much of the world. Australia weathered that pandemic with one of the world's lowest death rates, losing 15,000 people, or 2.7 per thousand in the population (the nearby island of Tasmania, which had isolated itself from Australia as well, had the world's lowest death rate, just 0.8 per thousand). In contrast, New Zealand, which did not implement similar border controls, had an overall death rate of 7.1 per thousand during the Spanish Flu; the island's indigenous Maori population suffered catastrophic losses, with 2,500 of the nation's 51,000 Maori perishing from the disease.[153] From New Zealand, the pandemic migrated to other Pacific islands, including Western Samoa, where one fifth of the population would die.[154] Public health research prior to Covid had suggested that island nations like Australia and New Zealand, if they were able to act quickly and thoroughly enough, might spare themselves from the worst of a novel pandemic and suffer less economic damage than more open nations. The border closure option was specifically included in New Zealand's pandemic plan, and in those of smaller island nations like the Cook Islands and Samoa. New Zealand's plan suggested that "such an intervention may be feasible because of New Zealand's geographical isolation, its limited number of entry points and its well-coordinated border management systems."[155]

That does not mean that the border closure decisions were easy, especially given Australia's economic dependence on China and the WHO's advice against travel restrictions. Prime Minister Morrison later said the cabinet debate over the initial border closure ran for three days. "When you have to shut your border to China, you realize you are in for quite a time economically." And China immediately blasted Australia for "overreaction."[156] But the border closure was popular. In an Ipsos poll in December 2020, nearly a year into the Covid shutdowns, 83% of Australians favored keeping the country's borders closed, "not letting anyone in or out."[157] Australia has a long history of using border restrictions to respond to perceived external threats, from diseases to asylum seekers. Elizabeth Hicks has argued that the Australian constitution explicitly rejects minority rights—the dominant view was that minorities "must trust to the sense of justice of the majority." A crisis like Covid further "re-orient[s] decision-making toward utilitarianism and the collective—majorities—toward which Australia's system is already tilted. They create an atmosphere of urgency and fear that deflects concern away from . . . minorities 'caught under the wheels' of measures benefiting the majority."[158]

Debates over the effectiveness of Australia's border measures will continue for many years. There were calls, not heeded, for a royal commission investigation of the sort that New Zealand decided to conduct.[159] Some argued that Australia had little choice but to resort to such draconian measures. The premier of the state of Victoria, Daniel Andrews, said "it is better to lock some people out than to lock everyone down." He added: "If you compare their discomfort, and the impact on them as a relatively small number of people with the damage and the pain of locking a whole city or a whole state down, there is no comparison."[160] In terms of deaths, Australia weathered the pandemic far better than the United States or Europe, though there was a sharp spike in both cases and deaths in early 2022 following the lifting of most travel restrictions. Others have argued that the border closures and hard lockdowns were a massive overreaction to a relatively mild health threat, and the measures were far more costly in both public health and economic costs than the putative benefits.[161] Australia's human rights commissioner Lorraine Finlay said: "While border closures have played an essential role in keeping Australians safe, there is also no doubt they have caused immeasurable harm to many people."[162]

The experience of Taiwan and South Korea and some other Asian countries suggest that similar results could have been achieved at much lower human and economic cost. But it required a strong and coordinated public health infrastructure that Australia largely lacked. As Chodor and Hameiri argue, the lack of prior investment in public health infrastructure and the divisions of federalism left Australia with little capacity to implement effective quarantine measures, set up complex testing and tracing, or roll out vaccines efficiently. Instead, they argue, federal and state leaders "turned to ad hoc measures that were simple to implement—international and internal border closures and lockdowns—to protect a health system unprepared for even a mild outbreak following decades of austerity."[163]

New Zealand

A New Zealand permanent resident, a mother of two teenage daughters identified only as "HW" in the court filing, flew to the UK in October 2020 to support her younger brother following the recent death of their father, leaving her children in the care of their grandmother.[164] She intended to return home to her daughters in about three months' time and immediately began seeking a slot in New Zealand's Managed Isolation and Quarantine (MIQ) system, required of all returning travelers (Figure 6.3). She checked the required sign-up website many times each day without success; in February 2021 she began setting an alarm in the middle of the night, thinking the time difference might be preventing her from securing a spot. Her mother and daughters were also checking regularly, still without success. "My mental health started deteriorating quite badly, I started having panic attacks and severe anxiety," she said. "For the first time in my life, I had become depressed." She was still trying to secure a spot two months later in April 2021, when New Zealand and Australia launched a "travel bubble," permitting quarantine-free travel (QFT) between the two countries. So, she booked a flight to Sydney, planning

Figure 6.3 Managed Isolation and Quarantine facility in Christchurch, NZ, March 2022. Lakeview Images/Shutterstock.

to quarantine there before returning home, but the soonest she could get a seat was November 2021. Then New Zealand suspended the arrangement just three months later amid the Delta outbreak in Australia.[165] HW wrote to Prime Minister Jacinda Ardern and received a reply from the office of Chris Hipkins, the minister for Covid-19 response, telling her only to keep checking the allocations page. In December 2021—when the vaccination rate in New Zealand had hit 90%, among the highest in the world—she was still trapped in the UK, living with her uncle. Her daughters had been left without their mother for more than fifteen months until New Zealand finally lifted its remaining quarantine restrictions in February 2022, and she was able to return home.

Throughout the pandemic, New Zealand maintained what could be called—North Korea excepted—the most severe border restrictions in the world, even more rigid than those in neighboring Australia. The measures helped keep Covid infections and deaths in New Zealand among the lowest in the world—for more than 100 days in 2020, there were no cases of community transmission at all. Prime Minister Ardern became "a global liberal icon" for doing what liberals had long denounced when the same measures were used by conservative governments—closing borders to keep out an external threat.[166] By the end of her tenure Ardern was facing growing protests over lockdowns and vaccine mandates, contributing to her January 2023 decision not to seek re-election. But New Zealand's success at containing Covid is still likely to be seen as a model in future pandemics.

Like neighboring Australia, New Zealand slow-walked into its near total shutdown. It had closed its borders first to travelers from China in early February 2020, following the lead of the United States and Australia; those measures barred Chinese citizens working or studying in New Zealand from returning if they had been in China, as many had been for the Chinese New Year.[167] The border restrictions were expanded to the rest of the world in mid-March 2020, exempting only New Zealand citizens, permanent residents, and some "essential workers."[168] The government also instituted a "Level 4" lockdown domestically—the highest level—which required New Zealanders to remain home for a month and leave only for buying groceries, seeking healthcare services, or brief outdoor exercise. All "non-essential" businesses and services, including schools, were closed.[169] The lockdown would succeed—over the next two months there were only 1,500 cases and twenty deaths, and by early May the country was reporting no further Covid cases at all.[170] For most of 2020, while the rest of the world was struggling through lockdowns, life was largely normal in New Zealand, with no restrictions on sporting events, concerts, and large parties.

The price for those outside the country, however, was steep—as political journalist Henry Cooke put it, elimination "relied on us essentially telling everyone outside the country to get lost."[171] Many with strong ties to New Zealand were barred from returning even by the first wave of border restrictions. Jeus Joquin worked as an emergency room nurse on New Zealand's North Island, battling the early outbreak of Covid cases. But his wife and two toddler children were stranded back in their home country, the Philippines; they had valid visas to return, but the government refused to grant them travel exemptions.[172] Wendy Harnett's Japanese husband was similarly barred from returning.[173] "I feel like New Zealand now has an iron curtain," Harnett told the *Washington Post*.

The government initially insisted that its own citizens would remain free to return. In March 2020 the health ministry had recommended closing the borders even to New Zealand citizens living overseas, but that suggestion was rejected by Prime Minister Ardern and her cabinet. "It would have been extraordinary for the government to make a decision to strand New Zealanders overseas," she said in April 2020 when the news emerged. "We couldn't entertain that. It is an extraordinary thing to deem someone stateless, we have international obligations to consider." Foreign Minister Winston Peters added that "it was and is inconceivable that we will ever turn our backs on our own."[174] But even as it was publicly denouncing the idea of barring its own citizens, the government began implementing measures that effectively did exactly that. On April 9, after the first lockdown, Prime Minister Ardern announced that all returning citizens and residents would be required to isolate at hotel facilities approved by the government, the so-called MIQ system. "Our borders are our biggest risk," she said, in announcing the new measures.[175] The government further tightened the system in June, putting the military in charge of the MIQ facilities after two visitors from the UK were released into the country before the end of the full fourteen days in order to see a dying relative, and later tested positive for Covid.[176] Then in August the government set up an online booking system for the MIQ, refusing to permit New Zealanders to book flights home unless they had successfully secured a hotel quarantine spot. Demand vastly exceeded the supply of quarantine spaces, and the system immediately backlogged and occasionally crashed.[177]

Petitions for emergency exemptions for those with an urgent need to return—including pregnant women like the journalist Charlotte Bellis who was stranded in Afghanistan pleading to come home—were often rejected or would languish for weeks without a response. One woman told the *New Zealand Herald* that she had applied to the MIQ lottery ten times unsuccessfully and had two emergency petitions rejected. She gave birth alone in Australia in December 2021 and told the newspaper the experience was "awful and traumatizing."[178] New Zealand barrister Tudor Clee represented thirty-five pregnant citizens who had to petition the nation's high court for permission to return. He said that of roughly 250 pregnant women who had applied for exemptions, only 10% had been accepted by the government. The decisions had effects beyond the physical and mental health of the expectant mothers—under New Zealand citizenship law, children born overseas cannot automatically transfer their citizenship to their own future children.[179] The officials running the MIQ system "seem to be absolutely steadfast that they will not recognize women's health as a priority," Clee said.[180] Despite such rigid restrictions, New Zealand—like Australia—frequently made exceptions for celebrity travelers; the Wiggles, a popular children's band, were granted a special exemption after promoters sold 40,000 tickets even though the group had not secured a space in the MIQ system.[181]

The public messaging was not subtle about the government's priorities—Prime Minister Ardern frequently referred to the country as "a team of 5 million," excluding the nearly 1 million citizens who were living abroad when Covid hit. "My passport clearly states my right to return home at any time, yet this right has been blocked by the MIQ system," said Antony Paine, who was teaching in the United Arab Emirates and as late as December 2021 had still been unable to return home to see family. He had applied three times under the system but had not been selected. "I simply can't come home because there is no room for me in MIQ, despite my vaccinated status."[182]

The success of the border measures and the initial lockdown in reducing Covid cases gave New Zealanders living on the island strong reasons to favor the toughest possible border controls. By early June 2020, New Zealand was reporting no new cases of the virus, and domestic restrictions eased all the way to Level 1, which permitted something close to a return to normal life. Even with the tough MIQ restrictions, returning citizens were therefore a threat to the island's blissful isolation, and social media highlighted the growing divide. Another pregnant New Zealander, identified only as "Kate," posted on

Facebook about her desperate need to return home and her inability to secure a place in the lottery. Quickly her feed filled with angry responses. "No
one wants your Covid bitch, you chose to leave and if your baby dies it's your
fault," one wrote. As the New Zealand news site *Stuff* put it: "From its concep-
tion the [MIQ] scheme has pitched would-be returnees against each other and
spawned a them-and-us mentality dividing those trapped outside Aotearoa,
and those safely ensconced within."[183]

The most puzzling and troubling aspect of New Zealand's severe border
restrictions was how long they remained in place. In August 2021, the
country entered another lockdown—with schools, restaurants, and businesses
shuttered—after an outbreak of the more contagious Delta virus. The government began pivoting away from its "elimination" strategy and pushing as
rapidly as possible to get the population vaccinated. In part because of the success in containment, New Zealand at the time had the lowest vaccination rates
of any developed country. Fewer than 25% of citizens were fully vaccinated by
August.[184] Even while pivoting away from elimination, the border restrictions
were further tightened. The government instituted a "virtual lobby" system—
a first-come, first-served online sign-up—that left many citizens, even those
who had been fully vaccinated, with no way to return home. When the virtual lobby was launched September 1, 2021, there were 30,000 people in the
queue vying for 3,000 spaces.[185] Many of the most wrenching stories are from
that period late in 2021, when most of the world was reopening to travel as
vaccinations were rolled out.

Since the waning of the pandemic, New Zealand has faced a partial reck-
oning over the severity of its measures. The nation's high court, in a case
brought by the advocacy group Grounded Kiwis, found that the restrictions
violated the explicit constitutional right of New Zealand citizens to enter
their own country in a way that could not properly be justified by the health
emergency.[186] The country's chief ombudsman, responding to hundreds of
complaints, found in a December 2022 report that, while the government
faced substantial challenges in managing "a novel and complex policy context,"
the quarantine system nonetheless "caused immense stress and frustration for
tens of thousands of people seeking to enter New Zealand."[187] In December
2022, the government agreed to launch a Royal Commission that will likely
be the most detailed investigation of any country on what worked and what
didn't in battling Covid-19.

But the government still remained unrepentant about the border restrictions. Troy Moon, a New Zealander working in Egypt, had booked flights to return to Auckland to visit his parents in February 2022. But despite repeated efforts, he could not get an MIQ voucher. Frustrated, he booked another leg on to Los Angeles to take a holiday instead. The United States had by then lifted all its restrictions on "non-essential" travel, and New Zealand was permitting some travelers to transit through the country. But he landed in Auckland to an urgent message from his mother that his father was sick, so he quickly told officials at the airport that he needed to stay in the country. They angrily accused him of "queue-jumping," but with no legal way to deport a New Zealand citizen, found a quarantine spot for him (the duration had by then been reduced to seven days).

Six months later, back working in Egypt, he received a letter from the New Zealand police, fining him $1,000 for breaching the voucher system. If he chose to fight the fine, he was warned, it would be increased to $4,000. Moon chose to fight, along with several others who had been fined; the New Zealand courts backed them, finding "a total absence of fault." Chris Knuth, a corporate executive who made a more deliberate decision to exploit the loophole to return home, was similarly unapologetic. "I was called selfish. But if it's selfish to want to go and see my mum and my daughters and my grandkids then fine, that means I'm selfish."[188]

7

China's Anti-Covid Great Wall

In late 2020, newspapers began reporting that China was quietly building a wall along its southern border with Laos, Myanmar, and Vietnam, a frontier that stretches for more than 3,000 miles. The first reports, from Radio Free Asia, showed images of new six-to-nine-foot-high barbed wire fences outside the city of Ruili (pronounced "Ray-lee") in the far southwest corner of China's Yunnan province (Figure 7.1).[1] The *Irrawaddy*, a Burmese publication, said that Chinese workers had started erecting the first sections in October in populous areas along the border of Myanmar's Kachin and Shan states, the two large districts bordering China.[2] The country's Ministry of Foreign Affairs had registered complaints with Beijing, arguing that some of the new fencing violated a 1960 agreement that barred either government from building permanent structures within ten meters of the border.[3] Since China began opening up commerce with the rest of the world in the early 1980s, the region's porous borders had become a conduit for illicit trade and undocumented crossings. Contraband goods included jade, luxury hardwoods, stolen cars, and chemical precursors for the methamphetamines being produced in labs in Shan. Human traffic included migrant workers, mostly Burmese working in China, and brides being smuggled in for Chinese husbands.[4] The many unpatrolled border crossings were sometimes used by critics of the regime of Chinese president Xi Jinping to escape the country.[5] Beijing could certainly have justified the new barriers in the way countries from the United States to Spain to Hungary have done over the past decade—as a tool for controlling the flow of irregular migrants, security threats, and contraband.

But Chinese officials did not cite any of those reasons when stories of the new wall began to spread. Burmese ministry officials were told instead that the fence was intended to keep out Covid-19. Some Chinese commentators dubbed it the "Southern Great Wall," but state media referred to it as the

Figure 7.1 Southern China border region. Courtesy Skylar Magee, Border Policy Research Institute.

"Anti-Covid Great Wall," a key fortification in China's unrivaled effort to keep the virus outside its borders.[6] Chinese leader Xi wrote an open letter to villagers along the border urging them to "safeguard the sacred land" by building an unbreachable barrier. Yunnan province raised some $500 million for fence construction, and assigned 100,000 soldiers, police, and civilians to patrol for illegal crossings.[7]

After containing the initial outbreak through sweeping lockdowns in Wuhan and neighboring cities, the Chinese government had adopted a "zero-Covid" strategy of stamping out the virus wherever it appeared in the country. That required not just a willingness to impose the world's most stringent domestic lockdowns when cases arose, but also tight control over national borders to prevent the introduction of new cases. The crossing between Ruili and the Myanmar town of Muse is a major node along China's southern border, and controlling cross-border movement was key to keeping out the virus. Local governments were under enormous pressure from Beijing to eliminate infections. Ruili faced four severe lockdowns from September 2020 to November 2021, with most of the new infections coming from Myanmar; the economy slumped by 8.4% in the first nine months of 2021.[8] Unofficial estimates suggest that more than half of the city's population of 500,000 fled to avoid the lockdowns and control measures, despite being required to quarantine at their own expense before leaving.[9] Ruili's Communist Party chief was fired for "severe negligence" in failing to control Covid outbreaks.[10]

By health metrics, China's border restrictions worked remarkably well. China's determination to contain infections for most of three years put its performance at least on par with the more successful Asian nations. China's official death count of just over 83,000 was on a per capita basis far below even countries like South Korea, Japan, and New Zealand; more realistic estimates, adjusting for the lack of transparency in the government's reporting, would still put Chinese deaths near the levels in Taiwan and Australia.[11] This comparative success gave Beijing a huge propaganda victory over the United States and Europe, which struggled with far higher rates of infections and deaths.

But the pursuit of zero-Covid also led the Chinese government to unprecedented extremes in border control. The Chinese southern border project was the first time since 1721 that a government had built a wall to control a pandemic. Then, officials in the French city of Avignon ordered construction of a twenty-two-mile stone barrier—remnants of which are still visible today—to keep out the infected during the last outbreak of the black plague. Some 500 men worked for five months to build the six-foot-high, 18-inch thick wall to keep the sick contained in Provence to the south. Travelers wishing to cross had to present soldiers patrolling the wall with a clean "health bill" demonstrating they were not carriers of the plague. The epidemic of course found its way to

Avignon anyway.[12] The outbreak would kill 100,000 people in the region over two years.[13]

The frontier between China and Myanmar, however, is a less likely place for such a barrier than the French countryside. Most of the 1,300 miles of the border is obscured by dense forest cover across hilly or even mountainous terrain. Scholar Alessandro Rippa, who visited the region in 2015, reported that the actual border between the two countries was almost impossible to identify, with hundreds of dirt roads crossing an indeterminate dividing line.[14] The line was first imagined in the late nineteenth century following the British invasion of Burma. Negotiations between the British and China's Qing dynasty recognized a rough location for the boundary, but it was not finalized until the 1960 agreement between Burmese prime minister U Nu and Chinese premier Zhou Enlai. Despite the formal demarcation, there was little to keep residents of the region from moving back and forth freely. By the end of the 1990s, China had begun to exercise greater control, requiring border crossing passes and at times cracking down on smuggling. But many families continued to live lives that straddled the border, with children from Myanmar permitted to attend Chinese schools, workers crossing daily to fill jobs in China, and trade—much of it unregulated—flowing in both directions.[15]

The pandemic brought an end to such freedoms. Those who stayed behind in Ruili as the wall was built were asked to man remote border stations and keep tabs on border crossers, with cash rewards for catching violators. The new barriers brought greater control—while much is just simple fencing, heavily trafficked areas include cameras and motion sensors that quickly alert nearby border guards to any breaches. In some cases, the barriers cut right through the middle of towns that span the border. Ruili was not the only place to see new barriers. A twelve-foot fence went up along sections of China's border with Vietnam, blocking Vietnamese villagers from selling their produce in China. In Guangxi, along the Vietnam border, party officials called for citizens to "race against time, go all out, resolutely win the battle against the pandemic, and defend the 'south gate" of China."[16] Some Vietnamese in the region responded by cutting portions of the fence, which were electrified with charges that could be lethal to both animals and human beings. The new fencing had separated families living on opposite sides of the border. "This has caused a lot of dissatisfaction in Vietnam, which is why they are demolishing it," a local businessman told Radio Free Asia.[17]

Gabriel Crossley of *The Economist*, who visited Ruili in early 2023, wrote that "what was once China's leakiest border has become one of its tightest." The lives of the people there have been made much harder, he reported; a Chinese watermelon farmer who once made a simple river crossing to manage his land in Myanmar now has to travel nearly 20 miles east to an official border crossing and the same distance back to his land. The jade trade was severely curtailed, with goods now having to go through official crossings and pay import duties. But many Chinese in the region saw the new barrier as a source of national pride. Some took to mocking US president Donald Trump online for his failure to complete his promised wall along the US border with Mexico. If Mr. Trump had outsourced construction to China, one wrote, the wall "would have been completed a long time ago."[18] For the government, controlling the remote border had long been a goal, Crossley says, but it took Covid to make it a top priority and free up the needed resources. "This was a golden opportunity to fix a problem that had been there for decades." But for the people who once crossed the region's borders freely, the price has been very high. "People talked with a certain amount of nostalgia about what Ruili used to be like," says Crossley. "You could cross the river to have a beer with a friend, move from one side to the other, sell your goods, meet some friends, meet some family, and not really feel like the national border impacted your life. . . . Covid really brought an end to that, and it's generally a less lively, sadder place to live."

The Mother of All Border Closures

China was the first country where Covid emerged, and the last to fully reopen its borders to foreign travelers as the threat from the virus waned. In pursuit of "zero-Covid," China maintained the world's most restrictive border regime for nearly three years—building walls, cutting most international flights, carefully controlling ports and imports of goods, and imposing the longest quarantine requirements of any country for the few who could get permission to enter (Figure 7.2). Other nations that were able to use border restrictions effectively to control the pandemic had the advantage of isolation—they were island nations or near islands that exercised something close to total control over who was permitted to enter the country. China stands alone as a nation with long land borders—indeed, the world's longest at nearly 14,000 miles in total—that

Figure 7.2 A section of China's "Anti-Covid Great Wall" along its southern border with Vietnam. Courtesy of Lam Le.

nonetheless managed until late in the pandemic to secure its frontier effectively against those infected with the virus. In doing so, Chinese authorities often went far beyond the science—requiring travelers to quarantine long after the incubation period had passed, and "disinfecting" incoming shipments of food and other goods that carried no risk of importing the disease. The border controls were mirrored by domestic controls that had no equivalent anywhere in the world. Small outbreaks of the virus triggered savage lockdowns in which millions of people were confined to their apartments, tested daily, and hauled away to government quarantine facilities in the event of a positive test.

Yet while China's border restrictions inflicted enormous human costs, they must be acknowledged as a triumph of border control. Securing borders on such a scale had never been attempted before—the closed borders of the Cold War era fenced in countries that interacted little with the rest of the world. The China of 2019 was the world's largest trading nation, the largest source of outbound tourists and one of largest recipients of foreign visitors. No country with such extensive borders and close economic ties to its neighbors, as well as enormous trade with the rest of the world, had ever before attempted to shut its borders in such a comprehensive way. Whatever the assessment of its effectiveness, and the dire consequences for millions of people locked out of the country or forced to endure the onerous entry requirements, China's Covid border controls were a historic accomplishment.

China showed that if a nation has both the capacity and will to deploy sufficiently rigorous measures—and faces no significant domestic dissent—it is possible even in a highly globalized world to all but shut down borders to the movement of people while maintaining robust trade. China's exports to the world actually grew by nearly 4% during 2020, the worst year of the pandemic, and then soared by more than 30% to near-record levels in 2021. China's ability to control human movement without doing significant short-term harm to the economy gave officials a free hand to keep borders closed. The most invasive and overreaching control measures occurred in 2022, when the rest of the world was opening up and China had vaccinated a large percentage of its population, though the effectiveness of Chinese-made vaccines was somewhat less than that of their Western counterparts. Success at controlling borders against the virus became, for the Chinese government, an end in itself, an argument for the superiority of its authoritarian system of governance. As Richard McGregor, an expert on China's Communist Party, has put it: "The battle over coronavirus in China was never just about public health. For the CCP like everything else, it was and remains primarily a contest of politics, in which the party-state benchmarks itself against other governing systems, especially the world's most powerful democracy, and its superpower rival, the US." China would not lift its restrictions until January 2023, when the more contagious Omicron variant finally overwhelmed its border defenses and public discontent was growing.

It is hard to imagine any other country with such vast land and sea borders, and such deep connections to the global economy, shutting its borders as China did. "Outside of military conflict, no country of any size or weight on the world stage has the ability to marshal resources like China, nor enforce a crackdown of a similar severity and dimension," says McGregor. "The mobilization of the state, businesses, and the people at such short notice was a potent reminder that the CCP has virtual war powers at its fingertips in any declared emergency, even in the absence of conflict with a foreign power." But even if the rest of the world is unlikely to emulate China in a future pandemic or other emergency, the experience will certainly be studied carefully. While few governments have the ability to run roughshod over civil liberties like

China's CCP, every country that closed its borders during Covid was testing the extremes of emergency powers, seeing how far it could stretch its authority to shut down the movement of people in the name of a greater public good. No country went as far or for as long as China in closing borders. But China showed the world the scale of control that is possible if a country is willing to force its own citizens, and many others, to pay a steep enough price.

China and the Failure of International Health Cooperation

As Covid-19 was spreading out from Wuhan as early as December 2019, few would have predicted that China would end up being the last country to reopen its borders to foreign travelers. China was the first target of travel controls by other nations, and Beijing objected vociferously, arguing that such measures violated broadly accepted norms in both the World Health Organization and the International Civil Aviation Organization (ICAO). At home, China was the first country to launch massive internal lockdowns that all but halted the movement of citizens in an effort to prevent the spread of the virus—lockdowns that became a model for much of the world. With the Chinese New Year approaching at the end of January 2020—an annual ritual in which hundreds of millions of Chinese go home to their families, the largest movement of people in the world—authorities took the drastic step of enforcing at-home isolation for some 50 million people across Hubei province and halted flights from Hubei to the rest of the country.[19]

But as other countries began to block flights leaving China, Chinese officials denounced the restrictions. Italy's ambassador to China was summoned following that country's January 31 ban on incoming flights from China. "Italy's decision to stop flights without contacting China in advance caused great inconvenience to citizens of both countries. Many Chinese are still stranded in Italy," said China's vice-minister of foreign affairs Qin Gang.[20] The US ban on travelers from China, imposed at the same time, was "neither based on facts nor helpful at this particular time," said the Foreign Ministry spokesperson.[21] "We deplore and oppose those countries who went against WHO's professional recommendations and ICAO's bulletins," said the spokesperson, Hua Chunying. "Their actions, which sowed panic among the public, will not help prevent and control the epidemic. They have gravely disrupted normal personnel exchanges, international cooperation, and order of the international market for air transportation."[22] Hua also accused the Trump administration of "overreacting," and praised Canada among other countries for not following the US lead. "Canada believes the ban of entry has no basis, which is a sharp contrast [to] the US behaviors," she said. Canada—which has a large population of Chinese immigrants—would not block travel from China until March 18, 2020, one of the later countries to do so. China would stick to its call for free travel for the first two months of the pandemic; it was among the last countries to impose restrictions on arriving visitors. On March 28, nearly two months after the United States and other countries had blocked travelers from China, the Beijing government suspended arrival by all foreign nationals except those conducting crucial "economic, trade, scientific, or technological activities" or fulfilling "emergency humanitarian needs." The National Immigration Administration called the border closure "an unfortunate temporary measure"; the Ministry of Foreign Affairs added that the decision was one "China is compelled to take in light of the outbreak situation and the practices of other countries."[23]

China's public outrage over the travel restrictions would have been more laudable if it had demonstrated the same cooperative spirit when the pandemic struck. As discussed in Chapter 3, the 2005 revisions to the International Health Regulations (IHR) agreed by member states in the WHO had two key pillars—first, that countries would beef up their domestic surveillance systems to help identify new pathogens, and then cooperate with other countries to quickly report novel diseases. The goal was to contain outbreaks at their source. Countries were expected to work closely with the WHO and its member states, welcoming foreign scientists and public health officials for whatever steps were needed to stem the danger before it could spread. In return, WHO member states agreed not to impose anything more than temporary and targeted travel restrictions, and to maintain cross-border mobility in order to ensure the flow of critical material and personnel to affected countries and to minimize economic damage. The failure of China to do the first, when for weeks it attempted to suppress news of the novel virus, broke that bargain. China's uncooperative response made it more likely that infected travelers would fan out across the rest of the country and the world in the early stages of the pandemic, leaving most other governments with little choice but to try to contain further infections through travel bans on China—however ineffective such measures were likely to be in most countries.

The revisions to the IHR had been influenced in large part by the experience of SARS in 2003. When the first SARS outbreak occurred in Guangdong province, China had not yet developed an effective disease surveillance system. On top of that, by law any occurrence of an infectious disease was considered a "state secret" that could only be publicized by the Ministry of Health. News of the SARS virus—which first broke out in November 2002 and would kill nearly 800 people around the world—would not reach the Chinese people, much less the rest of the world, for more than two months after the initial identification of the new threat.[24] Fuller reporting to the WHO would not happen until April 2003—and only after the WHO had issued its first travel advisory in its fifty-five-year-history, warning visitors to steer clear of Hong Kong and Guangdong province.

As with Covid, SARS was an existential challenge for the Chinese Communist Party—public health expert Yanzhong Huang called it "the most severe socio-political crisis for the Chinese leadership since the 1989 Tiananmen crackdown."[25] But instead of turning inward, China responded by expanding ties with foreign experts and investing heavily in new public health measures. In October 2003, just three months after the SARS pandemic waned, US Health and Human Services Secretary Tommy Thompson agreed to a partnership with China to strengthen its public health infrastructure. China's own Centers for Disease Control, modeled after its US counterpart, trained hundreds of public health officials and established a national reporting system in which any unexplained outbreaks would trigger alerts to local and national health officials. "I can confidently say there won't be another SARS incident," said Dr. Gao Fu, the Oxford- and Harvard-educated scientist who ran China's CDC, in 2019. "Because our country's infectious-disease surveillance network is very well-established, when a virus comes we can stop it."[26]

The progress China had made showed quickly during the outbreak of the H1N1 virus in 2009; the origins were in the United States and Mexico, but China became the first country to mass-produce a vaccine. That same year, health cooperation was formally incorporated into the new US-China Strategic and Economic Dialogue (S&ED), a forum for high-level cooperation launched by US president Barack Obama and Chinese president Hu Jintao. Over the next five years, China would expand its new Chinese National Influenza Center to include more than 400 laboratories and 500 "sentinel" hospitals to strengthen reporting on new outbreaks. The system also responded effectively in containing the H7N9 strain of avian influenza during a 2013 outbreak.[27]

Just when it was most needed, however, that cooperation had begun to break down. Rand Corporation health expert Jennifer Bouey testified to the US Congress in February 2020 that the cooperative mechanisms for reporting on disease outbreaks in China had badly eroded. Under Xi Jinping, Beijing had approved a 2017 law restricting the activities of foreign researchers and non-governmental organizations, weakening scientific cooperation on pandemic prevention. President Donald Trump launched a trade fight with China that would lead to billions of dollars in tariffs on goods moving both directions, and the S&ED and other high-level dialogues were suspended. Over the previous decade the US CDC had expanded its own presence in China—CDC officials were tasked with training and assisting their Chinese counterparts—but the staff was slashed by two-thirds during the first two years of the Trump administration. Bouey noted that the risks of global transmission were far higher in 2020 than they had been in 2003, and the need for international cooperation more urgent. In 2003, about 3 million people traveled in and out of China each year; by 2019 that number was 51 million. Wuhan, she noted, was "the Chicago of China," with tens of thousands of travelers moving through the city each day. "The environmental difference between the 2019 nCoV epidemic and SARS is the scale of mobility," she said, "which makes the global spreading of the disease much easier than that for SARS."[28]

But as they had done with SARS, Chinese officials again failed to promptly inform their own people, or the WHO, on the growing evidence of human-to-human transmission of Covid. The cover-up has been widely reported and documented. Local health officials in Wuhan delayed reporting to national health officials and worked to shut down online postings about a mysterious new disease. National officials in turn suppressed what they were learning, blocking Chinese scientists and doctors from sharing information with the outside world.[29] China also withheld for many days in January 2020 genetic sequences of the virus that would have allowed the world to more quickly develop tests and counter-measures; it was only shared because courageous Chinese scientists violated the government's prohibition.[30] WHO officials were privately recorded saying that China was withholding critical scientific information even as the agency was publicly praising the Chinese response.[31]

China's secrecy in the early days of the pandemic did much to sow the distrust that led countries to shut their borders. The IHR, which counseled strongly against countries imposing travel restrictions during a pandemic, were a compromise that had taken years of negotiations among the member states of the WHO. The norm against travel bans was meant primarily to incentivize prompt and accurate reporting of new outbreaks with pandemic potential. If countries felt they might be punished for transparency with costly travel bans—as happened to South Africa when it promptly reported its discovery of the new Omicron variant in late 2021—then they might attempt to suppress vital information. But there was a flip side to that deal; countries in which new diseases had emerged were expected to share their data fully and promptly so the world could cooperate in containing the outbreak at its source.

The consequence of this breakdown was that the United States, and the world, were essentially blind to the early development of the disease in China. As it had done with SARS, China delayed reporting on the severity of the Wuhan outbreak, insisting even as Wuhan hospitals were overflowing with patients with severe lung infections that there was no evidence of human-to-human transmission. The WHO—reluctant to anger Chinese officials and lose what little access to information it had—largely echoed the specious Chinese claims. The Associated Press obtained a recording of the WHO's chief of emergencies, Dr. Michael Ryan, telling colleagues in the second week of January that he feared a repeat of the SARS outbreak. "This is exactly the same scenario, endlessly trying to get updates from China about what was going on," he said. "WHO barely got out of that one with its neck intact given the issues that arose around transparency in southern China." It may never be clear whether China's suppression of information was simply another episode in the Communist Party's historic reluctance to share bad news with its own citizens and the world, or a deliberate effort to hide the origins of the virus.[32] Chinese leaders may have feared sowing panic at home, they may have fretted over the economic costs of travel bans, or they may have been trying to protect the reputation of the party. But the consequence was a repeat of the SARS episode on a much larger scale—a failure of international cooperation that almost certainly permitted the virus to spread more quickly and widely than it would have otherwise.

China Opens Its Borders

The gradual opening that China launched in 1978 is a story usually told in terms of trade and technology; China's embrace of foreign trade and a more market-oriented economy led to several decades of the strongest economic growth the world had ever seen, lifting hundreds of millions from poverty.[33] But it was also a revolution in mobility. China had a long history of tight border controls. Like the Soviet Union, revolutionary China largely restricted movement in and out of the country. About 200,000 foreigners were living in China in 1949 during the Communist Revolution; those who were not imprisoned or executed as spies either left voluntarily or were expelled under party leader Mao Zedong's dictum "first to clean out the room before inviting new guests."[34] It would be several decades before new guests were invited back. Until the early 1970s, only a handful of foreign students, journalists, and diplomats were admitted to the country. "Tourism" consisted of large official delegations whose activities were arranged and closely monitored by the government. Foreign business officials were largely excluded. Those foreigners permitted to visit or reside in China were carefully screened and closely monitored.[35] The United States did not lift its prohibition on Americans traveling to China until October 1971 following President Richard Nixon's historic visit. But following Mao's death in 1976 and the opening initiated under Deng, those numbers soared. More than 1 million foreigners visited China in 1978, a number that rose to more than 3 million by 1985 and to nearly 17 million by 1999. In 1985, the *Law of the People's Republic of China on the Control of the Exit and Entry of Citizens* was adopted, formally "safeguarding the legitimate rights and interests of Chinese citizens with respect to their exit from and entry into China's territory and to promoting international exchange."[36] In 1994, China began phasing out the requirement that foreigners live and work in separate places than resident Chinese. Longer-term foreign residents were primarily students, businesspeople, journalists, and foreign language teachers, and their numbers grew significantly.[37]

But the twentieth century was only a warm-up for the twenty-first. In 2019, China welcomed more than 65 million international tourists, the fourth largest number after France, Spain, and the United States.[38] That year, some 155 million Chinese traveled abroad, twice the number of American tourists, the next largest group. Most traveled to other Asian countries like Thailand, Japan, and South Korea, but the United States and Europe were also popular destinations.[39] For the United States and China alone, air travel grew from a few thousand passengers in the early 1980s to 15.2 million in 2019. The global losses from the halt in Chinese tourism during the pandemic are estimated at nearly $300 billion.[40] While immigration to China remained small by Western standards, by 2019 China was hosting roughly 1 million foreign residents, primarily international students, businesspeople, and spouses of Chinese cit-izens.[41] Shanghai was by far the biggest host city, accounting for about one-quarter of China's foreign-born workforce.[42] Those immigrant numbers were dwarfed, however, by the roughly 10.5 million Chinese living and working overseas.[43] China sent 369,000 students to American universities that year, while 11,000 Americans were studying in China.[44]

The growing, though still wary, welcoming of foreigners was part of a deliberate Communist Party strategy to modernize China by inviting and adopting the best ideas of the West. Opening China more fully to foreigners, and permitting Chinese to go abroad, was evidence of growing confidence in the strength of the Chinese party-state. It seemed that Chinese leaders had shed at least some of their fear that allowing Chinese citizens to be exposed to foreign influences would become a source of political instability. The govern-ment, for example, adopted a new passport law in April 2006 that lists overseas trade, business, study, or work abroad as legitimate reasons for travel.[45] While just 2% of Chinese held a passport in 2010, by 2019 that figure had grown to 15%.[46] China further codified its immigration regime in the 2012 Entry-Exit Administration Law, which mirrored many Western laws in strengthening the powers of the government to restrict entry at its borders and deport those who overstay visas, while also working to attract higher-skilled professionals.[47]

Before the pandemic, growing mobility was closely linked to China's ec-onomic progress. Expanded air travel and reduced restrictions made it easier for foreign companies to invest in China, easier for trade to flow in and out of China, and easier for students and academics to live and work abroad and acquire knowledge needed for China's progress. Chinese citizens in turn were "going out" as part of the huge Belt and Road Initiative to expand Chinese in-vestment in Asia and Africa; in 2019, nearly 200,000 Chinese were working in Africa.[48] Cutting off travel between China and the rest of the world appeared all but certain to do significant harm to the economy and to China's devel-opment prospects. But when Covid began to spread, the government did it anyway.

And Closes Them Again

By the time China chose to shut its international borders—on March 28, 2020—its harsh domestic lockdowns had gone a long way toward suppressing the virus at home. The lockdown in Wuhan would be lifted by mid-April as new infections fell to near zero. China then faced a greater threat from the importation of cases that were soaring abroad; on March 28, forty-four of the forty-five new confirmed cases in the country were brought from abroad, most by returning overseas Chinese.[49] China's border restrictions, which like other countries varied with the severity of outbreaks in different countries, were not the most exclusionary in the world—its broad ban on foreign nationals was lifted much earlier than in Japan, for example, and unlike Australia briefly, it never legally barred the return of its own citizens. China entered into various "fast-track" arrangements with nearby countries such as South Korea, Japan, and Singapore, and also began reducing restrictions on vaccinated travelers sooner than most countries.[50] But its quarantine regime was the most stringent in the world, going well beyond the science that suggested a maximum two-week incubation period for Covid. Arriving travelers were required to isolate in hotels for fourteen to twenty-one days upon arrival, at their own expense. If they traveled on to other cities such as the capital Beijing, they would be required to quarantine for another seven to fourteen days. China also cut the number of weekly international flights to just 200—a mere 2% of the 2019 level—leading to soaring ticket prices that effectively blocked all but wealthy Chinese from returning home.[51]

China also maintained stringent border restrictions long after most countries had eased up. In 2022—as controls were lifting in most of the world—two scholars from the United States and China decided to brave the travel requirements in an effort to restart scholarly exchanges between the two countries. In a joint report, Scott Kennedy of the Center for Strategic and International Studies in Washington, and Wang Jisi of Peking University, said they hoped that resumption of such exchanges might be a small step in mending a US–China relationship that had "deteriorated dramatically to levels of animosity not seen since the late 1960s."[52] Wang Jisi went first; he had been to the United States more than a hundred times before, but never in similar circumstances. Seventy-four years old at the time, and a diabetic, Wang said that his family and friends "feared the possible consequences of traveling from what they saw as the world's safest country (China) to the most dangerous place in the world (America)." After several canceled flights that required the intervention of the Chinese embassy in Washington to resolve, he arrived for what would be a thirty-five-day visit to Washington, New York, Boston, and Dallas. One planned meeting late in his itinerary, with the National Committee on US–China Relations in New York, was canceled at the last minute after a Covid exposure was reported in the office and Wang was "concerned that an exposure might jeopardize his ability to return." On the return trip to China, he was required to quarantine in hotels in Shanghai and Chengdu, and then isolate for another two weeks in a country home he owns outside Beijing. It took forty-two days to be reunited with his family, a week longer than the time he had spent in the United States.

Kennedy was set to reciprocate in April 2022 but was warned off by the US government as Shanghai was going into the most punishing lockdown of the entire pandemic—residents would be confined to their apartments for more than two months, many running short of fresh food and even medical supplies.[53] One of his friends, an American lawyer, ignored the warnings and ended up spending six weeks isolated in a Shanghai hotel room, meeting no one, before returning home. Kennedy instead chose to visit Japan, Taiwan, and South Korea, where quarantine requirements by then were shorter.[54] Kennedy had been to China many times since being a student there in 1988 and had lived in the country four separate times. But he too was worried about making the trip—the arbitrary arrest and detention of Canadians Michael Kovrig and Michael Spavor in 2018 as part of the US-China conflict over Huawei, the Chinese telecoms giant, had left many scholars feeling vulnerable.[55] His second attempt in mid-August was halted by China's "circuit-breaker policy"—if any arriving flight included infected passengers, that route was temporarily suspended.[56] He finally made it at the end of August. Compared to Wang, Kennedy got off easily, with China's quarantine requirements having been reduced in mid-2022—he was required to quarantine for three days in Taipei, where he flew first, and then another ten days in Beijing, being tested daily. From his first attempt to travel to China in April, he noted, it had taken him 163 days to make a journey that before the pandemic took fifteen hours.

Both Wang and Kennedy are well-known scholars and enjoyed every privilege in their travels. Wang flew business class both ways and quarantined in top hotels; his total expenses exceeded $65,000. Most of those affected by China's border restrictions were overseas Chinese, for whom the burdens of travel were far more onerous. As part of the Deng-initiated opening in the late 1970s, Chinese students had been encouraged to pursue study abroad—to learn from the West in order to make contributions to China's development. Roughly 1.4 million Chinese students were overseas when the travel restrictions were imposed, more than 400,000 in the United States alone.[57] Unlike many other countries, including India, which organized massive airlifts, China made no special efforts to help its overseas students return home.[58] Chinese students faced daunting obstacles in both directions—those wanting to return home were forced to pay sky-high airfares and endure long and costly quarantines on arrival. In April 2022, amid the Omicron outbreak that locked down Shanghai, the cheapest flights from Los Angeles to Guangzhou cost $20,000. Some overseas students fell for online scams, in which airline ticket "brokers" offered guaranteed flights back to China, with the tickets then never appearing after desperate travelers paid up; one student lost more than $3,000 just trying to return home from Japan.[59]

On top of that, travelers to China had to arrive in their departure city at least a week in advance for a PCR test, and take two more tests within forty-eight hours of departure.[60] Once in China, they were tested daily during quarantine; at times in 2021, Chinese officials insisted on invasive anal swabs to test for Covid on travelers from regions deemed high-risk, even using them on arriving US diplomats.[61] Travelers to Beijing faced still more quarantine time, since China for more than two years suspended direct overseas flights to protect the capital.[62] And until the United States eased its own restrictions on Chinese foreign students in May 2021, Chinese students would have been barred from returning to the United States to continue their studies unless they were willing to spend two weeks in another country not on the US travel ban list. Many Chinese students had little choice but to stay abroad separated from family, deterred by the cost of flights and the time required in quarantine. "I've been here the whole time, and for holidays," Meihua, a Chinese student in the United States, said eighteen months into the pandemic. "I just try to find a place to stay with friends and family friends." She said, "there are low periods where I feel so alone and I'm not near my family."[63]

Foreign students in China faced an even worse situation. Roughly half a million international students were studying in China when the country closed its borders. Like students around the world, most returned home and at best continued their studies online in 2021. Many countries, even Australia, began to welcome foreign students back as classes returned in-person in 2021. But China continued to block foreign students until August 2022.[64] One student in a PhD program at Jiangsu University in Zhenjiang was still barred from returning two years into the pandemic. "We have other colleagues who are studying in different countries other than China—in the US, in the UK, in the EU—they have been allowed to go back for on-campus studies," he said. "But we are still back home."[65] China was hosting some 70,000 foreign medical students in early 2020; those who were entering their fourth and fifth years, when clinical rotations are required, were unable to do their hands-on training. And many of their home countries would not permit local placements to allow them to complete their rotations. A group of foreign students went public with their complaints, forming a group called the China International Students Union and pressing for the Chinese government to ease restrictions under the Twitter hashtag #takeusbacktochina.

As in New Zealand and Australia, the Chinese restrictions exacerbated differences between Chinese living abroad and those at home.[66] James Liu had just graduated from a US midwestern university when China's travel controls were imposed. Wanting to return home, he discovered only canceled flights and unaffordable airfares. Worse, he told the *New York Times*, was that Chinese back home were making it clear in online posts that he and other foreign students were, as one put it, "spoiled brats who could jeopardize China's success in containing the epidemic." Liu had been an ardent nationalist, using his online platform to defend China's actions around the world, including the crackdown on pro-democracy protestors in Hong Kong. But he was shocked to discover, he wrote in mid-May 2020, that "the country I loved doesn't want me back." Much as with overseas citizens from New Zealand and Australia, China's overseas students became "a minority group that is expected to sacrifice for the benefit of the majority."[67] Wrote another online critic: "You were not here when we were developing the motherland, but you are the fastest to fly back thousands of miles to poison the Chinese here." Many Chinese students overseas found themselves caught between two hostile worlds, facing growing racism in Western countries that blamed China for the spread of the virus— Donald Trump repeatedly referred to Covid as "the China virus" or the "Kung Flu"—while being unwelcome back in China over fears they might bring Covid home with them.[68] Mr. Liu was still able to book a flight to Shanghai in April for just $900, but the flight was canceled; one friend paid $10,000 for a seat in coach. He was finally able to fly weeks later to the city of Xiamen, about 400 miles from his hometown, for $2,500. There were certainly thousands of similar stories throughout the pandemic, though most were never told. *New York Times* reporter Li Yuan was invited to join a WeChat group of about 500 students struggling to return home. But they warned each other not to talk to the news media, even Chinese media, for fear of retaliation from the Chinese government.[69]

Students were far from the only Chinese affected by the travel restrictions. Shi, an entrepreneur who moved to Cambodia in 2018 to invest in waste treatment plants under China's BRI, was one of thousands of Chinese who ended up trapped in Cambodia. Only two Chinese carriers continued to fly into China, so prices for return trips soared. In addition, in order to avoid triggering the "circuit breaker" halt on routes with infected passengers, the airlines required fourteen days of mandatory quarantine at assigned hotels in Phnom Penh before departure, also at the traveler's expense.[70] Liang, who had traveled to Sweden to visit her daughter, tried to book tickets back home in January 2022 to see her cancer-stricken mother. But one after another, the four flights she booked were canceled due to the circuit breaker policy. "Returning to China is like buying a lottery ticket," she said.[71] A Chinese academic working in the United States, who gave birth to a child in China in early 2020, was unable to bring him back with her to the United States; as part of the Covid shutdowns, the US government had suspended visa processing, so her son could not get a visa to travel back with her.[72] She had no choice but to continue running the gauntlet of costly flights and long quarantines during school term breaks to return to China to see her son, who was living with his grandparents. When US visa processing resumed, the backlogs were enormous; it would take nearly three years before the child's US visa came through and he was permitted to return to the United States with his mother.

Putting the Costs on Others: The Fate of Shipping Crews

On April 14, 2020, the WeChat account CNSeaman, which posts news about Chinese seafarers' welfare, training, and recruitment to its 50,000 followers on the most popular Chinese social media site, published an urgent plea. "I'm a Chinese seafarer; my mother passed away, but I cannot get off the ship," it said. The message—coming from a container vessel docked at the southern port of Zhoushan—was accompanied by a 15-second video in which two crewmen at the front held a Chinese flag while behind them was a giant white banner that read: "We are Chinese seafarers; we are healthy and request to go home." Aboard the ship were twelve workers who had been at sea for ten months and were scheduled for leave when they arrived at the port. Three of them were facing family emergencies. The one whose mother had died was expected home to arrange the funeral; another had just lost his grandfather and his mother was ill, and the father of the third was in hospital following a stroke. The ship had arrived April 1, and all had remained in strict quarantine on the vessel and tested negative for Covid. They had also agreed to remain in local quarantine for another two weeks before returning home. But on April 13, the day before the video was posted, local authorities denied their request, citing limited hotel quarantine and testing capacity. The video was viewed thousands of times and struck a nerve with online commentators. "Wake up!," said one. "In China, seafarers are low-class citizens, coolies at sea." Another wrote it was "completely irresponsible" for local authorities not to act. "It is lazy governance."[73]

Such symbolic protests were one of the few ways that Chinese citizens could object to their government's heavy-handed approach to lockdowns and quarantines in pursuit of zero-Covid. Some of the protests reverberated around the world. Residents of Shanghai trapped in their apartments during the two-month lockdown in the spring of 2022 pleaded that they were running short of food, water, and other basic necessities, and unable to access medical care; a six-minute video called "Voices of April" went viral despite Chinese censorship.[74] Online protests erupted in September 2022 after a bus headed to a quarantine facility crashed, killing twenty-seven people. Larger demonstrations, the so-called white paper protests, followed in November 2022 after the deaths of ten people in an apartment fire in Ürümqi, the capital of Xinjiang province. Strict anti-Covid measures that had been in place for three months blocked firefighters and rescue workers trying to get to the scene of the fire and may have barred residents from leaving the building.[75] The protests spread despite efforts by Chinese censors to block posts on sites like WeChat and Weibo, and likely contributed to President Xi Jinping's announcement on December 7, 2022, that China was abandoning the zero-Covid policy.[76] The seafarers' protests were never heard outside China, but they did reverberate locally. The *China Shipping Gazette* and *China Business Network* followed the story and interviewed the seamen. On April 17, 2020, local authorities in Zhoushan relented and permitted the men to come ashore.

The online protests from the Chinese seafarers were a small window into the suffering of a group of workers that paid an especially high price for the decisions by governments to shut borders during the pandemic. Like other countries, the Chinese government was determined to maintain the flow of traded goods even as borders were shutting to people. The EU established "green lanes" to speed freight through otherwise restricted borders; both cargo and health checks at borders were limited to no more than fifteen minutes.[77] In North America, truckers were declared essential and crossed borders without restrictions until January 2022, when Canada and the United States imposed vaccination requirements on truckers.[78] The move sparked massive protests by Canadian truckers that briefly shut down some border crossings. The World Trade Organization and other international organizations also worked to remove obstacles to trade and relieve supply chain shortages.[79]

No country was more committed to supporting trade than China; it managed throughout the pandemic to maintain the largest flow of trade goods in the world. As demand surged for Chinese-made products like electronics and home exercise equipment, trade between the United States and China reached a new record in 2022.[80] But unlike North America and Europe, where there was little health screening for truckers and dock workers, China expanded its trade while implementing stringent health measures. National, provincial, and local governments established an elaborate set of protocols to try to ensure that trade in goods would not become a vector for introduction of the virus. It was in many ways an astonishing accomplishment. While shipping bottlenecks and supply chain shortages persisted throughout the pandemic, China managed to serve the world's growing appetite for goods—its trade surplus of nearly $880 billion in 2022 was the largest ever recorded—while keeping the virus at bay for almost three years.[81]

But doing so meant imposing months of extra isolation and overwork on the nearly two million seafarers who man the container ships that ply the world's oceans, carrying nearly 90% of the world's traded goods.[82] In normal times, shipping companies facilitate crew changes across the world. International maritime law restricts workers to no more than eleven months on a ship, though most contracts are shorter. When contracts expire, workers are flown back home and replaced by new crews that are often flown in as well. A normal month would see roughly 100,000 crew changes across the world.[83] But Covid created multiple problems—flights were cut, visas were difficult to obtain, and quarantine requirements slowed crew changes. And countries often simply refused to let the seafarers come ashore, fearing they might be infected. China was far from alone in doing so—many countries initially imposed restrictions that made it impossible for seafarers to disembark in foreign ports and return home when their contracts expired. Dozens—including Canada, France, Kenya, Panama, and the Philippines—had responded to pressure from the shipping industry within several months of the shutdowns and began making exceptions for seafarers.[84] Most others moved slowly—by March 2021 only 56 of the 174 member states of the International Maritime Organization (IMO) had declared seafarers to be "key workers," permitting them to come ashore for crew changes.[85] But China was one of the few that maintained such restrictions throughout the pandemic. And as the world's largest trading nation, it was China's policies more than any other that kept hundreds of thousands of container ship workers trapped at sea. Conditions for those working on Chinese-owned fleets were especially grim.

Working aboard a container ship is one of the world's most dangerous, demanding, and lonely occupations. Even before Covid, seafarers struggled with difficult conditions. Most are from developing countries—the Philippines is the largest source, followed by Russia, Indonesia, China, and India. The pay is low—Filipino workers make about $1,000 a month. A British study found that workplace deaths among ship workers were fifteen times the level of the general population, and nearly five times that of British construction workers. Most ships have a skeleton staff of about twenty, so if a worker falls ill or is injured, others must pick up the slack. The 24/7 operation of container ships results in widespread fatigue. Mental health problems are endemic: 25% of seafarers say they suffer from depression, and suicide rates are nearly four times higher than in the general population.[86] One of the few perks of the job is shore leave, which allows seafarers to visit foreign countries, recharge after time on the ship, and reconnect with friends and family. That ended with Covid.

By September 2020, some 400,000 ship workers were trapped aboard their ships; even as the restrictions began to ease, roughly 250,000 were still working beyond their contracts in July 2021, many exceeding the legal limit of eleven months.[87] Only about one-fifth had voluntarily agreed to contract extensions.[88] Ralph Santillan, a Filipino seafarer, had boarded a bulk carrier hauling corn and barley in March 2019 and was coming to the end of his contract when the world shut down. He was supposed to disembark in Singapore but was told his flight back home had been canceled and he had no choice but to remain aboard. By September 2020 he had been separated from his wife and son for more than eighteen months. "I can see the fatigue and stress in their faces," he said of his shipmates. "I'm sure they can see it on my face."[89] Some seafarers were not even permitted to disembark when they were gravely ill. A Russian seafarer suffered a stroke in waters near Indonesia but was denied medical help by Indonesian authorities, who only relented two days later after intervention from the IMO and the International Labour Organization.[90] An officer with Anglo Eastern suffered a severe tooth abscess but was denied treatment where the ship was docked in China; he was not seen until they arrived in South Korea.[91] Said a top official of the International Transport Workers' Federation, the union for seafarers: "These governments refuse to accept that the globalized trade system that they rely on to get people their toothpaste, their shampoo, food and medical supplies, relies on these people who have been treated like a rubber band, stretched to the absolute limit and about to snap."[92]

Chinese workers deployed on ships owned by Chinese companies faced even greater indignities. Except where local officials intervened, China mostly did not bar its own seafarers from disembarking or returning from overseas. But there were lengthy testing requirements that made it difficult for ships to change crews and stay on schedule to avoid fines for late shipments. Those who were able to disembark faced huge obstacles. Return from abroad meant enduring two to three weeks of quarantine in foreign ports, and another two to four weeks upon arrival in China before they could return to their families.[93] When they arrived in Chinese ports, shore leaves were banned. And during time at port, the seafarers were required to don the full personal protective equipment (PPE) colloquially known as "big white"—a hazmat suit, protective goggles, disposable gloves, and an N95 mask—anytime they were outside their living quarters. The requirements even extended to portions of ocean travel. When pilots came aboard, as is required to transit the Suez Canal, for example, the ship's crew needed to wear full PPE. Seafarers complained that the suits were stiflingly hot, soaking them in sweat and making it hard to breathe. One officer, who was forced to stay in gear for a twelve-hour passage through the Suez Canal, said "all the clothes I was wearing underneath were soaked through."[94] Sometimes local authorities imposed additional restrictions; since officials were often punished for Covid outbreaks, there was a strong incentive to impose maximum precautions. And rather than easing the restrictions as vaccines became more wildly available, China doubled down. In the fall of 2021, in addition to continuing to outlaw international crew changes, China imposed a mandatory seven-week quarantine for returning Chinese seafarers— three weeks in a foreign port before their return, two weeks upon arrival, and another two weeks in their home province.[95]

China's measures went far beyond the science in trying to keep out the virus. China was the only country, for example, to set up a testing and tracing protocol for imports of frozen foods such as meats and seafood. Beginning in

November 2020, China required all overseas shipments of cold-chain products to be tested for Covid and undergo "disinfection"—dousing with disinfectant chemicals—upon arrival in China.[96] At various times during the pandemic, exports from Brazil, Ecuador, Indonesia, and Russia faced bans after the virus was detected on shipments.[97] While scientists and health experts were skeptical the virus could survive on surfaces during a long ocean journey, China's CDC later published research suggesting that several Covid outbreaks in China could plausibly be linked to imported frozen foods.[98] Chinese officials especially cited a major 2021 outbreak in Dalian, a port city that handles 70% of cold-chain imports. The flare-up resulted in a harsh lockdown of the city; retailers were ordered to destroy recently imported meat and seafood, and trade in cold-chain products was temporarily suspended through Dalian.[99] No other country implemented similar measures—a New Zealand cold storage worker tested positive in August 2020, but health authorities ruled out frozen food as the source. Scientists said that while some dead fragments of the virus could possibly survive on shipments, these would not be capable of infecting humans. "People should not fear food, food packaging or delivery of food," said Mike Ryan, head of the WHO's emergencies programme. "There is no evidence the food chain is participating in transmission of this virus." But China's disinfection and testing requirements would remain in place until January 2023.

Land-based trade was easier, but not by much. Domestic truckers in China—some 20 million in total—faced repeated Covid tests even as they crossed from one city boundary to another. Queues for the tests often stranded drivers in their trucks for six to eight hours at a time.[100] Drivers could be blocked entirely if they had recently traveled to a medium- or high-risk region in the country. The situation was especially dire in the spring of 2022, when Omicron cases were surging in China and Shanghai and other cities went into full lockdown. In addition to the testing, officials at some checkpoints would tape over the truck cab doors and windows with plastic, leaving drivers sealed inside temporarily. "I was stuck in my truck for almost twenty-four hours last weekend," one driver told Bloomberg News. "Like every other exhausted trucker who's helping out the supply shortage, I need to eat, drink, pee. They sealed our truck windows at almost every checkpoint."[101] Local closures would sometimes strand truckers on the highways. In March 2022, hundreds of drivers were blocked from delivering their supplies to Anshan, in Liaoning province. One driver said he was stuck for four nights with only a single steamed bun for food.[102] Another driver returning to his home village in Lianyungang, Jiangsu province, was blocked by local officials and told he would have to quarantine for fourteen days at his own expense. Not having the funds, he and other drivers had no choice but to isolate themselves in their truck cabs. Local officials delivered food twice daily, but there were no toilet or shower facilities.[103]

Cross-border truckers faced restrictions similar to those at the ocean ports. At China's border with Kyrgyzstan, truckers were not permitted to move freely back and forth. Importing goods from China required Kyrgyz drivers to undergo disinfection and screening at the border, and to cross briefly to pick up a Chinese container for the return trip. Imports from China fell by more than half in 2020, contributing to a 9% drop in Kyrgyzstan's GDP that year.[104] In December 2021 in the run-up to the Beijing Winter Olympics, China shut its borders to cargo from Vietnam, leading to backups of days and fresh fruit rotting in the containers.[105] Even when the border was opened, Vietnamese truckers were often required to turn their trucks over to Chinese drivers at the border.[106] In Yunnan province, where the land border fence was constructed, trucks coming from Myanmar had to stop at the border, have their cargo sanitized, and remain in Myanmar for forty-eight hours. Then a robot or crane would move the cargo onto Chinese trucks, where the goods would be moved onto the Chinese side, sanitized again, and held for another twenty-four hours before being permitted to continue into the rest of China.[107] Even with such precautions, when cases surged China would completely shut the border; the Wanding crossing, the region's largest, was shut to all traffic for 136 days in 2021.[108]

The Legacy of China's Border Closures

Michael Schuman, a veteran China journalist who contributes to *The Atlantic* and *Bloomberg*, lost his Chinese visa in early 2020, one of many journalists expelled from the country as relations between the United States and China deteriorated. He left for Hong Kong in the summer of 2020 while his wife, also an American journalist, stayed behind in Beijing. She was told she could not travel outside China and be permitted to return, and so they were separated—talking only by Zoom and telephone—for nearly two years. At one point, she was working on a story in Shenzen—a subway ride away from Hong

Kong—"yet she might as well have been in the Himalayas," Schuman wrote. In March 2022, the Chinese visa restrictions eased, and he was able to apply for a new visa. But the return was anything but smooth—he was forced to quarantine for twenty-one days in Shanghai, and then another two weeks in Beijing. The word itself—"quarantine"—has lost some of its horror since it became so ubiquitous during the pandemic. But Schuman wrote that after five weeks of isolation in China, "I came to the conclusion that Chinese quarantines are a form of torture." Over five weeks he was outside for a total of ten minutes, and his only visitors were the daily testers ramming swabs into his throat or up his nose. "I began to exhibit symptoms of the abused," he wrote: "recurring irrational bouts of terror for what might come, extreme lethargy that caused a loss of will and concentration, uncontrolled agitation and feelings of hostility toward my oppressors." Worse, he said, was the fear that the next knock on the door could be news of a positive test that would see him hauled away to a government quarantine facility. China, he said, has long been an autocracy backed by a powerful state machinery of repression. But the pandemic "offered the state further rationale and opportunity to expand this power." Modern technologies of control like the phone apps that tracked the movements of every citizen, coupled with the blunt force of millions of party and state officials, allowed China to impose both the world's most stringent border controls and the most sweeping and restrictive domestic lockdowns. "Only in a society like China's, where the individual has little recourse against the state, could zero-COVID operate as it has," Schuman wrote.[109]

The system was fallible, of course; the Omicron variant proved too contagious even for the world's most rigorous zero-Covid regime. And as it has done many times in the past, the Chinese government was able to pivot; when zero-Covid became impossible, China's pandemic controls were dismantled with astonishing speed. The sudden removal of both domestic lockdowns and border controls likely contributed to a late surge in cases and deaths in 2023 that sullied China's record. While the government abruptly stopped testing and counting, health experts estimate that more than 80% of Chinese were infected with Omicron, and perhaps a million or more lives were lost as the virus hit an immunologically naive population.[110] But little of that was made known to the Chinese people, and for the rest of the world the death counts are informed speculation. The heavily populated coastal Chinese province of Zhejiang reported that cremations in the first quarter of 2023 had jumped by 73% from the previous year, to 173,000, suggesting a surging death toll. The data was removed almost immediately, in keeping with China's decision to stop reporting cremation numbers.[111] For several months in early 2023, Hong Kong had some of the highest mortality rates seen anywhere in the world during the pandemic; barely half of the elderly population in the city was fully vaccinated when the Omicron variant began spreading ferociously.[112] But China's party leadership in February 2023 insisted that the country's death rate from Covid had been the lowest in the world, calling it "a major and decisive victory" and a "miracle in human history."[113]

China removed quarantine restrictions on incoming travelers on January 8, 2023, and lifted caps on the number of arriving international passengers. Travelers were required to have a negative PCR test within forty-eight hours of traveling; China was one of the last countries to lift that restriction.[114] In April 2023, travelers were permitted to substitute at-home rapid tests; airlines were no longer required to check the test results before boarding, however, and there were no testing requirements upon arrival in China.[115]

China has tried to lay out the welcome mat to the world again, but in the immediate aftermath of Covid the response was tepid. Chinese domestic tourism recovered quickly to 2019 levels, but foreign travel, both inward and outward, remained severely depressed. While international tourism recovered to 88% of pre-pandemic levels in 2023, and was expected to recover fully in 2024, China has lagged far behind. In the first quarter of 2023 after travel restrictions were lifted, just 52,000 foreigners came to the country on organized tours, compared with 3.7 million in the first quarter of 2019.[116] For the full year of 2023, the number of foreign visitors was just over one-third the level of 2019.[117] At the end of 2023, in an effort to boost numbers, China began offering fifteen days of visa-free travel to citizens of France, Germany, and several other European countries.[118] Travel to and from the United States remained especially low—at the end of 2023, the number of flights was still just one-third of the pre-pandemic level.[119] Chinese travel to the United States remained less than one-third of pre-pandemic levels in 2023. In June 2023, the US government issued a warning for Americans traveling to China, cautioning against the risk of wrongful detention, exit bans, and arbitrary enforcement of local laws.[120] Japan's visa-free travel to China was not restored after the Covid restrictions were lifted, and both inbound and outbound tourism with China is down sharply. The foreign population in China also fell significantly as a consequence of the Covid restrictions; Shanghai's expat population fell from about 80,000 in 2020 to 50,000 by the end of 2022.[121]

The Chinese economy also failed to see the post-Covid rebound that had been expected. The economy grew slowly for much of 2023 and youth unemployment soared to more than 20%, leading the government to stop reporting the figure.[122] Foreign investment in China in 2023, following the lifting of Covid restrictions, fell to its lowest level in thirty years.[123] Adam Posen, president of the Washington-based Peterson Institute, argued that China was suffering from a case of "economic long Covid"—ordinary Chinese were saving money rather than spending and investing, fearing that the next government crackdown could come at any time. The Covid restrictions under Xi Jinping, he wrote, broke the authoritarian bargain that if the people stayed out of politics, the government would largely stay out of their private affairs. Faced with uncertainty, households and small businesses began hoarding cash rather than risking it on illiquid investments. "The condition is systemic, and the only reliable cure—credibly assuring ordinary Chinese people and companies that there are limits on the government's intrusion into economic life—cannot be delivered," Posen wrote.[124]

It is harder to assess the longer-term consequences of China's actions during Covid. The pandemic is likely to mark the clearest dividing line between China's era of openness—dating roughly to 1978—and the greater self-sufficiency it has been pursuing over the past decade.[125] While China has for some years turned inward in pursuit of greater economic autonomy, the Covid years marked a dramatic swing back toward a more closed, more isolated nation. But others have argued that China's border measures, while certainly more extreme than most, were temporary measures designed to address a public health emergency.[126] As such, China's approach was different only in scale from many other countries and will pivot back to the pre-Covid normal. China has certainly signaled since the pandemic that it wants to reopen at least partially for foreign business and foreign tourists.

But more than anywhere else in the world, Covid in China laid bare the risks when governmental powers—even exercised in the name of a laudable goal like protecting public health—face no constraints. China is not alone in its growing capacity to close borders in the event of emergencies, real or perceived. As Schuman put it, the pandemic showed "what happens when an unfettered state is allowed free rein, unchecked by law or civil society."

8

Keeping the Doors Open

In the mid-1970s, Donna Ann Baker, a Canadian, fell in love with an American, John McCall; they were married in 1983 in Madoc, Ontario, a town of 2,200 people halfway between Toronto and Ottawa. The McCalls initially set up their lives in Chicago, where both their children were born and would take their father's American citizenship. They retired back to Ontario in 2017 after Donna worked for decades as an ICU nurse, and they would regularly drive to visit their adult children who lived across the border (Figure 8.1). In February 2020, just before the Covid border restrictions were implemented, Donna was diagnosed with liver failure. She was put on the transplant list, but as her condition worsened her family pleaded with the Canadian government for a compassionate exemption that would allow her children, Ian and Meghan, to come into the country to help with her care. Both children had birth certificates showing Canadian birthright to enter Canada based on their mother's citizenship, but their passports were American. They were told their best hope was to file for Canadian citizenship, but that they would not be allowed to cross the border until the applications were approved by Canada's Department of Immigration, Refugees and Citizenship. It did not happen in time. Donna's condition deteriorated rapidly, and she entered the hospital. With the applications still mired in the Ottawa bureaucracy, the decision was made to pull her off life support. "My children were denied the opportunity to be with their mother in the months before her death and I was forced to cope with the illness and the loss of my wife alone and without the direct support of immediate family," John recalled years later.[1] She said goodbye to her children and grandchildren on FaceTime before passing away August 10.[2] "I called the kids, and I held the phone up and they said goodbye. It was tough," John McCall said. "It's a tragedy that shouldn't have happened."[3] One week later, the citizenship applications were approved. Ian and Meghan traveled to

Figure 8.1 Donna McCall with her husband, John, and their descendants. Courtesy of John McCall.

Canada, quarantined for fourteen days, and then attended their mother's memorial service.

Donna's story inspired the creation of Faces of Advocacy, a Canadian grassroots organization set up in May 2020 to safely reunite Canadian families separated by the border restrictions. They gathered over 12,000 members who rallied for policy change, pleading that "we are not asking for open borders. We are just asking to be together. . . . 2020 is a rough year for all. Imagine going through it without your family."[4] Faces of Advocacy was led by Dr. David Edward-Ooi Poon, a Canadian physician born and raised in Saskatchewan to immigrant parents from China and Malaysia. Poon's girlfriend, Alexandria Aquino, had flown from Ireland to be with him in April 2020, but she was turned away at Toronto's Pearson airport. The organization garnered media attention, led a weekly letter writing campaign to government officials, and hosted a "Virtual Rally for Family Reunification" with Members of Parliament from every political party. Dr. Poon, who has training in mental health, also conducted a survey of 1,200 members regarding their emotional state during the pandemic. Eighty-four percent said their mental health was deteriorating the longer they were separated from their loved ones.[5] This information was presented to the House of Commons, accompanied by a petition signed by 5,300 Canadian citizens and residents. After Dr. Poon spoke on Parliament Hill, the Canadian government established a process to exempt extended families and unmarried couples from the restrictions on non-essential travel, which was enacted in the fall of 2020. The exemption established an application process for travel authorization to allow siblings, adult children, grandparents, and committed partners to reunite with their Canadian loved ones.

Dr. Poon and his group were not alone in winning small victories. In Europe, a similar online advocacy group—"Love Is Not Tourism"—was formed to fight for unmarried couples separated by the border closures.[6] It was founded by German programmer Felix Urbasik, whose partner, April, was trapped in Australia, barred by travel restrictions from leaving that country or from entering the EU. He set up a Facebook page and website in late June 2020 that would get 50,000 visits in the first week and ultimately attract 45,000 followers. The group's name was a direct criticism of government policies that excluded "non-essential" travelers. "We do not wish to travel and sightsee," Urbasik's website said. "We have one destination: the arms of our loved ones. We are willing to go into quarantine for however long it takes. We are willing to get tested as many times as it takes."[7] The campaign had some success in Europe—the European Commission endorsed travel exceptions for unmarried couples. Germany, France, Denmark, Norway, Spain, Italy, Denmark, and several other countries modified their restrictions in the summer of 2020 to permit the couples to reunite.[8]

The magazine *New Zealand Lawyer* named Tudor Clee, who represented Al-Jazeera journalist Charlotte Bellis and other pregnant women trying to return home, to its 2023 list of most influential lawyers. It credited his efforts with "hastening the end of the government's managed isolation and quarantine (MIQ) system." Clee was also the first to discover the loophole in the travel restrictions that allowed New Zealand citizens to purchase flights transiting the country, exit at the airports, and immediately be granted a quarantine slot so they could return home. Government efforts to fine those citizens were blocked by the courts.[9] The group "Grounded Kiwis" sued the government's MIQ lottery in court and won a partial victory that could strengthen the right of return for citizens in future border closures.[10] In a similar effort, the group "Stranded Aussies" representing Australian citizens unable to return home during the pandemic successfully challenged the government before the UN human rights committee for violating the 1966 International Covenant on

Civil and Political Rights, which requires that "no one shall be arbitrarily deprived of the right to enter his own country."[11]

Organized efforts to change Covid restrictions were not just limited to democratic countries. Even under the strict censorship laws in China, citizen action was able to move the needle. Pressure from the group China International Student Union likely played a role in Beijing permitting some foreign students to begin returning in late 2022 while zero-Covid restrictions were still in place.[12] The "white paper protests" against the lockdowns in China, one of the largest public uprisings since the Tiananmen Square protests, were forcefully suppressed by the government.[13] But they likely helped persuade the Communist Party leadership that its zero-Covid policy had become untenable in the face of the more contagious Omicron variants. China's Covid restrictions were removed quickly after the protests; restrictions for international arrivals were also phased out beginning in January 2023 and quarantine and testing requirements were lifted.[14]

Not every campaign was successful. Trump's press secretary Kayleigh McEnany, asked in July 2020 whether the United States would follow the European lead to help reunite cross-border couples and families, said, "this President will always put America first. This President put in place the travel bans to protect American lives, and they've done that."[15] The success of Faces of Advocacy in Canada inspired the spin-off of a similar group in the United States known as "Let Us Reunite!" The group consisted of about 2,000 members who lobbied the US government to reciprocate the travel exemptions that Canada enacted to allow family and those in committed relationships to cross the land border. "We wrote a letter to President Biden urging him to classify these exemptions as essential. There is nothing more essential than family," said Cary Whaley, co-founder of the organization. But, as his co-founder Devon Weber lamented after nearly a year of restrictions, "the U.S. government has done nothing."[16]

Australians like Shanika Carling, who was separated from her fiancé, Nathaniel Roark, in Reno, Nevada, were among thousands petitioning the Australian government to ease the restrictions for unmarried couples. The petition attracted more than 19,000 signatures.[17] "We're all saying we'd pay for our own quarantine, our own testing, pretty much whatever they require to establish we're a safe traveler," she said.[18] The petition won considerable support in Australia's Parliament, but the government continued to deny exemptions to non-married couples.[19] One of its few concessions was to add "overseas parents" to the definition of immediate family in October 2021, noting that "many families with parents overseas have missed weddings, funerals, the birth of grandchildren, and other significant events."[20] But unmarried couples were not allowed to reunite until Australia reopened for all travel in February 2022.

Successful or not, these efforts were unprecedented: citizens of countries who had largely enjoyed free travel organizing to fight for their right to live across borders, and in some cases for their right to return home. In doing so, they joined immigrant rights groups that for decades have been waging similar battles to reunite their families in the face of immigration restrictions and hostile bureaucracies. Covid reframed the issues around border controls in lasting ways. Borders, the pandemic made clear, are not just a barrier to those wishing to emigrate to foreign countries, but an obstacle to anyone trying to live a life outside national boundaries. "We feel marginalized by the simple fact that our love is not confined within borders," wrote Faces of Advocacy in a brief to the Canadian government. "In a world with advanced social technologies, it should be no surprise that loving relationships have blossomed across the globe."[21] As border scholar Rey Koslowski has argued, "global mobility" goes far beyond migration, encompassing cross-border workers, international students, temporary migrant workers, tourists, and those with family or other important relationships outside their countries.[22] Covid was the first crisis that disrupted that mobility on a global scale.

The activists who built alliances and helped move governments may go silent in the aftermath of the pandemic; most are back with their loved ones and life has returned to something like the pre-Covid normal. But Covid should serve as a wake-up call that in a world where borders are growing ever thicker, those relationships are precarious. Those living across borders should work to build new alliances and strengthen existing ones to demand stronger protections if they wish to prevent the same treatment in future crises. Many of those affected by the Covid closures were from wealthier countries, and they enjoy greater political and economic influence than most migrants from poorer countries. For the first time, governments took the same tools that have been used against less-privileged migrants and asylum seekers and turned them on their own citizens, and citizens from countries that had long enjoyed relatively unfettered travel. Covid showed the world that new restraints are needed, that left unchecked governments will continue to increase their capabilities to restrict borders, with too little regard to the damage and disruption they are doing to people's lives. These are the same governments, of course, that for decades have promoted globalization and are only too willing to profit from the movement of tourists, students, and migrant workers. Those competing goals—promoting mobility while tightening borders—offer an opening for the cross-border community to insist on stronger guarantees that recognize their contributions and protect their ways of life. But progress will not come easily. Governments jealously guard their sovereignty, and nowhere more than at their nation's borders.

Cross-Border Lives

As the disruptions of the pandemic fade to memory, the number of people living across borders is certain to keep accelerating. Migration has completely recovered from the collapse caused by Covid-19, according to the International Organization for Migration.[23] Many governments are encouraging more. Canada announced in early 2023 that it would admit the largest number of immigrants in its history—some 500,000 annually over three years, plus a new temporary worker program. Immigration to the United States rebounded sharply to pre-Covid levels by the end of 2022, and the Biden administration also admitted hundreds of thousands more under a special parole program designed to discourage illegal migration. Europe added more than 7 million new immigrants in 2022 and 2023, many of them Ukrainian refugees displaced by the war with Russia. Immigration to Australia similarly rebounded to levels higher than the pre-Covid numbers in 2023, with the government committed to "making up" for the declines in migration during Covid.[24] Even Japan's foreign-born population is rising sharply again, restoring pre-Covid trends that saw a doubling in the foreign workforce over the past decade.[25]

International education is similarly rebounding. Japan is aiming to host 400,000 foreign students by 2030 and wants more of them to remain after they graduate.[26] Foreign student populations recovered more strongly than expected in the United States, Canada, the UK, and Australia.[27] International tourism similarly reached nearly 90% of pre-pandemic levels in 2023 and was on track for a full recovery—though visa delays and the strong dollar slowed the return of tourists to the United States.[28] With the possible exception of China, the final story on Covid's effect on the global movement of people is likely to be a huge, but temporary, drop in a decades-long trend that has seen more people crossing borders for more reasons than ever before in history. The recovery is testament to the resilience of the human spirit—and to the very human inclination to hope that bad things are unlikely to be repeated. The predictable result is that millions more people will build cross-border lives for themselves—with their families, partners, jobs, and friends separated by national frontiers. And when the next crisis hits and governments again close or restrict their borders, the fate of these new arrivals will be very far down the list of priorities.

Can the world do better next time in protecting the well-being of those whose lives span borders, and in avoiding the economic damage from large-scale travel restrictions? There is unfortunately little reason to think so. "Travel measures are now squarely in the toolbox of policy options countries may use to respond to future public-health crises," states a report from the Migration Policy Institute.[29] International negotiators seeking greater cooperation in future crises have made it clear that they will not try to curb the use of travel and border restrictions. Countries have become increasingly determined to guard their prerogative to choose not just who is permitted to immigrate and settle in their countries, but who may cross their frontiers for any purpose. The one notable exception is the EU, but even there the last decade has demonstrated the limitations on the commitment by European nation-states to unfettered cross-border mobility. And the Covid crisis ruptured even well-established cooperative mechanisms like those between the United States and Canada. There seems little doubt that in a future pandemic of similar proportions governments would respond similarly. The Covid border closures were popular almost everywhere they were implemented, boosting the governments that embraced them. An Australian official told us that, despite the international controversy surrounding his country's especially harsh border restrictions, he had little doubt that Australia would do the same in a future outbreak.

Change will require a strong voice from those who are harmed by border restrictions. Those separated from homes and families by the Covid border closures organized themselves in unprecedented ways using the reach of modern social media; it will be harder for governments in the future to simply ignore their voices. People with the privilege of holding passports that permitted relatively free travel before Covid have hopefully gained a new awareness for the plight of more precarious migrants who routinely face the sort of border obstacles that became global during the pandemic. "We share our homes across an international border we never imagined would be closed to us," said Bobbi Hudson, who was separated from her partner in Canada.

"We never imagined our governments would tell us that our family isn't essential and prohibit our ability to be together as the family that we are."[30] Travelers and immigrants from wealthier countries discovered that, in extreme situations, they could face the same family separations that for decades have been endured by migrant workers, asylum seekers, and others from poorer countries. During Covid, all of those living their lives across borders faced massive discrimination by governments. From container and cruise ship workers to migrant workers to those with cross-border partners and families, they faced restrictions far beyond those forced on others outside of the most severe, and usually brief, domestic lockdowns. They played by the rules, and then the rules changed. People harmed by the border restrictions should make a simple demand for the future—an end to discrimination against those who choose to build their lives across borders.

Protections across Borders

There are three broad sets of changes that could go a long way to strengthening protections for those living across borders without unreasonably tying the hands of governments to respond to crises. These include strengthened international cooperation, constraints around the use of emergency powers, and better risk management.[31] Sadly, progress on all three has been minimal. The first is the hardest. Stronger collaboration among governments—almost wholly absent during Covid—could have minimized harm to those crossing borders. But the world is moving in the other direction. In revisions to the International Health Regulations and the push for a new global pandemic treaty in 2024, the issue of travel restrictions was removed from the agenda of international cooperation—a big step backward from the 2005 regulations that had discouraged border closures during pandemics. Governments instead focused on strengthening national health response capabilities and on equity issues like vaccine distribution, while leaving border and travel measures firmly in the hands of national governments. Trade remains, as it was during the pandemic, a striking exception—countries will be encouraged in future crises to keep any trade restrictions "temporary, targeted and proportionate" and "not create unnecessary barriers to trade or disruptions in supply chains of pandemic-related health products."[32] But negotiators have made clear that new international agreements on health cooperation will not require governments to take any specific actions such as "ban or accept travelers."[33]

There are certainly strong reasons why governments should cooperate in managing borders during future crises. The Covid shutdowns showed the catastrophic costs for countries that depended on tourist revenues and international students. Integrated cross-border regions were especially hard hit as border closures disrupted work, schooling, and access to medical care. In addition, many more countries are facing population pressures that create an urgent necessity for admitting more migrants. Others are competing to lure "digital nomads," remote tech workers with the freedom to work from anywhere in the world.[34] Yet the emergence of a mobile workforce points to novel challenges in updating social protections for a globalized world that lacks the systems to support people living cross-border lives. Stronger international norms to better protect the rights of those crossing borders would encourage such mobility, which would be a boost to the global economy. But set against those incentives is a deteriorating geopolitical landscape, with growing rivalry especially between the United States and China and millions of people on the move fleeing war, gang violence, corrupt governments, and environmental degradation from climate change. Any concessions to sovereignty, especially on a core issue like border control, will be immensely challenging to negotiate.

A second, somewhat more promising, path is changes in national laws and practices, in particular the rules around the use of emergency powers. If Covid showed us anything, it is that in the absence of constraints, governments will take the popular step of shutting borders and keep them closed for far longer than warranted. While no government would willingly deprive itself of tools like border closures to deal with emergencies, that does not mean that such powers should be immune to oversight by legislatures and courts. In particular, migrants and other border crossers faced massive discrimination throughout the pandemic despite international agreements that emergency powers should be used in a limited and non-discriminatory fashion.[35] Some legal scholars have called for courts to exercise greater scrutiny in evaluating the use of emergency powers—balancing the nature of the emergency against the rights being violated, and ensuring that government interventions are the least restrictive needed to achieve the public policy goal.[36] Yet in part because of historic deference to government actions at the border, and during public health emergencies, few courts did so during the pandemic. But those living

across borders are as deserving of legal protection as those whose choices have
kept them closer to home.

Finally, national officials need to take far more seriously their commitments
to limit social harm in pursuing broader public goods. The utilitarian logic
of the pandemic in which governments tried to protect the majority of their
people at the expense of outsiders—including at times their own citizens
living abroad—was the result in no small part of government incompetence.
As the Covid Crisis Group report into the US response argued, during the
pandemic the US government chose to "resort to the blunt instrument [of
border closures] because no better ones were available."[37] Governments need
to develop better tools to manage the risks of pandemics, much in the way
that better tools were developed after 9/11 to manage some of the risks of
terrorists crossing borders without resorting to economically and socially
harmful border closures. Targeted measures like those used in South Korea
and Taiwan show that more sensible, less costly approaches are possible. At the
least, governments should be able to achieve the benefits of travel restrictions
at much lower costs to their economies and to the individuals harmed by
border closures.

With rare short-term exceptions, rigid border controls should be understood
as a failure—a failure of governments to deploy more effective and less costly
measures to address the problem being faced. When dealing with any "threat"
that comes from abroad—diseases, harmful drugs, terrorism, unauthorized
migration—effective responses by governments require a broad range of measures, of which border control is only one part, and often a small one. Border
agents regularly interdict shipments of heroin, fentanyl, cocaine, and other
harmful drugs, but there are no examples of where such border seizures have
made an appreciable difference in the absence of domestic measures to reduce
demand for such drugs.[38] The United States and Europe have at times been
able to reduce unauthorized migration through deterrent measures at their
borders, but these have rarely lasted long and rely on harsh and often violent
means that endanger vulnerable migrant populations. More effective and du-
rable approaches require cooperation with neighboring states, aid to sending
countries, and greater opportunities for legal migration.[39] Border screening has
identified and thwarted terrorist and criminal threats, but border measures are
only a small part of a broader array of necessary actions including intelligence
gathering and sharing, domestic and international law enforcement, and diplomacy.[40] Heavy-handed and discriminatory border restrictions such as the

George W. Bush administration's National Security Entry Exit-Registration System (NSEERS) for Muslims or Trump's "Muslim ban" were political stunts that did not bolster counter-terrorism capabilities and harmed thousands of innocent individuals.[41] The same holds true for pandemics—except for a few island nations, and even here there are limitations, border controls will offer at best modest benefits in the absence of effective domestic public health strategies. Indeed, without effective public health measures, governments are more likely to resort to travel restrictions in response to public demands for action.[42]

Governments need to develop the capabilities to manage risks in all these dimensions. Sensible risk-management can reduce the need to resort to blunt instruments like border closures, but only if governments invest in developing the needed capabilities. Such efforts should be a priority because governments continue to encourage cross-border mobility without warning migrants and travelers of the risks they are assuming in building their lives across borders. Countries are competing aggressively for migrants, for foreign students, for remote workers, and for tourists, making an implicit promise that those individuals who play by the rules will enjoy something close to the protections they offer their own citizens. But Covid showed the hollowness of that promise. If governments are not working actively to do better in the next crisis, then those leaving their own countries at least need to clearly understand the risks they are taking.

Can Governments Cooperate on International Mobility?

Control over who and under what conditions people are permitted to cross borders has been called "the last major redoubt of unfettered national sovereignty."[43] The experience of the past several decades has only reinforced that observation. Digital technologies have enabled much closer tracking and scrutiny of migrants and travelers. Governments have built more physical barriers at their borders than ever before in history. The number of border walls has grown from fewer than ten in the 1950s to more than seventy-five today; their total span may be over 20,000 miles, though no one is quite sure.[44] Recent additions apart from China's southern wall include a 124-mile 10-foot fence with barbed wire on the border between Finland and Russia to "slow down illegal entry," and new fencing along the Lithuanian and Polish borders with Belarus after the government of Aleksandr Lukashenko in 2021 pushed asylum seekers across its border to Europe in retaliation for European sanctions.[45] Governments have become more assertive in expanding their capacities to control their borders, a trend that was greatly accelerated by the pandemic.

Against this, international efforts to build better rules to protect international mobility and migration have made scant progress. In 1990, for example, the United Nations General Assembly adopted the International Convention on the Protection of the Rights of All Migrant Workers and Members of Their Families (CMW), a historic achievement in extending basic human and civil rights to migrant workers. But fewer than seventy countries have ratified the agreement, and not a single large immigrant-receiving country.[46] Recently, many more nations—some 164 in total—adopted the Global Compact for Safe, Orderly, and Regular Migration, which spells out a limited set of non-binding obligations for governments in managing migration flows. The goal was to encourage countries to address problems arising from the chaotic mass movement of people; it urged signatory countries to "optimize the overall benefits of migration, while addressing risks and challenges for individuals and communities in countries of origin, transit and destination. No country can address the challenges and opportunities of this global phenomenon on its own."[47] Recommendations included strengthening data on migration, ensuring adequate documentation for migrants, combating trafficking and smuggling, and managing borders "in an integrated, secure and coordinated manner." But the compact explicitly reaffirmed "the sovereign right of States to determine their national migration policy."

Even at that, it managed to become controversial—the Trump administration walked away from the negotiations in 2017, and then in 2018 issued a blistering statement denouncing the compact: "[D]ecisions about how to secure its borders, and whom to admit for legal residency or to grant citizenship, are among the most important sovereign decisions a State can make, and are not subject to negotiation, or review, in international instruments, or fora."[48] Hungary withdrew from the compact, followed by several other Eastern European countries, as well as Austria, Israel, the Dominican Republic, Chile, and Brazil following the election of President Jair Bolsonaro.[49] The Biden administration partially reversed course, announcing in 2021 that it "endorsed the vision" of the agreement, while Brazil formally rejoined the pact in 2023 following the election of President Luiz Inácio Lula da Silva.[50]

In the public health sphere, it is also difficult to hold out hope for greater international cooperation. The 2005 International Health Regulations were explicitly intended to constrain government actions during global health crises, when international cooperation is most likely to break down. But the agreements failed egregiously; as David Fidler has put it, Covid was "devastating for global health governance."[51] Jeffrey Sachs, the Columbia University economist who chaired *The Lancet* COVID-19 Commission, said that "what we saw, rather than a cooperative global strategy, was basically each country on its own."[52] Members of the World Health Organization nonetheless optimistically reconvened in the wake of the pandemic to attempt to rewrite the regulations to take into account the lessons of Covid. Parallel negotiations were also launched on a separate overarching pandemic treaty spurred by "recognition of the catastrophic failure of the international community in showing solidarity and equity in response to the coronavirus disease."[53]

There seems little prospect for a significant strengthening of provisions to curtail travel restrictions through either venue. The 2005 IHR were negotiated at an especially propitious time of American geopolitical dominance, when US-China cooperation was far stronger than it is today, and when there was something close to an international consensus on the benefits of globalization. None of these is true today. Even if some new understandings can be reached, it is optimistic to predict that countries will comply in a future pandemic, which may well present conditions quite different from Covid. As Fidler puts it: "Claims that noncompliance with the IHR—the treaty most relevant to disease outbreaks—requires a pandemic treaty do not explain why a new treaty will generate the commitment that the IHR apparently did not." He argues that the "nationalism and populism [that] flared during the pandemic, damaged domestic and international responses, and have not dissipated."

Cooperation at the regional level may prove more fruitful. On border and travel restrictions, regional cooperation—like the mechanisms set up in North America following the 9/11 attacks—have made greater progress than global efforts. The United States and Canada, for example, pursued an integrated approach to data sharing and joint screening of arriving travelers. Importantly, the bilateral programs they developed are based on a shared—and agreed-upon—approach to risk management. Simple examples include the trusted trader and trusted traveler programs (known respectively as FAST and NEXUS), which incorporated the security concerns of both countries alongside a more efficient and streamlined process for the movement of people and goods.[54] During

Covid, under the framework of the North American Plan for Animal and Pandemic Influenza, the United States and Canada had the platforms, and the potential, to implement a joint approach to health screening that would have enabled greater cross-border mobility while still protecting public health.[55] They failed to use them.

But there is still potential for regional cooperation to bring innovation to the border, rather than stagnation. There are hopeful indicators of a renewed strategy of regional cooperation in North America. Recent meetings of the North American Leaders Summit have focused on discussions of building pandemic preparedness across these shared borders. This includes revising the North American Plan for Animal and Pandemic Influenza based on lessons learned from Covid.[56] However, it is not yet clear what lessons about border restrictions will be considered. At the very least, the United States and Canada should take the lessons learned—both in the aftermath of 9/11 and during Covid—to revive a bilateral approach to border management. Covid has shown us the costs of failing to do so.

In Europe, efforts at regional cooperation on border policy during the pandemic yielded positive, albeit geographically limited, benefits. The EU Digital Covid Certificate, launched in July 2021, provided a digital record of vaccinations, negative tests, and recoveries. It was adopted by all twenty-seven member states. "With more than two billion certificates issued, the EU Digital Covid Certificate has delivered tangible benefits for EU citizens," the EU Commission stated. "It has facilitated free movement when travel restrictions were still deemed necessary, and, at the same time, it has allowed for a coordinated lifting of these restrictions once possible."[57] The digital certificate, along with the traffic light map of regional infection rates, and the green lane border crossing system for freight, were beneficial at facilitating movement and creating metrics all EU countries could use to assess risk. While the lack of global coordination over digital health credentials during Covid inhibited interoperability on a larger scale, the benefits of regional cooperation could be spread to broader global networks.[58] The EU Digital Covid Certificate, for example, was eventually adopted by forty-nine countries and territories outside of the EU, making it a de facto global standard. And in July 2023, the WHO partnered with the European Commission to use the digital Covid certification to establish a global system that can be used during ongoing and future public health threats.[59]

The collapse of global health cooperation during Covid was so complete that rebuilding it will be an enormous challenge. Those whose lives were upended by the Covid border restrictions should keep pressure on governments to do better in future crises. The pandemic was a vast learning opportunity for governments, and they should take the opportunity—as the UK has been doing, for example, with its Covid-19 Inquiry or New Zealand is attempting through its Royal Commission—to assess what worked and what didn't in the "go it alone" approach.[60]

The Use and Misuse of Emergency Powers: A Call for Constraints for the Border

In democracies, emergency powers are vital during a crisis; the normal processes of government are often too slow and deliberative in the face of urgent threats, especially one as fast-moving as a pandemic. And governments were not hesitant to use them during Covid—some 112 countries declared emergencies.[61] Emergency powers can have broad utility, including freeing up funds for urgent problems that might otherwise be slow in coming through ordinary democratic decision-making. They can also permit governments to exercise powers that would be restricted in the absence of a declared emergency, such as enhanced surveillance of citizens, censorship of misinformation, and restrictions on movement.

But emergency declarations are not supposed to confer unlimited power on the executive branch of government. The United Nations High Commissioner for Human Rights has laid out parameters for their use. In the face of genuine emergencies that "threaten the life of the nation"—a reasonable judgment in the early days of the pandemic at least—governments can suspend individual rights, but they should do so in the least intrusive way possible. The enhanced authority should be proportional to the threat, limited in scope, temporary, and non-discriminatory.[62] Much of this is already codified in democratic systems, where emergency powers are authorized by the legislature, and most countries have built in constraints on how presidents or prime ministers can exercise that authority. The broadest survey to date of the use of emergency powers during the pandemic suggests that these constraints were reasonably effective—outside of authoritarian states or weak democracies like Hungary, legislatures and courts provided reasonably effective oversight on lockdowns, domestic mobility restrictions, and other measures taken by governments.[63]

The biggest exception to this restraint was borders, where emergency declarations fused with what Elizabeth Goitein has called "pseudo-emergency" powers—the essentially unlimited authority of national leaders to decide who and what can cross their borders. In the United States, she argues, President Trump took "full advantage of COVID-19 to deliver on longstanding promises to dramatically reduce the flow of lawful immigrants to the United States."[64] US statutes contain multiple provisions that permit the executive to close borders, without relying on emergency powers, or on explicit approval by the legislature. In the United States, Section 212(f) of the Immigration and Nationality Act clearly spells out the president's authority to "impose on the entry of aliens any restrictions he may deem to be appropriate." With the partial exception of the post-9/11 period, such powers have been used narrowly by presidents, to block individuals thought to pose a national security threat. The Department of Homeland Security further has explicit powers to close ports of entry "when necessary to respond to a national emergency" or "to respond to a specific threat to human life or national interests." Those were the authorities used to close the borders with Canada and Mexico during Covid.[65] Goitein argues that "there is ample evidence that at least some of these measures were driven by xenophobia and the prospect of political gain, rather than considerations of how best to address emergency conditions. In that sense, they should be viewed as an abuse of emergency powers."[66]

Other countries used different mechanisms. Australia's Biosecurity Act, the basis for the country's travel restrictions, was used to restrict both entry and exit of citizens. New Zealand rationed entry using authorities under its 1956 Health Act and the Covid-19 Public Health Response Act, which was quickly passed by the Parliament in May 2020.[67] In Canada, the border closures were authorized by the Public Health Agency of Canada (PHAC), set up in 2004 following the SARS outbreak. But unlike domestic restrictions—where courts sometimes struck down limitations on internal mobility, religious gatherings, and business openings—most courts refused to second-guess executive authorities on border closures. With rare exceptions, as discussed in more detail in Chapter 3, courts across the world declined to intervene to limit border or travel restrictions.

Curtailing such authorities is likely to be an uphill struggle. The global trend has been for legislatures to give executives greater authority to regulate borders.

In the United States, the Supreme Court has narrowed the ability of citizens to challenge the actions of officers at the border; non-citizens have long had little legal recourse in US courts.[68] Some would object that legislatures and courts cannot of course be expected to take actions that protect the interests of non-citizens. But if the pandemic proved anything, it was that citizens who have built their lives across borders can be deeply harmed if they are separated from family, work, medical care, schooling, and other necessities. Measures that arbitrarily exclude non-citizens can cause great harm to citizens. People who have built cross-border lives that were upended by the Covid closures should be able to expect some reasonable limitations on those authorities, either through legislative oversight or through reconsideration by the courts of their limited role.

Legislatures could, for example, authorize a greater role for the courts and for legislative bodies—with appropriate carve-outs for national security emergencies—in reviewing whether border restrictions are proportional to the threat, and implemented in a non-discriminatory way. They could require greater reporting and transparency by governments when extending such authorities, as opposed to the open-ended border closures imposed by so many countries during Covid. Legislatures could try to curb serious abuses, such as Trump's emergency declaration in 2019 permitting him to divert Pentagon money to construct the Mexican border wall after Congress refused to appropriate the funds.[69] The last serious effort by the US Congress to restrain federal emergency powers was in 1976, and that effort was partially struck down by the courts. Congress has never voted to terminate a presidential emergency declaration.[70] Ginsburg and Versteeg point out that in many nations, emergency authorities are drawn up with national security crises in mind, where it may not be prudent to allow a full public airing of the reasons for emergency actions.[71] The expansive nature of executive power at the borders similarly reflects a national security mindset in which only executive authorities are deemed competent to make judgments on risk. But with exceptions like imminent military invasion or terrorist infiltration, most border control issues are not matters of national security—they concern problems like documentation, drugs, disease, asylum seekers, and the movement of unauthorized migrants. Actions in those areas should be open to greater scrutiny and oversight by legislatures and courts.

Courts could also be more active in their oversight of existing laws. In several countries during the pandemic, court decisions suggest a way the judiciary could play a constructive oversight role. In an April 2021 decision, for example, a French administrative court ordered the suspension of border restrictions in the case of cross-border couples who wished to marry. The decision closely followed the proportionality tests laid out by the United Nations and the WHO. The plaintiffs argued that freedom of marriage is a fundamental freedom, and opening the doors for engaged couples would result in at most a few thousand entries per year. The health risks of such additional travel could be contained by "effective measures that are less detrimental to freedoms," they argued. The court agreed, finding that government travel restrictions should be "strictly proportionate to the health risks linked to the entry into France."[72] In March 2021, the Supreme Court of Israel struck down a government measure—implemented to stem the spread of new Covid variants—which limited new arrivals to 3,000 people per day, and restricted the exit of citizens who were not vaccinated or recovered from Covid. The court ruled that freedom of entry and exit was a fundamental right for Israeli citizens and, given the likelihood that Covid would linger for many years, "a balance must be struck between the damage that may be caused by the intrusion of an unknown strain of the virus and the violation of the basic rights of citizens." The restrictions, the court ruled, "do not pass the test of the least harmful means."[73]

Scholars have argued that such stricter scrutiny standards should be extended to examining certain sorts of mobility restrictions. In his book on the US "no fly" lists—which has barred even some American citizens from returning home—Jeffrey Kahn argues for a standard that would only permit such measures "by the least restrictive means necessary to achieve a compelling government purpose."[74] Victoria Ochoa has similarly argued that courts should use strict scrutiny in assessing state actions that infringe on fundamental rights. During the pandemic, for example, governors in Texas and Arizona "declared state emergencies to circumvent federal law on immigration and border security," matters that were in no direct way related to disease control. It is perfectly appropriate for courts to defer to public health experts, she argues, but only in the context of "assessing whether the government's interest is compelling and whether its actions are narrowly tailored to advancing that interest."[75]

US courts were not wholly immune to these considerations during Covid. The restriction most thoroughly vetted by the courts was Title 42, the law used to discourage crossings between the ports of entry from Mexico and Canada—a measure whose practical impact was to block many asylum seekers from their legal right to seek protection in the United States. The Supreme Court repeatedly declined to force the government to end or modify the restrictions, and for a time even backed Republican-led states that were fighting to prevent the Biden administration from lifting the provision. But in a blistering statement in May 2023, Justice Neil Gorsuch wrote that "the current border crisis is not a Covid crisis," and "the Court took a serious misstep when it effectively allowed nonparties to this case to manipulate our docket to prolong an emergency decree designed for one crisis in order to address an entirely different one." He went on to issue a stronger warning: "Make no mistake—decisive executive action is sometimes necessary and appropriate. But if emergency decrees promise to solve some problems, they threaten to generate others. And rule by indefinite emergency edict risks leaving all of us with a shell of a democracy and civil liberties just as hollow."[76]

Some reasonable limitations on emergency authorities at the border would help to close the yawning gap between domestic and international laws. Border closures are the area where domestic US actions during the pandemic were most egregiously at odds with international law—not just the scale and duration of the border closures, but also the absence of reasonable proportionality tests and the stark violation of international commitments such as the rights of asylum seekers.[77] Clearer direction from lawmakers and stricter scrutiny by courts is vital for closing that gap.

Managing Risk for Everyone

When Covid began to spread, governments around the world used border closures in an attempt to slow the spread of a novel virus whose dangers were still largely unknown. Despite WHO advice to the contrary, most of these measures were prudent given the circumstances in the early days of the pandemic. In the face of uncertainty, following the "precautionary principle" of taking preventive action with incomplete scientific knowledge can be viewed as a justifiable response by governments. This is not to say that a precautionary approach addresses many of the tough questions about how governments should respond in a crisis, but the principle of acting to forestall harm in the face of uncertainty makes particular sense for new diseases, which can quickly spiral out of control.[78] Beyond the early stages of the pandemic, however, travel restrictions made far less sense. Community spread in most countries meant that border measures brought little additional benefit in disease control at high economic and human costs, and too frequently became an excuse for governments to avoid more effective domestic mitigation measures. The rollout of vaccinations and widespread testing in 2021, while far from perfect in reducing the spread of Covid, allowed for more nuanced restrictions based on the risks posed by individual travelers. Yet many countries did not adjust their restrictions even as the risks changed and scientific knowledge on the spread and mitigation of Covid improved.

By late 2021, many countries had begun taking steps to reopen their borders to vaccinated travelers. But a survey of fifty travel markets, accounting for 92% of global traffic, revealed a messy and complex mishmash of travel rules. The International Air Transport Association (IATA), which conducted the survey, urged governments to implement simplified regimes to manage risks associated with Covid as international travel resumed. "Travel restrictions are a complex and confusing web of rules with very little consistency among them," said IATA's Director General Willie Walsh. "There is little evidence to support ongoing border restrictions and the economic havoc they create."[79] Other industry groups highlighted the fact that cross-border travel was still treated as high risk even as many domestic health precautions were lifted.[80] Too many countries maintained their early restrictions largely unmodified because it was easier—and more politically popular—than developing more refined strategies. A "wait and see" approach predominated, despite the enormous costs to those separated by the border restrictions.

The border management challenge during Covid was not unlike what the United States encountered following the 9/11 terrorist attacks. In the face of a novel—for the United States—threat of large-scale terrorist attacks on its territory, the initial response of the US government was similarly precautionary. It briefly shut its airspace and heavily restricted its land borders. Those measures were then followed up with crude and discriminatory restrictions—including travel bans and intrusive border screening—aimed largely at nationals of Muslim-majority countries that were deemed to pose the greatest threat. Gradually, however, such blanket measures were replaced with intelligence-driven targeting of individuals that expanded the options available to policymakers and enabled borders to be employed more as a sieve than as a shield.[81] What was originally perceived as a dichotomy between security and mobility eventually evolved into a risk management approach that has so far been successful at preventing similar attacks. In developing these approaches, Alan Bersin, who led international issues for the Department of Homeland

Security during the Obama administration, often used the analogy of looking for a needle in a haystack. Without having specific intelligence about where the threat is, "the only other way to find the needle in the haystack is to make the haystack smaller," he wrote. "And the only way to make the stack smaller is to differentiate routinely between high- and low-risk subjects."[82] The success of this risk management strategy depended largely on information sharing, strong international partnerships, and cooperation with the public and businesses.[83]

Covid presented similar challenges. In the early stages, the threat was broad and ill-defined; country-based travel restrictions were a crude tool, but for many countries the best option available. But after the initial stages, different nations varied widely in the degree to which they refined these initial approaches. Some opened travel based on specific vaccination and testing requirements, or reduced quarantine times to reflect new scientific evidence; others did not. In a review of countries that developed specific risk management criteria, a team of experts studying pandemics and borders found starkly different assessments of risk as the pandemic progressed.[84] For the first two and half years, for example, Hong Kong and New Zealand treated almost all non-nationals and non-residents as potentially high risk, regardless of their vaccination status or the extent of Covid infections in their countries. Others such as the EU treated vaccinated travelers, or those who recovered from a previous infection, as lower risk. There was also little consistency or predictability to the ways in which countries assessed risk. The lack of a clear and agreed-upon framework for risk analysis "contributed to highly varied, frequently changing, and poorly coordinated use of travel measures across jurisdictions, creating chaos for travelers," wrote the Pandemics and Borders Project research group.[85]

As with "precaution," there is no widely accepted definition of "risk management." For terrorism risk, the three foundational components are threat, vulnerability, and consequences. The threat represents the likelihood of an adverse event occurring, vulnerability refers to how prepared countries are to avoid serious damage, and consequences are the scale of the damage that could potentially occur.[86] All three are relevant for pandemic travel risks as well. During Covid, the threat was universal, though there was significant uncertainty and disagreement over its severity; vulnerability varied with the strength of national health systems, public trust, and pre-pandemic preparedness; and the consequences also varied enormously depending both on innate characteristics like the age of the population and variable ones like social distancing, masking, and access to treatment. Countries with stronger public health systems and contact tracing capabilities—South Korea was a standout example—were able largely to avoid domestic lockdowns and border closures, confident that outbreaks of the disease could be contained successfully. The Organization for Economic Cooperation and Development has laid out five criteria for travel risk assessments: local health conditions, volumes of travel, hospital capacity, effectiveness of public health interventions, and economic impacts. The OECD also encourages countries to respect both human rights and the impacts on vulnerable travelers such as refugees and seasonal workers.[87]

None of these approaches provides any definitive answers to appropriate levels of risk. Countries reached different conclusions about the risks they were prepared to run. In Europe and North America, maintaining robust flows of trade goods was deemed vital, so truckers and airline crews were largely exempted from quarantine and other restrictions. In contrast, China imposed strict restrictions on transportation workers in pursuit of its zero-Covid policy. But a defined risk management strategy at least identifies what level of risk governments are willing to accept, as well as the trade-offs that have been considered regarding cross-border travel. Such an approach was lacking in most countries during the pandemic, where travel was either considered "essential" or "non-essential" and nuanced distinctions were rare. This was exacerbated by the fact that the definitions of what governments and border agencies deemed essential or non-essential were inconsistent and often opaque. Within the EU, each country decided independently what type of travel was considered essential.[88] In the United States, such decisions were left up to the border officers, which resulted in subjective interpretations that varied widely. Such blunt and ill-defined approaches had huge costs, and there was often little effort made to support public understanding of the rationale behind those measures, which felt arbitrary and unfair to many forced to navigate them. The result, in many cases, was an erosion of public trust in government.[89]

Many governments also failed to communicate clearly the rationale for their travel measures and their decisions to maintain them. For many, the choice to use the blunt instrument of border restrictions and closures—and keep them in place even after community spread of the virus was widespread—had more to do with politics than with public health. In a review of the epidemiological and legal contexts for global border closures, researchers Hoffman, Weldon, and Habibi argue that "border closures represent an opportunity for political leaders to garner domestic support by complying with public opinion, delaying or avoiding scrutiny on underfunded public health systems, appearing thorough, diverting blame, and becoming champions of national security."[90] Such was the case in the United States, where "experts both outside and inside of the government knew that the system, from top to bottom, was unready for a pandemic."[91]

Covid has shown us that countries worldwide will employ border controls in the face of uncertainty, and that such actions are often politicized, with justifications framed in security terms. A publicly articulated risk management approach would at the least bring some greater transparency and accountability to those affected. Governments should be expected to assess continuously the impacts of their policy choices and communicate them effectively to the public. During times of crisis, governments owe it to the public to be transparent about their policymaking. This not only facilitates trust and compliance, but also helps to alleviate the anxiety and confusion that ensues during a crisis. "To strengthen future pandemic prevention, preparedness, response, and recovery," wrote the Pandemics and Borders Project team, "there is a need for improved transparency that enables the evaluation of decision-making processes."[92]

A Mobilized Population

As the number of people traversing borders grows, so do the prospects for disruptions. Whether in response to pandemics, terrorism, climate change, or state violence, the world has been moving toward increasingly restrictive borders as a way to deal with threats from abroad.[93] Protecting the well-being of those who live across borders is going to require sustained engagement by those whose lives were upended during Covid and those who will be vulnerable in a future crisis. Governments are unlikely to move toward greater international cooperation, more constrained emergency behavior, or more transparent risk management in the absence of steady pressure. And for the first time they face a mobilized community. "I think there are enough people who were affected that they will continue reminding the people working on this how important it is," said a former government official from Sweden.[94] This includes people like David Poon, who initiated the Faces of Advocacy group and ran for office "to make sure we are finally heard."[95] And Tudor Clee in New Zealand, who found new ways to speak up and fight for cross-border communities. They amplified the concerns not just of their communities but of millions of people around the world whose interests would otherwise have been ignored by governments during the pandemic.

Some of these voices were heard in Europe, where there is now a stronger push for carving out border regions as specific places that require a unique policy focus.[96] In response to the vocal outcries of citizens, regional governments, and businesses during the pandemic, revisions to the Schengen Borders Code aim to explicitly protect cross-border regions from future border disruptions by providing updated safeguards against the reintroduction of internal controls. If governments violate these codes, there will be more scrutiny and accountability. In Europe, advocates for more stable and predictable cross-border mobility say they "witness a real learning process."[97] And it is not just individuals or advocacy groups; there are also strong industry-led coalitions and organizations that came together during Covid, deepening awareness about the cross-border economic linkages across regions. In North America, a group called the Future Borders Coalition developed an ongoing bilateral dialogue between industry and government that continues to this day and advocates for "building a better U.S.-Canada border for travel and trade."[98] A "better border" for travel and trade demands more predictability and accountability alongside recognition by central governments of the significance of cross-border linkages—the same assurances that those harmed by the border restrictions are demanding.

At the US-Mexico border, where there is a long history of civic and political engagement on cross-border mobility that has developed for decades, during the pandemic, "local, state, and federal governments on both sides of the border overlooked the binational border region in favor of their own defined jurisdictions," wrote Paul Ganster in an assessment of the regional experience in CaliBaja during the pandemic. "Effective transborder response instead came from the non-profit, civil society, and private sectors."[99] These entities coordinated information sharing and organized donations of medical supplies and food, which helped to buffer against some of the impacts of the border restrictions on an otherwise highly interdependent cross-border community. These networks can provide a mechanism for those who depend on the border—be they individuals, companies, or communities—to "promote specific priorities with a consensus voice in federal legislation."[100]

A similar response played out at the regional scale between Canada and the United States. An emergency response group initiated by a border community in Washington State provided a key mechanism for ongoing dialogue and relationships across the border with British Columbia. The group, composed of local government officials, health authorities, and border agencies, was hastily formed in March 2020 and met consistently until the majority of restrictions were eased. This network provided a conduit between those impacted by the border restrictions and federal entities located far away in the capital cities, pushing for some exemptions and accommodations, for example, for those isolated in Point Roberts. Those ongoing conversations also kept border communities educated and updated on the state of the border—something both federal governments failed to do.

These common platforms for advocacy, advanced by those most harmed by border restrictions, are examples of the importance of ground-up action to pressure governments to make better decisions on the border. Such progress is likely to be slow and incremental. The recognition that those living across borders deserve protections for their way of life—much less the rights enjoyed by citizens—is a new development that was accelerated by the pandemic.

Conclusion

With the Covid pandemic squarely in the rearview mirror, many of us have attempted to look back and try to grasp what really happened during the whirlwind years when the world closed its doors. Our kids grew, our friends (and ourselves) aged, but time also collapsed and felt warped. It has been difficult to fully reflect on those years. The members of the Covid Crisis Group referred to this as "reflection deficit disorder." Their solution was to write a book that offers a "sketch of the whole picture, our sense of how we think the pieces fit together." They go on to say, "we think you, like us, want to get past the enormous jumble of information and make some sense of it all. What just happened to us, and why? How could we do better?"[101] In a similar vein, this book is an attempt to knit together the story of border closures and travel restrictions during the last global pandemic, and the ways those policy choices impacted millions of people around the world. Few governments are doing this type of post mortem. More important, by tracing why governments choose to use those policy tools, and pointing to alternatives, we hope to shape conversations that will inform better decisions in the future. Those conversations may echo in the halls of government buildings far from borderland communities but will be driven by the passion of people leading cross-border lives.

Unfortunately, border restrictions are spreading, even as more people now cross borders than ever before. This growing inconsistency—acutely accelerated by Covid—is our call to action to mobilize for cross-border rights. As the stories throughout this book demonstrate, those whose livelihoods and relationships depend on cross-border mobility face an unpredictable landscape. The different country case studies presented here also illustrate a disturbing tendency by governments—in liberal democratic societies with advanced border management regimes—to use borders to curtail individual rights and freedoms. This should concern even those whose lives are less impacted by cross-border mobility, yet whose rights may be equally impacted.

This disturbing trend may also give rise to an alliance between those who have long enjoyed more freedom of mobility and those, like asylum seekers, who attempt to cross borders out of desperation and face continued barriers and uncertainty. As the desire and need for cross-border mobility grows on a global scale, we are witnessing a confluence of demands for stronger safeguards around humanitarian concerns, economic necessity, and social connection. Our digitally globalized world offers a connected platform for engagement that can work to build such alliances.

The stories we carry forward from an unprecedented time of collective disruption will help to inform how we approach the future of borders, not just when the next pandemic arrives, but in other times of crisis when national security is invoked. "In the throes of it, you deal with it and you promise you are going to learn the lessons," said the Woodrow Wilson Center's Andrew Rudman. "But you get through the crisis and you are relieved and you move on."[102] Many have moved on. But many of us still live with the Covid tragedy. Those appalled by the situation faced by Donna McCall's family—who had no other choice but to say their last goodbyes online—have an opportunity to hold their governments accountable, to insist they do better the next time around. Governments certainly can and will close borders again during future crises, but they now face a far more engaged, determined, and passionate community that will not stay quiet.

Epilogue
The Next Pandemic

When Covid began spreading around the world, Dr. Martin S. Cetron—"Marty" to his colleagues and friends—had been the director of Global Migration and Quarantine at the Atlanta-based Centers for Disease Control and Prevention (CDC) for nearly a quarter century. His job was to lead teams of scientists and public health experts tasked with preventing the international spread of contagious diseases, and in particular to keep those diseases out of the United States. Part of that job was to draft and sign orders on whether and how to restrict travel, or even shut US borders, in the event of disease outbreaks overseas that could threaten the United States. While he had faced multiple crises, including the global spread of the deadly Ebola virus in 2014, he had never before invoked the full authority of his position to block foreign arrivals.

In March 2020 a memo arrived on his desk demanding he do just that. It did not come from the CDC's scientists or health experts; it came from the White House, routed through lawyers at the Department of Health and Human Services that houses the CDC. President Donald Trump had already acted on his own to bar travel from China and later from Europe, using the president's discretionary authority under Section 212 of the Immigration and Naturalization Act to stop the entry of foreign aliens deemed a security threat—the same authority he used for his "Muslim ban."[1] But this one needed the signature of someone at the CDC—it was an order under Title 42 of the Code of Federal Regulation that allowed the CDC to prohibit the entry of foreigners into the country if they are deemed a risk of spreading a communicable disease.[2] The order was narrowly targeted—empowering the Department of Homeland Security to turn back anyone crossing from Mexico or Canada who might be detained at the border because they lacked documents permitting entry into the United States; the likelihood that such crossers would be detained in "congregate settings" such as Border Patrol holding facilities made them a special risk, it said.[3]

The order, Cetron would later tell the House Select Subcommittee on the Coronavirus, "was not drafted by me or my team"; it was "handed to us." Its purpose was not a mystery—the Trump White House was looking for any tool available to slow the number of asylum seekers arriving at the southern border, a top campaign promise made by the president. In the days prior, Cetron told congressional investigators he had participated in several calls about Title 42 that included White House Senior Advisor Stephen Miller, Trump's hawkish advisor on immigration who had been pushing to use every available authority to shut the border with Mexico.[4] In a call with officials on March 17, Miller had warned that "the Southern Border is in crisis and will get worse as COVID-19 spreads in Mexico," according to an email from a deputy general counsel at Health and Human Services.[5] The next day the proposed order arrived on Cetron's desk.

Cetron wasn't the only CDC official who objected to the White House interference. Dr. Anne Schuchat, the principal deputy director of the CDC, told the subcommittee that triggering Title 42 made little sense. "There was a lot more disease in the U.S. than south of the border," she said. "The focus on reducing spread on our side of the border was critically needed."[6] Cetron added that, whatever the merits of the initial travel restrictions on China, with cases spreading widely in the United States by March the border measures would cause more harm than good. "It's one thing to use a travel ban in January with a single focus of infection," he said, but "[t]he continuation of the use of travel bans as a tool once there's widespread infection in the U.S. starts to become diminished." He said that "overreliance on border measures alone" had detracted from more needed steps like "testing, isolation, quarantine, cohorting, mask use, all of that other stuff" that "could mitigate the impact, alleviate the strain on health care systems," and "save lives."[7] Confronted with the White House demands, Cetron would later say that invoking Title 42 "was not justified based on the science. They were targeting the southern border and the population that was crossing."[8] So he did something he had never done in his decades of public service—he refused to sign the order.

The White House kicked it up to Cetron's boss, Trump-appointee Robert Redfield, who was director of the CDC. Vice President Mike Pence and Acting Homeland Security Secretary Chad Wolf called Redfield demanding that the order be approved. "They forced us," a former health official involved in the process told the Associated Press. "It is either do it or get fired."[9] Redfield authorized the border closure on March 20, 2020.

One of the many reasons that border and travel measures during Covid were handled in such a ham-handed fashion in much of the world—and nowhere more so than in the United States—was the conflict between experts and their political masters. It was not that the experts had all the answers—so little was known about Covid that much of the pre-pandemic response planning was thrown out the window and new approaches needed to be improvised. But in the countries that responded better, there was constant communication between scientists, doctors, and political leaders—the politicians deferring to experts in following the best science available, while making decisions about competing priorities in the face of enormously difficult trade-offs. That cooperation also made it easier to tell a consistent story to the public on why such measures were necessary. In the United States, a diminished scientific community—the CDC and other health agencies had faced years of budget constraints—faced off against political leaders who were distrustful of science and expertise. The result was a dangerously incompetent response to the most serious health threat the United States had experienced in generations.

The Education of Marty Cetron

Cetron should have been the official at or near the center of every decision on US travel restrictions during Covid. He had spent his whole career preparing for such an event. He wanted to be a doctor from a young age, attending Dartmouth College in New Hampshire and then medical school at Tufts University in Boston, focusing on international infectious diseases. He spent a good part of his fourth year in medical school in the south of India working on leprosy and other tropical diseases, and later lived and worked in Brazil. Early in his career he trained at the University of Washington in Seattle, working in clinics that were identifying and treating infectious diseases among returning travelers, recent migrants, and refugees. Impressed by the expertise of CDC officials working on the same issues, he joined the agency in June 1992 as part of the division of parasitic disease. He would play a key role in creating the Binational Border Infectious Disease Surveillance (BIDS) system that worked with local and state public health officials along the border zone with Mexico to monitor disease outbreaks.[10]

Then in 1996, he was asked to help rebuild what was then known as the Foreign Quarantine Service, an agency set up by the US government in 1878 with the task of keeping out imported infectious diseases. It had been more or less dismantled in the late 1960s as the eradication of smallpox, mass vaccinations, and other medical triumphs had appeared to all but eliminate the risk of future pandemics. But the world was changing. By the 1990s, he said, "the movement of people, animals and things was fundamentally different in every way" compared to just several decades before. Modern air travel meant that "people and pathogens could move around the globe shorter than the incubation period of most of those threats." That had undermined the classic notion behind quarantine, which was that seagoing vessels with infected crew or passengers aboard could be held offshore until the threats burned out. The new entity was renamed the Division of Global Migration and Quarantine, and it quickly began trying to assemble the data needed to monitor the new vectors of disease—air travel, border crossings, rail and cargo movement, and shipping records. While the United States was less likely than Africa or Southeast Asia to incubate new diseases, he said, "because we are so highly connected, maybe the most globally connected on the planet, we would likely be the next place it would be seen."[11]

In the coming years, Cetron would be on the front lines of the US government's response to the outbreaks of SARS, MERS, Monkeypox, Ebola, and other contagious diseases. He would rewrite and overhaul decades-old rules for quarantine—how and under what circumstances foreign travelers could be held involuntarily if they were suspected of carrying an infectious disease. He was the senior US official negotiating revisions to the International Health Regulations, and a senior advisor to the WHO sitting on the emergency committee tasked with determining the severity of new threats. He would go on to write or coauthor nearly 300 scientific papers as well. Some of the most influential work was his research with Howard Markel, a medical historian, into efforts to contain the 1918 Spanish Flu. They discovered that cities that had closed schools and canceled public gatherings early in the outbreak suffered far lower death tolls than those that didn't.[12] The two are credited with developing the concept of "flattening the curve"—using social distancing, masking, and isolation to slow the spread of a disease and avoid overwhelming the healthcare system.[13]

Cetron's work had quickly become compelling to top officials in Washington as well. For those who were in the nation's capital in the aftermath of the 9/11 attacks, the threat of bioterrorism arrived on their doorsteps when packages containing the deadly anthrax bacteria were mailed to the offices of Democratic senators Tom Daschle and Patrick Leahy with notes warning: "You cannot stop us. We have this anthrax. Death to America. Death to Israel. Allah is great." Similar packages were mailed to five new organizations; seventeen people were sickened by the attacks and five would die.[14] The perpetrator, who was not identified for seven years, turned out to be a disgruntled former US Army scientist, not a foreign terrorist. But the delay was more than enough time for the risks of terrorists wielding deadly pathogens to be put squarely on the agenda of the newly formed Department of Homeland Security. Cetron would share the stage with Michael Chertoff, a prosecutor turned DHS secretary, who told a Stanford conference in 2008 that "I think for the first time we've begun to think very seriously and in a disciplined fashion about how to plan for dealing with a major natural pandemic or a major biological attack. I wish I could tell you these things are unthinkable. But the one thing I've learned in the last seven years is there's pretty much nothing that's unthinkable."[15]

Figure E.1 Dr. Martin Cetron, former director of the Division of Global Migration and Quarantine for the US Centers for Disease Control. Courtesy of Martin Cetron.

The preparation effort got another boost when President George W. Bush in 2005 read an advance copy of John Barry's history of the Spanish Flu and ordered the development of a pandemic response plan. "A pandemic is a lot like a forest fire," Bush said in a speech at the National Institutes of Health. "If caught early it might be extinguished with limited damage. If allowed to smolder, undetected, it can grow to an inferno that can spread quickly beyond our ability to control it."[16] The plan called for the US government to have the capacity to do both entry and exit screening of travelers at air, sea, and land borders. Vice President Dick Cheney's office had gone further, requesting a study on full closure of the borders to stop a pandemic; the study found that "to do that we would basically have to bring all of our overseas military home and stand them up around the border," said Bradley Dickerson, who was biodefense advisor at DHS from 2007 to 2018. So, the plan was focused instead on border screening rather than a full closure, with special attention to entry screening and quarantine facilities at the largest US airports. The land borders were deemed too difficult. "The goal was to slow the spread of the disease—we knew you couldn't stop it—while not inordinately affecting travel and trade," Dickerson said. Critically, the scenario planning showed that restrictions needed to be imposed very early during any outbreak. "If you don't do it early," he said, "you don't get any bang for your buck."[17]

The Ebola Success

Prior to Covid, the most unthinkable crisis to hit the United States was the arrival of Ebola, a terrifying disease that, before the development of a vaccine in 2019, killed many of its victims in ghastly fashion—diarrhea, vomiting, and uncontrolled bleeding. The largest outbreak in history began in December 2013 in the African nation of Guinea—likely spread by bats—and traveled quickly to its neighbors in Sierra Leone and Liberia.[18] The region has some of the world's most porous and heavily crossed borders.[19] Extended families live across the borders, and those who got sick would frequently travel seeking help and support from their families in neighboring countries. Within six months, the virus had spread to the capitals in all three countries, the first time Ebola had escaped into Africa's cities. In August 2014 the WHO declared a Public Health Emergency of International Concern, warning of the danger of global spread.[20]

The CDC and Cetron's team were involved early, even before the WHO declaration. "One of the things that needed to be done was to figure out a strategy for containing further international spread," he later said.[21] The biggest alarm bell came in July 2014, when Patrick Sawyer, a Liberian-American, was sent to Lagos, Nigeria, to attend a conference on behalf of Liberia's ministry of finance. He had been reported to the ministry of health a few days before for possible exposure to Ebola after taking care of an ill sister who later died from the affliction. But the Liberian government did not block him from traveling.[22] He collapsed on the tarmac in Lagos and was taken to hospital; his wife later said he had traveled to Nigeria hoping to get better medical care than was available in Liberia.[23] Lagos is a megacity of more than 20 million people, the largest in Africa, with flights to everywhere in the world. Luciana Borio, who held senior pandemic preparedness positions in the US government for two decades, said the outbreak in such a globally connected city was what finally persuaded the international community to take action.[24] Nineteen people in Nigeria would become infected with Ebola and eight would die, including the doctor who first treated Sawyer.

Cetron's CDC team worked with the African nations to put in place exit and entry screening systems at airports to block known cases like Sawyer, and to identify and halt other symptomatic travelers. It was an enormous challenge. "They hadn't trained, prepared or exercised for an event like that," he said. And understandably, preventing the export of the disease was not the highest priority for those countries in the midst of the crisis. "The beneficiary of that type of screening is the international community," he said. "And the international community has a responsibility to provide this global assistance where the capacity exists."[25] The goal was both to fight the outbreak at its source and to create "buffers" of containment to ensure that no infected individuals flew out of Africa to other continents. There was one thing Cetron did not order—screening of passengers arriving at airports in the United States. Given the enormous resources that would be consumed in setting up such a system, he would argue later, it was better to focus on the countries facing outbreaks and screen passengers in those countries before they boarded their flights.

Then in September 2014, Thomas Eric Duncan flew from Liberia to visit his family in Dallas. He had no known exposures during his time in West Africa, had no symptoms, and passed the exit screening test at the airport in Monrovia. But eight days later he died from Ebola in Texas Health Presbyterian Hospital, passing the infection to two nurses, one of whom had already flown to Cleveland for a wedding. The country flew into a panic. Middle school students in Mississippi were kept home because their principal had come back from a family funeral in Zambia, on the opposite side of the African continent. An elementary school teacher in Maine was put on three weeks leave after attending a conference in Dallas.[26] Half of the public said they would avoid flying internationally, and the same number said they would steer clear of anyone who had traveled to Africa recently, sending airline stocks tumbling.[27]

Republicans slammed the Obama administration for not imposing a full ban on travel from West Africa. Donald Trump, long before he had declared his 2016 presidential candidacy, tweeted that: "The U.S. must immediately stop all flights from EBOLA infected countries, or the plague will start and spread inside our borders."[28] Governors in New York and New Jersey imposed a twenty-one-day quarantine for all arrivals from West Africa after a doctor treating patients in Guinea had returned to New York City with the infection. Kaci Hickox, a volunteer nurse who had worked in an Ebola treatment facility in Sierra Leone, was forced into an isolation tent in Newark, New Jersey, despite showing no signs of infection, and ended up in a highly public confrontation with Republican governor Chris Christie. With the 2014 midterm elections looming, many members of Congress were calling for a complete shutdown of flights from West Africa; 75% of the public agreed.[29] Around the world, despite calls from the WHO and the United Nations to avoid travel bans, forty-three countries implemented entry bans for individuals coming from countries with "widespread Ebola virus transmission," including Australia and Canada.[30]

But President Obama did not heed calls to close the United States to West Africans. "There were tremendous political pressures on President Obama at the time of Ebola," recalled Borio, who was the acting chief scientist at the Food and Drug Administration at the time. "He had to make decisions about border closures around Ebola, and I knew that there was one option that was scientifically sound, and one that was more politically sensitive. We were all on pins and needles waiting to see which way the president would go. And he chose the scientifically sound option, even at a political cost."[31] That option was to set up arrival screening at key airports in the United States, something that had never been done on such a scale. "On the books it was supposed to take six weeks to build," Cetron said. "I was told I had six days." Cetron spent hours talking with the Customs and Border Protection officers staffing the airports, many of whom "were way outside their comfort zone." He would ask groups of CBP officers if they were fearful, and every hand would go up. He would try to reassure them that the likelihood of encountering a traveler infected with Ebola was minuscule and that "the fears were in excess of the reality of the risk." But then "every time a shift turned over and new people came in, we would have to do it all over again." In the end, the mission was a success; the US government would screen 350,000 travelers over the next six months at five US airports without another Ebola-infected passenger escaping the screening net.[32]

The Covid Failure

Covid-19, said Cetron, "was the most challenging virus I had ever seen on the planet. It exploited all of our weaknesses." It was "highly, highly transmissible," and capable of multiple mutations that often outran therapeutic responses. Omicron, he said, was "almost a completely different virus." Those carrying the disease were at their most infectious in the early stages, often before they had begun to display any symptoms. Many others never developed symptoms at all. This meant that people were traveling while contagious, unaware they could be infecting others. The usual airport screening tools that had worked well for Ebola—such as fever and symptom checks—were certain to miss many of those infected. "Normally our border strategy is based on finding cases at the border and sorting the infected from the uninfected," he said. "But this virus broke all those rules. . . . It was totally overwhelming in its ability to take us by surprise."[33]

When the first reports started coming out of China in late December 2019, Cetron was enjoying the holidays with his family in New Hampshire. "My phone was starting to blow up with messages . . . all of the network was heating up," he said. He cut his vacation short and headed back to CDC headquarters in Atlanta. "Having been in this space for a long time, it had all the bad red flags. This was not something to ignore." In the early days of January, before the Trump White House had fully engaged, Cetron led the rollout of travel screening, and it looked much like the Ebola measures, though with an added sense of urgency. The Bush-era plan called for setting up a risk-based screening system that required mapping the likely sources of infection and the transportation networks. The playbook should have included, as with Ebola, CDC teams and others from around the world rushing to China to help contain the outbreak, but China refused to extend those invitations. At home, the agency moved quickly to set up passenger screening—though in retrospect not as quickly as it should have. On January 17, 2020, the CDC and CBP established entry health screening at the three airports—San Francisco, Los Angeles, and JFK International in New York—that received most of the travelers coming from Wuhan.[34] By the end of January the screening net had grown to twenty airports, targeting all travelers coming from China and not just those from Wuhan.[35] CDC's regional offices around the world were similarly alerted to be watching for new cases. "We had the whole system tuned up to different degrees as we could," he said.[36]

But the results were puzzling. The CDC's early failure to produce a reliable Covid test that could be processed quickly meant that airport screeners were flying blind. "We weren't finding a lot of sick people," Cetron said. "And even if we found a couple of people with fevers or other things, it was mostly things we had tools to diagnose, and we didn't have a good diagnostic for this." CDC officials were further trying to decide how to use quarantine, without firm knowledge of the incubation period. The CDC would not order a mandatory quarantine for returning travelers from China until January 31, when hundreds of citizens arriving from Wuhan were sent to be housed for fourteen days at the March Air Reserve Base in Riverside, California.[37] It was the first federal quarantine order since a smallpox outbreak in the 1960s.[38] Those arriving from other parts of China were told to self-quarantine at home for fourteen days, though there were few enforcement measures.[39]

Both the tools and resources at hand were hopelessly inadequate. By the 2010s, much of the post-9/11 urgency about biological threats had waned despite the Ebola scare. Ron Klain, the White House official who led the Ebola response for Obama, warned in 2016 that "the next President must act from Day One" to boost the nation's readiness. "If she or he waits until grim-faced aides file into the Oval Office to explain that a pandemic is unfolding, it will be far too late."[40] The Trump administration waited. There had been a big infusion of cash during the Ebola crisis, but that was all gone by 2019. Declining funding had forced the CDC to cut more than 300 posts overseas, including critical ones inside of China.[41] Trump's White House in 2018 disbanded the Obama-era directorate in the National Security Council responsible for pandemic prevention and preparedness.[42]

The United States was far behind countries like South Korea and Taiwan in its capability to implement the measures needed to reduce foreign introduction of such a stealthy virus. Cetron acknowledges that the United States had never done the preparation needed to impose large-scale quarantines and "still had not succeeded in setting up a digital contact tracing system" that might have allowed health officials to track and eliminate outbreaks. Deputy Director Schuchat told congressional investigators that "we were not ready for a very large-scale quarantine effort either at the federal level or the state level. We didn't have the systems. We didn't have the people. We didn't have the technology [to track cases and get needed information from the airlines], or the agreement on [using] the technology to do that in a swift and efficient way."[43] Outside of the big airports, local health officials complained they were getting very little guidance from the CDC on how to handle incoming passengers; Nevada's top public health official complained to CDC Director Redfield about "a breakdown in communication." The CDC would forward passenger data to the states, but antiquated systems were riddled with errors that made it difficult for public health officials to accurately identify incoming passengers and to monitor compliance with self-quarantine orders.[44] Americans returning from China said the airport screenings were minimal, and in most states there was little to no follow-up to ensure they remained isolated for two weeks after arriving.[45] A CDC review of the screening program in California found that local public health officials were overwhelmed by the volume of travelers, incomplete data, and the prevalence of asymptomatic transmission. "Despite intensive effort, the traveler screening system did not effectively prevent introduction of COVID-19 into California," the review concluded.[46]

But in January, at least, the CDC and the Trump leadership were still largely on the same page. Cetron worked with White House deputy national security advisor Matt Pottinger and others who were urging a ban on travel from China, which the president agreed to on January 31. As soon as Covid started moving into Europe, however, "it got much more complicated," Cetron said. The mass outbreak in Italy in early February especially showed the looming threat. "Our connections to the continent, to the EU, are huge. Anything that was going on in Italy was already here from all the migration maps that I had generated."[47] But in the White House, a ban on travel from Europe was seen for many weeks as a step too far. "There was a lot of animosity that we were overshooting," especially from Trump's top economic advisors like Larry Kudlow, he said.[48] "It was like he was personally responsible for the great economy, and we were going to destroy it." The debate over whether to impose travel restrictions on Europe went on for weeks. "That's where there was a huge rift with the White House," Cetron said. "We could not get the White House to take European travel seriously." The United States would not restrict visitors from Europe until March 13 following heated debates among Trump's top officials.[49] In February, 139,305 travelers arrived in the United States from Italy, and 1.74 million from all Schengen countries.[50] Later studies would show that most of the early infections in the country, including the massive outbreak that raged through New York City in March, were seeded by those arrivals from Europe.[51] But by this time CDC experts had been pushed to the side. "The White House started taking control of the whole response," he said.

The US travel restrictions remained essentially unchanged for the rest of the Trump administration. The United States did not initially adapt its border measures to the changing nature of the threat in the way many European and some Asian nations did over that first year. One of the few changes the CDC made was to drop airport health screenings in September 2020, which had proven wholly ineffective; the new approach would instead focus "on the continuum of travel and the individual passenger, including pre-departure and post-arrival education, efforts to develop a potential testing framework with international partners, and illness response."[52] It was a white flag.

When Joe Biden was elected, CDC officials were able to brief incoming officials on "mitigation measures short of border closures," including pre-departure testing and mandatory masking on airplanes. Cetron had tried to persuade Trump officials to endorse similar measures as early as the summer of 2020 that might have permitted an easing of border closures. But Trump was a vocal opponent of masking. "It all crumbled under the politics of the Trump administration," he said.[53] So the new measures waited until the Biden team implemented many of them early in the new administration. The day after taking office, the president rolled out a masking requirement for all transportation and directed DHS and the Secretary of Transportation to implement new pre-testing requirements for international air travel to the United States, including returning Americans.[54] Subsequent research by CDC scientists showed the new testing and masking measures resulted in more than a 50% decline in the introduction of new Covid cases from overseas.[55]

Cetron had no similar luck on Title 42. He urged the incoming CDC director Rochelle Walensky to lift the measure, and she "was totally behind it." But the White House balked. "They had no other solution for controlling flow on the southern border than a public health authority that was never justified in the beginning." None of this was scientifically rational, he said. "But public health doesn't operate in a vacuum of politics. It never has. It never does."[56]

Going Backwards

Well before Covid emerged in late 2019, Cetron had worried out loud about the eagerness of countries, including his own, to resort to border restrictions rather than do the hard work needed to shore up public health systems. Instead of investing in the public health capabilities needed to respond to infectious diseases, governments either ignore the risk of new outbreaks or hope they can just keep them out of their countries by shutting borders. "The problem with these knee-jerk over-reactions is they actually increase your risk," he said. "They play into that denial. The response to denial is we have a superpower, and we will build a fortress so strong it will be impenetrable. And that's fool's gold."[57]

It is not clear that any border and travel restrictions could have helped a country as large and open as the United States against a virus as stealthy and contagious as Covid-19. But if such measures are to be used effectively by more countries to slow the spread of future pandemics, there is nothing more important than early detection. Travel restrictions will almost certainly be part of future pandemic responses, but how the measures are implemented will determine if the benefits exceed the harm. And nothing is more important to better outcomes than strengthening the ability to identify and respond to new outbreaks as quickly as possible.

So, in early 2022, Cetron and his colleagues at the CDC launched the Traveler-Based Genomic Surveillance program (TGS). The program had been piloted at JFK, Newark, and San Francisco airports in September 2021, with the CDC cooperating with private partners to introduce voluntary screening of selected arriving travelers and rapid turnaround of the genetic sequencing. The immediate goal was to help identify the origins of new Covid variants; the pilot program was the first to identify the new BA.2 variant in the United States and discovered the BA.3 variant forty-three days before it was reported anywhere else in North America. These mechanisms are ones that could be used more widely for other diseases such as influenza and Monkeypox as well.[58] They have the potential, Cetron says, to identify novel diseases months before they show up in a clinical setting.[59] By the summer of 2023, genetic screening was being done at seven large US airports, and similar tracking systems were set up in Europe and Australia.[60]

The biggest innovation is the testing of wastewater recovered from airplane toilets, which requires no voluntary cooperation from passengers. The program was piloted at JFK in August and September 2022 and then fully launched at San Francisco Airport in January 2023. The sampling is cheap and adds just three minutes to normal aircraft maintenance times. With the active participation of private companies like Ginkgo Bioworks, it has been possible to do full genomic sequencing of novel diseases within a week. "Imagine how much better off the world might have been in January 2020 if a surveillance system like this could have picked up these strains of a new coronavirus in multiple countries after it was first detected in China," Cetron told *Time* magazine. "To know in advance would have helped in developing diagnostics and identifying outbreaks more quickly and would have been a game changer." Dr. Cindy Friedman, chief of the CDC's Travelers' Health Branch, said the sampling has identified new Covid variants before authorities in the countries where they originated were aware.[61] Cetron says the new program is an example of the sort of learning the United States needs to better respond to the inevitable future outbreak of diseases with pandemic potential. Wastewater tests can be the elusive "sentinel" that identifies these emerging threats, even without cooperation from the countries where those diseases are incubating. "If we are not wise in taking what we've learned and investing in anticipatory, proactive, 21st-century tools for surveillance, we're at risk of getting whacked again and repeating our mistakes."[62]

But as the program was being rolled out in 2023, political leaders in Washington were in the midst of a fierce battle over future funding for the government. House Republicans led by then Speaker Kevin McCarthy were calling for deep cuts in funding for most programs alongside a big increase in spending on border security, demands that were strongly resisted by Democrats and the Biden White House. Facing a potential default on US debt for the first time in history, President Biden cut short a visit to Asia and returned home to negotiate. With time running out, he and McCarthy reached a deal that avoided big cuts but would hold government spending flat for the next two years.[63] As part of the deal, the White House agreed to rescind nearly $30 billion that had been budgeted but not yet spent for Covid relief.

The CDC had planned to use that money for, among other things, the expansion of preventive measures such as traveler surveillance and airplane wastewater testing. Instead of ramping up a highly successful program, the agency was forced to cobble together whatever funding it could to keep the program alive. What was potentially the biggest breakthrough in early disease identification in decades was put on life support. The CDC has managed to find money to keep the program growing, adding new testing sites at airports in Boston, Washington, Miami, and Chicago, but the future is uncertain.[64] "We are in the inter-pandemic period, and there is this cycle of complacency and crisis that we live through over and over again," says Dr. Friedman of the CDC.[65] Cetron is more blunt: "It's pretty clear after doing this for so long that we make the same damn mistakes over and over again. As soon as the nightmare is over, everyone buries it as quickly as possible, and we go into denial." A 2020 Council on Foreign Relations task force, under direction of Obama Health and Human Services secretary Sylvia Mathews Burwell and Bush homeland security advisor Frances Fragos Townsend, said that despite a series of strategic plans dating back two decades, there remains "a repeated lack of urgency, resources, and political will. Rather than developing a standing capacity to prevent, respond to, and mitigate pandemics, the United States has too often paid lip service to readiness, resulting in a pattern of crisis response followed by policy drift."[66]

All of this has left Cetron fearing for the future of his life's work. "This is the kind of stuff that's really worrisome for people like me," he said. "The amnesia has set in; the denial has set in."[67] And there is little reason to believe the world will be granted another hundred years before a pandemic on the scale of Covid-19 and the Spanish Flu hits again. A study in the prestigious *Proceedings of the National Academy of Sciences* found that environmental change, much of it due to a warming planet, has already increased the risk of extreme epidemics, and those risks will grow in the coming decades.[68] Far from being a "once in a century" event, a comprehensive study by Ginkgo Bioworks and the Center for Global Development estimates a 50–50 chance of another Covid-scale pandemic occurring in the next twenty-five years.[69] "I think the next one is going to be a lot sooner than people would like to believe," Cetron said.

Crises like Covid-19 should be a chance for the world to learn, to examine what worked and what didn't—whether in domestic public health or in efforts to prevent the spread of diseases through border closures—and be ready to respond more effectively the next time around. But as in the aftermath of previous pandemics, amnesia has set in. Public health experts Yanzhong Huang and Rebecca Katz note a long-standing pattern in health emergencies—"decision-makers, the general public, and even the public health and scientific communities were fast to put the outbreaks behind them, move on to other problems, and neglect the challenges identified during the event." Despite more than 50 million deaths during the Spanish Flu, they note, within a few years "almost all mentions of the generation-defining pandemic [had] disappeared from popular culture."[70] Pandemic responses have historically been a "cycle of panic and neglect," says Ashley Bloomfield, the former director-general of health in New Zealand who co-chaired the WHO's recent effort to amend the International Health Regulations. "Because we are so good at moving on to the next things as humans—that's part of our survival strategy—there's almost this collective global amnesia."[71]

Nowhere has this been truer than in the United States, where there has been no serious evaluation of what went wrong during the Covid pandemic to leave more than a million Americans dead. Cetron still holds out hope for progress though. New technologies for early detection and rapid diagnostics offer "unprecedented promise" that the world can be more successful in fighting known and emerging disease threats, he says. "Humanity can win the battle against future pandemics." Friedman argues that incentives for improving early detection and initial responses are enormous. Early detection and mitigation "help avoid the border closures and travel and trade disruptions, which is in everybody's interest," she says.[72] But the challenges are enormous. The United States, Cetron worries, remains politically toxic, and is plagued by disinformation and false narratives that undermine the public trust needed for effective responses. "This is the first time in my experience of thirty years that we are coming out of a crisis less prepared than when we went in."[73] And if we are less prepared the next time, the world will once again close its doors.

Notes

CHAPTER 1

1. Tom Banse, "Couples and Families Separated by U.S.-Canada Border Closure Find Oasis at Peace Arch Park," *Northwest Public Broadcasting*, March 16, 2021, https://www.nwpb.org/2021/03/16/couples-and-families-separated-by-u-s-canada-border-closure-find-oasis-at-peace-arch-park/.

2. Feliks Banel, "Couples and Families Celebrate Peace Arch Centennial in Unexpected Ways," *Kiro News Radio*, July 23, 2021, https://mynorthwest.com/3048964/couples-and-families-celebrate-peace-arch-centennial-in-unexpected-ways/.

3. Edward Alden, "The Human Toll of Endless Pandemic Border Closures," *Foreign Policy*, February 26, 2021, https://foreignpolicy.com/2021/02/26/covid-19-pandemic-border-closures-travel-restrictions-human-cost/.

4. Chris Irlam (border community member) in discussion with the author, December 13, 2021.

5. Katie DeRosa, "Peace Arch Park: Rise of COVID-19 Variants Heighten Concerns around Cross-Border Meetups," *Vancouver Sun*, February 10, 2021, https://vancouversun.com/news/local-news/rise-of-covid-19-variants-heighten-concerns-around-cross-border-meetups-in-peace-arch-park.

6. Moira Warburton, "COVID-19: In a Time of Pandemic, Love Is in the Air at Peace Arch Park," *Vancouver Sun*, March 21, 2021, https://vancouversun.com/news/covid-19-in-a-time-of-pandemic-love-is-in-the-air-at-peace-arch-park.

7. Meghan Benton et al., *COVID-19 and the State of Global Mobility in 2021* (Washington, DC/Geneva: Migration Policy Institute and International Organization for Migration, 2022), 28, https://www.migrationpolicy.org/sites/default/files/publications/mpi-covid19-impact-global-mobility-2021_final.pdf.

8. Christina Farr and Michelle Gao, "How Taiwan Beat the Coronavirus," *CNBC*, July 15, 2020, https://www.cnbc.com/2020/07/15/how-taiwan-beat-the-coronavirus.html.

9. Peter Baldwin, *Fighting the First Wave: Why the Coronavirus Was Tackled So Differently across the Globe* (Cambridge: Cambridge University Press, 2021), 3.

10. M. A. Shiraef et al., "COVID Border Accountability Project, a Hand-Coded Global Database of Border Closures Introduced during 2020," *Scientific Data* 8 (2021): 253, https://doi.org/10.1038/s41597-021-01031-5.

11. Phillip Connor, "More than Nine-in-Ten People Worldwide Live in Countries with Travel Restrictions amid COVID-19," *Pew Research Center*, April 1, 2020, https://www.pewresearch.org/fact-tank/2020/04/01/

more-than-nine-in-ten-people-worldwide-live-in-countries-with-travel-restr ictions-amid-covid-19/; for an overview of the different databases tracking travel restrictions, see L. Piccoli et al., "Restricting Human Movement during the COVID-19 Pandemic: New Research Avenues in the Study of Mobility, Migration, and Citizenship," *International Migration Review* 57, no. 2 (2023): 505–520, https://doi.org/10.1177/01979183221118907.

12. See 5 IHR Review Committee, "Report of the Review Committee on the Functioning of the International Health Regulations (2005) during the COVID-19 Response," UN Doc A/74/9 Add.1 (May 5, 2021), 41 [83]; and Michael R. Kenwick and Beth A. Simmons, "Pandemic Response as Border Politics," *International Organization* 74, Supp. (December 2020): E41, doi:10.1017/S0020818320000363.

13. Benton et al., *COVID-19 and the State of Global Mobility in 2021*, 3.

14. See Michael Igoe, "Why the WHO Doesn't Like Travel Bans," *Devex*, May 1, 2020, https://www.devex.com/news/why-who-doesn-t-like-travel-bans-97149; and Adam Ferhani and Simon Rushton, "The International Health Regulations, COVID-19, and Bordering Practices: Who Gets In, What Gets Out, and Who Gets Rescued?," *Contemporary Security Policy* 41, no. 3 (2020), https://www.tandfonline.com/doi/full/10.1080/13523260.2020.1771955.

15. See Smriti Mallapaty, "What the Data Says about Border Closures and COVID Spread," *Nature*, December 22, 2020, https://www.nature.com/articles/d41586-020-03605-6; Karen Ann Grepin et al., "Evidence of the Effectiveness of Travel-Related Measures during the Early Phase of the COVID-19 Pandemic: A Rapid Systematic Review," *BMJ Global Health* (2021), 6, https://gh.bmj.com/content/6/3/e004537; and Matteo Chinazzi et al., "The Effect of Travel Restrictions on the Spread of the 2019 Novel Coronavirus (COVID-19) Outbreak," *Science*, March 6, 2020, https://www.science.org/doi/10.1126/science.aba9757.

16. Baldwin, *Fighting the First Wave*, 5.

17. Wikipedia has compiled a comprehensive list of national lockdowns across the world; most typically lasted two to three months in total. See https://en.wikipedia.org/wiki/COVID-19_lockdowns. In the United States, there was a strong public consensus on "social distancing" restrictions between March and May 2020, but after that opinion began to fragment along partisan lines, with Republican opposition growing strongly. See Yiqian Alice Wang, "Public Opinion on the COVID-19 Pandemic: From Consensus to Conflict," in *Who Governs: Emergency Powers in the Time of Covid*, ed. Morris P. Fiorina (Stanford, CA: Hoover Institution Press, 2023), 175–206.

18. Darrel Bricker, "Majority (67%) of Global Citizens Support the Closing of Their Borders as Few (33%) Believe COVID-19 Is Contained," *Ipsos*, November 22, 2020, https://www.ipsos.com/en-ca/news-polls/majority-of-global-citizens-support-closing-of-borders-few-believe-covid-is-contained.

19. Ipsos, "World Divided on Whether COVID Is Contained, but Increasing Optimism We Are Turning the Corner," November 20, 2021, https://www.ipsos.com/en-us/news-polls/2021-hisf-covid-response.

20. Michael R. Kenwick and Beth A. Simmons, "Pandemic Response as Border Politics," *International Organization* 74, S1 (2020): 36–58, https://doi.org/10.1017/S0020818320000363.

21. Kenwick and Simmons, "Pandemic Response as Border Politics."

22. Glenn Kessler, "Trump's Claim That He Imposed the First 'China Ban,'" *Washington Post*, April 7, 2020.

23. Cf. Uri Friedman, "New Zealand's Prime Minister May Be the Most Effective Leader on the Planet," *The Atlantic*, April 19, 2020, https://www.theatlantic.com/politics/archive/2020/04/jacinda-ardern-new-zealand-leadership-coronavirus/610237/.

24. "Victims of the Wall," State of Berlin, accessed January 31, 2023, https://www.berlin.de/mauer/en/history/victims-of-the-wall/.

25. Katy Long, "In Search of Sanctuary: Border Closures, 'Safe' Zones and Refugee Protection," *Journal of Refugee Studies* 26, no. 3 (2013): 458–476, doi:10.1093/jrs/feso50, https://academic.oup.com/jrs/article/26/3/458/1587140.

26. "COVID-19 Related Travel Restrictions: A Global Review for Tourism," UNWTO, 2020, https://webunwto.s3.eu-west-1.amazonaws.com/s3fs-public/2020-04/TravelRestrictions%20-%2028%20April.pdf.

27. Jonathan Cheng, "China to Open Borders as Covid-19 Cases Rise," *Wall Street Journal*, December, 26, 2022, https://www.wsj.com/articles/china-to-open-borders-despite-surge-in-covid-19-cases-11672073476.

28. On North America, see Edward Alden, *The Closing of the American Border: Terrorism, Immigration and Security since 9/11* (New York: HarperCollins, 2008); on Europe, see Anita Orav and Alessandro D'Alfonso, "Smart Borders: EU Entry/Exit System," *European Parliamentary Research Service*, January 12, 2018, http://brexitlegal.ie/wp-content/uploads/2019/08/Smart-Borders-People.pdf.

29. See International Monetary Fund, *World Economic Outlook*, April 2022, esp. Ch. 4, "Global Trade and Value Chains in the Pandemic," https://www.imf.org/en/Publications/WEO/Issues/2022/04/19/world-economic-outlook-april-2022.

30. See Adrien Delmas and David Goeury, "Bordering the World in Response to Emerging Infectious Disease: The Case of SARS-CoV-2," *Borders in Globalization Review* 2, no. 1 (Fall/Winter 2020): 12–20.

31. Alex Irwin-Hunt, "The Great Competition for International Students," FDI Intelligence, March 27, 2024, https://www.fdiintelligence.com/content/data-trends/the-great-competition-for-international-students-83628.

32. "International Tourism to Reach Pre-Pandemic Levels in 2024," UN World Tourism Organization, January 19, 2024, https://www.unwto.org/news/international-tourism-to-reach-pre-pandemic-levels-in-2024.

CHAPTER 2

1. Jeffrey D. Sachs et al., "The *Lancet* Commission on Lessons for the Future from the Covid-19 Pandemic," *Lancet Commission* 400, no. 10359 (September 2022), https://www.thelancet.com/journals/lancet/article/PIIS0140-6736(22)01585-9/fulltext.

2. World Health Organization, "Middle East Respiratory Syndrome Coronavirus (MERS-CoV)," https://www.who.int/health-topics/middle-east-respiratory-syndrome-coronavirus-mers#tab=tab_1.

3. Richard Horton, *The Covid-19 Catastrophe: What's Gone Wrong and How to Stop It Happening Again* (Cambridge: Polity Press, 2021), 43.

4. World Health Organization, "WHO Statement regarding Cluster of Pneumonia Cases in Wuhan, China," January 9, 2020, https://www.who.int/china/news/detail/09-01-2020-who-statement-regarding-cluster-of-pneumonia-cases-in-wuhan-china.

5. Kelly Drews, "A Brief History of Quarantine," *Virginia Tech Undergraduate Historical Review* 2 (2013), doi:10.21061/vtuhr.v2i0.16, https://vtuhr.org/articles/10.21061/vtuhr.v2i0.16.

6. Dave Roos, "Social Distancing and Quarantine Were Used in Medieval Times to Fight the Black Death," *History*, March 25, 2020, https://www.history.com/news/quarantine-black-death-medieval.

7. Eugenia Tognotti, "Lessons from the History of Quarantine, from Plague to Influenza A," *Emerging Infectious Diseases* (February 2013), 254–259, https://www.ncbi.nlm.nih.gov/pmc/articles/PMC3559034/.

8. Joshua Loomis, *Epidemics: The Impact of Germs and Their Power over Humanity* (Nashville: Turner Publishing, 2018), 18.

9. Melissa A. McLeod et al., "Protective Effect of Maritime Quarantine in South Pacific Jurisdictions, 1918–19 Influenza Pandemic," *Emerging Infectious Diseases* 14, no. 3 (March 2008): 468–470, doi:10.3201/eid1403.070927, https://www.ncbi.nlm.nih.gov/pmc/articles/PMC2570822/.

10. McLeod et al., "Protective Effect of Maritime Quarantine."

11. John M. Barry, *The Great Influenza: The Story of the Deadliest Pandemic in History* (New York: Penguin Books, 2004).

12. David M. Bell and World Health Organization Working Group on International and Community Transmission of SARS, "Public Health Interventions and SARS Spread, 2003," *Emerging Infectious Diseases* 10, no. 11 (November 2004): 1900–1906, doi:10.3201/eid1011.040729, https://www.ncbi.nlm.nih.gov/pmc/articles/PMC3329045/; and Ronald K. St. John et al., "Border Screening for SARS," *Emerging Infectious Diseases* 11, no. 1 (January 2005): 6–10, doi:10.3201/eid1101.040835, https://www.ncbi.nlm.nih.gov/pmc/articles/PMC3294328/.

13. David P. Fidler, *SARS, Governance and the Globalization of Disease* (New York: Palgrave Macmillan, 2004).

14. David P. Fidler, "SARS: Political Pathology of the First Post-Westphalian Pathogen," *Journal of Law and Medical Ethics* 31, no. 4 (Winter 2003): 485–505, https://pubmed.ncbi.nlm.nih.gov/14968652/.

15. A. Ferhani and S. Rushton, "The International Health Regulations, COVID-19, and Bordering Practices: Who Gets In, What Gets Out, and Who Gets Rescued?," *Contemporary Security Policy* 41, no. 3(2020): 458–477, doi:10.1080/13523260.2020.1771955; see also B. von Tigerstrom and B. K. Wilson, "COVID-19 Travel Restrictions and the *International Health Regulations* (2005)," *BMJ Global Health* 5, no. 5 (May 2020): e002629, doi:10.1136/bmjgh-2020-002629, https://gh.bmj.com/content/5/5/e002629.

16. See the review of pre-January 2020 research in David J. Bier, "Research Provides No Basis for Pandemic Travel Bans," *Cato Institute*, April 15, 2020, https://www.cato.org/publications/research-provides-no-basis-pandemic-travel-bans.

17. See L. Forman and R. Habibi, "Revisiting the Legality of Travel Restrictions under International Law during Covid-19," *International & Comparative Law Quarterly* 71, no. 3 (2022): 743–760, doi:10.1017/S0020589322000240, https://www.cambridge.org/core/journals/international-and-comparative-law-quarterly/article/revisiting-the-legality-of-travel-restrictions-under-international-law-during-covid19/78D8D2DF06E659D2BC3C529954DB7E59.

18. Benjamin Wallace-Wells, "Will the Omicron Travel Restrictions Work," *New Yorker*, December 4, 2021, https://www.newyorker.com/news/annals-of-inquiry/will-the-omicron-travel-restrictions-work; see also Smriti Mallapaty, "Omicron-Variant Border Bans Ignore the Evidence, Say Scientists," *Nature*, December 2, 2021, https://www.icpcovid.com/sites/default/files/2021-12/Ep%20197-4%20Omicron-variant%20border%20bans%20ignore%20the%20evidence%2C%20say%20scientists.pdf.

19. Krzysztof Pelc, "Can COVID-Era Export Restrictions Be Deterred?" *Canadian Journal of Political Science* 53, no. 2 (June 2020): 1–8, doi:10.1017/S0008423920000578.

20. Ferhani and Rushton, "The International Health Regulations."

21. "Statement from the Travel and Transport Task Force on Ebola Virus Disease Outbreak in West Africa," World Health Organization, November 7, 2014, https://www.who.int/news/item/07-11-2014-statement-from-the-travel-and-transport-task-force-on-ebola-virus-disease-outbreak-in-west-africa.

22. World Health Organization, "Updated WHO Recommendations for International Traffic in Relation to Covid-19 Outbreak," February 29, 2020, https://www.who.int/news-room/articles-detail/updated-who-recommendations-for-international-traffic-in-relation-to-covid-19-outbreak.

23. Max Roser and Bastian Herre, "Tourism," Our World in Data, 2017, https://ourworldindata.org/tourism.

24. Mark Honigsbaum, "Revisiting the 1957 and 1968 Influenza Pandemics," *The Lancet*, May 25, 2020, https://www.thelancet.com/journals/lancet/article/PIIS0140-6736(20)31201-0/fulltext.

25. Elizabeth Becker, *Overbooked: The Exploding Business of Travel and Tourism* (New York: Simon & Schuster, 2013), 14.

26. Matthew Carr, *Fortress Europe: Dispatches from a Gated Continent* (New York: New Press, 2012), 26.

27. Daniel Scott and Stefan Gössling, "What Could the Next 40 Years Hold for Global Tourism?" *Tourism Recreation Research* 40, no. 3 (2015): 269–285, doi:10.1080/02508281.2015.1075739.

28. Bureau of Transportation Statistics, "Border Crossing/Entry Data," https://www.bts.gov/browse-statistical-products-and-data/border-crossing-data/border-crossingentry-data.

29. "Air Transport, Passengers Carried," The World Bank, https://data.worldbank.org/indicator/IS.AIR.PSGR.

30. The official slogan of the Madrid-based United Nations World Tourism Organization is "Tourism—Passport to Peace." Becker, *Overbooked*, 9.

31. Derek Thompson, "How Airline Ticket Prices Fell 50 Percent in 30 Years (And Why Nobody Noticed)," *The Atlantic*, February 28, 2013, https://www.theatlantic.com/business/archive/2013/02/how-airline-ticket-prices-fell-50-in-30-years-and-why-nobody-noticed/273506/.

32. "Air Transport, Passengers Carried," The World Bank, https://data.worldbank.org/indicator/IS.AIR.PSGR.

33. "Are Americans Well Traveled? New Study Follows the Passports," Business Traveler USA, September 24, 2019, https://www.businesstravelerusa.com/business-traveler-usa-story/are-americans-well-traveled-new-study-follows-the-passports/.

34. "68% Have Visited up to 10 Countries: Agoda.com Study," Agoda, January 29, 2020, https://www.agoda.com/press/well-traveled-survey-2019?cid=1844104.

35. Daniel Avery, "A Record Number of Americans Are Traveling Abroad," *Newsweek*, March 28, 2019, https://www.newsweek.com/record-number-americans-traveling-abroad-1377787.

36. Becker, *Overbooked*, 17.

37. World Tourism Organization, *The Economic Contribution of Tourism and the Impact of COVID-19* (Madrid: UNWTO, 2021), doi:10.18111/9789284423200.

38. Gian Maria Milesi-Ferretti, "The COVID-19 Travel Shock Hit Tourism-Dependent Economies Hard," *Brookings Institution*, August 12, 2021, https://www.brookings.edu/research/the-covid-19-travel-shock-hit-tourism-dependent-economies-hard/.

39. "Travel: America's Unsung Hero of Job Creation," US Travel Association, March 2020, https://www.ustravel.org/system/files/media_root/document/Research_Fact-Sheet_Travel-Jobs.pdf.

40. Tariro Mzezewa, "In Hawaii, Reimagining Tourism for a Post-Pandemic World," *New York Times*, March 7, 2021, https://www.nytimes.com/2021/03/07/travel/hawaii-covid-tourism.html; Jen Murphy, "Hawaii Is Rethinking Tourism. Here's What That Means for You," *Bloomberg*, December 30, 2021, https://

www.bloomberg.com/news/features/2021-12-30/hawaii-is-rethinking-tour ism-here-s-what-that-means-for-you.

41. "Enrollment Trends," Open Doors, 2022, https://opendoorsdata.org/data/in ternational-students/enrollment-trends/.

42. "Enrollment Trends," Open Doors.

43. "Leading Places of Origin," Open Doors, 2022, https://opendoorsdata.org/ data/international-students/leading-places-of-origin/.

44. "New NAFSA Data: Despite Stagnant Enrollment, International Students Contribute Nearly $41 Billion to the U.S. Economy," NAFSA, November 18, 2019, https://www.nafsa.org/about/about-nafsa/new-nafsa-data-despite-stagn ant-enrollment.

45. International Labour Organization, "ILO Global Estimates on International Migrant Workers: Results and Methodology" (Geneva: ILO, 2021), https:// www.ilo.org/wcmsp5/groups/public/---dgreports/---dcomm/---publ/docume nts/publication/wcms_808935.pdf.

46. "Migration and Remittance Data Update: Remittances to Low- and Middle-Income Countries on Track to Reach $551 Billion in 2019 and $597 Billion by 2021," KNOMAD, October 2019, https://www.knomad.org/publication/ migration-and-remittance-data-update-remittances-low-and-middle-income-countries-track; "Global Remittances Guide," Migration Policy Institute, https:// www.migrationpolicy.org/programs/data-hub/global-remittances-guide.

47. "270 Million People Are Migrants, Who Send Home a Staggering $689 Billion," UN News, November 27, 2019, https://news.un.org/en/story/2019/11/ 1052331.

48. International Labour Organization, "ILO Global Estimates."

49. "COVID-19 Impact on Stranded Migrants," IOM UN Migration, September 30, 2020, https://www.iom.int/sites/g/files/tmzbdl486/files/documents/ issue_brief_return_task_force.pdf.

50. "Migration Data Relevant for the COVID-19 Pandemic," Migration Data Portal, April 1, 2022, https://www.migrationdataportal.org/themes/migration-data-relevant-covid-19-pandemic; "COVID-19 Impact on Stranded Migrants," IOM UN Migration.

51. Mina Kaji, "300,000 Seafarers Still Stuck on Ships: 'We Feel Like Hostages,'" ABC News, September 11, 2020, https://abcnews.go.com/Politics/300000-seafarers-stuck-ships-feel-hostages/story?id=72948111.

52. "Herr and Madame, Señor and Mrs," The Economist, November 12, 2011, https://www.economist.com/international/2011/11/12/herr-and-madame-senor-and-mrs.

53. Li Wenchao and Yi Junjian, "The Globalisation of Marriage Markets," The Straits Times, July 12, 2017, https://fass.nus.edu.sg/ecs/wp-content/uploads/ sites/4/2020/11/MARRIAGE-st-12jul-pA20.pdf.

54. So Yoon Ahn, "Matching across Markets: An Economic Analysis of Cross-Border Marriage," Working Paper No. 047 (Chicago: University of Illinois at Chicago, September 2021), https://syahn.people.uic.edu/JMP_SA.pdf.

55. Michelle Ye Hee Lee, "I Live in Tokyo. He Lives in D.C. Omicron Forced Us to Marry if We Ever Wanted to See Each Other," *Washington Post*, February 1, 2022, https://www.washingtonpost.com/lifestyle/2022/02/01/pandemic-marri age-separation-japan/; Thisanka Siripala, "What's behind Japan's Continued COVID-19 Border Restrictions," *The Diplomat*, May 2, 2022, https://thediplo mat.com/2022/05/whats-behind-japans-continued-covid-19-border-restricti ons/; Sheila A. Smith, "Japan Has Weathered COVID-19 Better than Many, but Problems Persist," *Council on Foreign Relations*, March 18, 2022, https://www. cfr.org/in-brief/japan-covid-19-pandemic-response-restrictions-two-years.

56. Stacy Leasca, "With Land Borders Closed Canadian Snowbirds Are Taking Helicopters to Get into the U.S. This Winter," *Travel & Leisure*, January 8, 2021, https://www.travelandleisure.com/travel-news/canadians-taking-helicopt ers-across-border-to-get-into-us.

57. Barbara Wojazer, "They Love Each Other but Covid Has Torn Them Apart," *CNN*, February 14, 2021, https://www.cnn.com/travel/article/couples-torn-apart-by-covid/index.html.

58. Adit Sarin, "India to Atlanta via Mexico," *Lestacindia*, June 19, 2021, https:// lestacindia.com/india-to-atlanta-via-mexico/.

59. Musafir, "Quarantine Packages," https://in.musafir.com/holidays/quarantine-packages.aspx.

60. Zofeen Maqsood, "Beat U.S. Travel Bans with Quarantine Holiday in Exotic Lands!" *The American Bazaar*, June 13, 2021, https://www.americanbazaaronline.com/ 2021/06/12/beat-us-travel-ban-with-quarantine-holiday-in-exotic-lands-445787/.

61. Horton, *The Covid-19 Catastrophe*, 68.

62. Nick Corasaniti, Alexander Burns, and Binyamin Appelbaum, "Donald Trump Vows to Rip Up Trade Deals and Confront China," *New York Times*, June 28, 2016, https:// www.nytimes.com/2016/06/29/us/politics/donald-trump-trade-speech.html.

63. In announcing the new travel restrictions, Secretary Azar and the rest of the Trump administration made no reference to the WHO, or to its declaration two days previously that Covid was a "Public Health Emergency of International Concern." As such, it blatantly ignored US obligations under the International Health Regulations. Gian Luci Burci, "The Outbreak of Covid-19 Coronavirus: Are the International health Regulations fit for purpose?" *European Journal of International Law*, February 27, 2020. See https://www.ejiltalk.org/the-outbreak-of-covid-19-coronavirus-are-the-international-health-regulations-fit-for-purpose/.

64. Myah Ward, "15 Times Trump Praised China as Coronavirus Was Spreading across the Globe," *Politico*, April 15, 2020, https://www.politico.com/news/ 2020/04/15/trump-china-coronavirus-188736.

65. The internal deliberations leading to the China travel ban have been well documented in several books by journalists closely following the Trump White

House, including Bob Woodward, *Rage* (New York: Simon & Schuster, 2020); Yasmeen Abutaleb and Damian Paletta, *Nightmare Scenario: Inside the Trump Administration's Response to the Pandemic That Changed History* (New York: HarperCollins, 2021); and Carol Leonnig and Philip Rucker, *I Alone Can Fix It: Donald J. Trump's Catastrophic Final Year* (New York: Penguin, 2021). See also Michael D. Shear, Sheri Fink, and Noah Weiland, "Inside Trump Administration, Debate Raged over What to Tell Public," *New York Times*, March 7, 2020, https://www.nytimes.com/2020/03/07/us/politics/trump-coronavirus.html.

66. "Proclamation on Suspension of Entry as Immigrants and Nonimmigrants of Persons Who Pose a Risk of Transmitting 2019 Novel Coronavirus," Trump White House Archives, January 31, 2020, https://trumpwhitehouse.archives. gov/presidential-actions/proclamation-suspension-entry-immigrants-nonimm igrants-persons-pose-risk-transmitting-2019-novel-coronavirus/.

67. Stephen Braun, Hope Yen, and Calvin Woodward, "AP Fact Check: Trump and the Virus-Era China Ban That Isn't," *AP News*, July 18, 2020, https://apnews. com/article/asia-pacific-anthony-fauci-pandemics-politics-ap-fact-check-d227b 34b168e576bf5068b92a03c003d.

68. Thomas Bollyky and Jennifer B. Nuzzo, "Trump's Early Travel Bans Weren't Early, Weren't Bans, and Didn't Work," *Washington Post*, October 1, 2020, https://www.washingtonpost.com/outlook/2020/10/01/debate-early-travel-bans-china/; Glenn Kessler, "Trump's Claim That He Imposed the First 'China Ban,'" *Washington Post*, April 7, 2020, https://www.washingtonpost.com/polit ics/2020/04/07/trumps-claim-that-he-imposed-first-china-ban/.

69. Abutaleb and Paletta, *Nightmare Scenario*, 123; see also Deborah Birx, *Silent Invasion: The Untold Story of the Trump Administration, Covid-19, and Preventing the Next Pandemic Before It's Too Late* (New York: HarperCollins, 2022), 113–117.

70. "Department of Homeland Security Outlines New Process for Americans Returning from Certain European Countries, China, and Iran," Department of Homeland Security, March 13, 2020, https://www.dhs.gov/news/2020/03/ 13/department-homeland-security-outlines-new-process-americans-returning-certain.

71. "Mount Sinai Study Finds First Cases of COVID-19 in New York City Are Primarily from European and US Sources," Mount Sinai, June 2, 2020, https:// www.mountsinai.org/about/newsroom/2020/mount-sinai-study-finds-first-cases-of-covid-19-in-new-york-city-are-primarily-from-european-and-us-sour ces-pr.

72. Bill Chappell, "Coronavirus: Chaos Follows Trump's European Travel Ban; EU Says It Wasn't Warned," *NPR*, March 12, 2020 https://www.npr.org/secti ons/goatsandsoda/2020/03/12/814876173/coronavirus-trump-speech-creates-chaos-eu-says-it-wasnt-warned-of-travel-ban.

73. "Prime Minister Announces Temporary Border Agreement with the United States," Government of Canada, March 20, 2020, https://pm.gc.ca/en/news/

news-releases/2020/03/20/prime-minister-announces-temporary-border-agreement-united-states.

74. Meghan Benton et al., *COVID-19 and the State of Global Mobility in 2021* (Washington, DC/Geneva: Migration Policy Institute and International Organization for Migration, 2022), 28, https://www.migrationpolicy.org/sites/default/files/publications/mpi-covid19-impact-global-mobility-2021_final.pdf.

75. "Displacement Tracking Matrix," IOM UN Migration, https://migration.iom.int/.

76. "Japan to Expand Entry Ban to 73 Countries, Regions amid Virus Spread," *The Mainichi*, April 1, 2020, https://web.archive.org/web/20200404082806/https://mainichi.jp/english/articles/20200401/p2g/00m/0na/103000c; and Magdalena Osumi, "Foreign Residents Stranded Abroad by Japan's Coronavirus Controls," *Japan Times*, May 19, 2020, https://www.japantimes.co.jp/news/2020/05/19/national/social-issues/japan-foreign-residents-stranded-abroad-coronavirus/.

77. Andrew Rettman, "Nine EU States Close Borders Due to Virus," *EU Observer*, March 16, 2020, https://euobserver.com/coronavirus/147742.

78. Michael Birnbaum, "Europe Is Closing Borders amid Coronavirus Outbreak. They May Be Hard to Reopen," *Washington Post*, March 17, 2020, https://www.washingtonpost.com/world/europe/europe-closing-borders-coronavirus/2020/03/17/131a6f56-67c8-11ea-b199-3a9799c54512_story.html.

79. Victoria Klesty, "Border Town Pays Price for Sweden's No-Lockdown as Norway Reopens," *Reuters*, July 2, 2020, https://www.reuters.com/article/us-health-coronavirus-norway-sweden/border-town-pays-price-for-swedens-no-lockdown-as-norway-reopens-idUSKBN24319R.

80. Adrian Øhrn Johansen, "Between Norway and Sweden, Two Countries Proud of Their Freedom of Movement, a Closed Border Separates Families, *Washington Post*, May 28, 2021, https://www.washingtonpost.com/photography/2021/05/28/norway-sweden-two-countries-proud-their-freedom-movement-closed-border-separates-families/.

81. Richard Milne, "Nordic Co-operation Crumbles at the Norway-Sweden Border," *Financial Times*, June 19, 2020, https://www.ft.com/content/af311c89-95f6-48fd-beb9-0ac10f21eacc.

82. "COVID-19 Travel Restrictions Output—09 July 2020," IOM UN Migration, https://migration.iom.int/reports/covid-19-travel-restrictions-output-%E2%80%94-09-july-2020.

83. Meghan Benton, *Future Scenarios for Global Mobility in the Shadow of Pandemic* (Washington, DC: Migration Policy Institute, July 2021), https://www.migrationpolicy.org/sites/default/files/publications/mpi-mobility-future-scenarios-updated-2021_final.pdf.

84. Tamara Hardingham-Gill, "The People Waiting Out Covid-19 in Dark, Frozen Antarctica," *CNN*, May 8, 2020, https://www.cnn.com/travel/article/life-in-antarctica-during-the-pandemic/index.html; "Coronavirus and COVID-19: What

You Should Know," WebMD, https://www.webmd.com/lung/news/20201224/antarctica-reports-first-covid-19-outbreak.

CHAPTER 3

1. A timeline of the New Zealand government's use of quarantine, known as the "Managed Isolation and Quarantine" (MIQ) system, is at "MIQ Timeline," Government of New Zealand, Ministry of Business, Innovation and Employment, accessed September 14, 2022, https://www.mbie.govt.nz/immigration-and-tourism/isolation-and-quarantine/managed-isolation-and-quarantine/about-miq/miq-timeline/.

2. Charlotte Bellis, "Exclusive: Pregnant TV Reporter Charlotte Bellis' Full, Open Letter on MIQ—'NZ Said You're Not Welcome,'" *New Zealand Herald*, January 28, 2022, https://www.nzherald.co.nz/nz/covid-19-omicron-charlotte-bellis-an-open-letter-on-miq/U4WQGYTJHUP36AGVOBN3F6PJSE/.

3. "'Dying every two hours': Afghan Women Risk Life to Give Birth," *Al Jazeera*, December 7, 2023, https://www.aljazeera.com/gallery/2023/12/27/photos-dying-every-two-hours-afghan-women-risk-life-to-give-birth.

4. Annabelle Timsit, "Pregnant Journalist Says She's Returning to New Zealand after Strict Covid Rules Left Her in Afghanistan," *Washington Post*, February 1, 2022, https://www.washingtonpost.com/world/2022/02/01/charlotte-bellis-return-new-zealand-afghanistan-taliban/.

5. Nicole Trian, "Stranded Abroad, Australians Lodge UN Petition against Government for 'Right to Return Home,'" *France 24*, April 6, 2021, https://www.france24.com/en/asia-pacific/20210406-stranded-abroad-australians-lodge-un-petition-against-govt-for-right-to-return-home.

6. John Power, "No Way Home: Overseas New Zealanders Despair at Tightened Borders," *Al-Jazeera*, December 22, 2021, https://www.aljazeera.com/economy/2021/12/22/no-way-home-overseas-new-zealanders-despair-at-border-rules.

7. Relief Web, "Chile: Return Migration to Bolivia (COVID-19 Context) Information Bulletin No. 1," May 25, 2020, https://reliefweb.int/report/chile/chile-return-migration-bolivia-covid-19-context-information-bulletin-no-1.

8. L. Budrie and A. Narinesingh, "Locked Out: An Ethical Analysis of Trinidad and Tobago's COVID-19 Border Closure," *Ethics, Medicine and Public Health* 20 (February 2022): 100749, https://www.sciencedirect.com/science/article/pii/S2352552521001262.

9. Yader Luna, "Régimen de Ortega Impide Retorno al País a 92 Nicas Varados en el Salvador," *Confidencial*, April 19, 2020, https://www.confidencial.digital/nacion/regimen-de-ortega-impide-retorno-al-pais-a-92-nicas-varados-en-el-salvador/; OACNUDH, "Hemos conocido la situación que enfrentan alrededor de 850 nicaragüenses en zonas fronterizas en Costa Rica, Nicaragua, Guatemala, y Panamá en condiciones precarias a la espera de la autorización por parte de las

autoridades de #Nicaragua para retornar a su país (1)" [Tweet], July 27, 2020, https://twitter.com/OACNUDH/status/1287821412124766208.

10. Austin Carr, "The Cruise Ship Suicides," *Bloomberg*, December 30, 2020, https://www.bloomberg.com/features/2020-cruise-ship-suicides/.

11. Mina Kaji, "300,000 Seafarers Still Stuck on Ships: 'We Feel Like Hostages,'" *ABC News*, September 11, 2020, https://abcnews.go.com/Politics/300000-seafarers-stuck-ships-feel-hostages/story?id=72948111; on the COVID preventative measures taken by Mauritius, see Marie Chan Sun and Claude Bernard Lan Cheong Wah, "Lessons to Be Learnt from the COVID-19 Public Health Response in Mauritius," *Public Health in Practice* 1 (November 2020), https://www.sciencedirect.com/science/article/pii/S2666535220300227.

12. UN Press Release, "Bachelet Urges Latin American States to Allow Their Nationals to Return Home," OHCHR, April 15, 2020, https://www.ohchr.org/en/press-releases/2020/04/bachelet-urges-latin-american-states-allow-their-nationals-return-home.

13. Shiori Shakuto and Flavia Baldari, "Japan's Migrants Are Not Allowed to Go 'Home,'" *Open Democracy*, November 3, 2020, https://www.opendemocracy.net/en/pandemic-border/japans-migrants-are-not-allowed-to-go-home/; Magdalena Osumi, "All Japan's Foreign Residents Can Travel in and out from September," *Japan Times*, August 28, 2020, https://www.japantimes.co.jp/news/2020/08/28/national/social-issues/japan-stranded-foreign-residents-free/.

14. Ben Dooley, "Japan's Locked Borders Shake the Trust of Its Foreign Workers," *New York Times*, updated May 18, 2021, https://www.nytimes.com/2020/08/05/business/japan-entry-ban-coronavirus.html; Ryotaro Nakamaru, "Japan's Coronavirus Entry Ban Disrupting Lives of Foreign Residents," *Kyodo News*, June 5, 2020, https://english.kyodonews.net/news/2020/06/29bd4e7ac3ee-feature-japans-coronavirus-entry-ban-disrupting-lives-of-foreign-residents.html.

15. "30,000 Foreign Students Entered Japan since Covid Border Curbs Eased," *Japan Times*, April 12, 2022, https://www.japantimes.co.jp/news/2022/04/12/national/japan-students-covid-ease/; Julian Ryall, "Foreign Student Ban Raises Concern over Lost Talent: Interest in Languages and Humanities Dwindles with Travel Restrictions," *South China Morning Post*, August 5, 2022.

16. David Nikel, "Norway Closes Border to All but Essential Travel," *Forbes*, January 27, 2021, https://www.forbes.com/sites/davidnikel/2021/01/27/norway-closes-border-to-all-but-essential-travel/?sh=5ce67b4d212a.

17. Sanjay Maru, "Ontario Man Fined $3.8K at Land Border Crossing amid Confusion over Who's 'Essential'," *CBC News*, February 27, 2021, https://www.cbc.ca/news/canada/windsor/border-ticket-tunnel-quarantine-act-1.5926311.

18. Michelle Maluske, "COVID Test Confusion at Border Leaves Canadian Family Stuck in Michigan," *CTV News Windsor*, December 11, 2021, https://windsor.ctvnews.ca/covid-test-confusion-at-border-leaves-canadian-family-stuck-in-michigan-1.5703872.

19. Piccoli et al. point out that the loss of international mobility during the pandemic was felt most acutely by those from wealthier countries who had enjoyed relatively open travel prior to the pandemic. For Americans, Germans, and Japanese, for example, the closing of borders was sudden and abrupt, whereas those holding passports from Afghanistan or Iran or many African nations had long faced significant international travel restrictions. See Lorenzo Piccoli et al., "Restricting Human Movement during the COVID-19 Pandemic: New Research Avenues in the Study of Mobility, Migration, and Citizenship," *International Migration Review* (November 2022), doi:10.1177/01979183221118907.

20. John C. Torpey, *The Invention of the Passport: Surveillance, Citizenship and the State*, 2nd ed. (India: Cambridge University Press, 2018).

21. Alan Dowty, *Closed Borders: The Contemporary Assault on Freedom of Movement* (New Haven, CT: Yale University Press, 1969), 62.

22. Andrea M. Chandler, *Institutions of Isolation: Border Controls in the Soviet Union and Its Successor States, 1917–1993* (Montreal: McGill-Queen's Press, 1998).

23. Jeffrey Kahn, *Mrs. Shipley's Ghost: The Right to Travel and Terrorist Watchlists* (Ann Arbor: University of Michigan Press, 2013), 82.

24. "Timeline: Travel Documents at the Canada-U.S. Border," *CBC News*, May 12, 2009, https://www.cbc.ca/news/canada/timeline-travel-documents-at-the-can ada-u-s-border-1.834929.

25. "From Threat to Threat," National Commission on Terrorist Attacks upon the United States, https://govinfo.library.unt.edu/911/report/911Rep ort_Ch6.htm.

26. "ePassport Basics," ICAO, https://www.icao.int/Security/FAL/PKD/Pages/ePassport-Basics.aspx.

27. Beth A. Simmons and Michael R. Kenwick, "Border Orientation in a Globalizing World," *American Journal of Political Science* 66, no. 4 (October 23, 2022): 853–870, https://scholarship.law.upenn.edu/faculty_scholarship/2254/.

28. Ayelet Shachar, "Borders in the Time of COVID-19," *Max Planck Institute for the Study of Religious and Ethnic Diversity*, April 4, 2020, https://www.mpg.de/14650555/borders-in-the-time-of-covid-19; Matthew Longo, *The Politics of Borders: Sovereignty, Security and the Citizen after 9/11* (Cambridge: Cambridge University Press, 2018).

29. "U.S. Border Patrol Fiscal Year Staffing Statistics (FY1992–FY 2020)," US Customs and Border Protection, accessed September 15, 2022, https://www.cbp.gov/sites/default/files/assets/documents/2021-Aug/U.S.%20Border%20Patrol%20Fiscal%20Year%20Staffing%20Statistics%20%28FY%201992%20-%20FY%202020%29%20%28508%29.pdf.

30. Frontex, "Key Facts," https://www.frontex.europa.eu/assets/Publications/General/Frontex_at_a_Glance.pdf.

31. Gabriela Baczynska and Sara Ledwith, "How Europe Built Fences to Keep People Out," *Reuters*, April 4, 2016, https://www.reuters.com/article/us-eur

ope-migrants-fences-insight/how-europe-built-fences-to-keep-people-out-idUSKCN0X10U7.

32. "Deaths during Migration Recorded since 2014, by Region of Incident," Missing Migrants Project, https://missingmigrants.iom.int/.

33. "Australia: 8 Years of Abusive Offshore Asylum Processing," Human Rights Watch, July 15, 2021, https://www.hrw.org/news/2021/07/15/australia-8-years-abusive-offshore-asylum-processing.

34. "Offshore Processing Statistics," Refugee Council of Australia, February 10, 2023, https://www.refugeecouncil.org.au/operation-sovereign-borders-offsh ore-detention-statistics/.

35. James Kirchick, "European Populism and Immigration," *Great Decisions* (2019): 51–58, https://www.jstor.org/stable/26739052; Martin A. Schain, "Shifting Tides: Radical-Right Populism and Immigration Policy in Europe and the United States," *Migration Policy Institute*, August 2018; Michelle Mittelstadt, "Pushing Migration to the Forefront, Populists Make New Strides," *Migration Policy Institute*, December 20, 2018, https://www.migrationpolicy.org/article/top-10-2018-issue-2-populists-make-new-strides.

36. Gabriel Popescu, *Bordering and Ordering the Twenty-first Century* (Lanham, MD: Rowman & Littlefield, 2012), 3.

37. Stephen E. Flynn, "Beyond Border Control," *Foreign Affairs*, November/December 2000.

38. Edward Alden, *The Closing of the American Border: Terrorism, Immigration and Security since 9/11* (New York: HarperCollins, 2008).

39. Delmas and Goeury write that: "The so-called smart borders promoted by international organizations have allowed for the filtering of indispensables (merchandise, data, capital and key workers) from dispensables (human beings)." See Adrien Delmas and David Goeury, "Bordering the World in Response to Emerging Infectious Disease: The Case of SARS-CoV-2," *Borders in Globalization Review* 2, no. 1 (Fall/Winter 2020): 12–20, https://doi.org/10.18357/bigr21202019760.

40. As Delmas and Goeury put it, the response to the pandemic "demonstrated the superfluous nature of the movement of men and women as long as goods themselves can circulate."

41. Alexander Panetta, "How the Shutdown after 9/11 Paved the Way for the New Canada-U.S. Border Response to Covid-19," *CBC News*, March 20, 2020, https://www.cbc.ca/news/world/coronavirus-covid-19-border-canada-united-states-trade-1.5503192.

42. Camila Valdivieso, "Constitution-Free Zones: How the Fourth Amendment Rights of Americans Are Violated at and near the Border," *GGU Race, Gender, Sexuality, and Social Justice Law Journal*, September 20, 2021, https://digital commons.law.ggu.edu/cgi/viewcontent.cgi?article=1009&context=rgssj-law-journal.

43. Reece Jones, *Nobody Is Protected: How the Border Patrol Became the Most Dangerous Police Force in the United States* (Berkeley: Counterpoint, 2022).

44. "CBP Enforcement Statistics Fiscal Year 2023," US Customs and Border Protection, https://www.cbp.gov/newsroom/stats/cbp-enforcement-statistics; Drew Harwell, "Customs Officials Have Copied Americans' Phone Data at Massive Scale," *Washington Post*, September 15, 2022, https://www.washingtonpost.com/technology/2022/09/15/government-surveillance-database-dhs/.

45. See *Almeida-Sanchez v. United States*, 413 U.S. 266 (1973), https://supreme.justia.com/cases/federal/us/413/266/; and Deborah Anthony, "The U.S. Border Patrol's Constitutional Erosion in the '100-Mile Zone,'" *Penn State Law Review* 124, no. 2 (2020), https://elibrary.law.psu.edu/pslr/vol124/iss2/3. There is more controversy over the Department of Homeland Security's assertion that searches without probable cause can be carried out at interior checkpoints far away from the physical border. The government asserts special authority over a border zone that stretches 100 miles from the country's land borders or ocean and lake perimeters. That 100-mile zone includes about 65% of the entire US population.

46. The US government told the commission investigating the attacks that some 140,000 people had been registered under NSEERS and that eleven of them had some connection to terrorism. But the commission was skeptical of the claims. Six of those, it said, were arrested under circumstances unconnected to NSEERS. Two came up as hits on the separate terrorist watch lists. And the other three claims were even more ambiguous. See Alden, *Closing American Border*; and Tomas R. Eldridge et al., "9/11 and Terrorist Travel: Staff Report of the National Commission on Terrorist Attacks upon the United States," August 21, 2004, https://govinfo.library.unt.edu/911/staff_statements/911_TerrTrav_Monograph.pdf.

47. Alden, *Closing American Border*.

48. Jay Shooster, "What Did the Courts Say When Bush Was Accused of Targeting Muslim Immigrants," *Just Security*, January 25, 2017, https://www.justsecurity.org/36737/courts-bush-accused-targeting-muslim-immigrants/. Also Muzaffar Chisti and Claire Bergeron, "DHS Announces End to Controversial Post-9/11 Immigrant Registration and Tracking Program," *Migration Policy Institute*, May 17, 2011, https://www.migrationpolicy.org/article/dhs-announces-end-controversial-post-911-immigrant-registration-and-tracking-program.

49. Michael D. Shear, "New Order Indefinitely Bars Almost All Travel from Seven Countries," *New York Times*, September 24, 2017, https://www.nytimes.com/2017/09/24/us/politics/new-order-bars-almost-all-travel-from-seven-countries.html.

50. Adam Liptak and Michael D. Shar, "Trump's Travel Ban Is Upheld by Supreme Court," *New York Times*, June 26, 2018, https://www.nytimes.com/2018/06/26/us/politics/supreme-court-trump-travel-ban.html.

51. Amy Howe, "Opinion Analysis: Divided Court Upholds Trump Travel Ban (Updated)," *SCOTUS Blog*, June 26, 2018, https://www.scotusblog.com/2018/06/opinion-analysis-divided-court-upholds-trump-travel-ban/.

52. 8 U.S. Code § 1182—Inadmissible Aliens, https://www.law.cornell.edu/uscode/text/8/1182.

53. "Instrumentalising Citizenship: In the Fight against Terrorism," Institute on Statelessness and Inclusion and EU Global Citizenship Observatory, March 2022, https://files.institutesi.org/Instrumentalising_Citizenship_Global_Trends_Report.pdf.

54. "English Translation of Magna Carta," British Library, July 28, 2014, https://www.bl.uk/magna-carta/articles/magna-carta-english-translation#:~:text=*%20(42)%20In%20future%20it,common%20benefit%20of%20the%20realm.

55. Joel D. Ingles, "Study of Discrimination in Respect of the Right of Everyone to Leave Any Country, Including His Own, and Return to His Country," *Special Rapporteur of the Sub-Commission on Protection of Discrimination and Protection of Minorities* (New York: United Nations, 1963), https://en.calameo.com/books/000953612851odcf87bf5, 3.

56. "Right of Return," *Wikipedia*, https://en.wikipedia.org/wiki/Right_of_return, accessed July 23, 2022.

57. Noah Smith-Drelich, "The Constitutional Right to Travel under Quarantine," *Southern California Law Review* 94, no. 6 (2022): 1367–1405.

58. Martin Bauml Duberman, *Paul Robeson* (New York: Alfred A. Knopf, 1988), 399. In 1952, the United States was still officially under a state of national emergency called by the US government during World War II that was not lifted until April 1952.

59. *Kent v. Dulles*, 357 U.S. 116 (1958), https://supreme.justia.com/cases/federal/us/357/116/.

60. Charlie Savage, "Judge Rules Terrorism Watchlist Violates Constitutional Rights," *New York Times*, September 4, 2019, https://www.nytimes.com/2019/09/04/us/politics/terrorism-watchlist-constitution.html.

61. "U.S. Citizens Exiled Are Allowed to Return Home," ACLU of Northern California, October 2, 2006, https://www.aclunc.org/blog/us-citizens-exiled-are-allowed-return-home.

62. Murtaza Hussain, "One Man's No-Fly List Nightmare," *The Intercept*, May 30, 2021, https://theintercept.com/2021/05/30/no-fly-list-terrorism-watchlist/.

63. Timothy Bella, "The FBI's Terrorism Watch List Violates the Constitution, Federal Judge Says," *Washington Post*, September 5, 2019, https://www.washingtonpost.com/nation/2019/09/05/fbi-terror-watch-list-unconstitutional/.

64. "Federal Appeals Court Says Government Can Put Americans on Terror Watchlist without Notice or Chance to Rebut," Law and Crime, https://lawandcrime.com/high-profile/federal-appeals-court-says-government-can-put-americans-on-terror-watchlist-without-notice-or-chance-to-rebut/.

65. Smith-Drelich, "The Constitutional Right to Travel under Quarantine," 1367.

66. Adam Klein and Benjamin Wittes, "The Long History of Coercive Health Responses in American Law," *Lawfare*, April 13, 2020, https://www.lawfareb log.com/long-history-coercive-health-responses-american-law.

67. Smith-Drelich, "The Constitutional Right to Travel under Quarantine," 1372.

68. *Wong Wai v. Williamson et al.*, 103 F.1 (U.S. Circuit Court, N.D. California 1900), http://libraryweb.uchastings.edu/library/research/special-collections/ wong-kim-ark/103%20F.%201.pdf.

69. Quoted in Regina Jefferies and Jane McAdam, "Can We Still Call Australia Home? The Right to Return and the Legality of Australia's COVID-19 Travel Restrictions," *Australian Journal of Human Rights* 27 (2021): 211–231, https:// www.tandfonline.com/doi/full/10.1080/1323238X.2021.1996529.

70. Jefferies and McAdam, "Can We Still Call Australia Home?," 9.

71. Rod McGuirk, "Australian Court Upholds Ban on Most International Travel," *AP News*, June 1, 2021, https://apnews.com/article/asia-pacific-australia-lifest yle-travel-coronavirus-pandemic-a1d239e80be05c8cf393ec67d1b6cce2.

72. "India Labour Migration Update 2018," International Labour Organization, https://www.ilo.org/wcmsp5/groups/public/---asia/---ro-bangkok/---sro-new_ delhi/documents/publication/wcms_631532.pdf.

73. Irudaya Rajan and H. Arokkiaraj, "Return Migration from the Gulf Region to India amidst COVID-19," in *Migration and Pandemics: Spaces of Solidarity and Spaces of Exception*, ed. Anna Triandafyllidou (Cham, Switzerland: Springer, 2022), 209–211; "Stay Where You Are: Supreme Court to Indians Abroad," *Indian Express*, April 14, 2020, https://indianexpress.com/article/india/coronavirus-lockdownstay-where-you-are-supreme-court-to-indians-abroad-6361229.

74. The US Department of Transportation, however, blocked the rescue flights for Indian citizens. The US government argued that, because India was charging its citizens for the return flights at a time when India was barring US airlines from flying to the country, the actions were "unfair and discriminatory" and "create a competitive disadvantage for U.S. carriers." See Alan Levin, "US Restricts Air India's 'Vande Bharat' Flights Citing 'Unfair' Limits on Its Airlines," *The Print*, June 23, 2020, https://theprint.in/india/us-restricts-air-indias-vande-bharat-flig hts-citing-unfair-limits-on-its-airlines/446832/.

75. Schain, "Shifting Tides," 55.

76. Sergio Carrera and Ngo Chun Luk, "Love Thy Neighbour? Coronavirus Politics and Their Impact on EU Freedoms and Rule of Law in the Schengen Area," *CEPS*, April 3, 2020, https://www.ceps.eu/ceps-publications/love-thy-neighbour/.

77. "Coronavirus: Commission Recommends Partial and Gradual Lifting of Travel Restrictions to the EU after 30 June, Based on Common Coordinated Approach," European Commission, June 11, 2020, https://ec.europa.eu/com mission/presscorner/detail/en/ip_20_1035.

78. Francesco Guarascio, "EU Health Agency Slams Border Closures as Too Late and Costly to Tame Coronavirus," *Skift*, May 27, 2020, https://skift.com/2020/

05/27/eu-health-agency-slams-border-closures-as-too-late-and-costly-to-tame-coronavirus/.

79. Smith-Drelich, "The Constitutional Right to Travel under Quarantine."

80. Katherine Florey, "The Tribal COVID-19 Response," *Regulatory Review*, March 17, 2021, https://www.theregreview.org/2021/03/17/florey-tribal-covid-19-response/.

81. "Atlantic Bubble," *Wikipedia*, https://en.wikipedia.org/wiki/Atlantic_Bubble, accessed November 9, 2022; "In Canada's 'Atlantic Bubble,' COVID Is a Distant Reality," *VOA News*, November 11, 2020, https://www.voanews.com/a/americas_canadas-atlantic-bubble-covid-distant-reality/6198251.html.

82. The Canadian Charter of Rights and Freedoms, Government of Canada, https://www.justice.gc.ca/eng/csj-sjc/rfc-dlc/ccrf-ccdl/check/art6.html.

83. Danielle Hopkins, "Taylor v Newfoundland and Labrador: Mobility Rights in the Age of a Global Pandemic," *Saskatchewan Law Review*, December 9, 2021, https://sasklawreview.ca/comment/taylor-v-newfoundland-and-labrador-mobility-rights-in-the-age-of-a-global-pandemic.php.

84. David Hume, "Palmer v Western Australia (2021) 95 ALJR 229; [2021] HCA 5: Trade, Commerce and Intercourse Shall Be Absolutely Free (except When It Need Not)," *Australian Public Law*, June 23, 2021, https://www.auspublaw.org/blog/2021/06/palmer-v-western-australia-2021-95-aljr-229-2021-hca-5.

85. "Palmer v The State of Western Australia," High Court of Australia, February 24, 2021, https://cdn.hcourt.gov.au/assets/publications/judgment-summaries/2021/hca-5-2021-02-24.pdf.

86. Paul Karp, "Clive Palmer's Challenge against Western Australia's Border Ban Rejected by High Court," *The Guardian*, November 5, 2020, https://www.theguardian.com/australia-news/2020/nov/06/clive-palmers-challenge-against-western-australias-border-ban-rejected-by-high-court.

87. Benjamen Gussen, "On the Constitutionality of Hard State Border Closures in Response to the COVID-19 Pandemic," HeinOnline, https://heinonline.org/HOL/LandingPage?handle=hein.journals/jlah35&div=5&id=&page=.

88. Nina Haug et al., "Ranking the Effectiveness of Worldwide COVID-19 Government Interventions," *Nature Human Behavior* 5 (2020): 1303–1312, https://www.nature.com/articles/s41562-020-01009-0.pdf.

89. See, e.g., Nate Cohn, "Americans Are Frustrated with the Pandemic. These Polls Show How Much," *New York Times*, February 8, 2022, https://www.nytimes.com/2022/02/08/us/politics/covid-restrictions-americans.html; "A Year of Public Opinion on the Coronavirus Pandemic," Pew Research Center, March 5, 2021, https://www.pewresearch.org/2021/03/05/a-year-of-u-s-public-opinion-on-the-coronavirus-pandemic/; and Owen Jones, "Public Support for Lockdown Measures Is Disintegrating—A New Approach Is Needed," *The Guardian*, December 22, 2021, https://www.theguardian.com/commentisfree/2021/dec/22/omicron-covid-restrictions-young-people.

90. "Global Travel Restrictions Imposed amid COVID-19 Outbreak," Swisscham, July 2020, https://www.swisscham.org/hongkong/wp-content/uploads/sites/5/2020/07/Global-Travel-Restrictions-Jul-27.pdf.

91. "Guidelines Concerning the Exercise of the Free Movement of Workers during the COVID-19 Outbreak," *Official Journal of the European Union*, March 30, 2020, https://eur-lex.europa.eu/legal-content/EN/TXT/?uri=CELEX%3A52020XC0330%2803%29#ntr7-CI2020102EN.01001201-E0007.

92. Moti (Mordehai) Mironi and Monika Schlachter, *Regulating Strikes in Essential Services: A Comparative "Law in Action" Perspective* (Alphen aan den Rijn, The Netherlands: Wolters Kluwer, 2018).

93. "Substantive Provisions of Labour Legislation: The Right to Strike," International Labour Organization, https://www.ilo.org/legacy/english/dialogue/ifpdial/llg/noframes/ch5.htm#6.

94. Joanna Gaitens et al., "COVID-19 and Essential Workers: A Narrative Review of Health Outcomes and Moral Injury," *International Journal of Environmental Research and Public Health* 18, no. 4 (2021): 1446, https://www.ncbi.nlm.nih.gov/pmc/articles/PMC7913818/.

95. See Chih-Fu Wei et al., "Risk of SARS-CoV-2 Infection among Essential Workers in a Community-Based Cohort in the United States," *Frontiers in Public Health* 10 (2022), https://www.ncbi.nlm.nih.gov/pmc/articles/PMC9169416/.

96. "Guidance on Essential Services and Functions in Canada during the COVID-19 Pandemic," Government of Canada, https://www.publicsafety.gc.ca/cnt/ntnl-scrt/crtcl-nfrstrctr/esf-sfe-en.aspx.

97. Shelby Thevenot, "Canada Redefines Definition of 'Essential Travel' during Coronavirus," *CIC News*, May 1, 2020, https://www.cicnews.com/2020/05/canada-refines-definition-of-essential-travel-during-coronavirus-0514270.html#gs.n6hynj.

98. Anna Triandafyllidou, ed., *Migration and Pandemics* (Cham, Switzerland: Springer, 2022), https://link.springer.com/content/pdf/10.1007/978-3-030-81210-2.pdf?pdf=button, 28.

99. "Travel Restrictions Fact Sheet," US Embassy and Consulates in Canada, updated October 26, 2021, https://ca.usembassy.gov/travel-restrictions-fact-sheet/#:~:text=Individuals%20traveling%20for%20emergency%20response,%2D19%20or%20other%20emergencies.

100. Meghan Benton et al., *COVID-19 and the State of Global Mobility in 2021* (Washington, DC/Geneva: Migration Policy Institute and International Organization for Migration, 2022), 28, https://www.migrationpolicy.org/sites/default/files/publications/mpi-covid19-impact-global-mobility-2021_final.pdf.

101. Shelby Thevenot, "How CBSA Determines 'Essential Travel' Revealed in Internal Memo," *CIC News*, May 27, 2020, https://www.cicnews.com/2020/05/how-cbsa-determines-essential-travel-revealed-in-internal-memo-0514463.html#gs.n6fwyn.

102. Frances Mao, "Celebrities in Australia Anger Stranded Citizens over 'Double Standard,'" *BBC News*, April 1, 2021, https://www.bbc.com/news/world-australia-55851074; and Josh Taylor, "'No Exemptions' but Nicole Kidman and Keith Urban Reportedly Allowed to Quarantine at NSW Holiday Home," *The Guardian*, July 22, 2020, https://www.theguardian.com/australia-news/2020/jul/22/no-exemptions-but-nicole-kidman-and-keith-urban-allowed-to-quarantine-at-separate-nsw-location.

103. Novak Djokovic, "The Australian Public Have Felt There's One Rule for the Rich and Another for the Rest throughout the Pandemic," *The Guardian*, January 6, 2022, https://www.theguardian.com/commentisfree/2022/jan/07/the-australian-public-have-felt-theres-one-rule-for-the-rich-and-another-for-the-rest-throughout-the-pandemic.

104. Brad Japhe, "Celebrities Are Traveling Where We're Banned. These Loopholes May Be How," *Washington Post*, October 7, 2020, https://www.washingtonpost.com/travel/2020/10/22/celebrity-travel-covid-19/.

105. Alice Newbold, "Now We Know What Hailey and Bella Were Doing in Sardinia," *Vogue*, September 14, 2020, https://www.vogue.co.uk/news/article/hailey-bieber-bella-hadid-versace-campaign.

106. Justin Mohammed, "If Canada Can Welcome the NHL, It Can Welcome Refugees," *Toronto Star*, August 4, 2020, https://www.thestar.com/opinion/contributors/2020/08/04/if-canada-can-welcome-the-nhl-it-can-welcome-refugees.html.

107. Jonathan Gatehouse, Madeline McNair, and Albert Leung, "UPS Executive Granted Special Ministerial Exemption from Canada's COVID-19 Quarantine," *CBC*, October 29, 2020, https://www.cbc.ca/news/canada/ups-executive-quarantine-exemption-1.5780753.

108. "International Health Regulations Enter into Force," PAHO, June 17, 2007, https://www.paho.org/en/news/17-6-2007-international-health-regulations-enter-force.

109. Agustina Calatayud et al., "Containing the Spatial Spread of COVID-19 through the Trucking Network," *Transport Policy* 15 (2022): 4–13, https://www.ncbi.nlm.nih.gov/pmc/articles/PMC8558009/.

110. Francis Bajunirwe, Jonathan Izudi, and Stephen Asiimwe, "Long-Distance Truck Drivers and the Increasing Risk of COVID-19 Spread in Uganda," *International Journal of Infectious Diseases* 98 (2020): 191–193, https://www.sciencedirect.com/science/article/pii/S1201971220305221; Thobile Malinga et al., "A Scoping Review of the Impact of Long-Distance Truck Drivers on the Spread of COVID-19 Infection," *Pan African Medical Journal* 38, no. 27 (2021), https://www.ncbi.nlm.nih.gov/pmc/articles/PMC7955595/.

111. Dakshana Bascaramurty, "Deemed Essential, Long-Haul Truckers Risk Infection and Spreading COVID-19 with Every Shift," *Globe and Mail*, January 25, 2021, https://www.theglobeandmail.com/canada/article-deemed-essential-long-haul-truckers-risk-infection-and-spreading-covid/.

112. "Temporary Relaxation of EU Truck Driving and Resting Time Rules Due to COVID-19," *Fleet*, https://fleet.ie/temporary-relaxation-of-eu-truck-driving-and-resting-time-rules-due-to-covid-19/; "Transportation Emergency Fact Sheet 2—Regulatory Relief," US Department of Transportation, updated September 2, 2020, https://www.transportation.gov/emergency/transportation-emergency-response-factsheet-2-regulatory-relief.

113. "COVID-19 and Road Transport," International Labour Organization, June 2020, https://www.ilo.org/wcmsp5/groups/public/---ed_dialogue/---sector/documents/briefingnote/wcms_746914.pdf; "COVID-19 Pandemic: Rest Stops Must Remain Open, Trucking Stakeholders Contend," *Safety and Health Magazine*, April 8, 2020, https://www.safetyandhealthmagazine.com/articles/19671-covid-19-pandemic-rest-stops-must-remain-open-trucking-stakeholders-contend.

114. Paul Anand et al., "Work-Related and Personal Predictors of COVID-19 Transmission: Evidence from the UK and USA," *Journal of Epidemiology and Community Health* (2021), https://www.ncbi.nlm.nih.gov/pmc/articles/PMC8277485/.

115. "400,000 Seafarers Stuck at Sea as Crew Change Crisis Deepens," International Maritime Organization, September 25, 2020, https://www.imo.org/en/MediaCentre/PressBriefings/pages/32-crew-change-UNGA.aspx.

116. Consumer Good Forum, "Letter to Antonio Guterres, Secretary-General, United Nations," September 23, 2020. https://www.theconsumergoodsforum.com/wp-content/uploads/202009-cgf-letter-to-un-general-secretary-on-maritime-crew-changes.pdf.

117. "Frequently Asked Questions about How COVID-19 Is Impacting Seafarers," International Maritime Organization, https://www.imo.org/en/MediaCentre/HotTopics/Pages/FAQ-on-crew-changes-and-repatriation-of-seafarers.aspx.

118. Laura Schumm, "Food Rationing in Wartime America," *History*, May 23, 2014, https://www.history.com/news/food-rationing-in-wartime-america.

119. The Trump administration invoked the "national security" exemption of the WTO to impose tariffs on imports of steel and aluminum in 2018. Those actions were vigorously defended in the WTO by the Biden administration, insisting such actions cannot be reviewed by the WTO's dispute settlement panels. See William Reinsch and Jack Caporal, "The WTO's First Ruling on National Security: What Does It Mean for the United States?," CSIS, April 5, 2019, https://www.csis.org/analysis/wtos-first-ruling-national-security-what-does-it-mean-united-states; and "Statement from USTR Spokesperson Adam Hodge," Office of the United States Trade Representative, https://ustr.gov/about-us/policy-offices/press-office/press-releases/2022/december/statement-ustr-spokesperson-adam-hodge.

120. Vincent Chetail, "The Transnational Movement of Persons under General International Law—Mapping the Customary Law Foundations of International Migration Law," Office of the United Nations High Commissioner for Human

Rights (2014), https://www.ohchr.org/sites/default/files/Documents/Issues/Migration/StudyMigrants/CivilSociety/VincentChetailTransnationalMovement.pdf.

121. Universal Declaration of Human Rights, United Nations at Art. 13, https://www.un.org/en/universal-declaration-human-rights.

122. Quoted in Susan Martin and Jonas Bergmann, "(Im)mobility in the Age of COVID-19," *International Migration Review* 55, no. 3 (2021): 660–687, https://journals.sagepub.com/doi/epub/10.1177/01979183209841041.

123. None of the migrant worker treaties has more than fifty signatory nations, and the members do not include any of the major immigrant-receiving countries. The 1990 International Convention on the Protection of the Rights of All Migrant Workers and Members of Their Families is the least-ratified of all the major international human rights treaties. See Martin Ruhs, "The Human Rights of Migrant Workers: Why Do So Few Countries Care?," *American Behavioral Scientist* 56, no. 9 (2012): 1277–1293, https://journals.sagepub.com/doi/10.1177/0002764212443815.

124. Gian Luca Burci, "The Outbreak of COVID-19 Coronavirus: Are the International Health Regulations Fit for Purpose?," *EJIL Talk*, February 27, 2020, https://www.ejiltalk.org/the-outbreak-of-covid-19-coronavirus-are-the-international-health-regulations-fit-for-purpose/.

125. Fernando Dias Simoes, "COVID-19 and International Freedom of Movement: A Stranded Human Right?," *Yale Journal of Health Policy, Law, and Ethics* 20, no. 2 (2022): 362–432, https://papers.ssrn.com/sol3/papers.cfm?abstract_id=3781792.

126. Roojin Habibi et al., "Do Not Violate the International Health Regulations during the COVID-19 Outbreak," *The Lancet* 395, no. 10225 (2020): 664–666, https://www.thelancet.com/journals/lancet/article/PIIS0140-6736(20)30373-1/fulltext.

127. "Extraordinary G20 Leaders' Summit Statement on COVID-19," World Trade Organization, 2020, https://www.wto.org/english/news_e/news20_e/dgra_26mar20_e.pdf.

128. "WTO Issues Report on Measures to Expedite Access to COVID-19 Critical Goods, Services," World Trade Organization, https://www.wto.org/english/news_e/news20_e/serv_16sep20_e.htm.

129. "Trade Facilitation and the COVID-19 Pandemic," OECD, April 22, 2020, https://www.oecd.org/coronavirus/policy-responses/trade-facilitation-and-the-covid-19-pandemic-094306d2/.

130. "The Principle of *Non-Refoulment* under International Human Rights Law," Office of the United Nations High Commissioner for Human Rights, January 1, 2018, https://www.ohchr.org/sites/default/files/Documents/Issues/Migration/GlobalCompactMigration/ThePrincipleNon-RefoulementUnderInternationalHumanRightsLaw.pdf.

131. "The Principle of *Non-Refoulement* under International Human Rights Law"; see also Oona A. Hathaway, Preston Lim, Alasdair Phillips-Robins, and Mark Stevens, "The COVID-19 Pandemic and International Law," *Cornell International Law Journal* 54, no. 2 (2021), https://ssrn.com/abstract=3815164 or http://dx.doi.org/10.2139/ssrn.3815164.

132. Lawrence O. Gostin and Eric A. Friedman, "Title 42 Exclusions of Asylum Seekers—A Misuse of Public Health Powers," *JAMA Forum*, January 19, 2023, https://jamanetwork.com/journals/jama-health-forum/fullarticle/2800821.

133. Reuters, "New Zealand to Resume Taking Refugees a Year after Covid Border Closure," *The Guardian*, February 5, 2021, https://www.theguardian.com/world/2021/feb/05/new-zealand-to-resume-taking-refugees-a-year-after-covid-border-closure.

134. Elise Mercier and Sean Rehaag, "The Right to Seek Asylum in Canada (during a Global Pandemic)," *HeinOnline* (2020), https://heinonline.org/HOL/Land ingPage?handle=hein.journals/ohlj57&div=32&id=&page=.

135. Alexander Aleinikoff, "COVID-19 and the Protection of Refugees and Asylum-Seekers," *University of Pennsylvania* (2021), https://global.upenn.edu/sites/defa ult/files/perry-world-house/AleinikoffGSC21ThoughtPiece.pdf.

136. "G20 Tourism Ministers' Statement on COVID-19," University of Toronto, April 24, 2020, http://www.g20.utoronto.ca/2020/2020-g20-tourism-0424.html.

CHAPTER 4

1. Frank Jacobs, "A Not-So-Straight Story," *New York Times*, November 28, 2011, https://archive.nytimes.com/opinionator.blogs.nytimes.com/2011/11/28/a-not-so-straight-story/.

2. Libby Denkmann and Alec Cowan, "After Two Years of Isolation, Point Roberts Is Open for Business—Sort of," *KUOW*, June 14, 2022, https://www.kuow.org/stories/after-two-years-of-isolation-point-roberts-is-open-for-business-sort-of.

3. Alec Regimbal, "'We've been treated the worst': Residents in Point Roberts, Washington Fight to Open Northern Border," *SeattlePi*, July 7, 2021, https://www.seattlepi.com/local/seattlenews/article/point-roberts-wash-protest-can ada-border-closure-16299988.php.

4. Pat Grubb, "Point Roberts Students Attending School in B.C. Are Subject to 14-Day Quarantine," *All Point Bulletin*, August 13, 2020, https://www.allpo intbulletin.com/stories/point-roberts-students-attending-school-in-bc-are-subj ect-to-14-day-quarantine,11224.

5. Moira Warburton, "U.S.-Canada Towns Marooned by Border Closure Brace for Winter Trapped in Isolation," *Reuters*, September 6, 2020, https://www.reuters.com/article/uk-health-coronavirus-canada-towns-featu-idUKKBN25X0JD.

6. Pseudonym used to protect privacy.

7. Author correspondence with Point Roberts resident, September 18, 2020. The name is withheld by mutual agreement.

8. Author correspondence with Point Roberts resident, September 18, 2020. The name is withheld by mutual agreement.

9. Author correspondence with Point Roberts resident, September 18, 2020. The name is withheld by mutual agreement.

10. Jacob Resneck, "Canada's Relaxes COVID-19 Border Rules for Alaskans in Hyder," *Alaska Public Media*, November 2, 2020, https://alaskapublic.org/2020/11/02/canadas-relaxes-covid-19-border-rules-for-alaskans-in-hyder/.

11. Mitch Smith, "Caught between Two Countries, a Minnesota Resort Area Still Feels Lockdown Blues," *New York Times*, May 30, 2021, https://www.nytimes.com/2021/05/30/us/minnesota-covid-tourism.html.

12. Greg Mercer, "'We're basically trapped here': Campobello Struggles as U.S. Border Restrictions Keep N.B. Community Off Limits," *Globe and Mail*, October 1, 2021, https://www.theglobeandmail.com/canada/article-were-basically-trapped-here-campobello-struggles-as-us-border/.

13. Ian Holliday, "Point Roberts Records Its First Case of COVID-19, Health Officials Confirm," *CTV News*, February 11, 2021, https://bc.ctvnews.ca/point-roberts-records-its-first-case-of-covid-19-health-officials-confirm-1.5306081.

14. "Washington Delegation Members Urge President to Prioritize Safely Reopening Canada-U.S. Border," US Congresswoman Suzan DelBene Press Release, February 22, 2021, https://delbene.house.gov/news/documentsingle.aspx?DocumentID=2727.

15. "ICYMI: Canada Makes Border Exemption for Point Roberts Residents," Washington governor Jay Inslee, February 17, 2021, https://governor.wa.gov/news/2021/icymi-canada-makes-border-exemption-point-roberts-residents.

16. Michelle Esteban, "Feds Say Washington State Has Reached 70 Percent Vaccination, but State Metrics Differ," *KOMO News,* June 7, 2021, https://komonews.com/news/coronavirus/feds-say-washington-state-has-reached-70-percent-vaccination-but-state-metrics-differ.

17. Tom Banse, "Ferry Service Boosted to U.S. Enclave of Point Roberts, Which Is Cut Off by Canada," *Northwest News Network*, September 2, 2020, https://www.nwnewsnetwork.org/international-affairs/2020-09-02/ferry-service-boosted-to-u-s-enclave-of-point-roberts-which-is-cut-off-by-canada.

18. Regimbal, "We've been treated the worst."

19. Passengers include those in cars, buses, and trains. See US Department of Transportation, Bureau of Transportation Statistics, "Border Crossing/Entry Data," https://data.bts.gov/Research-and-Statistics/Border-Crossing-Entry-Data/keg4-3bc2/about_data.

20. US Department of Commerce, International Trade Administration, *APIS/I-92 MONITOR*, https://www.trade.gov/data-visualization/apisi-92-monitor.

21. "The Border between the U.S. and Mexico," Smart Border Coalition, https://smartbordercoalition.com/about-the-border.

22. Laurie Trautman, "Strengthening the Ties That Bind Us in North America across Our Borders," https://www.wilsoncenter.org/publication/strengthening-ties-bind-us-north-america-across-our-borders.

23. See Edward Alden, *The Closing of the American Border: Terrorism, Immigration and Security since 9/11* (New York: HarperCollins, 2008).

24. "Week 52: Measuring the Regional Impacts of the Canada-U.S. Border Restrictions," Wilson Center, March 18, 2021, YouTube video, 1:27:17, https://www.wilsoncenter.org/event/week-52-measuring-regional-impacts-canada-us-border-restrictions.

25. US Department of Homeland Security, *Beyond the Border: A Shared Vision for Perimeter Security and Economic Competitiveness*, December 5, 2011, i, https://www.dhs.gov/publication/beyond-border.

26. Chappell Lawson, "The Trusted and the Targeted: Segmenting Flows by Risk," in *Beyond 9/11: Homeland Security for the Twenty-First Century*, ed. Chappell Lawson, Alan Bersin, and Juliette Kayyem (Cambridge, MA: MIT Press, 2020), 101–120.

27. Christian Leuprecht and Todd Hataley, eds., *Security. Cooperation. Governance: The Canada–United States Open Border Paradox* (Ann Arbor: University of Michigan Press, 2023).

28. See "Border Security: U.S.-Mexico Border Partnership Agreement," George W. Bush White House, https://georgewbush-whitehouse.archives.gov/infocus/usmxborder/; and Peter Andreas, "U.S.-Mexico Border Control in a Changing Economic and Security Context," Wilson Center, December 2004, https://www.wilsoncenter.org/publication/us-mexico-border-control-changing-economic-and-security-context.

29. Matthew Longo, *The Politics of Borders: Sovereignty, Security, and the Citizen after 9/11* (Cambridge: Cambridge University Press, 2017); and Alden, *The Closing of the American Border*.

30. See, e.g., T. Eldridge et al., *9/11 and Terrorist Travel: Staff Report of the National Commission on Terrorist Attacks upon the United States* (Washington, DC: National Commission on Terrorist Attacks, 2004).

31. Alden, *The Closing of the American Border*.

32. US Department of Health and Human Services, Office of the Assistant Secretary for Preparedness and Response, *North American Plan for Animal Pandemic and Influenza* (2012), 38, https://www.phe.gov/Preparedness/international/Pages/napapi.aspx.

33. Government of Canada, *North American Plan for Animal Pandemic and Influenza*, Chapter 5, https://www.publicsafety.gc.ca/cnt/rsrcs/pblctns/nml-pndmc-nflnz/index-en.aspx#a5.

34. Government of Canada, *North American Plan for Animal Pandemic and Influenza*, Chapter 5.

35. René Kladzyk, "Border Travel Restrictions in Detroit and El Paso Show the Uneven Impacts of COVID-19," *Borderzine*, March 19, 2021, https://bor

derzine.com/2021/03/border-travel-restrictions-in-detroit-and-el-paso-show-the-uneven-impacts-of-covid-19/; and Katherine Richardson and Francesco Cappellano, "Sieve or Shield? High Tech Firms and Entrepreneurs and the Impacts of COVID 19 on North American Border Regions," *Journal of Borderlands Studies* 37, no. 4 (2022): 805–824, https://www.tandfonline.com/doi/full/10.1080/08865655.2022.2038230.

36. Martin Armstrong, "Where Trust in Government Is Highest and Lowest," *Statista*, January 19, 2022, https://www.statista.com/chart/12634/where-trust-in-government-is-highest-and-lowest/.

37. Michelle Ye Hee Lee, "Donald Trump's False Comments Connecting Mexican Immigrants and Crime," *Washington Post*, July 8, 2015, https://www.washingtonpost.com/news/fact-checker/wp/2015/07/08/donald-trumps-false-comments-connecting-mexican-immigrants-and-crime/; Vanda Felbab-Brown, "AMLO's Feeble Response to COVID-19 in Mexico," *Brookings*, March 30, 2020, https://www.brookings.edu/articles/amlos-feeble-response-to-covid-19-in-mexico/.

38. Mary Sheridan, "Mexico's Pandemic Policy: No Police. No Curfews. No Fines. No Regrets," *Washington Post*, January 26, 2021, https://www.washingtonpost.com/world/the_americas/coronavirus-mexico-lockdown-lopez-obrador/2021/01/25/8d6311aa-50fc-11eb-a1f5-fdaf28cfca90_story.html.

39. Mary Sheridan, "Mexico Has Refused to Close Its Borders during the Covid-19 pandemic. Does That Make Sense?" *Washington Post*, January 12, 2022, https://www.washingtonpost.com/world/2022/01/12/mexico-coronavirus-pandemic-open-border/.

40. Kimberly Collins, "Governance in Imperial County and Mexicali at the U.S.-Mexico Border during the COVID-19 Pandemic," *Borders in Globalization Review* 2, no. 1 (2020): 38–41, https://journals.uvic.ca/index.php/bigreview/article/view/19856.

41. Anne McLellan et al., "Report of the Wilson Center Task Force on Public Health and the U.S.-Canadian Border," *Wilson Center*, October 29, 2021, 21, https://www.wilsoncenter.org/publication/report-wilson-center-task-force-public-health-and-us-canadian-border.

42. Department of Homeland Security, *Fact Sheet: DHS Measures on the Border to Limit the Further Spread of Coronavirus*, March 23, 2020, https://www.dhs.gov/news/2020/10/19/fact-sheet-dhs-measures-border-limit-further-spread-coronavirus.

43. US Embassy & Consulates in Mexico, *COVID-19 Information for U.S. Citizens in Mexico*, COVID-19 Information for U.S. Citizens in Mexico - U.S. Embassy & Consulates in Mexico (COVID-19 Archives - U.S. Embassy & Consulates in Mexico (usembassy.gov)).

44. Richardson and Cappellano, "Sieve or Shield?"

45. Carrie Kahn, "'We Feel Safe': Americans Keep Visiting Mexico despite Pandemic Risks," *NPR*, December 25, 2020, https://www.npr.org/2020/12/25/949557

976/we-feel-safe-americans-keep-visiting-mexico-despite-pandemic-risks;   and Natalie Compton, "Should Travelers Avoid Mexico as Delta Surges? For Locals Who Need Them, It's Complicated," *Washington Post*, September 1, 2021, https://www.washingtonpost.com/travel/tips/mexico-travel-covid-delta-cdc/.

46. Lauren Villagran, "Back-to-School on the Border Means Long Wait Times for US Citizen Children," *El Paso Times*, August 6, 2021, https://www.elpasotimes.com/story/news/2021/08/06/us-mexico-paso-del-norte-ysleta-zaragoza-bridge-face-long-wait-times-students-back-to-school/5501714001/.

47. "The Southern Border Region at a Glance," *Southern Border Communities Coalition*, updated June 28, 2023, https://www.southernborder.org/border_lens_southern_border_region_at_a_glance.

48. Rafael Fernández de Castro, Paul Ganster, and Carlos González Gutiérrez, eds., "CaliBaja: Emerging Stronger after COVID-19," *University of California San Diego, School of Global Policy and Strategy*, 2021, https://usmex.ucsd.edu/research/usmex_calibaja_after-covid-19_report-2020-21_en.pdf; and Julian Resendiz, "Juarez Trying to Keep Mexican Shoppers from Making Trip to El Paso after U.S. Rolls Back Travel Restrictions," *Border Report*, November 10, 2021, https://www.borderreport.com/news/trade/juarez-trying-to-keep-mexican-shoppers-from-making-trip-to-el-paso-after-u-s-rolls-back-travel-restrictions/.

49. Jose Rodriguez-Sanchez, "Mexican Consumption and the Economic Impact of the Coronavirus on Texas Border Countries," *Rice University's Baker Institute for Public Policy*, December 4, 2020, https://www.bakerinstitute.org/research/mexican-consumption-and-economic-impact-coronavirus-texas-border-counties; and Imelda García, "Mexican Shoppers Have Returned along the Border, but Not in the Massive Numbers Expected," *Dallas Morning News*, November 20, 2021, https://www.dallasnews.com/news/2021/11/20/mexican-shoppers-have-returned-along-the-border-but-not-in-the-massive-numbers-expected/.

50. Roberto Coronado and Keith Phillips, "Dollar-Sensitive Mexican Shoppers Boost Texas Border Retail Activity," *Federal Reserve Bank of Dallas*, 2012, https://www.dallasfed.org/~/media/documents/research/swe/2012/swe1204g.pdf.

51. Lauren Villagran, "A Year into Border Restrictions over COVID-19, Still No Public Plan for Reopening," *El Paso Inc*, March 16, 2021, https://www.elpasoinc.com/news/local_news/paywall_exempt/a-year-into-border-restrictions-over-covid-19-still-no-public-plan-for-reopening/article_5b4a6cec-866a-11eb-9288-07d7ac3e590a.html; and María Méndez, Angela Kocherga, and Paul Flahive, "The Feds Targeted the Border for Pandemic Enforcement. Did It Work?" *TPR*, December 21, 2020, https://www.tpr.org/government-politics/2020-12-21/border-economies-saw-more-coronavirus-enforcement-than-other-communities-why.

52. Alexandra Mendoza, "Some Cross-Border Workers Are Sleeping in Their Cars to Get to Work on Time," *San Diego Union Tribune*, May 25, 2020, https://

www.sandiegouniontribune.com/news/border-baja-california/story/2020-05-25/cross-border-workers-sleeping-inside-cars.

53. Wendy Fry, "Four Months In, Coronavirus Travel Restrictions Strain Cross-Border Relationships," *Los Angeles Times*, July 25, 2020, https://www.latimes.com/california/story/2020-07-25/coronavirus-us-mexico-border-regulations-straining-families.

54. US Department of Health and Human Services, Centers for Disease Control and Prevention, "Order Suspending Introduction of Certain Persons from Countries Where a Communicable Disease Exists," 1, https://www.cdc.gov/quarantine/pdf/CDC-Order-Prohibiting-Introduction-of-Persons_Final_3-20-20_3-p.pdf.

55. See "Emails Show Stephen Miller Led Efforts to Expel Migrants at Border under Title 42," *American Oversight*, March 21, 2022, https://www.americanoversight.org/emails-show-stephen-miller-led-efforts-to-expel-migrants-at-the-border-under-title-42.

56. US Select Subcommittee on the Coronavirus Crisis, "New Select Subcommittee Report Details Trump Administration's Assault on CDC and Politicization of Public Health during the Coronavirus Crisis," October 17, 2022, https://coronavirus-democrats-oversight.house.gov/news/press-releases/clyburn-trump-cdc-redfield-caputo-report.

57. "Epidemiologists and Public Health Experts Reiterate Urgent Call to End Title 42," Columbia University Mailman School of Public Health, January 14, 2022, https://www.publichealth.columbia.edu/research/programs/program-forced-migration-health/voices/epidemiologists-public-health-experts-reiterate-urgent-call-end-title-42.

58. "Epidemiologists and Public Health Experts Reiterate Urgent Call to End Title 42."

59. Arelis Hernández and Nick Miroff, "Facing Coronavirus Pandemic, Trump Suspends Immigration Laws and Showcases Vision for Locked-Down Border," *Washington Post*, April 3, 2020, https://www.washingtonpost.com/national/coronavirus-trump-immigration-border/2020/04/03/23cb025a-74f9-11ea-ae50-7148009252e3_story.html; and Natalia Banulescu-Bogdan, Meghan Benton, and Susan Fratzke, "Coronavirus Is Spreading across Borders, but It Is Not a Migration Problem," *Migration Policy Institute*, March 2020, https://www.migrationpolicy.org/news/coronavirus-not-a-migration-problem.

60. Nicole Ellis and Casey Kuhn, "What Is Title 42 and What Does It Mean for Immigration at the Southern Border?" *PBS*, January 13, 2023, https://www.pbs.org/newshour/nation/what-is-title-42-and-what-does-it-mean-for-immigration-at-the-southern-border.

61. John Gramlich, "Monthly Encounters with Migrants at U.S.-Mexico Border Remain Near Record Highs," *Pew Research Center*, January 13, 2023, https://www.pewresearch.org/short-reads/2023/01/13/monthly-encounters-with-migrants-at-u-s-mexico-border-remain-near-record-highs/.

62. Muzaffar Chishti and Jessica Bolter, "Controversial U.S. Title 42 Expulsions Policy Is Coming to an End, Bringing New Border Challenges," *Migration Policy Institute*, March 31, 2022, https://www.migrationpolicy.org/article/title-42-expulsions-end-unwinding-unprecedented.

63. "Title 42: 'Human Rights Stain, Public Health Farce,'" Human Rights First, December 16, 2022, https://humanrightsfirst.org/library/title-42-human-rig hts-stain-public-health-farce/.

64. "The Human Cost of Title 42: Stories from the US-Mexico Border," Doctors without Borders, March 28, 2022, https://www.doctorswithoutborders.org/lat est/human-cost-title-42-stories-us-mexico-border.

65. Nicole Narea, "Another 50 Migrant Deaths and an Ever-Climbing Body Count on the Border," *Vox*, June 28, 2022, https://www.vox.com/policy-and-politics/2022/6/28/23187056/san-antonio-migrant-death-truck-border.

66. "CDC Public Health Determination and Termination of Title 42 Order," Centers for Disease Control and Prevention, https://www.cdc.gov/media/relea ses/2022/s0401-title-42.html.

67. Michael McDaniel, "Red States Sue to Stop Biden Administration from Ending Title 42 Asylum Policy," *Courthouse News Service*, April 4, 2022, https://www.courthousenews.com/three-republican-led-states-sue-to-stop-biden-administrat ion-from-ending-title-42-asylum-policy.

68. *Arizona, et al. v. Alejandro Mayorkas*, 598 U.S. 22 (2022), https://www.supre mecourt.gov/opinions/22pdf/22-592_5hd5.pdf.

69. US Department of Health and Human Services, "Fact Sheet: End of the COVID-19 Public Health Emergency," May 9, 2023, https://www.hhs.gov/about/news/2023/05/09/fact-sheet-end-of-the-covid-19-public-health-emergency.html.

70. "Border Barometer," Border Policy Research Institute, Western Washington University, April 9, 2021, https://cedar.wwu.edu/bpri_publications/127/.

71. Evan Dyer, "How Canada Changed Its Position on Pandemic Travel Bans," *CBC*, November 30, 2021, https://www.cbc.ca/news/politics/travel-ban-africa-covid-omicron-trudeau-1.6268299.

72. Kathleen Harris, "Canada to Bar Entry to Travellers Who Are Not Citizens, Permanent Residents or Americans," *CBC*, March 16, 2020, https://www.cbc.ca/news/politics/cbsa-border-airports-screening-trudeau-covid19-coronavirus-1.5498866; and "Canadian COVID-19 Intervention Timeline," *CIHI*, October 13, 2022, https://www.cihi.ca/en/canadian-covid-19-intervention-timeline.

73. Harris, "Canada to Bar Entry to Travellers Who Are Not Citizens."

74. Aaron Wherry, "Thinking the Unthinkable: How Canada and the U.S. Agreed on Border Restrictions in a Hurry," *CBC*, March 19, 2020, https://www.cbc.ca/news/politics/trump-trudeau-covid-19-coronavirus-pandemic-border-1.5502192.

75. Gordon Lubold and Paul Vieira, "U.S. Drops Proposal to Put Troops at Canadian Border," *Wall Street Journal*, updated March 26, 2020, https://www.wsj.com/articles/canada-objects-to-u-s-plan-to-put-troops-at-border-11585247654.

76. Lauren Gardner, "Canada's New Ambassador in D.C. Learns Art of Covid-19 Diplomacy," *Politico*, April 23, 2020, https://www.politico.com/news/2020/04/23/canadas-new-ambassador-in-dc-learns-art-of-covid-19-diplomacy-205710.

77. "Huizenga, Higgins Statement on U.S. Canada Border Restrictions Being Extended until at Least July 21," Congressman Bill Huizenga Press Releases, June 18, 2021, https://huizenga.house.gov/news/documentsingle.aspx?DocumentID=401318.

78. Anne McLellan et al., "Report of the Wilson Center Task Force on Public Health and the U.S.-Canadian Border."

79. Border Policy Research Institute, Western Washington University, "Emerging from the Pandemic: Understanding the Canada-US Land Border Requirements" (2021), *Border Policy Research Institute Publications* 129, https://cedar.wwu.edu/bpri_publications/129.

80. "Improving the Process of Adjudicating TN Status," Border Policy Research Institute, Western Washington University, 2015.

81. Author correspondence with Point Roberts resident, September 18, 2020. Name is withheld by mutual agreement. See also Cara Ball, "On the Border: Essential Workers Commuting between the US, Canada Reflect on Border Closure a Year Later," *WXYZ*, March 10, 2021, https://www.wxyz.com/news/coronavirus/on-the-border-essential-workers-reflect-on-a-year-of-travel-between-canada-and-the-us.

82. Grace McCarthy, "What Defines Essential? A Year with a Closed Border," *The Northern Light*, March 17, 2021, https://thenorthernlight.com/stories/what-defines-essential-a-year-with-a-closed-border,16166.

83. Author correspondence, Aimee Beachamp, February 10, 2021.

84. Author correspondence, border resident, December 9, 2021. Name withheld by mutual agreement.

85. Annie Hall (Canadian resident) in discussion with the author, November 29, 2021.

86. US Department of Transportation, Bureau of Transportation Statistics, "Border Crossing/Entry Data."

87. Kelley Lee et al., "Expert Advisory Panel Report on COVID-19 Testing and Quarantine at Canada's Borders: Comments on Analysis and Recommendations," *Pandemics & Borders, Global Canada*, June 2021, 60e9368c02e522753398ca7c_advisorypanel-report-comments.pdf (website-files.com); and "Border Barometer," Border Policy Research Institute, Western Washington University, April 9, 2021, https://cedar.wwu.edu/bpri_publications/127/.

88. Office of the Auditor General of Canada, "Report 15—Enforcement of Quarantine and COVID-19 Testing Orders—Public Health Agency of Canada" (2021), 20, https://www.oag-bvg.gc.ca/internet/English/parl_oag_202112_04_e_43968.html.

89. Kelley Lee, Julianne Piper, and Jennifer Fang, "Using Risk Analysis to Shape Border Management: A Review of Approaches during the COVID-19 Pandemic," *Migration Policy Institute* (January 2023), 1, https://www.migratio npolicy.org/research/risk-analysis-border-covid19.

90. Cecily Fasanella and Xavier Delgado, "What's the Plan? U.S. Land Border Restrictions during the COVID-19 Pandemic," Wilson Center, September 1, 2021, https://www.wilsoncenter.org/article/whats-plan-us-land-border-restricti ons-during-covid-19-pandemic.

91. Brent Griffiths, "Navarro: 'Special Place in Hell' for Trudeau," *Politico*, June 10, 2018, https://www.politico.com/story/2018/06/10/special-place-hell-trump-trudeau-navarro-635100.

92. "COVID-19 Border Measures," Government of Canada, September 2022, https://www.canada.ca/en/public-health/news/2022/09/covid-19-border-measures.html.

93. "Mandatory Quarantine," Public Safety Canada, August 6, 2020, https://www.publicsafety.gc.ca/cnt/trnsprnc/brfng-mtrls/prlmntry-bndrs/20201201/010/index-en.aspx.

94. Christine Van Geyn and Joanna Baron, *Pandemic Panic: How Canadian Government Responses to Covid 19 Changed Civil Liberties Forever* (Ontario: Optimum Publishing International, 2023).

95. Sophia Harris, "More than 200 Travellers Fined for Refusing to Quarantine in Hotels after Landing in Canada," *CBC*, April 16, 2021, https://www.cbc.ca/news/business/quarantine-hotel-covid-19-travel-canada-fine-1.5988378.

96. Harris, "More than 200 Travellers Fined."

97. Van Geyn and Baron, *Pandemic Panic*.

98. Adrian Humphreys, "Quarantine Hotels on Trial as Federal Court Hears Constitutional Challenge of COVID Restrictions," *National Post*, June 1, 2021, https://nationalpost.com/news/canada/quarantine-hotels-on-trial-as-federal-court-hears-constitutional-challenge-of-covid-restrictions.

99. Office of the Auditor General of Canada, "Report 15—Enforcement of Quarantine and COVID-19 Testing Orders."

100. Office of the Auditor General of Canada, "Report 15—Enforcement of Quarantine and COVID-19 Testing Orders."

101. Catharine Tunney, "Hotel Quarantine Measures for Air Travellers Come into Effect Feb. 22: Trudeau," *CBC*, February 12, 2021, https://www.cbc.ca/news/politics/travel-restictions-border-1.5911845.

102. Border Policy Research Institute, Western Washington University, "Emerging from the Pandemic."

103. "Strong Majority of Canadians Want the Canada-US Border to Remain Closed for the Foreseeable Future," Nanos Research (2021), 2, https://nanos.co/wp-content/uploads/2021/05/2021-1897-Border-April-Populated-Report-with-tabs.pdf.

104. Steven Chase, "Majority of Canadians Support Scrapping All COVID-19 Restrictions at U.S.-Canada Border by Fall, Poll Suggests," *Globe and Mail*, July 9, 2021, https://www.theglobeandmail.com/politics/article-majority-of-canadi ans-support-scrapping-all-pandemic-restrictions-at/.

105. Office of the Auditor General of Canada, "Report 8—Pandemic Preparedness, Surveillance, and Border Control Measures" (2021), 5, https://www.oag-bvg. gc.ca/internet/English/parl_oag_202103_03_e_43785.html.

106. Julianne Piper, Benoît Gomis, and Kelley Lee, "'Guided by Science and Evidence'? The Politics of Border Management in Canada's Response to the COVID-19 Pandemic," *Frontiers in Political Science* 4 (2022): 12, 16, https:// www.frontiersin.org/articles/10.3389/fpos.2022.834223/full#B25.

107. "Here's the Johns Hopkins Study President Trump Referenced in His Coronavirus News Conference," Johns Hopkins University, February 27, 2020, https://hub.jhu.edu/2020/02/27/trump-johns-hopkins-study-pandemic-coron aviruscovid-19-649-emo-art1-dtd-health/.

108. John Iskander et al., "Pandemic Influenza Planning, United States, 1978–2008," *Emerging Infectious Diseases* 19, no. 6 (2013): 879–885, https://www.ncbi.nlm. nih.gov/pmc/articles/PMC3713824/; and "America's Pandemic," *Washington Post* (2020), https://www.washingtonpost.com/graphics/2020/national/admi nistrations-pandemic-documentary/.

109. Bradley Dickerson (former senior biodefense officer at DHS), in discussion with authors, June 29, 2023.

110. The Covid Crisis Group, *Lessons from the Covid War: An Investigative Report* (New York: Public Affairs, 2023), 79.

111. Homeland Security Council, "National Strategy for Pandemic Influenza," May 2006, https://www.cdc.gov/flu/pandemic-resources/pdf/pandemic-influenza- implementation.pdf, 72, 18.

112. "Canadian Pandemic Influenza Preparedness: Planning Guidance for the Health Sector," Government of Canada, https://www.canada.ca/en/public-health/servi ces/flu-influenza/canadian-pandemic-influenza-preparedness-planning-guida nce-health-sector/table-of-contents.html#pre.

113. Authors' interview with Luciana Borio (former director for Medical and Biodefense Preparedness at the National Security Council from 2017 to 2019), July 31, 2023.

114. The Covid Crisis Group, *Lessons from the Covid War*, 67.

115. David Shepardson, "U.S. to Lift Restrictions Nov 8 for Vaccinated Foreign Travelers," *Reuters*, October 15, 2021, https://www.reuters.com/world/us/ exclusive-us-partly-lift-international-travel-curbs-nov-8-official-2021-10-15/.

116. Denkmann and Cowan, "After Two Years of Isolation, Point Roberts Is Open for Business."

117. Phil Melnychuk, "Border Is Open, but Point Roberts Still Recovering from Pandemic," *Delta Optimist*, October 3, 2022, https://www.delta-optimist.com/

local-news/border-is-open-but-point-roberts-still-recovering-from-pandemic-5888662.

118. Simone Higashi, "Point Roberts Labor Shortages Persist with Few Solutions," *Cascadia Daily News*, July 2, 2023, https://www.cascadiadaily.com/news/2023/jul/02/point-roberts-labor-shortages-persist-with-few-solutions.

119. US Bureau of Transportation Statistics, "Border Crossing/Entry Data."

CHAPTER 5

1. David Nikel, "Norway Hands Out $2,000 Fines or Jail for Ignoring Coronavirus Quarantine," *Forbes*, March 17, 2020, https://www.forbes.com/sites/davidnikel/2020/03/17/norway-hands-out-2000-fines-or-jail-for-ignoring-coronavirus-quarantine/?sh=7e4e441a4f42.

2. Kamilla Thue (member of the municipal council of Eidskog), in discussion with the authors, August 31, 2022.

3. Interview with Norwegian government official, August 30, 2022. Name is withheld by mutual agreement.

4. Kamilla Thue, in discussion with the authors, August 31, 2022.

5. "History of the European Union 1990–99," European Union, https://european-union.europa.eu/principles-countries-history/history-eu/1990-99_en.

6. "Towards a Stronger and More Resilient Schengen Area," European Commission, June 2, 2021, https://ec.europa.eu/commission/presscorner/detail/en/ip_21_2708.

7. European Union, European Centre for Disease Prevention and Control, "Considerations for Travel-Related Measures to Reduce Spread of COVID-19 in the EU/EEA," May 26, 2020, 3, https://www.ecdc.europa.eu/en/publications-data/considerations-travel-related-measures-reduce-spread-covid-19-eueea.

8. European Commission, "Temporary Reintroduction of Border Control," https://home-affairs.ec.europa.eu/policies/schengen-borders-and-visa/schengen-area/temporary-reintroduction-border-control_en.

9. This includes Norway, Austria, Germany, Sweden, Denmark, and France. See "Several Schengen Countries Reintroduce Border Controls in Context of COVID-19," *Schengen Visa News*, February 18, 2021, https://www.schengenvisainfo.com/news/several-schengen-countries-reintroduce-border-controls-in-context-of-covid-19/.

10. Florian Weber, "Cross-Border Cooperation in the Border Region of Germany, France, and Luxembourg in Times of Covid-19," *European Societies* 24, no. 3 (2022): 354–381, doi: 10.1080/14616696.2022.2076894.

11. Some exceptions existed, such as the efforts in Benelux to facilitate cross-border commuters into Luxembourg.

12. Martin Guillermo-Ramirez (Secretary General of the Association of European Border Regions), in discussion with the authors, September 5, 2022.

13. Until recently, these included Bulgaria, Romania, and Croatia. For a list of EU, EEA, and Schengen countries, see: "What Countries are in the EU, EEA, EFTA and the Schengen Area?," https://www.netherlandsworldwide.nl/eu-eea-efta-schengen-countries.

14. European Parliament, Committee on Regional Development, "Report on EU Border Regions: Living Labs of European Integration," July 27, 2022, https://www.europarl.europa.eu/doceo/document/A-9-2022-0222_EN.html.

15. Sergio Carrera and Ngo Chun Luk, "Love Thy Neighbour?" *CEPS*, April 3, 2020, https://www.ceps.eu/ceps-publications/love-thy-neighbour/.

16. Border controls, or checks, are defined in the Schengen Borders Code to be "checks carried out at border crossing points, to ensure that persons, including their means of transport and the objects in their possession, may be authorised to enter the territory of the member states or authorised to leave it." See European Parliament, Directorate-General for Internal Policies, "Internal Border Controls in the Schengen Area: Is Schengen Crisis-Proof?," 2016, https://www.europarl.europa.eu/RegData/etudes/STUD/2016/571356/IPOL_STU(2016)571356_EN.pdf.

17. Elspet Guild, "Schengen Borders and Multiple National States of Emergency: From Refugees to Terrorism to COVID-19," *European Journal of Migration and Law* 23, no. 4 (2021): 385–404, at 385, https://brill.com/view/journals/emil/23/4/article-p385_2.xml?language=en.

18. European Court of Auditors, "Free Movement in the EU during the COVID-19 Pandemic: Limited Scrutiny of Internal Border Controls, and Uncoordinated Actions by Member States together with the Replies of the Commission and the European Centre for Disease Prevention and Control (ECDC)," 2022, https://op.europa.eu/webpub/eca/special-reports/free-movement-13-2022/en/#chapter3.

19. Transfrontier Operational Mission (MOT), "The Effects of Covid-19 Induced Border Closures on Cross-Border regions," 2021, Annex, https://budapest.cesci-net.eu/wp-content/uploads/_publications/CBR/CBR_Y2021.pdf.

20. Martin Barthel et al., "Cross-Border Review 2020," *CESCI European Institute*, 2020, https://budapest.cesci-net.eu/en/cross-border-review-2020/.

21. "Immigration," *Brexit Legal*, https://brexitlegal.ie/immigration/.

22. Heather Stewart and Rowena Mason, "Nigel Farage's Anti-Migrant Poster Reported to Police," *The Guardian*, June 16, 2016, https://www.theguardian.com/politics/2016/jun/16/nigel-farage-defends-ukip-breaking-point-poster-queue-of-migrants.

23. See Laura Zanfrini, "Europe and the Refugee Crisis: A Challenge to Our Civilization," United Nations, https://www.un.org/en/academic-impact/europe-and-refugee-crisis-challenge-our-civilization; J. Laine, "Ambiguous Bordering Practices at the EU's Edges," in *Borders and Border Walls: In-Security, Symbolism, Vulnerabilities*, ed. Andréanne Bissonnette and Élisabeth Vallet

(New York: Routledge, 2021); Martin Klatt, "The So-Called 2015 Migration Crisis and Euroscepticism in Border Regions: Facing Re-Bordering Trends in the Danish-German Borderlands," *Geopolitics* 25, no. 3 (2020): 567–586, https://www.tandfonline.com/doi/full/10.1080/14650045.2018.1557149; and Jeanne Park, "Europe's Migration Crisis," *Council on Foreign Relations*, updated September 23, 2015, https://www.cfr.org/backgrounder/europes-migration-crisis.

24. Lorne Cook, "EU Defends Its Libya Migrant Work as UN Points the Finger," *AP News*, March 28, 2023, https://apnews.com/article/eu-libya-migration-uni ted-nations-5e5a95611fca61db0126dbb5827c0283.

25. Zanfrini, "Europe and the Refugee Crisis."

26. International Organization for Migration, UN Migration, www.iom.int.

27. Deutsche Welle News, "Germany Suspends 'Dublin Rules' for Syrians," *DW*, August 25, 2015, https://www.dw.com/en/germany-suspends-dublin-rules-for-syrians/a-18671698.

28. Deutsche Welle News, "Germany Suspends 'Dublin Rules' for Syrians."

29. Luke Harding, "Refugee Crisis: Germany Reinstates Controls at Austrian Border," *The Guardian*, September 13, 2015, https://www.theguardian.com/world/2015/sep/13/germany-to-close-borders-exit-schengen-emergency-measures.

30. "Europe Starts Putting Up Walls," *The Economist*, September 19, 2015, https://www.economist.com/europe/2015/09/19/europe-starts-putting-up-walls.

31. A. Giacometti, M. Meijer, and J. Moodie, "Trust: The Social Capital of Border Communities in the Nordic Region," in *Cross-Border Review: Yearbook 2021*, ed. James W. Scott (Budapest: Central European Service for Cross-Border Initiatives, 2021), 33–41.

32. European Parliament, Directorate-General for Internal Policies, "Internal Border Controls in the Schengen Area."

33. European Parliament, Directorate-General for Internal Policies, "Internal Border Controls in the Schengen Area"; and European Commission, "Temporary Reintroduction of Border Control."

34. Jeanne Park, "Europe's Migration Crisis," *Council on Foreign Relations*, updated September 23, 2015, https://www.cfr.org/backgrounder/europes-migration-crisis.

35. Sébastien Platon, "30 Days, Six Months . . . Forever? Border Control and the French Council of State," *Verfassungsblog*, January 9, 2018, https://verf assungsblog.de/30-days-six-months-forever-border-control-and-the-french-council-of-state/; and Sergio Carrera and Ngo Chun Luk, "In the Name of COVID-19: An Assessment of the Schengen Internal Border Controls and Travel Restrictions in the EU," *European Parliament*, September 2020, https://www.europarl.europa.eu/RegData/etudes/STUD/2020/659506/IPOL_STU(2020)659506_EN.pdf.

36. Edward Delman, "How Not to Welcome Refugees," *The Atlantic*, January 27, 2016, https://www.theatlantic.com/international/archive/2016/01/denmark-refugees-immigration-law/431520/.

37. European Parliament, Legislative Train Schedule, "Back to Schengen Roadmap," Carriages Preview, April 2022, https://www.europarl.europa.eu/legislative-train/carriage/back-to-schengen-roadmap/report?sid=5801.

38. European Commission, "Back to Schengen: Commission Proposes Roadmap for Restoring Fully Functioning Schengen System," March 4, 2016, https://ec.europa.eu/commission/presscorner/detail/en/IP_16_585.

39. European Court of Auditors, "Free Movement in the EU during the COVID-19 Pandemic."

40. Platon, "30 Days, Six Months . . . Forever?"

41. Danilo Cereda et al., "The Early Phase of the COVID-19 Epidemic in Lombardy, Italy," *Epidemics* 37 (2021), https://www.sciencedirect.com/science/article/pii/S1755436521000724.

42. Jason Horowitz, Emma Bubola, and Elisabetta Povoledo, "Italy, Pandemic's New Epicenter, Has Lessons for the World," *New York Times*, March 21, 2020, https://www.nytimes.com/2020/03/21/world/europe/italy-coronavirus-center-lessons.html.

43. Jason Horowitz and Emma Bubola, "Italy's Coronavirus Victims Face Death Alone, with Funerals Postponed," *New York Times*, Marcy 19, 2020, https://www.nytimes.com/2020/03/16/world/europe/italy-coronavirus-funerals.html?searchResultPosition=5.

44. Hanneke van Eiken and Jorrit J. Rijpma, "Stopping a Virus from Moving Freely: Border Controls and Travel Restrictions in Times of Corona," *Utrecht Law Review* 17, no. 3 (2021): 34–50.

45. European Commission, "COVID-19: Temporary Restriction on Non-Essential Travel to the EU," March 16, 2020, 2, https://eur-lex.europa.eu/legal-content/EN/TXT/PDF/?uri=CELEX:52020DC0115&from=IT.

46. Steven Erlanger, "Macron Declares France 'at War' with Virus, as E.U. Proposes 30-Day Travel Ban," *New York Times*, March 16, 2020, https://www.nytimes.com/2020/03/16/world/europe/coronavirus-france-macron-travel-ban.html.

47. European Court of Auditors, "Free Movement in the EU during the COVID-19 Pandemic."

48. European Court of Auditors, "Free Movement in the EU during the COVID-19 Pandemic"; and Daniel Thym and Jonas Bornemann, "Schengen and Free Movement Law during the First Phase of the COVID-19 Pandemic: Of Symbolism, Law and Politics," *European Papers* 5, no. 3 (2020): 1143–1170, https://www.europeanpapers.eu/en/system/files/pdf_version/EP_eJ_2020_3_4_Articles_Daniel_Thym_Jonas_Bornemann_00420_0.pdf.

49. European Court of Auditors, "Free Movement in the EU during the COVID-19 Pandemic."

50. Van Eijken and Rijpma, "Stopping a Virus from Moving Freely."

51. Christina Gonzalez, "Seehofer Rebuffs EU Criticism of New German Border Controls," *Politico*, February 13, 2021, https://www.politico.eu/article/germany-travel-coronavirus-border-austria-czech-republic-horst-seehofer-rebuffs-eu-criticism/.

52. Carrera and Chun Luk, "Love Thy Neighbour?"; and European Court of Auditors, "Free Movement in the EU during the COVID-19 Pandemic."

53. Carrera and Chun Luk, "Love Thy Neighbour?"

54. "Poland's Borders Closed from 15 March Due to Coronavirus," Government of Poland, https://www.gov.pl/web/qatar/polands-borders-closed-from-15-march-due-to-coronavirus.

55. "In Europe, Coronavirus Spread Creates Border Chaos, Choked Supply Lines," *VOA*, March 17, 2020, https://www.voanews.com/a/science-health_coronavirus-outbreak_europe-coronavirus-spread-creates-border-chaos-choked-supply/6185953.html.

56. European Court of Auditors, "Free Movement in the EU during the COVID-19 Pandemic."

57. Alberto Alemanno, "The European Response to COVID-19: From Regulatory Emulation to Regulatory Coordination?" *European Journal of Risk Regulation* (2020): 1–10, https://www.ncbi.nlm.nih.gov/pmc/articles/PMC7218191/.

58. Angela Merkel, "An address to the nation by Federal Chancellor Merkel," Bundesregierung, https://www.bundesregierung.de/breg-en/service/archive/statement-chancellor-1732302.

59. Council of the European Union, "Prolongation of the Temporary Reintroduction of Border Controls at the French Internal Borders in Accordance with Articles 25 and 27 of Regulation (EU) 2016/399 on a Union Code on the Rules Governing the Movement of Persons across Borders (Schengen Borders Code)," https://www.parlament.gv.at/gegenstand/XXVII/EU/179686.

60. "Transportation during the Pandemic," European Commission, https://commission.europa.eu/strategy-and-policy/coronavirus-response/transportation-during-pandemic_en.

61. European Commission, "Upgrading the Transport Green Lanes to Keep the Economy Going during the COVID-19 Pandemic Resurgence," October 28, 2020, https://eur-lex.europa.eu/legal-content/EN/TXT/HTML/?uri=CELEX:52020DC0685&rid=1.

62. MOT, "The Effects of COVID-19 Induced Border Closures on Cross-Border Regions," Annex.

63. Jean Peyrony (Director General of the Transfrontier Operational Mission), in discussion with the authors, September 7, 2022.

64. Birte Wassenberg, "'Return of Mental Borders': A Diary of COVID-19 Closures between Kehl, Germany and Strasbourg, France," *Borders in Globalization Review* 2, no. 1 (2020), https://journals.uvic.ca/index.php/bigreview/article/view/19886.

65. Wassenberg, "'Return of Mental Borders.'"

66. Wassenberg, "'Return of Mental Borders,'" 117.

67. Wassenberg, "'Return of Mental Borders,'" 115.

68. It is notable that a number of border controls had been in place since 2016, but movement had been relatively unrestricted. See Jean Peyrony, Jean Rubio, and Raffaele Viaggi, "The Effects of COVID-19 Induced Border Closures on Cross-Border Regions—An Empirical Report Covering the Period March to June 2020" (Luxembourg: Publications Office of the European Union, 2021), https://data.europa.eu/doi/10.2776/092793.

69. Martin Klatt, "The Danish-German Border in Times of COVID-19," *Borders in Globalization Review* 2, no. 1 (2020): 70–73.

70. MOT, "The Effects of COVID-19 Induced Border Closures on Cross-Border Regions," Annex.

71. Iva Pires, "The Portuguese-Spanish Border . . . Back Again?!," *Borders in Globalization Review* 2, no. 1 (2020), https://journals.uvic.ca/index.php/bigreview/article/view/19871.

72. Peyrony, Rubio, and Viaggi, "The Effects of COVID-19."

73. Peyrony, Rubio, and Viaggi, "The Effects of COVID-19."

74. Peyrony, Rubio, and Viaggi, "The Effects of COVID-19."

75. The Czech government required Czech commuters to stay in their country of employment for three weeks, followed by a two-week quarantine upon returning home.

76. Peyrony, Rubio, and Viaggi, "The Effects of COVID-19."

77. Peyrony, Rubio, and Viaggi, "The Effects of COVID-19," 66.

78. Peyrony, Rubio, and Viaggi, "The Effects of COVID-19."

79. Wassenberg, "'Return of Mental Borders.'"

80. "Coronavirus: Baltic States Open a Pandemic 'Travel Bubble,'" *BBC*, May 15, 2020, https://www.bbc.com/news/world-europe-52673373.

81. "Hungary, Slovenia Allow Travel by Citizens between the Two Countries," *Reuters*, May 28, 2020, https://www.reuters.com/article/us-health-coronavirus-hungary-slovenia/hungary-slovenia-allow-travel-by-citizens-between-the-two-countries-idUSKBN234277.

82. Francesco Guarascio, "EU Health Agency Slams Border Closures as Too Late and Costly to Tame Coronavirus," *Skift*, May 27, 2020, https://skift.com/2020/05/27/eu-health-agency-slams-border-closures-as-too-late-and-costly-to-tame-coronavirus/.

83. European Commission, Secretariat-General, "Joint European Roadmap towards Lifting COVID-19 Containment Measures 2020/C 126/01," April 17, 2020, https://op.europa.eu/en/publication-detail/-/publication/14188cd6-809f-11ea-bf12-01aa75ed71a1/language-en.

84. European Court of Auditors, "Free Movement in the EU during the COVID-19 Pandemic."

85. Peter van Elsuwege, "Lifting Travel Restrictions in the Era of COVID-19: In Search of a European Approach," *Verfassungsblog*, June 5, 2020, https://verfassu

ngsblog.de/lifting-travel-restrictions-in-the-era-of-covid-19-in-search-of-a-europ
ean-approach/.

86. Notable exceptions were the countries bordering Sweden. Peyrony, Rubio, and
Viaggi, "The Effects of COVID-19."

87. Elena Sánchez Nicolás, "EU Warning after Hungary Unilaterally Shuts Borders,"
EUobserver, September 1, 2020, https://euobserver.com/health-and-society/
149282.

88. Sánchez Nicolás, "EU Warning."

89. Marta Rodriguez Martinez and Gregoire Lory, "Coronavirus: EU Agrees Traffic
Light System for Travel amid COVID-19 Second Wave," *Euronews*, October 13,
2020, https://www.euronews.com/my-europe/2020/10/13/coronavirus-eu-agr
ees-traffic-light-system-for-travel-amid-covid-19-second-wave.

90. Justine Blanford et al., "Navigating Travel in Europe during the Pandemic: From
Mobile Apps, Certificates and Quarantine to Traffic-Light System," *Journal of
Travel Medicine* 29, no. 3 (2022), https://www.ncbi.nlm.nih.gov/pmc/articles/
PMC9155998/.

91. Joshua Posaner and Hanne Cokelaere, "Berlin Bats Away EU Concern over
'Painful' Coronavirus Border Curbs," *Politico*, February 15, 2021, https://www.
politico.eu/article/germany-border-controls-coronavirus-reaction/.

92. "EU Digital COVID Certificate," European Commission, https://commission.
europa.eu/strategy-and-policy/coronavirus-response/safe-covid-19-vaccines-eu-
ropeans/eu-digital-covid-certificate_en.

93. "EU Lifts Non-Essential Travel Ban for Vaccinated & Recovered Travellers
from Third Countries from March 1," *Schengen Visa News*, February 22, 2022,
https://schengen.news/eu-lifts-non-essential-travel-ban-for-vaccinated-recove
red-travellers-from-third-countries-from-march-1/.

94. "Timeline of EU Member States Reopening Their Borders," *Schengen Visa
News*, May 5, 2021, https://schengen.news/timeline-of-eu-member-states-re-
opening-their-borders/.

95. Holly Ellyatt, "Lawmakers Slam UK's Covid Response, Say 'Herd Immunity'
Strategy a Public Health Failure," *CNBC*, October 12, 2021, https://www.cnbc.
com/2021/10/12/uks-herd-immunity-covid-strategy-a-public-health-failure-
inquiry.html; and Martin Lindström, "The New Totalitarians: The Swedish
COVID-19 Strategy and the Implications of Consensus Culture and Media
Policy for Public Health," *SSM-Population Health* 14 (2021), https://www.
sciencedirect.com/science/article/pii/S235282732100063X.

96. Hazel Shearing, "Covid: Use Common Sense on Overseas Travel, Says Shapps,"
BBC, May 20, 2021, https://www.bbc.com/news/uk-57183259.

97. Alex Ledsom, "U.K. to Lift Covid Restrictions but Travel Bans to Stay in Place,
for Now," *Forbes*, July 5, 2021, https://www.forbes.com/sites/alexledsom/2021/
07/05/uk-to-lift-covid-restrictions-but-travel-bans-to-stay-in-place-for-now/
?sh=43464b6d6c07.

98. While a transition period was in place for the rest of 2020, this was largely in regard to the movement of goods and enabled the UK to remain part of the single market while trade deals and arrangements were negotiated.

99. Nordregio, *State of the Nordic Region 2022* (Stockholm: Nordregio, 2022).

100. Bjarge Schwenke Fors, "The Swedish-Norwegian Cross-Border Region," *Nordregio* magazine, https://nordregio.org/nordregio-magazine/issues/cross-border-co-operation/the-swedish-norwegian-cross-border-region/.

101. Giacometti, Meijer, and Moodie, "Trust."

102. Giacometti, Meijer, and Moodie, "Trust."

103. Lise Helsingen et al., "The COVID-19 Pandemic in Norway and Sweden—Threats, Trust, and Impact on Daily Life: A Comparative Survey," *BMC Public Health* 20, art. 1597 (2020), https://bmcpublichealth.biomedcentral.com/artic les/10.1186/s12889-020-09615-3.

104. Martin Lindström, "The COVID-19 Pandemic and the Swedish Strategy: Epidemiology and Postmodernism," *SSM-Public Health* 11 (2020), https://www.sciencedirect.com/science/article/pii/S2352827320302809.

105. Gøril Ursin, Ingunn Skjesol, and Jonathan Tritter, "The COVID-19 Pandemic in Norway: The Dominance of Social Implications in Framing the Policy Response," *Health Policy and Technology* 9, no. 4 (2020): 663–672, https://www.ncbi.nlm.nih.gov/pmc/articles/PMC7452841/.

106. Kasper Kepp et al., "Estimates of Excess Mortality for the Five Nordic Countries during the Covid-19 Pandemic 2020–2021," *International Journal of Epidemiology* 51, no. 6 (2022): 1722–1732, https://www.medrxiv.org/content/10.1101/2022.05.07.22274789v1.full.pdf.

107. Ben Cohen, "Norway Was a Pandemic Success. Then It Spent Two Years Studying Its Failures," *Wall Street Journal*, June 29, 2022, https://www.wsj.com/articles/norway-covid-pandemic-commission-11656453506.

108. Sara Stebbings et al., "Experience with Open Schools and Preschools in Periods of High Community Transmission of COVID-19 in Norway during the Academic Year of 2020/2021," *BMC Public Health* 22, art. 1454 (2022), https://bmcpubli chealth.biomedcentral.com/articles/10.1186/s12889-022-13868-5.

109. Helsingen et al., "The COVID-19 Pandemic in Norway and Sweden."

110. Bojan Pancevski, "Finland and Norway Avoid Covid-19 Lockdowns but Keep the Virus at Bay," *Wall Street Journal*, November 18, 2020, https://www.wsj.com/articles/finland-and-norway-avoid-covid-19-lockdowns-but-keep-the-virus-at-bay-11605704407?mod=article_inline.

111. Lars Jonung, "Sweden's Constitution Decides Its Exceptional Covid-19 Policy," *CEPR*, June 18, 2020, https://cepr.org/voxeu/columns/swedens-constitution-decides-its-exceptional-covid-19-policy.

112. Jostein Askim and Tomas Bergström, "Between Lockdown and Calm Down. Comparing the COVID-19 Responses of Norway and Sweden," *Local Government Studies* 48, no. 2 (2022): 291–311, https://www.tandfonline.com/doi/pdf/10.1080/03003930.2021.1964477?src=getftr.

113. Alberto Giacometti, "New Report: Nordic Cooperation amid Pandemic Travel Restrictions," *Nordregio*, December 2, 2021, https://nordregio.org/new-report-nordic-cooperation-amid-pandemic-travel-restrictions/.

114. Nordregio, *State of the Nordic Region 2022*.

115. Marta Paterlini, "'Closing Borders Is Ridiculous': The Epidemiologist behind Sweden's Controversial Coronavirus Strategy," *Nature*, April 21, 2020, https://www.nature.com/articles/d41586-020-01098-x.

116. "New Measures against Covid-19," *KrisInformation*, December 21, 2021, https://www.krisinformation.se/en/news/2021/december/new-measures-against-covid-19; and "Sweden Bans Travellers from Denmark & UK until January 21, 2021," *Schengen Visa News*, December 22, 2020, https://www.schengenvisainfo.com/news/sweden-bans-travellers-from-denmark-uk-until-january-21-2021/.

117. Excess mortality rate is defined as the number of deaths from all causes that are above what is typically experienced.

118. Johan Ahlander, "Sweden Saw Lower 2020 Death Spike than Much of Europe—Data," *Reuters*, March 24, 2021, https://www.reuters.com/business/healthcare-pharmaceuticals/sweden-saw-lower-2020-death-spike-than-much-europe-data-2021-03-24/.

119. "European Statistical Recovery Dashboard," Eurostat, updated August 17, 2023, ec.europa.eu/eurostat/cache/recovery-dashboard/.

120. Finnish Institute of International Affairs, "Nordic Cooperation amid Pandemic Travel Restrictions," November 2021, https://www.fiia.fi/en/publication/nordic-cooperation-amid-pandemic-travel-restrictions.

121. Finnish Institute of International Affairs, "Nordic Cooperation."

122. "Coronavirus: Baltic States Open a Pandemic 'Travel Bubble,'" *BBC*, May 15, 2020, https://www.bbc.com/news/world-europe-52673373.

123. Interviews with residents in Svinesund region, August 31–September 3, 2022. All interviews were conducted in confidentiality, and the names of interviewees are withheld by mutual agreement.

124. Giacometti, Meijer, and Moodie, "Trust"; and "Sweden: Unemployment Rate from 2003 to 2022," *Statista*, https://www.statista.com/statistics/375284/unemployment-rate-in-sweden/.

125. A. Giacometti and M. Meijer, "Closed Borders and Divided Communities: Status Report and Lessons from COVID-19 in Cross-Border Areas" (Stockholm: Nordregio 2021), https://nordregio.org/publications/closed-borders-and-divided-communities-status-report-and-lessons-from-covid-19-in-cross-border-areas/.

126. Richard Milne, "Nordic Co-operation Crumbles at the Norway-Sweden Border," *Financial Times*, June 18, 2020, https://www.ft.com/content/af311c89-95f6-48fd-beb9-0ac10f21eacc.

127. Giacometti and Meijer, "Closed Borders and Divided Communities."

128. Giacometti and Meijer, "Closed Borders and Divided Communities."

129. Interview with Swedish resident, September 1, 2022. All interviews were conducted in confidentiality, and the names of interviewees are withheld by mutual agreement.

130. Finnish Institute of International Affairs, "Nordic Cooperation amid Pandemic Travel Restrictions," November 2021.

131. Alberto Giacometti (Nordic cooperation researcher), in discussion with the author, August 26, 2022.

132. Giacometti and Meijer. "Closed Borders and Divided Communities."

133. Linda Engsmyr (Swedish elected official), in discussion with the authors, September 2, 2022.

134. Mari Wøien Meijer and Alberto Giacometti, "Nordic Border Communities in the Time of COVID-19," *Nordregio*, 2021, https://nordregio.org/publications/nordic-border-communities-in-the-time-of-covid-19/.

135. Kamilla Thue (member of the municipal council of Eidskog), in discussion with the authors, August 31, 2022.

136. Giacometti, in discussion with the author, August 26, 2022.

137. Nordic Cooperation, "Our Vision 2030," https://www.norden.org/en/our-vision-2030.

138. Meijer and Giacometti, "Nordic Border Communities in the Time of COVID-19."

139. Nordregio, *State of the Nordic Region 2022*.

140. Interview with representative from Freedom of Movement Council, August 29, 2022.

141. Kamilla Thue, in discussion with the authors, August 31, 2022.

142. "Freedom of movement," Nordic Co-operation, https://www.norden.org/en/freedom-movement.

143. "Towards a Stronger and More Resilient Schengen Area," *EUreporter*, February 3, 2022, https://www.eureporter.co/politics/schengen/2022/02/03/towards-a-stronger-and-more-resilient-schengen-area-2/.

144. Costica Dumbrava, European Parliamentary Research Service, "Revision of the Schengen Borders Code," April 2022, https://www.europarl.europa.eu/RegData/etudes/BRIE/2022/729390/EPRS_BRI(2022)729390_EN.pdf.

145. "Towards a Stronger and More Resilient Schengen Area," *EUreporter*, February 3, 2022.

146. Jean Peyrony, in discussion with the authors, September 7, 2022.

147. Martin Guillermo-Ramirez (Secretary General of AEBR), email message to author, September 5, 2023.

148. Kikki Lindset (Grensetjänsten), in discussion with the authors, August 31, 2022.

149. Jean Peyrony, Jean Rubio, and Raffaele Viaggi, "Analysis of the Impact of Border-Related Measures Taken by Member States in the Fight against COVID-19," 2022, https://www.researchgate.net/publication/364637975_Analysis_of_the_impact_of_border-related_measures_taken_by_Member_States_in_the_fight_against_COVID-19_Update_and_follow-up_Written_by.

150. Jean Peyrony et al., "Analysis of the Impact of Border-Related Measures Taken by Member States in the Fight against COVID-19," 5.

151. Peyrony, Rubio, and Viaggi, "The Effects of COVID-19," 102.

152. European Parliament, Legislative Train Schedule, "Back to Schengen Roadmap"; and Fabian Gülzau, "A 'New Normal' for the Schengen Area. When, Where and Why Member States Reintroduce Temporary Border Controls?," *Journal of Borderlands Studies* 38, no. 5 (2023): 785–803, https://www.tandfonline.com/doi/full/10.1080/08865655.2021.1996260.

153. Gülzau, "A 'New Normal' for the Schengen Area."

154. Gülzau, "A 'New Normal' for the Schengen Area."

155. Authors' correspondence with representative from Freedom of Movement Council, August 29, 2022. Names withheld by mutual agreement.

156. Interview with Swedish resident, September 1, 2022. Names withheld by mutual agreement.

157. European Commission, "Temporary Reintroduction of Border Control."

158. Emil Wannheden (formerly with Sweden's Ministry of Foreign Affairs), in discussion with the authors, September 8, 2022.

CHAPTER 6

1. Cf. Jay Patel and Devi Sridhar, "We Should Learn from the Asia-Pacific Responses to COVID-19," *The Lancet Regional Health—Western Pacific* 5 (2020), https://www.sciencedirect.com/science/article/pii/S2666606520300626; and I-wei Jennifer Chang, "Taiwan's Model for Combatting COVID-19: A Small Island with Big Data," *Middle East Institute*, November 10, 2020, https://www.mei.edu/publications/taiwans-model-combating-covid-19-small-island-big-data.

2. "Mortality in the Most Affected Countries," Johns Hopkins University, https://coronavirus.jhu.edu/data/mortality.

3. "The Worst Covid Strategy Was Not Picking One," *Bloomberg*, March 15, 2023, https://www.bloomberg.com/graphics/2023-opinion-lessons-learned-from-covid-pandemic-global-comparison.

4. Thomas Bollyky et al., "Pandemic Preparedness and COVID-19: An Exploratory Analysis of Infection and Fatality Rates, and Contextual Factors Associated with Preparedness in 177 Countries, from January 1, 2020, to September 20, 2021," *The Lancet* 399, no. 10334 (2022): 1489–1512, https://www.thelancet.com/action/showPdf?pii=S0140-6736%2822%2900172-6.

5. Swee Kheng Khor and David Heymann, "An Asian Pandemic Success Story," *Foreign Affairs*, September 21, 2020, https://www.foreignaffairs.com/articles/united-states/2020-09-21/asian-pandemic-success-story; and Thomas Bollyky et al., "Pandemic Preparedness and COVID-19"; Michael Penn, "How Some Asian Countries Beat Back COVID-19," *Duke Global Health Institute*, August 12, 2020, https://globalhealth.duke.edu/news/how-some-asian-countries-beat-back-covid-19.

6. Richard Horton, *The Covid-19 Catastrophe: What's Gone Wrong and How to Stop It Happening Again*, 2nd ed. (Cambridge: Polity Press, 2021), 97.

7. Khor and Heymann, "An Asian Pandemic Success Story"; Julie Rafferty, "Lessons from Asia on COVID-19: What the U.S. Can Learn from Successes Abroad," *Tufts Now*, June 8, 2022, https://now.tufts.edu/2022/06/08/lessons-asia-covid-19-what-us-can-learn-successes-abroad; Brian An and Shui-Yan Tang, "Lessons from COVID-19 Responses in East Asia: Institutional Infrastructure and Enduring Policy Instruments," *American Review of Public Administration* 50, no. 6–7 (2020): 790–800, https://journals.sagepub.com/doi/pdf/10.1177/0275074020943707:

8. Lawrence Huang, "Mobility Shutdown: The Impacts of Covid-19 on Migration in Asia and the Pacific," *Migration Policy Institute*, March 2024, https://www.migrationpolicy.org/research/covid-19-migration-asia-pacific.

9. Yen Nee Lee, "Asia's Top-Performing Economy in 2020 Could Grow Even Faster This Year," *CNBC*, February 22, 2021, https://www.cnbc.com/2021/02/23/taiwan-asias-top-performing-economy-in-2020-could-grow-faster-in-2021.html; Era Dabla-Norris and Yuanyan Sophia Zhang, "Vietnam: Successfully Navigating the Pandemic," *International Monetary Fund*, March 10, 2021, https://www.imf.org/en/News/Articles/2021/03/09/na031021-vietnam-successfully-navigating-the-pandemic:

10. "World Economic Outlook Update," International Monetary Fund, January 2021, https://www.imf.org/en/Publications/WEO/Issues/2021/01/26/2021-world-economic-outlook-update; in Asia, India was the hardest-hit major country economically, seeing an 8% GDP decline.

11. "COVID-19 and the Future of Tourism in Asia and the Pacific," Asian Development Bank, March 2022, https://www.adb.org/publications/covid-19-future-tourism-asia-pacific:

12. "COVID-19 and the Future of Tourism."

13. B. M. Meier et al., "Travel Restrictions and Variants of Concern: Global Health Laws Need to Reflect Evidence," *Bull World Health Organ* 100, no. 3 (March 1, 2022): 178–178A, doi:10.2471/BLT.21.287735, https://www.ncbi.nlm.nih.gov/pmc/articles/PMC8886257/.

14. Lisa Forman and Roojin Habibi write that: "[T]he WHO's travel guidance has evolved from strictly endorsing the futility of travel restrictions to gradually promoting a 'risk-based approach to international travel', while still denouncing discriminatory manifestations of travel restrictions insufficiently rooted in public health evidence." See Lisa Forman and Roojin Habibi, "Revisiting the Legality of Travel Restrictions under International Law during COVID-19," *International & Comparative Law Quarterly* 71, no. 3 (2022): 743–760, https://www.cambridge.org/core/journals/international-and-comparative-law-quarterly/article/revisiting-the-legality-of-travel-restrictions-under-international-law-during-covid19/78D8D2DF06E659D2BC3C529954DB7E59.

15. Kelley Lee, "The World Needs a Better Strategy for COVID Travel Restrictions," *Foreign Affairs*, December 9, 2021, https://www.foreignaffairs.com/articles/world/2021-12-09/world-needs-better-strategy-covid-travel-restrictions.

16. D. Lai et al., "How to Organise Travel Restrictions in the New Future: Lessons from the COVID-19 Response in Hong Kong and Singapore," *BMJ Global Health* 7 (2022): e006975, doi:10.1136/bmjgh-2021-006975.

17. Damien Cave, "How Covid's Bitter Divisions Tarnished a Liberal Icon," *New York Times*, January 19, 2023, https://www.nytimes.com/2023/01/19/world/asia/jacinda-ardern-resigns-covid.html.

18. Damien Cave, "How Australia Saved Thousands of Lives While Covid Killed a Million Americans," *New York Times*, May 15, 2022, https://www.nytimes.com/2022/05/15/world/australia/covid-deaths.html; Aaron Odysseus Patrick, "Australia Has Almost Eliminated the Coronavirus—by Putting Faith in Science," *Washington Post*, November 5, 2020, https://www.washingtonpost.com/world/asia_pacific/australia-coronavirus-cases-melbourne-lockdown/2020/11/05/96c198b2-1cb7-11eb-ad53-4c1fda49907d_story.html.

19. Edward Alden, "The Meaningless Mantra of 'Border Security,'" *Wall Street Journal*, June 1, 2010, https://www.wsj.com/articles/SB10001424052748704269204575270810940585150.

20. Edward Alden, "Immigration and Border Control," *Cato Journal* 32, no. 1 (2013), https://papers.ssrn.com/sol3/papers.cfm?abstract_id=2245030#.

21. "Precautionary Measures in Response to Severe Pneumonia Cases in Wuhan, China," Singapore Ministry of Health, January 2, 2020, https://www.moh.gov.sg/news-highlights/details/precautionary-measures-in-response-to-severe-pneumonia-cases-in-wuhan-china; Tom Benner, "Singapore Closes Borders to Keep Virus at Bay, but No Shutdown," *Aljazeera*, March 22, 2020, https://www.aljazeera.com/news/2020/3/22/singapore-closes-borders-to-keep-virus-at-bay-but-no-shutdown.

22. Legislative Council of the Hong Kong Special Administrative Region of the People's Republic of China, "Easing of Travel Restrictions," 2020, https://www.legco.gov.hk/research-publications/english/essentials-2021ise05-easing-of-travel-restrictions.htm.

23. Ayman Falak Medina, "The Indonesia-Singapore Reciprocal Green Lane: Salient Features," ASEAN Briefing, November 3, 2020, https://www.aseanbriefing.com/news/the-indonesia-singapore-reciprocal-green-lane-salient-features/; Niluksi Koswanage, "Singapore, Germany to Start Green Lane for Business Travel," *Bloomberg*, October 22, 2020, https://www.bloomberg.com/news/articles/2020-10-23/singapore-germany-to-start-green-lane-for-business-travel.

24. "COVID-19: Stay-Home Notice Extended to 21 Days, Policies Updated," *BAL*, May 6, 2021, https://www.bal.com/bal-news/singapore-covid-19-stay-home-notice-extended-to-21-days-policies-updated.

25. Rachel Rosenthal, "The Half-Million People Left Behind by Singapore's Travel Lanes," *Bloomberg*, October 21, 2021, https://www.bloomberg.com/opinion/

articles/2021-10-21/singapore-s-new-covid-travel-lanes-will-be-missing-half-a-million-people.

26. Raymond Zhong, "How Taiwan Plans to Stay (Mostly) Covid-Free," *New York Times*, January 2, 2021, https://www.nytimes.com/2021/01/02/world/asia/tai wan-coronavirus-health-minister.html.

27. Kris Hartley, Sarah Bales, and Azad Singh Bali, "COVID-19 Response in a Unitary State: Emerging Lessons from Vietnam," *Policy Design and Practice* 4, no. 1 (2021): 152–168, https://www.tandfonline.com/doi/full/10.1080/25741292.2021.1877923; Emma Willoughby, "An Ideal Public Health Model? Vietnam's State-Led, Preventative, Low-Cost Response to COVID-19," *Brookings*, June 29, 2021, https://www.brookings.edu/blog/order-from-chaos/2021/06/29/an-ideal-public-health-model-vietnams-state-led-preventative-low-cost-response-to-covid-19/.

28. Julia Belluz, "Vietnam Defied the Experts and Sealed Its Border to Keep COVID-19 Out. It Worked," *Vox*, April 23, 2021, https://www.vox.com/22346085/covid-19-vietnam-response-travel-restrictions.

29. Khor and Heymann, "An Asian Pandemic Success Story."

30. Todd Pollack et al., "Emerging COVID-19 Success Story: Vietnam's Commitment to Containment," *Our World in Data*, March 5, 2021, https://ourworldindata.org/covid-exemplar-vietnam.

31. Mark Barnes, "Explained: The Slow Recovery of Vietnam's Tourism Industry," *Vietnam Briefing*, April 6, 2023, https://www.vietnam-briefing.com/news/viet nam-tourism-industry-2023.html/; "Vietnam Tourism Annual Report 2019," Vietnam National Administration of Tourism, 2019, https://images.vietnam tourism.gov.vn/vn/dmdocuments/2020/E-BCTNDLVN_2019.pdf.

32. Wannaphong Durongkaveroj, "Lifting the Veil on Thailand's COVID-19 Success Story," *East Asia Forum*, August 6, 2020, https://www.eastasiaforum.org/2020/08/06/lifting-the-veil-on-thailands-covid-19-success-story/.

33. Caleb Quinley, "Thailand's Empty Beach Resorts Hope Vaccines Will Put Them Back in the Sun," *The Guardian*, March 20, 2021, https://www.theg uardian.com/world/2021/mar/20/thailands-empty-beach-resorts-hope-vacci nes-will-put-them-back-in-the-sun.

34. Richard Paddock, "Thailand's Quarantine-Island Experiment Is Showing (Modest) Results," *New York Times*, October 4, 2021, https://www.nytimes. com/2021/10/04/world/asia/thailand-phuket-covid-quarantine.html; for the experience of an early American visitor, see Alison Fox, "I Was One of the First Vaccinated Americans to Visit Thailand in More than a Year—Here's What It Was Like," *Travel and Leisure*, July 29, 2021, https://www.travelandleisure. com/travel-news/thailand-phuket-sandbox-program.

35. Steve Saxon, Jan Sodprasert, and Voramon Sucharitakul, "Reimagining Travel: Thailand Tourism after the COVID-19 Pandemic," *McKinsey and Company*, November 30, 2021, https://www.mckinsey.com/industries/travel-logist

ics-and-infrastructure/our-insights/reimagining-travel-thailand-tourism-after-the-covid-19-pandemic.

36. "Israel Confirms First Coronavirus Case as Cruise Ship Returnee Diagnosed," *The Times of Israel*, February 21, 2020, https://www.timesofisrael.com/israel-confirms-first-coronavirus-case-as-cruise-ship-returnee-diagnosed/.

37. "Israel Returns Non-Israelis on Flight from South Korea amid Coronavirus Fears," *Middle East Eye*, February 22, 2020, https://www.middleeasteye.net/news/israel-returns-non-israelis-flight-south-korea-amid-coronavirus-fears.

38. David Meyer, "Italy and South Korea Join China as Coronavirus Pariahs as Countries Close Borders," *Fortune*, February 27, 2020, https://fortune.com/2020/02/27/coronavirus-travel-ban-italy-south-korea/.

39. Robert Kelly, "South Korea's Struggle with Coronavirus," *The Interpreter*, February 27, 2020, https://www.lowyinstitute.org/the-interpreter/south-korea-s-struggle-coronavirus.

40. Charlie Campbell, "South Korea's Health Minister on How His Country Is Beating Coronavirus without a Lockdown," *Time*, April 30, 2020, https://time.com/5830594/south-korea-covid19-coronavirus/.

41. Dasl Yoon and Timothy Martin, "Why a South Korean Church Was the Perfect Petri Dish for Coronavirus," *Wall Street Journal*, March 2, 2020, https://www.wsj.com/articles/why-a-south-korean-church-was-the-perfect-petri-dish-for-coronavirus-11583082110.

42. Anthony Kuhn, "Secretive Church Sect at the Center of South Korea's Coronavirus Outbreak," *NPR*, February 24, 2020, https://www.npr.org/sections/goatsandsoda/2020/02/24/808914718/secretive-church-sect-at-the-center-of-south-koreas-coronavirus-outbreak.

43. Dennis Normile, "Coronavirus Cases Have Dropped Sharply in South Korea. What's the Secret to Its Success?" *Science*, March 17, 2020, https://www.science.org/content/article/coronavirus-cases-have-dropped-sharply-south-korea-whats-secret-its-success.

44. Choe Sang-Hun, "Shadowy Church Is at Center of Coronavirus Outbreak in South Korea," *New York Times*, February 21, 2020, https://www.nytimes.com/2020/02/21/world/asia/south-korea-coronavirus-shincheonji.html.

45. Hyonhee Shin and Hyun Young Yi, "Secretive Church at Center of South Korea's Explosive Coronavirus Outbreak," *Reuters*, February 26, 2020, https://www.reuters.com/article/us-china-health-southkorea-church/secretive-church-at-center-of-south-koreas-explosive-coronavirus-outbreak-idUSKCN20L0Q8; Kim Se-jeong, "Shincheonji Vows to Collaborate with Gov't on Coronavirus," *Korea Times*, February 23, 2020, https://www.koreatimes.co.kr/www/nation/2020/02/119_283920.html.

46. Eunsun Jeong et al., "Understanding South Korea's Response to the COVID-19 Outbreak: A Real-Time Analysis," *International Journal of Environmental Research and Public Health* 17, no. 24 (2020): 9571, https://www.ncbi.nlm.nih.gov/pmc/articles/PMC7766828/.

47. Dylan Scott and Jun Michael Park, "South Korea's COVID-19 Success Story Started with Failure," *Vox*, April 19, 2021, https://www.vox.com/22380161/south-korea-covid-19-coronavirus-pandemic-contact-tracing-testing.

48. "In Focus: OECD Economic Survey of Korea 2022," OECD, 2022, https://www.oecd.org/country/korea/.

49. June-Ho Kim et al., "Emerging COVID-19 Success Story: South Korea Learned the Lessons of MERS," *Our World in Data*, March 5, 2021, https://ourworldindata.org/covid-exemplar-south-korea.

50. Myungji Yang, "Behind South Korea's Success in Containing COVID-19: Surveillance Technology Infrastructures," *Social Science Research Council*, January 21, 2021, https://items.ssrc.org/covid-19-and-the-social-sciences/covid-19-in-east-asia/behind-south-koreas-success-in-containing-covid-19-surveillance-technology-infrastructures/.

51. Yang, "Behind South Korea's Success."

52. Min Joo Kim and Simon Denyer, "A 'Travel Log' of the Times in South Korea: Mapping the Movements of Coronavirus Carriers," *Washington Post*, March 13, 2020, https://www.washingtonpost.com/world/asia_pacific/coronavirus-south-korea-tracking-apps/2020/03/13/2bed568e-5fac-11ea-ac50-18701e14e06d_story.html.

53. Dyani Lewis, "Why Many Countries Failed at COVID Contact-Tracing—but Some Got It Right," *Nature* 588, no. 7838 (2020): 384–387, https://pubmed.ncbi.nlm.nih.gov/33318682/.

54. Steven Borowiec, "How South Korea's Nightclub Outbreak Is Shining an Unwelcome Spotlight on the LGBTQ Community," *Time*, May 14, 2020, https://time.com/5836699/south-korea-coronavirus-lgbtq-itaewon/.

55. Eunsun Jeong et al., "Understanding South Korea's Response to the COVID-19 Outbreak: A Real-Time Analysis," *International Journal of Environmental Research and Public Health* 17, no. 24 (2020): 9571, https://www.ncbi.nlm.nih.gov/pmc/articles/PMC7766828/.

56. Jennifer Couzin-Frankel and Gretchen Vogel, "Not Open and Shut: School Openings across the Globe Suggest Ways to Keep the Coronavirus at Bay, despite the Outbreaks," *Science*, July 7, 2020, https://www.science.org/content/article/school-openings-across-globe-suggest-ways-keep-coronavirus-bay-despite-outbreaks.

57. Will Davies, "These Are the World's Busiest Airline Routes during Covid Times," *Bloomberg*, November 16, 2020, https://www.bloomberg.com/news/articles/2020-11-17/these-are-the-world-s-busiest-airline-routes-during-covid-times.

58. Byeongho Lim et al., "COVID-19 in Korea: Success Based on Past Failure," *Asian Economic Papers* 20, no. 2 (2021): 41–62, https://direct.mit.edu/asep/article/20/2/41/97312/COVID-19-in-Korea-Success-Based-on-Past-Failure.

59. Sangmi Cha, Jack Kim, and Muralikumar Anantharaman, "South Korea to Lift Ban on Travelers from Hubei, China," *Reuters*, August 6, 2020, https://www.

reuters.com/article/us-health-coronavirus-southkorea-china/south-korea-to-lift-ban-on-travellers-from-hubei-china-idUSKCN253097.

60. Simon Denyer et al., "Coronavirus Infections on Diamond Princess Cruise Ship Swell to 174," *Washington Post*, February 11, 2020, https://www.washingtonp ost.com/world/asia_pacific/coronavirus-china-live-updates/2020/02/11/2b8de 3ba-4c5c-11ea-b721-9f4cdc90bc1c_story.html.

61. Morten Soendergaard Larsen, "South Korea's President Tried to Help China Contain the Coronavirus. Now People Want Him Impeached," *Foreign Policy*, March 9, 2020, https://foreignpolicy.com/2020/03/09/moon-jae-in-china-coro navirus-impeachment-south-korea-president/.

62. "Special Entry Procedure to All Travelers Entering Korea," Consulate General of the Republic of Korea in Vancouver, March 19, 2020, https://mex.mofa.go.kr/ ca-vancouver-en/brd/m_4543/view.do?seq=750854; "South Korea: Authorities to Introduce New COVID-19 Restrictions Scheme, Ease Measures Nationwide from July 1st/update 62," *Crisis 24*, June 29, 2021, https://crisis24.garda.com/ alerts/2021/06/south-korea-authorities-to-introduce-new-covid-19-restricti ons-scheme-ease-measures-nationwide-from-july-1-update-62; and Erica Zohar, "Quarantining in Korea: One Young American's Unique Travel Adventure during the COVID-19 Pandemic," *Forbes*, July 10, 2020, https://www.forbes. com/sites/ericawertheimzohar/2020/07/10/quarantining-in-korea-one-young-americans-unique-travel-adventure-during-covid-19.

63. Kilkin Ko, *Managing the Covid-19 Pandemic in South Korea* (London: Routledge, 2023).

64. Digi Therese K J and Flory Ann Tacuban, "The Pandemic and Its Effect on South Korea's Tourism Industry," *Diinsider*, December 1, 2021, https://www. changemag-diinsider.com/blog/the-pandemic-and-its-effect-on-south-korea-s-tourism-industry.

65. "Fast Track Business Programs with Korea," FKCCI, October 17, 2020, https://www.fkcci.com/actualites/n/news/fast-track-business-programs-with-korea.html.

66. William Sposato, "Japan and Korea Won't Let a Pandemic Stop Them Fighting," *Foreign Policy*, March 12, 2020, https://foreignpolicy.com/2020/03/12/japan-and-korea-wont-let-a-pandemic-stop-them-fighting/.

67. "South Korea: Officials Extend International Travel Curbs through Feb. 3 due to COVID-19 Activity/update 81," *Crisis 24*, December 30, 2021, https://crisi s24.garda.com/alerts/2021/12/south-korea-officials-extend-international-tra vel-curbs-through-feb-3-due-to-covid-19-activity-update-81.

68. Kim Tong-Hyung, "South Korea Extends Restrictions on Travelers from China," *ABC*, January 26, 2023, https://abcnews.go.com/Business/wireStory/ south-korea-extends-restrictions-travelers-china-96708624.

69. John Power, "South Korea Offers Quarantine-Free Travel as Asia's 'Zero-Covid' Economies Stay Isolated," *South China Morning Post*, July 2, 2021, https://

www.scmp.com/week-asia/health-environment/article/3139607/south-korea-offers-quarantine-free-travel-asias-zero.

70. "Record COVID Cases in S Korea as 'Immunity Wanes among Elderly,'" *Aljazeera*, December 8, 2021, https://www.aljazeera.com/news/2021/12/8/rec ord-covid-cases-in-s-korea-as-immunity-wanes-among-elderly.

71. Jennifer Bouey et al., *Public Health and Soft Power: The Republic of Korea's Initial COVID-19 Response and Its Implication for Health Diplomacy* (Santa Monica, CA: RAND Corporation, 2022), https://www.rand.org/pubs/resea rch_reports/RRA1415-1.html.

72. Clarissa Wei, "The Topsy-Turvy End of Zero Covid In Taiwan," *New Yorker*, May 23, 2022, https://www.newyorker.com/news/dispatch/the-topsy-turvy-end-of-zero-covid-in-taiwan; Robert Anderson, "2020 Final Death Statistics: COVID-19 as an Underlying Cause of Death vs. Contributing Cause," National Center for Health Statistics, Center for Disease Control and Prevention, 2020, https://www.cdc.gov/nchs/pressroom/podcasts/2022/20220107/20220107.htm.

73. Chang, "Taiwan's Model for Combatting COVID-19."

74. "Security Alert Level Raised for All International and Cross-Strait Ports of Entry/Exit," Taiwan Ministry of Health and Welfare, January 8, 2020, https://covid19.mohw.gov.tw/en/cp-4868-53697-206.html; "Timely Border Control," Taiwan Ministry of Health and Welfare, May 14, 2020, https://covid19.mohw.gov.tw/en/cp-4774-53783-206.html.

75. "All Airlines of Taiwan Suspended Direct Flights to and from Wuhan, and Chinese Nationals Residing in Wuhan Were Prohibited from Entry into Taiwan," Taiwan Ministry of Health and Welfare, https://covid19.mohw.gov.tw/en/cp-4868-53725-206.html.

76. Nick Aspinwall, "Taiwan Closes Borders in Preparation for Possible 'Second Wave' of the Coronavirus," *The Diplomat*, March 20, 2020, https://thediplo mat.com/2020/03/taiwan-closes-borders-in-preparation-for-possible-second-wave-of-the-coronavirus/; "Restrictions on All Foreigners from Entering into Taiwan. All Inbound Travelers Were Requested to Undergo Home Quarantine for 14 Days," Taiwan Ministry of Health and Welfare, March 19, 2020, https://covid19.mohw.gov.tw/en/cp-4868-53890-206.html.

77. "Foreign Visitor Visas Extended for Fourth Time," *Taipei Times*, June 16, 2020, https://www.taipeitimes.com/News/taiwan/archives/2020/06/16/200 3738305.

78. "MOFA Adjusts Entry Regulations for Foreign Nationals in Response to Worldwide Efforts to Resume Economic Activity and International Exchanges Following COVID-19 Outbreak," Ministry of Foreign Affairs Republic of China (Taiwan), June 24, 2020, https://en.mofa.gov.tw/News_Content.aspx?n=1eadd cfd4c6ec567&s=cd55a0d12ea00ea7.

79. Nick Aspinwall, "Taiwan Tightens Pandemic Measures after First Local COVID-19 Case since April," *The Diplomat*, January 1, 2021, https://thediplomat.com/

2021/01/taiwan-tightens-pandemic-measures-after-first-local-covid-19-case-since-april/.

80. "MOFA Announces Adjustments to Regulations for Foreign Nationals Entering Taiwan Beginning March 1, 2021, in Line with the Continuation of CECC Fall–Winter COVID-19 Prevention Program," Bureau of Consular Affairs, Ministry of Foreign Affairs, Republic of China (Taiwan), February 25, 2021, https://www.boca.gov.tw/cp-220-6342-02525-2.html; "COVID-19: Entry Suspended for Foreign Nationals and Transit Travelers," *BAL*, May 18, 2021, https://www.bal.com/bal-news/taiwan-covid-19-entry-suspended-for-foreign-nationals-and-transit-travelers/.

81. "COVID-19: Entry Suspended for Foreign Nationals and Transit Travelers," *BAL*, May 18, 2021, https://www.bal.com/bal-news/taiwan-covid-19-entry-suspended-for-foreign-nationals-and-transit-travelers/; Helen Davidson, "How Did Covid Slip through Taiwan's 'Gold Standard' Defenses?," *The Guardian*, May 17, 2021, https://www.theguardian.com/world/2021/may/17/how-did-covid-slip-through-taiwans-gold-standard-defences.

82. "Taiwan Opens Borders to Tourists as Restrictions after 2.5 Years," *The Guardian*, October 12, 2022, https://www.theguardian.com/world/2022/oct/13/taiwan-opens-borders-to-tourists-as-restrictions-eased-after-25-years; "Tourists Flock to Taiwan as COVID Entry Restrictions Ease," *VOA*, October 13, 2022, https://www.voanews.com/a/tourists-flock-to-taiwan-as-covid-entry-restrictions-ease/6787917.html; "Taiwan to End COVID Quarantine for Arrivals, Welcome Back Tourists," *Reuters*, September 29, 2022, https://www.reuters.com/world/asia-pacific/taiwan-confirms-mid-october-end-covid-quarantine-arrivals-2022-09-29/.

83. Authors' interview with Shih-Fen Chen, Kaiser Professor of International Business, Western Washington University, April 11, 2023.

84. Helen Davidson, "Speed, Decisiveness, Cooperation: How a Tiny Taiwan Village Overcame Delta," *The Guardian*, September 5, 2021, https://www.theguardian.com/world/2021/sep/05/speed-decisiveness-cooperation-how-a-tiny-taiwan-village-overcame-delta.

85. "Taiwan Records First Omicron Case in Traveler from Africa," *AP News*, December 11, 2021, https://apnews.com/article/coronavirus-pandemic-health-taiwan-68ee3b70b79ab3e8d4b09c23b0e29d40.

86. Interview with Shih-Fen Chen, April 11, 2023.

87. Annabel Uhlman, "COVID-19, Migrant Workers, and the Fight Equality in Taiwan," *Global Taiwan Institute*, June 16, 2021, https://globaltaiwan.org/2021/06/covid-19-migrant-workers-and-the-fight-for-equality-in-taiwan/.

88. "Rights Groups Urge Government to Ease Migrant Worker Vacation Rules," *Focus Taiwan*, February 20, 2023, https://focustaiwan.tw/society/202302200010; "CORONAVIRUS/Taiwan to Loosen COVID-19 Protocols for Migrant Worker Entry," *Focus Taiwan*, March 8, 2023, https://focustaiwan.tw/society/202303080011.

89. Pei-Chia Lan, "Shifting Borders and Migrant Workers' Im/mobility: The Case of Taiwan during the COVID-19 Pandemic," *Asian Pacific Migration Journal* 31, no. 3 (2022): 225–246, https://www.ncbi.nlm.nih.gov/pmc/articles/PMC 9490386/.

90. Erin Hale, "Taiwan's COVID Rules Bar Foreign Workers from Entering or Leaving," *Nikkei Asia*, August 14, 2021, https://asia.nikkei.com/Spotlight/ Coronavirus/Taiwan-s-COVID-rules-bar-foreign-workers-from-entering-or-leaving.

91. Chiang Yi-ching, "CORONAVIRUS/Taiwan's Foreign Residents Hope for End to Family Entry Ban," *CEDAW*, October 24, 2021, http://www.cedaw.org. tw/en/en-global/news/detail/287.

92. Diaa Hadid, "Aussies Stranded Abroad Include Hundreds of Kids, Folks Short on Cash," *NPR*, July 4, 2021, https://www.npr.org/sections/goats andsoda/2021/07/04/1010891117/aussies-stranded-abroad-include-hundr eds-of-kids-folks-short-on-cash.

93. Anna Larson, "'You Should Have Come Back Earlier': The Divisive Effect of Australia's COVID-19 Response on Diaspora Relations," *Australian Geographer* 53, no. 2 (2022): 131–148, https://www-tandfonline-com.ezproxy.library.wwu. edu/doi/full/10.1080/00049182.2022.2082038.

94. Jocelyne Basseal et al., "Key Lessons from the COVID-19 Public Health Response in Australia," *The Lancet Regional Health—Western Pacific* 30, no. 100616 (2022), https://www.thelancet.com/journals/lanwpc/article/PIIS2666-6065(22)00231-0/fulltext.

95. Open Society, Common Purpose Taskforce 2022, "The Great Australian Renovation," Sydney Policy Lab, University of Sydney, 2022, https://www.syd ney.edu.au/content/dam/corporate/documents/sydney-policy-lab/our-research/ report_great-australian_-renovation.pdf.

96. "U.S. Raises Travel Alert to Japan due to 'Community Spread' of Virus," *Kyodo News*, February 23, 2020, https://english.kyodonews.net/news/2020/02/36799 dcc49ca-urgent-us-raises-travel-alert-to-japan-due-to-community-spread-of-virus.html.

97. M. Osumi, "Tokyo's Pandemic Border Policy Highlights Insecure Status of Foreign Residents," *The Japan Times*, January 1, 2021, https://www.japantimes. co.jp/news/2020/12/30/national/japan-pandemic-foreign-residents/.

98. "The Independent Investigation Commission on the Japanese Government's Response to COVID-19," API Initiative, https://apinitiative.org/en/project/ covid19/#part2.

99. "Japan to Expand Entry Ban to 73 Countries, Regions amid Virus Spread," *The Mainichi*, April 1, 2020, https://web.archive.org/web/20200404082806/ https://mainichi.jp/english/articles/20200401/p2g/00m/0na/103000c.

100. Magdalena Osumi, "Foreign Residents Stranded Abroad by Japan's Coronavirus Controls," *Japan Times*, May 19, 2020, https://www.japantimes.co.jp/news/

2020/05/19/national/social-issues/japan-foreign-residents-stranded-abroad-coronavirus/..

101. Magdalena Osumi, "Tokyo's Pandemic Border Policy Highlights Insecure Status of Foreign Residents," *Japan Times*, December 30, 2020, https://www.japanti mes.co.jp/news/2020/12/30/national/japan-pandemic-foreign-residents/.

102. Osumi, "Tokyo's Pandemic Border Policy."

103. "The Independent Investigation Commission on the Japanese Government's Response to COVID-19," API Initiative, https://apinitiative.org/en/project/covid19/.

104. Saya Soma and Yves Tiberghien, "Japan Slams the Borders Shut on Omicron," *East Asia Forum*, February 6, 2022, https://www.eastasiaforum.org/2022/02/06/japan-slams-the-borders-shut-on-omicron/.

105. Mirza Shehnaz, "What Pandemic Border Closures Say about Japan's View of Outsiders," *The Economist*, July 7, 2022, https://www.economist.com/asia/2022/07/07/what-pandemic-border-closures-say-about-japans-view-of-outsiders.

106. Osumi, "Tokyo's Pandemic Border Policy."

107. "Japanese Departures Overseas Totaled 512,000, down 84% over 2020 or down 97.4% over 2019," *Travel Voice*, January 26, 2022, https://www.travelvoice.jp/english/japanese-departures-overseas-tota led-512-000-down-84-over-2020-or-down-97-4-over-2019.

108. Soma and Tiberghien, "Japan Slams the Borders Shut on Omicron."

109. Justin McCurry, "'I Cried All Day': The Anguish of People Locked Out of Japan by Covid," *The Guardian*, January 22, 2022, https://www.theg uardian.com/world/2022/jan/22/i-cried-all-day-the-anguish-of-people-loc ked-out-of-japan-by-covid.

110. Isabel Reynolds, "Xenophobia Spills into Japan's Covid-Era Debate on Immigration," *Bloomberg*, December 26, 2021, https://www.bloomberg.com/news/articles/2021-12-26/xenophobia-spills-into-japan-s-covid-era-debate-on-immigration.

111. "Japan's COVID Border Ban Alienates Friends and Allies," East Asia Forum, February 7, 2022, https://www.eastasiaforum.org/2022/02/07/japans-covid-border-ban-alienates-friends-and-allies/.

112. Soma and Tiberghien, "Japan Slams the Borders Shut on Omicron"; Kate Sameulson, "'Neo-Sakoku': How Has Japan's Border Experiment Worked?" *The Week*, February 11, 2022, https://www.theweek.co.uk/news/world-news/asia-pacific/955731/neo-sakoku-japan-border-experiment-covid-19.

113. Kanako Takahara, "Japan Says It Will 'Lift Entry Ban on 106 Countries,' but Tourists Still Can't Enter," *Japan Times*, April 6, 2022, https://www.japantimes.co.jp/news/2022/04/06/national/lift-entry-ban-106-countries/.

114. Leonard Schoppa, "Calling on Japan to Open to Foreign Students and Scholars," *GoPetition*, January 15, 2022, https://www.gopetition.com/petitions/calling-on-japan-to-open-to-foreign-students-and-scholars.html.

115. "Poll Finds 89% in Japan Back Kishida's Ban on New Foreign Arrivals," *Japan Times*, December 6, 2021, https://www.japantimes.co.jp/news/2021/12/06/national/kishida-arrivals-ban-support/; Miho Inada and Peter Landers, "Japan's Foreigner Ban over Omicron Raises Memories of Isolation History," *Wall Street Journal*, updated January 11, 2022, https://www.wsj.com/articles/japan-extends-entry-ban-for-foreigners-citing-omicron-11641874059.

116. Takumi Kato, "Opposition in Japan to the Olympics during the COVID-19 Pandemic," *Humanities and Social Sciences Communications* 8, no. 327 (2021), https://www.nature.com/articles/s41599-021-01011-5; Matt Alt, "Tokyo's Olympics Have Become the Anger Games," *New Yorker*, July 22, 2021, https://www.newyorker.com/sports/sporting-scene/tokyos-olympics-have-become-the-anger-games.

117. Linda Sieg, "Explainer: As COVID-19 Cases Surge, Japan Sticks to 'Lockdown-Lite,'" *Reuters*, August 5, 2021, https://www.reuters.com/world/asia-pacific/covid-19-cases-surge-japan-sticks-lockdown-lite-2021-08-06/.

118. "The Independent Investigation Commission on the Japanese Government's Response to COVID-19," API Initiative, https://apinitiative.org/en/project/covid19/.

119. Irwin Wong, "Welcome Back to Japan," *Washington Post*, November 11, 2022, https://www.washingtonpost.com/travel/2022/11/11/japan-travel-open-restrictions-tourism/; Mari Yamaguchi, "Japan to Lift COVID-19 Border Controls before Holiday Week," *AP News*, April 28, 2023, https://apnews.com/article/japan-coronavirus-lift-border-control-tourism-331fdd3a1268a1d56118d4a5d2b49c1c.

120. "Chapter 2: Preparation and Initial Response," Parliament of Australia, https://www.aph.gov.au/Parliamentary_Business/Committees/Senate/COVID-19/COVID19/Interim_Report/section?id=committees%2freportsen%2f024513%2f73496.

121. Will Ziebell, "Australia Bars Entry to Foreign Nationals Traveling from Mainland China," *Reuters*, January 31, 2020, https://www.reuters.com/article/us-china-health-australia/australia-bars-entry-to-foreign-nationals-traveling-from-mainland-china-idUSKBN1ZV3F1; Dan Conifer, "Australia Announces Iran Travel Ban amid COVID-19 Coronavirus Outbreak," *Australian Broadcasting Corporation*, February 28, 2020, https://www.abc.net.au/news/2020-02-29/australia-announces-iran-travel-ban/12013884; "Australia Bans Travelers from South Korea in Bid to Slow Coronavirus," *Reuters*, March 4, 2020, https://jp.reuters.com/article/us-health-coronavirus-australia-southkor-idUKKBN20S07D.

122. Alice Klein, "Australia Axes Overseas Travel and Large Gatherings to Slow Covid-19," *New Scientist*, March 18, 2020, https://www.newscientist.com/article/2237798-australia-axes-overseas-travel-and-large-gatherings-to-slow-covid-19/.

123. Australia's Senate Select Committee on Covid-19, which looked in-depth at the government's response, concluded in its first interim report that with two-thirds

of the new cases then coming from overseas, the government should have acted sooner in imposing more comprehensive travel restrictions. "Senate Select Committee on COVID-19," Parliament of Australia, https://www.aph.gov.au/ Parliamentary_Business/Committees/Senate/COVID-19/COVID19.

124. Lauren Smiley, "27 Days in Tokyo Bay: What Happened on the *Diamond Princess*," *Wired*, April 30, 2020, https://www.wired.com/story/diamond-princ ess-coronavirus-covid-19-tokyo-bay/.

125. Frances Mao, "Coronavirus: How Did Australia's Ruby Princess Cruise Debacle Happen?" *BBC*, March 24, 2020, https://www.bbc.com/news/world-australia-51999845.

126. Harriet Alexander and Sarah McPhee, "Scars and Redemption: The Ruby Princess Legacy a Year On," *Sydney Morning Herald*, March 11, 2021, https:// www.smh.com.au/national/scars-and-redemption-the-ruby-princess-legacy-a-year-on-20210309-p57904.html.

127. See Lily McCann et al., "Police, Permits and Politics: Navigating Life on Australia's State Borders during the COVID-19 Pandemic," *Australian Journal of Rural Health* 30, no. 3 (2022): 363–372, https://onlinelibrary.wiley.com/doi/ 10.1111/ajr.12845.

128. Covid-19 Hotel Quarantine Inquiry, Final Report and Recommendations, Volume I, Victorian Government Printer, December 2020, https://www.quaran tineinquiry.vic.gov.au/covid-19-hotel-quarantine-inquiry-final-report, 17; Paul Karp and Katherine Murphy, "Overseas Arrivals to Australia to Be Quarantined in Hotels for Two Weeks over Coronavirus," *The Guardian*, March 27, 2020, https://www.theguardian.com/world/2020/mar/27/overseas-arrivals-to-austra lia-to-be-quarantined-in-hotels-for-two-weeks-over-coronavirus.

129. Covid-19 Hotel Quarantine Inquiry, 32.

130. "The Latest: 2nd Wave of Cases Traced to 2 Australian Hotels," *AP News*, August 17, 2020, https://apnews.com/article/virus-outbreak-australia-health-latin-amer ica-victoria-699d82eeb3bf88079f6b5d8dd8a43e8b.

131. The Senate Select Committee on Covid-19, Final Report, Commonwealth of Australia, April 2022, https://www.aph.gov.au/Parliamentary_Business/Com mittees/Senate/COVID-19/COVID19/Report, 38.

132. "All the Melbourne Lockdown Rules Explained," *Australian Financial Review*, August 3, 2020, https://www.afr.com/politics/federal/all-the-melbourne-lockd own-rules-explained-20200803-p55hz8.

133. "Victoria Coronavirus Cases Rise by 108 as Daniel Andrews Strengthens Lockdown at Nine Public Housing Estates," *Australian Broadcasting Corporation*, July 3, 2020, https://www.abc.net.au/news/2020-07-04/victo ria-coronavirus-cases-rise-by-108-lockdown-new-postcodes/12422456; and "Lockdown of Victoria's Public Housing Towers during COVID Crisis Breached Human Rights, Ombudsman Finds," *Australian Broadcasting Corporation*, December 16, 2020, https://www.abc.net.au/news/2020-12-17/lockdown-pub lic-housing-towers-breached-human-rights-ombudsman/12991162.

134. Senate Select Committee on Covid-19, Final Report, 90.

135. Paul Smith, "Hard Lockdown and a 'Health Dictatorship': Australia's Lucky Escape from COVID-19," *BMJ*, December 23, 2020, https://www.bmj.com/content/371/bmj.m4910.full.

136. Bianca Hall, "Victoria's Contact Tracing System to Be Bolstered after String of Failures," *The Age*, July 10, 2020, https://www.theage.com.au/politics/victoria/victoria-s-contact-tracing-system-to-be-bolstered-after-string-of-failures-20200710-p55aud.html.

137. Hall, "Victoria's Contact Tracing System."

138. Adam Ang, "Government-Backed Study Finds Australia's COVIDSae App Ineffective for Contact Tracing," *Healthcare IT News*, February 7, 2022, https://www.healthcareitnews.com/news/anz/government-backed-study-finds-australias-covidsafe-app-ineffective-contact-tracing.

139. Colin Packham and Sonali Paul, "Australia Restricts Number of Citizens Returning as Virus Surges," *Reuters*, July 9, 2020, https://www.reuters.com/article/us-health-coronavirus-australia-idUSKBN24B00F; Cailey Rizzo, "Australia Will No Longer Cover the Cost of Coronavirus Quarantine for Travelers Arriving in Sydney," *Travel and Leisure*, July 13, 2020, https://www.travelandleisure.com/travel-news/australia-new-south-wales-mandatory-quarantine-costs. While the government required citizens to foot their hotel bills, more than 20,000 of those forced to endure the two-week quarantine refused to pay. The government footed a bill estimated at A$140 million. Eathan Rix, "Hotel Quarantine Debt Is Estimated at $140 Million—but Some Are Contesting Their Bills," *Australian Broadcasting Corporation*, November 16, 2022, https://www.abc.net.au/news/2022-11-17/hotel-quarantine-debt-challenged-by-returned-travelers/101659300.

140. Senate Select Committee on Covid-19, Final Report, 3.

141. Caitlin Fitzsimmons, "The Inside Story of How Celebrities Organise Alternative Quarantine," *Sydney Morning Herald*, March 21, 2021, https://www.smh.com.au/national/nsw/the-inside-story-of-how-celebrities-organise-alternative-quarantine-20210312-p57a52.html; Nadia Daly, "Australia's Hotel Quarantine Exemptions Explained: Who Can Get Them, What Are the Reasons, and Who Is Making the Decisions," *Australian Broadcasting Corporation*, January 20, 2021, https://www.abc.net.au/news/2021-01-21/australia-hotel-quarantine-exemptions-rules-reasons-process/13078830.

142. Steve McMorran and Bruce Matthews, "Djokovic Out, but Vaccine Debate Stays in Australian Open," *AP News*, January 17, 2022, https://apnews.com/article/coronavirus-pandemic-novak-djokovic-sports-health-tennis-12144853eef39464285c9ee636341b7e.

143. Liam Mannix and Rachel Eddie, "Mum Dies While Son Pleads for Quarantine Exemption to Be by Her Side," *Sydney Morning Herald*, June 21, 2021, https://www.smh.com.au/national/mum-dies-while-son-pleads-for-quarantine-exemption-to-be-by-her-side-20210620-p582n1.html.

144. Kathina Ali et al., "A Cross-Sectional Investigation of the Mental Health and Wellbeing among Individuals Who Have Been Negatively Impacted by the COVID-19 International Border Closure in Australia," *Globalization and Health* 18, no. 12 (2022), https://globalizationandhealth.biomedcentral.com/articles/10.1186/s12992-022-00807-7.

145. Hannah Ritchie, "'Even Prisoners Get Fresh Air': Inside Australia's 'Lucky Dip' Hotel Quarantine System," *CNN*, March 10, 2021, https://www.cnn.com/travel/article/australia-hotel-quarantine-system/index.html.

146. Ritchie, "'Even Prisoners Get Fresh Air.'"

147. "Chapter 2: Preparation and Initial Response," Parliament of Australia, https://www.aph.gov.au/Parliamentary_Business/Committees/Senate/COVID-19/COVID19/Interim_Report/section?id=committees%2freportsen%2f024513%2f73496.

148. Olivera Simic, "Locked In and Locked Out: A Migrant Woman's Reflection on Life in Australia during the COVID-19 Pandemic," *Journal of International Women's Studies* 22, no. 9 (2021), https://vc.bridgew.edu/cgi/viewcontent.cgi?article=2646&context=jiws.

149. Damien Cave and Livia Albeck-Ripka, "Australia Tells Its Citizens in India amid Covid Crisis: Don't Come Home," *New York Times*, May 3, 2021.

150. Senate Select Committee on Covid-19, Final Report, 42.

151. Olivera Simic and Kim Rubenstein, "The Challenge of 'COVID-19 Free' Australia: International Travel Restrictions and Stranded Citizens," *International Journal of Human Rights* 27, no. 5 (2022): 830–843, https://www.tandfonline.com/doi/abs/10.1080/13642987.2022.2058496?journalCode=fjhr20.

152. James Glynn, "A Year after COVID-19 Emerged, Australians Still Can't Get Home," *Wall Street Journal*, updated January 7, 2021, https://www.wsj.com/articles/a-year-after-covid-19-emerged-australians-still-cant-get-home-11610015403.

153. Geoffrey Rice, "How Reminders of the 1918–19 Pandemic Helped Australia and New Zealand Respond to COVID-19," *Journal of Global History* 15, no. 3 (2020): 421–433, doi:10.1017/S1740022820000285.

154. Rice, "How Reminders of the 1918–19 Pandemic Helped Australia and New Zealand."

155. M. Boyd, M. G. Baker, and N. Wilson, "Border Closure for Island Nations? Analysis of Pandemic and Bioweapon-Related Threats Suggests Some Scenarios Warrant Drastic Action," *Australian and New Zealand Journal of Public Health*, 44 (2020): 89–91, doi:10.1111/1753-6405.12991; M. Boyd et al., "Economic Evaluation of Border Closure for a Generic Severe Pandemic Threat Using New Zealand Treasury Methods," *Australian and New Zealand Journal of Public Health* 42, no. 5 (October 2018): 444–446, doi:10.1111/1753-6405.12818; Ministry of Health, *Responding to Public Health Threats of International Concern at New Zealand Air and Sea Ports: Guidelines for Public Health Units,*

Border Agencies and Health Service Providers (Wellington: Government of New Zealand, 2016).

156. Katharine Murphy, *The End of Certainty: Scott Morrison and Pandemic Politics* (Carlton, Victoria: Quarterly Essay, 2020).

157. "Majority (83%) of Australians Support the Closing of Their International Borders as Few (21%) Believe COVID-19 Is Contained," *Ipsos*, December 4, 2020, https://www.ipsos.com/en-au/majority-83-australians-support-closing-their-international-borders-few-21-believe-covid-19.

158. Elizabeth Hicks, "A Right to Come Home? Repatriation Rights and Policy in Australia," *Melbourne School of Government*, April 20, 2021, https://papers.ssrn.com/sol3/papers.cfm?abstract_id=3829313.

159. Paul Karp, "Australia's Covid Response Should Be Examined by Royal Commission, Senate Inquiry Recommends," *The Guardian*, April 7, 2022, https://www.theguardian.com/world/2022/apr/07/australias-covid-response-should-be-examined-by-royal-commission-senate-inquiry-recommends.

160. Melissa Iaria, "Premier Daniel Andrews Has 'Lock-Out, Not Down' Plan to Stop Delta," *The Australian*, July 1, 2021, https://www.theaustralian.com.au/breaking-news/premier-daniel-andrews-has-lock-out-not-down-plan-to-stop-delta/news-story/9cb5036c4d650ee34ed84c90aa827703.

161. Gigi Foster, *Do Lockdowns and Border Closures Serve the "Greater Good"?* (Redland Bay, Queensland: Connor Court Publishing, 2022); Pippa McDermid et al., "Stranded Abroad during the COVID-19 Pandemic: Examining the Psychological and Financial Impact of Border Restriction," *MedRxiv*, 2021, https://www.medrxiv.org/content/10.1101/2021.12.08.21267218v1.

162. "Time for Review on COVID-19 Border and Quarantine Restrictions," Australian Human Rights Commission, December 18, 2021, https://humanrights.gov.au/about/news/opinions/time-review-covid-19-border-and-quarantine-restrictions.

163. Tom Chodor and Shahar Hameiri, "COVID-19 and the Pathologies of Australia's Regulatory State," *Journal of Contemporary Asia* 53, no. 1 (2023): 28–52, doi:10.1080/00472336.2022.2106883.

164. High Court of New Zealand, "Grounded Kiwis Group Inc v Minister of Health," April 27 2022, 60, http://www.nzlii.org/nz/cases/NZHC/2022/832.html.

165. Jamie Freed and Renju Jose, "New Zealand Suspends Quarantine-Free Travel with Australia," *Reuters*, July 22, 2021, https://www.reuters.com/world/asia-pacific/new-zealand-suspends-quarantine-free-travel-with-australia-2021-07-23/.

166. Natasha Frost, "Jacinda Ardern, New Zealand's Leader, Says She Will Step Down," *New York Times*, January 18, 2023, https://www.nytimes.com/2023/01/18/world/asia/jacinda-ardern-new-zealand.html.

167. Charlotte Graham-McLay, "Coronavirus Outbreak: New Zealand Bans Foreign Travelers from China," *The Guardian*, February 2, 2020, https://www.theguard

ian.com/world/2020/feb/03/coronavirus-outbreak-new-zealand-bans-foreign-travellers-from-china.

168. "New Zealand Shuts Border to All Foreigners to Curb Spread of Coronavirus," *Reuters*, March 18, 2020, https://www.reuters.com/article/us-health-coronavirus-newzealand-ban/new-zealand-shuts-border-to-all-foreigners-to-curb-spread-of-coronavirus-idUSKBN2160KX.

169. Praveen Menon, "'Act Like You Have COVID-19': PM Ardern Says as New Zealand Heads into Lockdown," *Reuters*, March 24, 2020, https://www.reuters.com/article/us-health-coronavirus-newzealand-emergen/act-like-you-have-covid-19-pm-ardern-says-as-new-zealand-heads-into-lockdown-idUSKBN21C061.

170. Sophie Cousins, "New Zealand Eliminates COVID-19," *Lancet* 395, no. 10235 (2020): 1474, https://www.ncbi.nlm.nih.gov/pmc/articles/PMC7252131/.

171. Henry Cooke, "A Royal Commission Gives New Zealand a Chance to Reckon with What Covid Did to Us," *The Guardian*, December 7, 2022, https://www.theguardian.com/world/2022/dec/08/a-royal-commission-gives-new-zealand-a-chance-to-reckon-with-what-covid-did-to-us.

172. Miriam Berger, "New Zealand Beat Back the Coronavirus, but Families Were Left Divided and Migrant Workers Stranded," *Washington Post*, June 22, 2020, https://www.washingtonpost.com/world/2020/06/20/new-zealand-coronavirus-migrants-borders/.

173. "Immigration Minister on the Government's Plans for Migrants," *RNZ*, June 9, 2020, https://www.rnz.co.nz/national/programmes/ninetonoon/audio/2018749867/immigration-minister-on-the-government-s-plans-for-migrants.

174. Charlotte Graham-McLay, "New Zealand Health Ministry Floated Closing Borders to Citizens over COVID-19," *The Guardian*, April 29, 2020, https://www.theguardian.com/world/2020/apr/29/new-zealand-health-ministry-floated-closing-borders-to-citizens-over-covid-19.

175. "COVID-19: Quarantine or 'Managed Isolation' Compulsory for All Arrivals into NZ, PM Says," *RNZ*, April 9, 2020, https://www.rnz.co.nz/news/national/413866/covid-19-quarantine-or-managed-isolation-compulsory-for-all-arrivals-into-nz-pm-says.

176. Mia Jankowicz, "New Zealand's Prime Minister Put the Military in Charge of New Arrivals, Saying Letting 2 New COVID-19 Cases Travel the Country without Being Tested Was an 'Unacceptable Failure,'" *Business Insider*, June 17, 2020, https://www.businessinsider.com/new-zealand-military-in-charge-border-quarantine-new-uk-cases-2020-6; "Government Strengthens Managed Isolation System," *Scoop*, June 28, 2020, https://www.scoop.co.nz/stories/PA2006/S00269/government-strengthens-managed-isolation-system.htm.

177. Katie Todd, "Covid 19 Coronavirus: MIQ Receiving about 100 Complaints Each Week," *NZ Herald*, March 21, 2021, https://www.nzherald.co.nz/nz/covid-19-coronavirus-miq-receiving-about-100-complaints-each-week/ZFOH7DYRG27URA6PY5CKZE3KDY/.

178. Katie Todd, "Covid 19 Omicron: MIQ Assessment Adds 'Insult to Injury' for Women Forced to Give Birth Abroad," *NZ Herald*, April 20, 2022, https://www.nzherald.co.nz/nz/covid-19-omicron-miq-assessment-adds-insult-to-injury-for-women-forced-to-give-birth-abroad/N2FWZK4JMZMDGHJ7L2FL6TUOMQ/.

179. "Registering for New Zealand Citizenship by Descent," New Zealand Ministry of Foreign Affairs and Trade, https://www.mfat.govt.nz/en/countries-and-regions/africa/ethiopia/new-zealand-embassy-to-ethiopia/new-zealand-documents/#:~:text=A%20child%20born%20outside%20New,applying%20for%20Citizenship%20by%20Descent.

180. "Covid-19: Lawyer Fighting to Get Pregnant New Zealanders into MIQ," *RNZ*, January 31, 2022, https://www.rnz.co.nz/national/programmes/morningreport/audio/2018828685/covid-19-lawyer-fighting-to-get-pregnant-new-zealanders-into-miq.

181. "Covid-19 Coronavirus: The Wiggles Received Death Threats over MIQ Spots for NZ Tour," *NZ Herald*, March 18, 2021, https://www.nzherald.co.nz/entertainment/covid-19-coronavirus-the-wiggles-received-death-threats-over-miq-spots-for-nz-tour/VYVP3I7JT4E7HAANTNATW76UNY/.

182. John Power, "No Way Home: Overseas New Zealanders Despair at Tightened Borders," *Al-Jazeera*, December 22, 2021, https://www.aljazeera.com/economy/2021/12/22/no-way-home-overseas-new-zealanders-despair-at-border-rules.

183. Virginia Fallon, "When Being Kind Stops at the Border: How MIQ Made Kiwis Mean," *Stuff*, February 6, 2022, https://www.stuff.co.nz/national/health/coronavirus/127663968/when-being-kind-stops-at-the-border--how-miq-made-kiwis-mean. "Aotearoa" is the Maori word for New Zealand.

184. Natasha Frost, "An Impossible Task? New Zealand Tries to Eliminate Delta," *New York Times*, September 1, 2021, https://www.nytimes.com/2021/09/01/world/australia/delta-new-zealand-lockdown.html.

185. New Zealand Parliament, Ombudsman, "Chief Ombudsman's Opinion under the Ombudsman Act," December 9, 2022, https://www.ombudsman.parliament.nz/sites/default/files/2022-12/Final%20opinion%20on%20Managed%20Isolation%20Allocation%20System.pdf.

186. Grounded Kiwis Group In. v Min of Health.

187. "Chief Ombudsman's Opinion."

188. Jonathan Milne, "Accused MIQ 'Queue Jumpers' Prosecuted—but Vindicated in Court," *Newsroom*, December 16, 2022, https://www.newsroom.co.nz/accused-miq-queue-jumpers-prosecuted-but-vindicated-in-court.

CHAPTER 7

1. John Feng, "China Building 1200-Mile Southern Great Wall along Myanmar Border: Reports," *Newsweek*, December 15, 2020, https://www.newsweek.com/

china-building-1200-mile-southern-great-wall-along-myanmar-border-reports-1554793.

2. Nan Lwin Hnin Pwint, "Myanmar Says Chinese 'COVID-19' Fence Breaches Border Agreement," *Irrawaddy*, December 23, 2020, https://www.irrawaddy.com/news/burma/myanmar-says-chinese-covid-19-fence-breaches-border-agreement.html.

3. Pwint, "Chinese 'COVID-19' Fence."

4. Sebastian Strangio, "China Building Massive Myanmar Border Wall: Reports," *The Diplomat*, December 17, 2020, https://thediplomat.com/2020/12/china-building-massive-myanmar-border-wall-reports/.

5. Didi Tang, "Great Border Wall of China Stops Critics Escaping to Burma," *The Times*, December 15, 2020, https://www.thetimes.co.uk/article/great-border-wall-of-china-stops-critics-escaping-to-burma-r7dkdf76n.

6. Liyan Qi, Keith Zhai, and Lam Le, "China Fortifies Its Borders with a 'Southern Great Wall,' Citing Covid-19," *Wall Street Journal*, February 2, 2022, https://www.wsj.com/articles/china-fortifies-its-borders-with-a-southern-great-wall-citing-covid-19-11643814716.

7. Qi et al., "China Fortifies Its Borders."

8. Qi et al., "China Fortifies Its Borders."

9. Voice of America, "A Chinese City on Myanmar Border Vows Covid Curbs despite Disruptions," *VOA*, October 29, 2021, https://www.voachinese.com/a/chinese-city-on-myanmar-border-vows-covid-curbs-despite-disruption-20211029/6290837.html.

10. Liyan Qi and Natasha Khan, "Covid-19 Lockdowns Ripple across China—'I Wonder How Long I Can Hang On,'" *Wall Street Journal*, November 4, 2021, https://www.wsj.com/articles/covid-19-lockdowns-ripple-across-chinai-wonder-how-long-i-can-hang-on-11636025787?mod=article_inline.

11. James Glanz, Mara Hvistendahl, and Agnes Chang, "How Deadly Was China's Covid Wave?" *New York Times*, February 15, 2023, https://www.nytimes.com/interactive/2023/02/15/world/asia/china-covid-death-estimates.html.

12. "Mur de la Peste: When the Epidemic Struck, They Built a Wall," Offbeat France, https://www.offbeatfrance.com/mur-de-la-peste-plague-wall.html; Keith Van Sickle, "The Plague Wall of Provence—Mur de la Peste," Perfectly Provence, https://perfectlyprovence.co/plague-wall-provence-mur-peste/.

13. "Great Plague of Marseille," *Wikipedia*, https://en.wikipedia.org/wiki/Great_Plague_of_Marseille.

14. Alessandro Rippa, "Imagined Borderlands: Terrain, Technology and Trade in the Making and Managing of the China-Myanmar Border," *Singapore Journal of Tropical Geography* 43, no. 3 (2022): 287–308, https://onlinelibrary.wiley.com/doi/full/10.1111/sjtg.12429.

15. "How Life Has Changed along China's Border with South-East Asia," *The Economist*, March 16, 2023, https://www.economist.com/china/2023/03/16/how-life-has-changed-along-chinas-border-with-south-east-asia.

16. Qi et al., "China Fortifies Its Borders."

17. Qiao Long and Chingman, "Vietnamese Border Region Residents Remove China's Electrified Fencing," *Radio Free Asia*, September 21, 2021, https://www.rfa.org/english/news/china/vietnam-border-09212021095446.html.

18. "How Life Has Changed along China's Border."

19. Sandip Sen, "How China Locked Down Internally for COVID-19, but Pushed Foreign Travel," *The Economic Times*, April 30, 2020, https://economictimes.indiatimes.com/blogs/Whathappensif/how-china-locked-down-internally-for-covid-19-but-pushed-foreign-travel/.

20. Sen, "How China Locked Down."

21. Yuliya Talmazan, "China Criticizes U.S. Border Closure as Coronavirus Death Toll Rises," *NBC*, February 1, 2020, https://www.nbcnews.com/news/world/china-criticizes-u-s-border-closure-coronavirus-death-toll-rises-n1128161.

22. Lain Marlow, "China Lashes Out at Countries Restricting Travel over Virus," *Bloomberg*, February 6, 2020, https://www.bloomberg.com/news/articles/2020-02-06/china-lashes-out-at-countries-restricting-travel-over-virus.

23. Tabitha Speelman, "Unfortunate or Convenient? Contextualizing China's Covid-19 Border Restrictions," *Made in China Journal*, March 8, 2022, https://madeinchinajournal.com/2022/03/08/unfortunate-or-convenient-contextualising-chinas-covid-19-border-restrictions-2/; and "Ministry of Foreign Affairs of the People's Republic of China National Immigration Administration Announcement on the Temporary Suspension of Entry by Foreign Nationals Holding Valid Chinese Visas or Resident Permits," Ministry of Foreign Affairs of the People's Republic of China, March 26, 2020, https://web.archive.org/web/20200327173542/https://www.fmprc.gov.cn/mfa_eng/wjbxw/t1761867.shtml.

24. Jennifer Bouey, *From SARS to 2019-Coronavirus (nCoV): U.S.-China Collaborations on Pandemic Response*, Testimony before the Committee on Foreign Affairs Subcommittee on Asia, the Pacific, and Nonproliferation United States House of Representatives (Santa Monica, CA: RAND Corporation, 2020), https://www.rand.org/pubs/testimonies/CT523.html.

25. Yanzhong Huang, "The SARS Epidemic and Its Aftermath in China: A Political Perspective," in *Learning from SARS: Preparing for the Next Disease Outbreak: Workshop Summary*, ed. S. Knobler, A. Mahmound, and S. Lemon (Washington, DC: National Academies Press, 2004).

26. Jeremy Page and Lingling Wei, "China's CDC, Built to Stop Pandemics Like Covid, Stumbled When It Mattered Most," *Wall Street Journal*, August 17, 2020, https://www.wsj.com/articles/chinas-cdc-built-to-stop-pandemics-stumbled-when-it-mattered-most-11597675108; and Jasper Becker, *Made in China: Wuhan, Covid and the Quest for Biotech Supremacy* (London: Hurst & Co., 2021), 209-210.

27. Becker, *Made in China*.

28. Buoy, *From SARS to 2019-Coronavirus*.

29. Page and Wei, "China's CDC."

30. Becker, *Made in China*; Jane McMullen, *China's Covid Secrets* (2022; PBS Frontline), https://www.pbs.org/wgbh/frontline/documentary/chinas-covid-secrets/; "China Delayed Releasing Coronavirus Info, Frustrating WHO," *Associated Press*, June 1, 2020, https://apnews.com/article/united-nations-health-ap-top-news-virus-outbreak-public-health-3c061794970661042b18d5aea aed9fae.

31. *AP*, "China Delayed Releasing Coronavirus Info."

32. The question of whether Covid was the result of animal-to-human transmission, or the accidental leak of a genetically engineered virus, has been the subject of several detailed political, intelligence, and journalistic investigations. The conclusions remain indeterminate. See "McCaul's Final Report: The Origins of the Global Pandemic, Including the Roles of the CPP & WHO," United States Congressional House Foreign Affairs Committee, September 21, 2020, https://foreignaffairs.house.gov/finalcovid-19pandemicoriginsreport/; US Select Subcommittee on the Coronavirus Pandemic Democrats, " 'They Played No Role': Select Subcommittee Republicans' Own Investigation Disproves Allegations That Dr. Fauci and Dr. Collins Suppressed the Lab Leak Theory through the 'Proximal Origin' Paper," Democratic Staff, 2023, https://www.dropbox.com/sh/bml8xlaw8s4kqoo/AAAGY23vzhA-pODdcBM4Yg8na?dl= 0&preview=For+Distribution-2023.07.11+Proximal+Origin+Democratic+ Staff+Report.pdf; US Office of the Director of National Intelligence, "Potential Links between the Wuhan Institute of Virology and the Origin of the COVID-19 Pandemic," 2023, https://www.dni.gov/files/ODNI/documents/assessments/ Report-on-Potential-Links-Between-the-Wuhan-Institute-of-Virology-and-the-Origins-of-COVID-19-20230623.pdf; Katherine Eban and Jeff Kao, "COVID-19 Origins: Investigating a 'Complex and Grave Situation' inside a Wuhan Lab," *ProPublica*, October 28, 2022, https://www.propublica.org/article/senate-rep ort-covid-19-origin-wuhan-lab; and "Intelligence Report Says Safety Training at Chinese Government Lab Complex in Wuhan before the Pandemic Appears Routine," *ProPublica*, July 7, 2023, https://www.propublica.org/article/safety-training-wuhan-china-lab-covid-appears-routine.

33. Ezra F. Vogel, *Deng Xiaoping and the Transformation of China* (Cambridge, MA: Belknap Press, 2013).

34. Frank Pieke, "Immigrant China," *Modern China* 38, no. 1 (2012): 40–77, https://journals-sagepub-com.ezproxy.library.wwu.edu/doi/full/10.1177/ 0097700411424564.

35. See Anne-Marie Brady, *Making the Foreign Serve China* (Lanham, MD: Rowman & Littlefield, 2003).

36. People's Republic of China Administrative Law, "Law of the People's Republic of China on the Control of the Exit and Entry of Citizens," http://www.npc. gov.cn/zgrdw/englishnpc/Law/2007-12/13/content_1383959.htm.

37. People's Republic of China Administrative Law, "Law of the People's Republic of China on the Control of the Exit and Entry of Citizens."

38. "Most Visited Countries 2023," World Population Review, 2023, https://worldp opulationreview.com/country-rankings/most-visited-countries.

39. Thomas Hale, "'There Is a Lot of Pent Up Demand': World Awaits Return of Chinese Tourists," *Financial Times*, January 6, 2023, https://www.ft.com/cont ent/c58661a7-4516-441b-9dc1-6186bac76aa6.

40. "UNWTO Looks to 'Re-Write Tourism History' at Official Reopening of China," UN World Tourism Organization, February 24, 2023, https://www. unwto.org/news/unwto-looks-to-re-write-tourism-history-at-official-re-open ing-of-china.

41. Frank Pieke, "How Immigration Is Shaping Chinese Society," *Merics*, November 27, 2019, https://www.merics.org/en/report/how-immigration-shaping-chin ese-society.

42. Pieke, "How Immigration Is Shaping Chinese Society."

43. Heidi Ostbo Haugen and Tabitha Speelman, "China's Rapid Development Has Transformed Its Migration Trends," *Migration Policy Institute*, January 28, 2022, https://www.migrationpolicy.org/article/china-development-transfor med-migration.

44. Scott Kennedy and Wang Jisi, "Breaking the Ice: The Role of Scholarly Exchange in Stabilizing U.S.-China Relations," *Center for Strategic and International Studies*, 2023, https://csis-website-prod.s3.amazonaws.com/s3fs-public/2023-04/230407_Kennedy_Breaking_Ice.pdf.

45. People's Republic of China Administrative Law, "Passport Law of the People's Republic of China," http://www.npc.gov.cn/zgrdw/englishnpc/Law/2008-01/02/content_1388000.htm.

46. Speelman, "Unfortunate or Convenient?"

47. Heidi Ostbo Haugen, "Destination China: The Country Adjusts to Its New Migration Reality," *Migration Policy Institute*, March 4, 2015, https://www. migrationpolicy.org/article/destination-china-country-adjusts-its-new-migrat ion-reality.

48. Haugen and Speelman, "China's Rapid Development Has Transformed Its Migration Trends."

49. Speelman, "Unfortunate or Convenient?"

50. Arendse Huld, "China Travel Restrictions 2021/2022: An Explainer (Updated)," *China Briefing*, December 30, 2021, updated December 16, 2022, https://www. china-briefing.com/news/china-travel-restrictions-2021-2022-an-explainer-updated/.

51. Speelman, "Unfortunate or Convenient?"

52. Kennedy and Jisi, "Breaking the Ice."

53. See Han Zhang, "How Shanghai Residents Endured the Covid Lockdown," *New Yorker*, June 7, 2022, https://www.newyorker.com/news/news-desk/how-shanghai-residents-endured-the-covid-lockdown; and Cissy Zhou et al.,

"Inside Shanghai's COVID Lockdown Nightmare," *Nikkei Asia*, June 22, 2022, https://asia.nikkei.com/Spotlight/The-Big-Story/Inside-Shanghai-s-COVID-lockdown-nightmare.

54. Scott Kennedy, "China's Neighbors Are Navigating COVID-19, Beijing and Washington," *Foreign Policy*, September 13, 2022, https://foreignpolicy.com/2022/09/13/south-korea-japan-taiwan-china-covid-travel/.

55. The best account of the struggle over Huawei and the arrest of the "two Michaels" is the thirteen-part podcast from the Canadian Broadcasting Corporation, *Sanctioned: The Arrest of a Telecom Giant*, https://www.cbc.ca/listen/cbc-podcasts/365-radio-sanctioned.

56. "Circuit Breaker Measures for Scheduled International Passenger Flights Adjusted," Civil Aviation Administration of China, August 8, 2022, http://www.caac.gov.cn/en/XWZX/202208/t20220808_214894.html.

57. "Ministry of Foreign Affairs: 1.42 Million International Students Are Still Abroad, We Must Do Everything Possible to Ensure Their Safety," *CCTV News*, April 2, 2022, http://m.news.cctv.com/2020/04/02/ARTI5TUyUMofRLPdef7uDKbB200402.shtml.

58. Jeffery Gettleman and Sameer Yasir, "India Starts Bringing Home Hundreds of Thousands Stranded amid Coronavirus," *New York Times*, May 8, 2020, https://www.nytimes.com/2020/05/08/world/asia/india-coronavirus-repatriation.html.

59. Xinlu Liang, "With Few Options to Get Home, Chinese Students Abroad Fall Victim to Ticket Scams," *Los Angeles Times*, July 29, 2020, https://www.latimes.com/california/story/2020-07-29/with-few-options-to-get-home-chinese-students-abroad-fall-victim-to-ticket-scams.

60. Jasmine Yu, "The Quad: International Students from China Face Challenges Returning Home," *Daily Bruin*, April 7, 2022, https://dailybruin.com/2022/04/07/the-quad-international-students-from-china-face-challenges-returning-home.

61. Vivian Wang, "China Subjects Some Travelers to Anal Swabs, Angering Foreign Governments," *New York Times*, March 5, 2021, https://www.nytimes.com/2021/03/04/world/asia/china-anal-swab-tests.html.

62. "Beijing Reopens for International Flights after Covid Isolation," *Bloomberg*, July 27, 2022, https://www.bloomberg.com/news/articles/2022-07-27/beijing-reopens-for-international-flights-after-covid-isolation.

63. Christina Shen, "Experiences of Chinese International Students during COVID-19," *San Francisco State University*, 2021, https://scholarworks.calstate.edu/downloads/kh04dw182.

64. Belinda Cao and Linda Lew, "China Reopens to Foreign Students after More than Two Years," *Bloomberg*, August 23, 2022, https://www.bloomberg.com/news/articles/2022-08-24/china-reopens-to-foreign-students-after-more-than-two-years.

65. Tripti Lahiri, "China Has Abandoned Its Foreign Students over Covid Zero," *Quartz*, March 17, 2022, https://qz.com/2126939/china-has-forgotten-about-its-foreign-graduate-students.

66. See Shuli Ren, "Beijing's Covid Paranoia Is Alienating China's Diaspora," *Bloomberg*, October 28, 2021, https://www.bloomberg.com/opinion/articles/2021-10-28/keeping-china-covid-free-is-keeping-overseas-chinese-from-the-mainland?sref=5clhGucw.

67. Li Yuan, "Trapped Abroad, China's 'Little Pinks' Rethink Their Country," *New York Times*, June 24, 2020, https://www.nytimes.com/2020/06/24/business/china-nationalist-students-coronavirus.html.

68. Jing Yu, "Caught in the Middle? Chinese International Students' Self-Formation amid Politics and Pandemic," *International Journal of Chinese Education* 10, no. 3 (2021), https://journals.sagepub.com/doi/full/10.1177/2212586821 1058911; and Yu Tao, "Chapter 10: Chinese Students Abroad in the Time of Pandemic: An Australian View," *Australian Centre on China in the World*, 2020, https://www.thechinastory.org/yearbooks/yearbook-2020-crisis/chapter-10-chinese-students-abroad-in-the-time-of-pandemic-an-australian-view/.

69. Li Yuan, "'The Last Generation': The Disillusionment of Young Chinese," *New York Times*, May 24, 2022, https://www.nytimes.com/2022/05/24/business/china-covid-zero.html.

70. Wu Peiyue, "The Plight of Chinese Workers in Cambodia Waiting to Return Home," *Sixth Tone*, November 5, 2021, https://www.sixthtone.com/news/1008882.

71. Zhang Wanqing, "'Returning to China Is Like Buying a Lottery Ticket,'" *Sixth Tone*, January 17, 2022, https://www.sixthtone.com/news/1009463.

72. "Suspension of Routine Visa Services," US Department of State, https://travel.state.gov/content/travel/en/us-visas/visa-information-resources/visas-news-archive/suspension-of-routine-visa-services.html.

73. We are indebted here to the superb account contained in: Lijun Tang, "Defending Workers' Rights on Social Media: Chinese Seafarers during the COVID-19 Pandemic," *Industrial Relations Journal* 53, no. 2 (2022): 110–125, https://onlinelibrary.wiley.com/doi/10.1111/irj.12357.

74. Rina Chandran, "Shanghai Residents Use Code Words, Video to Protest COVID Lockdown," *Thomson Reuters Foundation*, April 26, 2022, https://news.trust.org/item/20220426124738-69pln/; "The Voice of April," *YouTube*, April 22, 2022, https://www.youtube.com/watch?v=llP2qTXJFBc&list=PPSV.

75. See Kathy Huang and Mengyu Han, "Did China's Street Protests End Harsh COVID Policies?" *Council on Foreign Relations*, December 14, 2022, https://www.cfr.org/blog/did-chinas-street-protests-end-harsh-covid-policies; Rebecca Wright, Ivan Watson, and Enwer Erdem, "'I Hold China Accountable': Uyghur Families Demand Answers over Fire That Triggered Protests," *CNN*, December 1, 2022, https://www.cnn.com/2022/12/01/china/china-protests-urumqi-fire-deaths-covid-dst-intl-hnk/index.html.

76. Kerry Allen, "How China's Covid Protests Are Being Silenced," *BBC*, November 28, 2022, https://www.bbc.com/news/world-asia-china-63788477; William Taipei, "How Social Media Is Helping China's COVID Protests," *DW*, December 8, 2022, https://www.dw.com/en/how-soliscial-media-is-helping-chinas-covid-protests/a-64031424; Christian Shepherd, "What You Need to Know about China's Covid Protests," *Washington Post*, November 28, 2022, https://www.washingtonpost.com/world/2022/11/28/what-know-china-protests-covid/.

77. "Coronavirus: Commission Presents Practical Guidance to Ensure Continuous Flow of Goods across EU via Green Lanes," European Commission, March 23, 2020, https://ec.europa.eu/commission/presscorner/detail/%5Beuropa_tokens:europa_interface_language%5D/ip_20_510.

78. "New Canadian Border Vaccination Requirement for Exempt Essential Travelers, including Commercial Truck Drivers," US Federal Motor Carrier Safety Administration, https://www.fmcsa.dot.gov/international-programs/canada/new-canadian-border-vaccination-requirement-exempt-essential; Deon Hampton, "U.S. Vaccine Mandate on Freight Drivers Coming from Canada May Worsen Auto Supply Chain Shortage," *NBC*, January 19, 2022, https://www.nbcnews.com/news/us-news/us-vaccine-mandate-freight-drivers-coming-canada-may-exacerbate-auto-s-rcna12649.

79. "COVID-19 Trade Facilitation Repository," Trade Facilitation Agreement Facility, https://www.tfafacility.org/media-resources/covid-19-trade-facilitation-repository.

80. Eric Martin and Ana Monteiro, "US-China Goods Trade Hits Record Even as Political Split Widens," *Bloomberg*, February 7, 2023, https://www.bloomberg.com/news/articles/2023-02-07/us-china-trade-climbs-to-record-in-2022-despite-efforts-to-split.

81. Joe McDonald, "China's Trade Surplus Swells to $877.6B as Exports Grow," *AP*, January 12, 2023, https://apnews.com/article/inflation-shanghai-business-0c0f7946bc3c08db1df13eb78911f4aa.

82. "Frequently Asked Questions about How COVID-19 Is Impacting Seafarers," International Maritime Organization, https://www.imo.org/en/MediaCentre/HotTopics/Pages/FAQ-on-crew-changes-and-repatriation-of-seafarers.aspx.

83. Emmanuel Faber et al. to António Guterres, September 23, 2020, The Consumer Goods Forum, https://www.theconsumergoodsforum.com/wp-content/uploads/202009-cgf-letter-to-un-general-secretary-on-maritime-crew-changes.pdf.

84. "400,000 Seafarers Stuck at Sea as Crew Change Crisis Deepens," International Maritime Organization, September 25, 2022, https://www.imo.org/en/MediaCentre/PressBriefings/pages/32-crew-change-UNGA.aspx.

85. Taylor Telford and Jacob Bogage, "Essential, Invisible: Covid Has 200,000 Merchant Sailors Stuck at Sea," *Washington Post*, April 9, 2021, https://www.washingtonpost.com/health/2021/04/09/maritime-workers-pandemic-global-trade/.

86. Desai Shan, "Occupational Safety and Health Challenges for Maritime Key Workers in the Global COVID-19 Pandemic," *International Labour Review* 161, no. 2 (2022), https://www.ncbi.nlm.nih.gov/pmc/articles/PMC8444828/pdf/ILR-161-267.pdf.

87. "Frequently Asked Questions about How COVID-19 Is Impacting Seafarers."

88. Anish Hebbar and Nitin Mukesh, "COVID-19 and Seafarers' Rights to Shore Leave, Repatriation and Medical Assistance: A Pilot Study," *International Maritime Health* 71, no. 4 (2020): 217–228, https://pubmed.ncbi.nlm.nih.gov/33394486/.

89. Aurora Almendral, "Trapped by Pandemic, Ships' Crews Fight Exhaustion and Despair," *New York Times*, September 9, 2020, https://www.nytimes.com/2020/09/09/business/coronavirus-sailors-cargo-ships.html.

90. Lee Kok Leong, "Seafarer Suffering from Stroke Did Not Get Immediate Evacuation," *Maritime Fairtrade*, May 1, 2020, https://maritimefairtrade.org/seafarer-suffering-from-stroke-did-not-get-immediate-evacuation/.

91. K. Oanh Ha and Jack Wittels, "China's Covid Zero Policy towards Seafarers Escalates Supply Chain Crisis," *Bloomberg*, November 24, 2021, https://gcaptain.com/chinas-covid-zero-policy-seafarers-escalates-supply-chain-crisis/.

92. Charissa Isidro, "Coronavirus Nightmare at Sea for the World's Most Essential Workers," *Daily Beast*, March 20, 2021, https://www.thedailybeast.com/virus-nightmare-at-sea-for-the-worlds-most-essential-workers.

93. Zhiwei Zhao, Lijun Tang, and Yueyan Wu, "Fatigue during the COVID-19 Pandemic: The Experiences of Chinese Seafarers," *Marine Policy* 153 (2023), https://www.ncbi.nlm.nih.gov/pmc/articles/PMC10150193/.

94. Zhao, Tang, and Wu, "Fatigue during the COVID-19 Pandemic."

95. K. Oanh Ha and Jack Wittels, "Supply-China Crisis Only Getting Worse with China's 7-Week Port Quarantine," *Bloomberg*, November 24, 2021, https://www.bloomberg.com/news/articles/2021-11-24/china-s-seven-week-port-quarantine-is-blocking-shipping-recovery?srnd=premium-asia&sref=5clhGucw.

96. Simone McCarthy, "China Is Obsessed with Disinfection against Covid. But Is It Causing More Harm than Good?" *CNN*, May 2, 2022, https://www.cnn.com/2022/05/02/china/china-covid-disinfection-intl-hnk-mic/index.html.

97. Luna Sun, "China to Drop Covid-19 Screening on Imported Cold-Chain Food after 3 Years of Contamination Fears," *South China Morning Post*, December 29, 2022, https://www.scmp.com/economy/china-economy/article/3204962/china-drop-covid-19-screening-imported-cold-chain-food-after-3-years-contamination-fears.

98. Jiahui Wang et al., "Perspectives: COVID-19 Outbreaks Linked to Imported Frozen Food in China: Status and Challenge," *China CDC Weekly* 4, no. 22 (2022): 483–487, https://weekly.chinacdc.cn/en/article/doi/10.46234/ccdcw2022.072.

99. Orange Wang, "China Trade: US, Europe Frozen Seafood Exports under Threat as Dalian's Covid-19 Cases Halt Cold Chain Food Trading," *South China Morning*

Post, November 12, 2021, https://www.scmp.com/economy/china-economy/article/3155736/dalian-suspends-cold-chain-food-operations-amid-covid-19.

100. Wang, "US, Europe Frozen Seafood Exports."

101. "Truckers Caught in Covid Controls Snarl China Supply Chains," *Bloomberg*, April 13, 2023, https://www.bloomberg.com/news/articles/2022-04-14/truckers-caught-in-covid-controls-snarl-china-s-supply-chains.

102. "Truck drivers Stranded across China Are Unable to Earn an Income, Lack Food and Bare Necessities," *China Labour Bulletin*, May 16, 2022, https://clb.org.hk/en/content/truck-drivers-stranded-across-china-are-unable-earn-income-lack-food-and-bare-necessities.

103. Martin Quin Pollard, "Chinese Truckers Left Stranded for Days at Highway Exit by Hardline COVID Curbs," *Reuters*, April 15, 2022, https://www.reuters.com/world/china/chinese-truckers-left-stranded-days-highway-exit-by-hardline-covid-curbs-2022-04-15/.

104. Reid Standish, "Squeezed on Both Sides: Kyrgyz Truckers Protest New Rules to Restart Trade with China," *Radio Free Europe Radio Liberty*, November 13, 2021, https://www.rferl.org/a/kyrgyzstan-china-trade-covid/31559872.html.

105. Niharika Mandhana, "How China's Zero-Covid Policies Are Disrupting Cross-Border Trade," *Wall Street Journal*, updated January 18, 2022, https://www.wsj.com/articles/chinas-zero-covid-policies-cause-a-traffic-jam-in-vietnam-as-farmers-suffer-11642503601; Vo Kieu Bao Uyen, Sui-Lee Wee, and Muktita Suhartono, "A Side-Effect of China's Strict Virus Policy: Abandoned Fruit," *New York Times*, February 5, 2022, https://www.nytimes.com/2022/02/05/world/asia/virus-vietnam-china-fruit.html.

106. Emily C., "COVID-19 Protocols Tightened at Chinese-Vietnam Border," *Produce Report*, August 31, 2021, https://www.producereport.com/article/covid-19-protocol-tightened-china-vietnam-border.

107. Qi et al., "China Fortifies Its Borders."

108. "China-Myanmar Border Port Resumes Trade after Four-Month Closure—CCTV," *Reuters*, November 26, 2021, https://www.reuters.com/world/china/china-myanmar-border-port-resumes-trade-after-four-month-closure-cctv-2021-11-26/.

109. Michael Schuman, "What Returning to China Taught Me about China," *Atlantic*, June 14, 2022, https://www.theatlantic.com/international/archive/2022/06/china-zero-covid-restrictions-quarantine/661226/.

110. See Yanzhong Huang, "China's Hidden COVID Catastrophe," *Foreign Affairs*, February 16, 2023, https://www.foreignaffairs.com/china/chinas-hidden-covid-catastrophe; Emma Goldberg et al., "Swift and Extensive Omicron Outbreak in China after Sudden Exit from 'Zero-COVID Policy,'" *Nature Communications* 14, art. 3888 (2023), https://www.nature.com/articles/s41467-023-39638-4.

111. Ryan McMorrow and Nian Liu, "China Deletes Covid-19 Death Data," *Financial Times*, July 18, 2023, https://on.ft.com/3QTMnU7.

112. Luke Taylor, "Covid-19: Hong Kong Reports World's Highest Death Rate as Zero-Covid Strategy Fails," *BMJ* 2022 (March 2022): 376, https://www.bmj.com/content/376/bmj.o707; Kan Chun Chung et al., "Changes in All-Cause and Cause-Specific Excess Mortality before and after the Omicron Outbreak of COVID-19 in Hong Kong," *Journal of Global Health*, April 28, 2023, https://pubmed.ncbi.nlm.nih.gov/37114968/.

113. Simone McCarthy, "China Calls Its Covid Response a 'Miracle in Human History.' The Data Isn't So Clear," *CNN*, February 17, 2023, https://www.cnn.com/2023/02/17/china/china-covid-decisive-victory-xi-jinping-death-rate-intl-hnk/index.html.

114. "China to Scrap COVID Quarantine Rule for Inbound Travellers," *Reuters*, December 26, 2022, https://www.reuters.com/world/china/china-drop-covid-quarantine-rule-inbound-travellers-jan-8-2022-12-26/.

115. When it lifted the testing requirement in April 2023, the only other countries with remaining testing requirements were Angola, Myanmar, Turkmenistan, Tuvalu, Comoros, and the Solomon Islands. See Yanzhong Huang, "Breaking Down the Barriers: A Call to Drop the Forty-Eight Hour PCR Test Requirement for Inbound Travelers to China," *Council on Foreign Relations Blog Post*, April 24, 2023, https://www.cfr.org/blog/breaking-down-barriers-call-drop-forty-eight-hour-pcr-test-requirement-inbound-travelers-china; see also Arendse Huld, "Traveling to China after Reopening—What's Changed?" *China Briefing*, June 9, 2023, https://www.china-briefing.com/news/traveling-to-china-after-reopening-whats-changed/; Vivian Wang, "China Drops Covid P.C.R. Test Rule for Inbound Travelers," *New York Times*, April 25, 2023, https://www.nytimes.com/2023/04/25/business/china-travel-covid-test.html?smid=nytcore-ios-share&referringSource=articleShare.

116. Wenxin Fan, "China's Latest Problem: People Don't Want to Go There," *Wall Street Journal*, August 3, 2023, https://www.wsj.com/articles/chinas-latest-problem-people-dont-want-to-go-there-7d17a83a.

117. Jasmine Tse and Ralph Jennings, "Tourism Trouble: Post-Pandemic Hurdles of China Travel," *South China Morning Post*, April 9, 2024.

118. Ethan Wang and Joe Cas, "China Offers Visa-Free Entry for Citizens of France, Germany and Italy," *Reuters*, November 24, 2023.

119. Economist Intelligence Unit, "In Charts: China's Outbound Tourism in 2024," March 27, 2024, https://www.eiu.com/n/in-charts-chinas-outbound-tourism-in-2024/.

120. US State Department, "China Travel Advisory," June 30, 2023, https://travel.state.gov/content/travel/en/traveladvisories/traveladvisories/china-travel-advisory.html.

121. "Shanghai Expat Exodus Shows Covid Zero's Enduring Scars," *Bloomberg*, March 26, 2023, https://www.bloomberg.com/news/articles/2023-03-26/shanghai-expat-exodus-shows-covid-zero-s-enduring-scars.

122. Claire Fu, "China Suspends Reporting on Youth Unemployment, Which Was at a Record High," *New York Times*, August 15, 2023, https://www.nytimes.com/2023/08/15/business/china-youth-unemployment.html.

123. Iori Kawate and Shunsuke Tabeta, "Foreign Direct Investment in China Falls to 30-Year Low," *Nikkei Asia*, February 19, 2024. https://asia.nikkei.com/Economy/Foreign-direct-investment-in-China-falls-to-30-year-low.

124. Adam Posen, "The End of China's Economic Miracle," *Foreign Affairs*, September/October 2023, https://www.foreignaffairs.com/china/end-china-economic-miracle-beijing-washington.

125. See Edward White, James Kynge, and Tom Mitchell, "China Turns Inward: Xi Jinping, COP26 and the Pandemic," *Financial Times*, November 5, 2021, https://www.ft.com/content/17314336-b7df-453a-b2ca-25a58e26ca3e; and Gideon Rachman, "China's Self-Isolation Is a Global Concern," *Financial Times*, November 8, 2021, https://www.ft.com/content/1d00bff4-ac9d-486a-9a50-ae819e106d4c.

126. Speelman, "Unfortunate or Convenient?"

CHAPTER 8

1. John McCall, in correspondence with the author, May 10, 2024.

2. David Poon, February 9, 2021; David Edward-Ooi Poon and Erin Avenant, "Mental Health Index Report," Faces of Advocacy, 2020, https://www.ourcommons.ca/Content/Committee/432/HESA/Brief/BR11045599/br-external/FacesOdAdvocacy-Poon-2020-11-30-10347117-f.pdf.

3. Rodrigo De Azevedo, "Coronavirus: Ottawa to Ease Border Restrictions for Compassionate Visits by Foreign Nationals," *Vasto Mundo Intercâmbio*, October 3, 2020, vmintercambio.com/2020/10/03/coronavirus-ottawa-to-ease-border-restrictions-for-compassionate-visits-by-foreign-nationals/.

4. David Edward-Ooi Poon and Erin Avenant, "Emergency Situation Facing Canadians in Light of the Second Wave of the COVID-19," *Faces of Advocacy*, 2020, https://www.facesofadvocacy.com/wp-content/uploads/2021/07/English-Health-Committee-Nov.-30-Policy-Brief.pdf.

5. Poon and Avenant, "Mental Health Index Report."

6. Priscilla Lalisse-Jespersen, "'Love Is Not Tourism': Couples Separated by Pandemic Travel Bas Are Fighting to Be Reunited," *Washington Post*, August 5, 2020, https://www.washingtonpost.com/travel/2020/08/05/love-is-not-tourism-how-couples-separated-by-pandemic-are-fighting-be-reunited/.

7. Michael Safi, "'Like a Prison Sentence': The Couples Separated by Covid-19," *The Guardian*, August 12, 2020, https://www.theguardian.com/world/2020/aug/12/like-a-prison-sentence-the-couples-separated-by-covid-19.

8. Alice Tidey, "'Love Is Not Tourism': EU Bids to Reunite Couples Split by Coronavirus Restrictions," *Euronews*, July 8, 2020, https://www.euronews.

com/2020/08/07/love-is-not-tourism-eu-bids-to-reunite-couples-split-by-coro navirus-restrictions.

9. "Profile: Tudor Clee," *The Lawyer Magazine*, 2023, https://premium.thela wyermag.com/nz-nzl-most-influential-lawyers-2023-tudor-clee/p/1.

10. "Get Informed," Grounded Kiwis, https://www.groundedkiwis.com/get-informed.

11. Daniel Hurst, "UN Urges Australia to Act Quickly to Bring Stranded Australians Home," *The Guardian*, April 16, 2021, https://www.theguardian.com/austra lia-news/2021/apr/16/un-urges-australia-to-act-quickly-to-bring-stranded-aust ralians-home.

12. Pola Lem, "China Will Again Welcome International Students," *Inside Higher Ed*, August 31, 2022, https://www.insidehighered.com/news/2022/09/01/ china-will-again-welcome-international-students.

13. Jessie Yeung and Tara Subramaniam, "What's Happening in China after Zero-Covid Protests? Here's What You Need to Know," *CNN*, December 1, 2022, https://www.cnn.com/2022/12/01/china/china-protests-lockdown-softening-covid-explainer-intl-hnk/index.html; Jessie Yeung, Carlotta Dotto, and Henrik Pettersson, "How a Deadly Fire Ignited Dissent over China's Zero-Covid Policy," *CNN*, December 3, 2022, https://www.cnn.com/2022/12/02/china/china-covid-lockdown-protests-2022-intl-hnk-dst/index.html.

14. Gian Volpicelli, "China Reopens Borders after 3 Years of COVID Travel Restrictions," *Politico*, January 8, 2023, https://www.politico.eu/article/china-reopen-border-travel-restrictions-coronavirus-zero-covid-policy/.

15. "Press Briefing by Press Secretary Kayleigh McEnany," Trump White House, July 31, 2020, https://trumpwhitehouse.archives.gov/briefings-statements/ press-briefing-press-secretary-kayleigh-mcenany-7-31-2020/.

16. "Barred at the Border: Compassionate Policy Options for Safe Family Reunification," Wilson Center, February 8, 2021, https://www.wilsoncen ter.org/event/barred-border-compassionate-policy-options-safe-family-reunif ication.

17. Emily Styers, "Safely Reunite Committed Binational Couples & Families," *Change.org*, October 1, 2020, https://www.change.org/p/scott-morrison-safely-reunite-committed-binational-couples-families.

18. Jessica Warriner, "The Coronavirus Pandemic Has Separated Lovers across the Globe—Now They Want the Government to Help," *ABC*, July 7, 2020, https:// www.abc.net.au/news/2020-07-08/coronavirus-separated-lovers-seek-travel-ban-exemption/12431716.

19. Emily McPherson, "'Just Give Us a Chance': Couples Plead for Travel Exemptions to End Marriage Limbo," *9News*, June 24, 2021, https://www.9news.com.au/ national/prospective-marriage-visa-couples-plead-for-travel-exemptions-to-end-marriage-limbo/8a4673d8-fbe4-4d54-aea1-e90598d347b2.

20. "Travel Exemption Applications Open for Overseas Parents of Australians Separated by COVID-19," *Xinhua*, October 22, 2021, http://www.news.cn/english/asiapacific/2021-10/22/c_1310261863.htm.

21. Poon and Avenant, "Mental Health Index Report."

22. Rey Koslowski, "Global Mobility Regimes: A Conceptual Framework," in *Global Mobility Regimes*, ed. Rey Koslowski (New York: Palgrave Macmillan, 2011), 1–25.

23. Meghan Benton et al., *The State of Global Mobility in the Aftermath of the Covid-19 Pandemic* (Washington, DC: International Organization for Migration and Migration Policy Institute, 2024).

24. "Population Growth and the Economy: A Mixed Blessing?" University of Sydney, August 7, 2023, https://www.sydney.edu.au/business/news-and-events/news/2023/08/07/population-growth-and-the-economy-a-mixed-blessing.html.

25. Gearoid Reidy, "Japan Is Bringing In More Foreigners than You Think," *Washington Post*, August 3, 2023, https://www.washingtonpost.com/business/2023/08/03/foreign-workers-japan-quietly-prepares-for-more-immigration/06841b84-3245-11ee-85dd-5c3c97d6acda_story.html.

26. "Japan Unveils Ambitious Plan to Welcome 400,000 International Students by 2033," *Erudera*, March 18, 2023, https://erudera.com/news/japan-unveils-ambitious-plan-to-welcome-400000-international-students-by-2033/.

27. Carmeli Argana, "Universities Race to Recapture Lucrative International Students," *Bloomberg*, March 17, 2023, https://www.bloomberg.com/news/articles/2023-03-17/universities-race-to-recapture-international-students-in-australia-us-uk.

28. "Tourism on Track for Full Recovery as New Data Shows Strong Start to 2023," *UNWTO*, May 9, 2023, https://www.unwto.org/news/tourism-on-track-for-full-recovery-as-new-data-shows-strong-start-to-2023; and Lebawit Girma, "Visa Delays, Divisive Politics Dampen US International Travel Recovery," *Bloomberg*, July 27, 2023, https://www.bloomberg.com/news/articles/2023-07-27/lack-of-international-tourists-slow-visas-are-hurting-us-travel-recovery.

29. Meghan Benton and Lawrence Huang, "Lessons from Covid-19: Managing Borders in the Next Global Public Health Crisis" (Washington, DC: Migration Policy Institute, 2024), https://www.migrationpolicy.org/research/lessons-covid-19-borders.

30. "Barred at the Border: Compassionate Policy Options for Safe Family Reunification," Wilson Center, February 8, 2021, https://www.wilsoncenter.org/event/barred-border-compassionate-policy-options-safe-family-reunification.

31. Benton and Huang, "Lessons from COVID-19."

32. World Health Organization, "Proposals for the WHO Pandemic Agreement," A/INB/9/3 Rev.1, April 2024, https://apps.who.int/gb/inb/pdf_files/inb9/A_inb9_3Rev1-en.pdf.

33. WHO, "Proposals for the WHO Pandemic Agreement," Art. 24.

34. Kate Hooper and Meghan Benton, "The Future of Remote Work: Digital Nomads and the Implications for Immigration Systems," *Migration Policy Institute*, June 2022, https://www.migrationpolicy.org/sites/default/files/publi cations/mpi-remote-work-2022_final.pdf.

35. Katherine Ellena and Erica Shein, "Emergency Powers and the COVID-19 Pandemic: Protecting Democratic Guardrails," *International Foundation for Electoral Systems*, March 30, 2020, https://www.ifes.org/news/emergency-pow ers-and-covid-19-pandemic-protecting-democratic-guardrails.

36. Cf. Victoria Ochoa, "Court Evaluation of COVID-19 State Emergency Orders: Upholding Fundamental Rights during Times of Crisis," in *Who Governs: Emergency Powers in the Time of Covid*, ed. Morris P. Fiorina (Stanford, CA: Hoover Institution Press, 2023), 207–232; and Jeffrey Kahn, *Mrs. Shipley's Ghost: The Right to Travel and Terrorist Watchlists* (Ann Arbor: University of Michigan Press, 2013).

37. The Covid Crisis Group, *Lessons from the Covid War: An Investigative Report* (New York: PublicAffairs, 2023), 102.

38. A comprehensive 2015 study of drug seizures at the US southwest border found that an increase in border enforcement had no impact on the street price of marijuana in the United States and was correlated with a slight *decrease* in the price of cocaine and heroin. Michelle Keck and Guadalupe Correa-Cabrera, "U.S. Drug Policy and Supply-Side Strategies: Assessing Effectiveness and Results," *Norteamérica* 10, no. 2 (2015): 47–67, https://www.sciencedirect.com/science/ article/pii/S1870355016300209. The smuggling of fentanyl, which is fueling tens of thousands of overdose deaths in the United States, occurs almost entirely through legal ports of entry. The pandemic border controls led to a huge increase in fentanyl smuggling, since the drug is smaller and easier to conceal than heroin and other drugs. David Bier, "Fentanyl Is Smuggled for U.S. Citizens by U.S. Citizens, Not Asylum Seekers," *CATO Institute*, September 14, 2022, https:// www.cato.org/blog/fentanyl-smuggled-us-citizens-us-citizens-not-asylum- seekers.

39. See Andrew Selee et al., "Laying the Foundation for Regional Cooperation: Migration Policy & Institutional Capacity in Mexico and Central America," *Migration Policy Institute*, April 2021, https://www.migrationpolicy.org/resea rch/regional-cooperation-migration-capacity-mexico-central-america; Silva Mathema and Zefitret Abera Molla, "Taking Migration Seriously: Real Solutions to Complex Challenges at the Border," *Center for American Progress*, October 26, 2022, https://www.americanprogress.org/article/taking-migration-seriou sly-real-solutions-to-complex-challenges-at-the-border/; Melanie Bennett, "The Refugee Crisis and the EU's Externalisation of Integrated Border Management to Libya and Turkey," *College of Europe*, 2018, http://aei.pitt.edu/97355/1/edp- 6-2018_bonnicibennett.pdf,

40. On Europe, see Sarah Léonard, "Border Controls as a Dimension of the European Union's Counter-Terrorism Policy: A Critical Assessment," *Intelligence and*

National Security 30, no. 2–3 (2015): 306–332, https://www.taylorfrancis.com/chapters/edit/10.4324/9781315674360-12/border-controls-dimension-european-union-counter-terrorism-policy-critical-assessment-sarah-l%C3%A9onard; on the United States, see Mark Helbling and Daniel Merierrieks, "Terrorism and Migration: An Overview," *British Journal of Political Science* 52, no. 2 (2020): 977–996, https://www.cambridge.org/core/journals/british-journal-of-political-science/article/terrorism-and-migration-an-overview/2D92D099D870D7D8E606C39E683D3E89.

41. See Edward H. Alden, *The Closing of the American Border* (New York: Harper, 2009); Thomas R. Eldridge et al., *9/11 and Terrorist Travel: Staff Report of the National Commission on Terrorist Attacks upon the United States*, August 21, 2004, https://govinfo.library.unt.edu/911/staff_statements/911_TerrTrav_Monograph.pdf; and Penn State Law Immigrants' Rights Clinic and Rights Working Group, "The NSEERS Effect: A Decade of Racial Profiling, Fear, and Secrecy," Pennsylvania State University, June 4, 2012, https://elibrary.law.psu.edu/irc_pubs/11/.

42. See Catherine Z. Worsnop, "Domestic Politics and the WHO's International Health Regulations: Explaining the Use of Trade and Travel Barriers during Disease Outbreaks," *Review of International Organizations* 12 (2017): 365–395, luhttps://link.springer.com/article/10.1007/s11558-016-9260-1 12.

43. David Martin, "Effects of International Law on Migration Policy and Practice: The Uses of Hypocrisy," *International Migration Review* 23, no. 3 (1989): 547–578, https://www.jstor.org/stable/2546428.

44. Élisabeth Vallet, "The World Is Witnessing a Rapid Proliferation of Border Walls," *Migration Policy Institute*, March 2, 2022, https://www.migrationpolicy.org/article/rapid-proliferation-number-border-walls.

45. Júlia Ledur, "The 'Barbed-Wire Curtain' Dividing Europe from Russia and Belarus, Visualized," *Washington Post*, March 15, 2023, https://www.washingtonpost.com/world/2023/03/15/europe-russia-belarus-fence/; and Loveday Morris, "At Center of Europe's Migrant Crisis, Tales of How Belarus Clears the Way—and Punishes 'Pawns' Sent Back," *Washington Post*, November 13, 2021, https://www.washingtonpost.com/world/2021/11/13/belarus-migrants-europe-lukashenko-poland/.

46. United Nations Treaty Collection, https://treaties.un.org/pages/ViewDetails.aspx?src=IND&mtdsg_no=IV-13&chapter=4&clang=_en.

47. "Global Compact for Safe, Orderly and Regular Migration," Global Compact For Migration, July 13, 2018, 3, https://refugeesmigrants.un.org/sites/default/files/180713_agreed_outcome_global_compact_for_migration.pdf.

48. United States Mission to the United Nations, "National Statement of the United States of America on the Adoption of the Global Compact for Safe, Orderly, and Regular Migration," December 7, 2018, https://usun.usmission.gov/national-statement-of-the-united-states-of-america-on-the-adoption-of-the-global-compact-for-safe-orderly-and-regular-migration/.

49. Ulf Laessing and Andreas Rinke, "U.N. Members Adopt Global Migration Pact Rejected by U.S. and Others," *Reuters*, December 10, 2018, https://www. reuters.com/article/us-europe-migrants-un-pact/u-n-members-adopt-global-migration-pact-rejected-by-u-s-and-others-idUSKBN1O90YS; Francesca Paris, "Brazilian President Bolsonaro Withdraws from U.N. Compact on Migration," *NPR*, January 9, 2019, https://www.npr.org/2019/01/09/683634412/brazil ian-president-bolsonaro-withdraws-from-u-n-compact-on-migration; Kathleen Newland, "An Overheated Narrative Unanswered: How the Global Compact for Migration Became Controversial," *Migration Policy Institute*, December 2018, https://www.migrationpolicy.org/news/overheated-narrative-unanswe red-how-global-compact-became-controversial.

50. U.S. Department of State, "Revised National Statement of the United States of America on the Adoption of the Global Compact for Safe, Orderly and Regular Migration," December 17, 2021, https://www.state.gov/wp-content/ uploads/2021/12/GCM.pdf; and Cedê Silva, "Lula Brings Brazil Back to Global Migration Pact," *The Brazilian Report*, January 8, 2023, https://brazilian.rep ort/liveblog/2023/01/08/lula-back-migration-pact/.

51. David Fidler, "The Case against a Pandemic Treaty," *Think Global Health*, November 26, 2021, https://www.thinkglobalhealth.org/article/case-against-pandemic-treaty.

52. Dan Diamond, "'Untrustworthy and Ineffective': Panel Blasts Governments' Covid Response," *Washington Post*, September 14, 2022, https://www.washing tonpost.com/health/2022/09/14/lancet-covid-commission-report-who/.

53. "Zero Draft of the WHO CA+ for the Consideration of the Intergovernmental Negotiating Body at Its Fourth Meeting," World Health Organization, February 1, 2023, 1, https://apps.who.int/gb/inb/pdf_files/inb4/A_INB4_3-en.pdf.

54. Chappell Lawson, "The Trusted and the Targeted: Segmenting Flows by Risk," in *Beyond 9/11: Homeland Security for the Twenty-First Century*, ed. Chappell Lawson, Alan Bersin, and Juliette Kayyem (Cambridge, MA: MIT Press, 2020), 101–120.

55. "The U.S.-Canadian Border: Recovery from COVID-19," Wilson Center, October 29, 2021, https://www.wilsoncenter.org/event/us-canadian-border-recovery-covid-19.

56. White House Briefing Room, November 29, 2022, https://www.whitehouse. gov/briefing-room/statements-releases/2022/11/29/fact-sheet-biden-harris-administration-announces-expansion-of-global-health-security-partnerships-and-releases-annual-progress-report/.

57. "Commission's Report on EU Digital COVID Certificate Highlights Tangible Benefits of the Document," Schengen Visa, December 22, 2022, https://www. schengenvisainfo.com/news/commissions-report-on-eu-digital-covid-certificate-highlights-tangible-benefits-of-the-document/.

58. Lawrence Huang, "Digital Health Credentials and Covid-19: Can Vaccine and Testing Requirements Restart Global Mobility?" *Migration Policy Institute*,

April 2022, https://www.migrationpolicy.org/sites/default/files/publications/mpi-digital-health-credentials_final.pdf.

59. "EU Digital COVID Certificate," European Commission, https://commission.europa.eu/strategy-and-policy/coronavirus-response/safe-covid-19-vaccines-europeans/eu-digital-covid-certificate_en.

60. "What Is the UK Covid-19 Inquiry?" UK Covid-19 Inquiry, https://covid19.public-inquiry.uk; and "Welcome to the NZ Royal Commission COVID-19 Lessons Learned | Te Tira Ārai Urutā," Royal Commission, https://www.covid19lessons.royalcommission.nz.

61. "COVID-19 Civic Freedom Tracker," International Center for Not-For-Profit Law, https://www.icnl.org/covid19tracker/.

62. "Emergency Measures and COVID-19: Guidance," United Nations Human Rights Office of the High Commissioner, 2020, https://www.ohchr.org/sites/default/files/Documents/Events/EmergencyMeasures_COVID19.pdf.

63. Tom Ginsburg and Mila Versteeg, "The Bound Executive: Emergency Powers during the Pandemic," *Virginia Public Law and Legal Theory Research Paper no. 2020-52* (2020), https://papers.ssrn.com/sol3/papers.cfm?abstract_id=3608974.

64. "Can the President Close the Border? Relevant Laws and Considerations," Congressional Research Service, April 12, 2019, https://crsreports.congress.gov/product/pdf/LSB/LSB10283.

65. Elizabeth Goitein, "Emergency Powers, Real and Imagined: How President Trump Used and Failed to Use Presidential Authority in the COVID-19 Crisis," *Journal of National Security Law & Policy* 11, no. 27 (2020), https://jnslp.com/wp-content/uploads/2020/12/Emergency-Powers-Real-and-Imagined_2.pdf.

66. Goitein, "Emergency Powers, Real and Imagined."

67. Dean Knight, "New Zealand: Legal Response to Covid-19," *The Oxford Compendium of National Legal Responses to Covid-19* (2021), https://oxcon.ouplaw.com/display/10.1093/law-occ19/law-occ19-e4.

68. See Shaw Drake and Katie Hoeppner, "Four Things to Know about the Supreme Court's Ruling in Egbert v. Boule," ACLU, June 27, 2022, https://www.aclu.org/news/civil-liberties/four-things-the-supreme-court-ruling-egbert-v-boule-ice.

69. Peter Baker, "Trump Declares a National Emergency, and Provokes a Constitutional Clash," *New York Times*, February 15, 2019, https://www.nytimes.com/2019/02/15/us/politics/national-emergency-trump.html.

70. David Welna, "Yes, the President Can Declare a 'National Emergency' to Build a Wall," *NPR*, January 9, 2019, https://www.npr.org/2019/01/09/683501440/congress-aims-to-control-presidents-emergency-powers.

71. Ginsburg and Versteeg, "The Bound Executive."

72. "France, Council of State, 9 April 2021, No. 450884," Covid-19 Litigation, https://www.covid19litigation.org/case-index/france-council-state-no-450884-2021-04-09.

73. "Israel, The Supreme Court Sitting as High Court of Justice, 17 March 2021, HCJ 1107/21 O. S. v. Prime Minister, Covid-19 Litigation," https://www. covid19litigation.org/case-index/israel-supreme-court-sitting-high-court-justice-hcj-110721-0-s-v-prime-minister-2021-03.

74. Kahn, *Mrs. Shipley's Ghost*.

75. Ochoa, "Court Evaluation of COVID-19 State Emergency Orders."

76. Arizona, et al. v. Alejandro Mayorkas, Secretary of Homeland Security, et al., 598 U.S. 1 (2023), https://www.supremecourt.gov/opinions/22pdf/22-592_5 hd5.pdf.

77. Vincent Chetail, "Crisis without Borders: What Does International Law Say about Border Closure in the Context of Covid-19?" *Frontiers in Political Science* 2 (2020), https://www.frontiersin.org/articles/10.3389/fpos.2020.606307/full.

78. Cf. David Kriebel et al., "The Precautionary Principle in Environmental Science," *Environmental Health Perspectives* 109, no. 9 (2001): 871–876, https://www. ncbi.nlm.nih.gov/pmc/articles/PMC1240435/.

79. "Risk Management Will Allow Borders to Re-open," International Air Transport Association, October 5, 2021, https://www.iata.org/en/pressroom/pressroom-archive/2021-releases/2021-10-04-02/.

80. David Carr et al., "Evaluating Canada's Pandemic Border and Travel Policies: Lessons Learned," Tourism Industry Association of Canada, https://www. newswire.ca/news-releases/infectious-disease-and-medical-experts-declare-federal-government-travel-restrictions-ineffective-at-protecting-canadians-from-covid-19-spread-813481354.html.

81. Alden, *The Closing of the American Border*.

82. Alan D. Bersin, "Lines and Flows: The Beginning and End of Borders," *Brooklyn Journal of International Law* 37, no. 2 (2012): 389–406, at 401.

83. Christopher Wilson, "The Lessons of Post-9/11 Border Management," *Wilson Center*, November 18, 2015, https://www.wilsoncenter.org/article/the-lessons-post-911-border-management.

84. Kelley Lee, Julianne Piper, and Jennifer Fang, "Using Risk Analysis to Shape Border Management: A Review of Approaches during the COVID-19 Pandemic," *Migration Policy Institute*, January 2023, https://www.migratio npolicy.org/sites/default/files/publications/mpi-covid-travel-risk-analysis_fi nal.pdf.

85. Lee et al., "Using Risk Analysis to Shape Border Management," 17.

86. Henry H. Willis et al., "Estimating Terrorism Risk," *Rand Center for Terrorism Risk Management Policy*, 2005, https://www.rand.org/content/dam/rand/ pubs/monographs/2005/RAND_MG388.pdf.

87. "Multilayer Risk Management for COVID-19: A Risk-Based Approach to Public Health Measures in International Travel," OECD, 2022, https:// www.oecd.org/health/safe-international-travel/Multilayer-risk-managem ent-for-COVID-19.pdf.

88. Sergio Carrera and Ngo Chun Luk, "Love Thy Neighbour?" *CEPS*, April 3, 2020, https://www.ceps.eu/ceps-publications/love-thy-neighbour/.

89. Julianne Piper, Benoît Gomis, and Kelley Lee, "'Guided by Science and Evidence'? The Politics of Border Management in Canada's Response to the COVID-19 Pandemic," *Frontiers in Political Science* 4 (2022), https://www.fron tiersin.org/articles/10.3389/fpos.2022.834223/full.

90. Steven Hoffman, Isaac Weldon, and Roojin Habibi, "A Virus Unites the World While National Border Closures Divide It: Epidemiologic, Legal, and Political Analysis on Border Closures during COVID-19," *International Journal* 77, no. 2 (2022): 188–215, https://doi.org/10.1177/00207020221135323.

91. Covid Crisis Group, *Lessons from the Covid War*, 79.

92. Lee et al., "Using Risk Analysis to Shape Border Management," 17.

93. Alexander Murphy, "Taking Territory Seriously in a Fluid, Topologically Varied World: Reflections in the Wake of the Populist Turn and the COVID-19 Pandemic," *Geografiska Annaler: Series B, Human Geography* 104, no. 1 (2022): 27–42.

94. Emil Wannheden (formerly with Sweden's Ministry of Foreign Affairs), in discussion with the author, September 8, 2022.

95. David Poon, "A Thank You from Our Founder," *Faces of Advocacy*, https://www.facesofadvocacy.com/.

96. Birte Wassenberg, "INTRODUCTION—Frontiers in Motion (Frontem): Comparative Perspectives on European Borders, Cross-Border Cooperation, and Integration," *Borders in Globalization Review* 4, no. 2 (2023): 8–13, https://doi.org/10.18357/bigr42202321507; and Jean Peyrony et al., "Analysis of the Impact of Border-Related Measures Taken by Member States in the Fight against COVID-19," 2022, https://www.researchgate.net/publication/364637975_Analysis_of_the_impact_of_border-related_measures_taken_by_Member_States_in_the_fight_against_COVID-19_Update_and_follow-up_Written_by.

97. Jean Peyrony et al., "Analysis of the Impact of Border-Related Measures Taken by Member States in the Fight against COVID-19," 5.

98. "Our Story," Future Borders Coalition, https://www.futureborderscoalit ion.org/.

99. Rafael Fernández de Castro, Paul Ganster, and Carlos González Gutiérrez, eds., "CaliBaja: Emerging Stronger after COVID-19," University of California San Diego, 2021, p.9, https://usmex.ucsd.edu/research/usmex_calibaja_after-covid-19_report-2020-21_en.pdf

100. Fernández de Castro et al., "CaliBaja," 3.

101. Covid Crisis Group, *Lessons from the Covid War*, 2–3.

102. Puente News Collective, March 30, 2022, "Missed Opportunity: Comprehensive North American Plan to Battle Pandemics Largely Ignored," https://elpasomatt ers.org/2022/03/30/missed-opportunity-comprehensive-north-american-plan-to-battle-pandemics-largely-ignored/.

EPILOGUE

1. "Proclamation on Suspension of Entry of Immigrants and Nonimmigrants of Persons Who Pose a Risk of Transmitting 2019 Novel Coronavirus," Trump White House, January 31, 2020, https://trumpwhitehouse.archives.gov/presi dential-actions/proclamation-suspension-entry-immigrants-nonimmigrants-persons-pose-risk-transmitting-2019-novel-coronavirus/.
2. "COVID-Related Restrictions on Entry into the United States under Title 42: Litigation and Legal Considerations," Congressional Research Service, updated March 13, 2023, https://crsreports.congress.gov/product/pdf/LSB/LSB10874#.
3. "Notice of Order under Sections 362 and 365 of the Public Health Service Act Suspending Introduction of Certain Persons from Countries Where a Communicable Disease Exists," Centers for Disease Control and Prevention, 2020, https://www.govinfo.gov/content/pkg/FR-2020-03-26/pdf/2020-06327.pdf.
4. "Preparing for and Preventing the Next Public Health Emergency: Lessons Learned from the Coronavirus Crisis," US Select Subcommittee on the Coronavirus Crisis, 2022, https://coronavirus-democrats-oversight.house.gov/sites/democrats.coronavirus.house.gov/files/2022.12.09%20Preparing%20 for%20and%20Preventing%20the%20Next%20Public%20Health%20Emerge ncy.pdf.
5. James Bandler et al., "Inside the Fall of the CDC," *ProPublica*, October 15, 2020, https://www.propublica.org/article/inside-the-fall-of-the-cdc.
6. Arizona, et al., v. Alejandro Mayorkas, Secretary of Homeland Security, et al., 22-592 (2022), https://www.supremecourt.gov/DocketPDF/22/22-592/254410/20230209144505687_No.%2022-592_AmiciFormerCDCOfficials.pdf.
7. "Preparing For and Preventing the Next Public Health Emergency."
8. Authors' interview with Martin Cetron (former director of Global Migration and Quarantine at the CDC), July 20, 2023.
9. Jason Dearen and Garance Burke, "Pence Ordered Borders Closed after CDC Experts Refused," *Associated Press*, October 3, 2020, https://apnews.com/arti cle/virus-outbreak-pandemics-public-health-new-york-health-4efoc6c526381 5a26f8aa17f6ea490ae.
10. Michelle Weinberg et al., "The U.S.-Mexico Border Infectious Disease Surveillance Project: Establishing Binational Border Surveillance," *EID Journal* 9, no. 1 (2003), https://wwwnc.cdc.gov/eid/article/9/1/02-0047_article.
11. "Cetron, Martin (Interview 1)," *CDC Museum Digital Exhibits*, January 10, 2018, http://cdcmuseum.org/items/show/629.
12. Eric Lipton and Jennifer Steinhauer, "The Untold Story of the Birth of Social Distancing," *New York Times*, April 22, 2020, https://www.nytimes.com/2020/04/22/us/politics/social-distancing-coronavirus.html.
13. Geoff Manaugh and Nicola Twilley, *Until Proven Safe: The History and Future of Quarantine* (New York, Farrar, Straus & Giroux, 2021), 142–143.

14. Edward H. Alden, *The Closing of the American Border* (New York: Harper, 2009), 117–118.

15. Lisa Trei, "Preparation Is Key to Avoiding 'Worst-Case Outcome,' Chertoff Says," *Stanford University Center for International Security and Cooperation*, April 16, 2008, https://cisac.fsi.stanford.edu/news/preparation_is_key_to_avoiding_worstcase_outcome_chertoff_says_20080416.

16. "President Outlines Pandemic Influenza Preparations and Response," President George W. Bush White House, November 1, 2005, https://georgewbush-whitehouse.archives.gov/news/releases/2005/11/20051101-1.html.

17. Bradley Dickerson (biodefense advisor at DHS from 2007 to 2018), in discussion with the authors, June 20, 2023.

18. Rebecca Kilberg, "Building Borders around Ebola," *Migration Policy Institute*, https://www.migrationpolicy.org/article/building-borders-around-ebola.

19. "Factors That Contributed to Undetected Spread of the Ebola Virus and Impeded Rapid Containment," World Health Organization, 2015, https://www.who.int/news-room/spotlight/one-year-into-the-ebola-epidemic/factors-that-contributed-to-undetected-spread-of-the-ebola-virus-and-impeded-rapid-containment.

20. "2014–2016 Ebola Outbreak in West Africa," Centers for Disease Control and Prevention, https://www.cdc.gov/vhf/ebola/history/2014-2016-outbreak/index.html.

21. "Cetron, Martin (Interview 2)," *CDC Museum Digital Exhibits*, April 30, 2018, http://cdcmuseum.org/items/show/630.

22. "Nigeria 'on Red Alert' over Ebola death in Lagos," *BBC*, July 26, 2014, https://www.bbc.com/news/world-africa-28498665; "Key Events in the WHO Response to the Ebola Outbreak," World Health Organization, https://www.who.int/news-room/spotlight/one-year-into-the-ebola-epidemic/key-events-in-the-who-response-to-the-ebola-outbreak.

23. Nicholas Ibekwe, "Ebola: Why Patrick Sawyer Travelled to Nigeria—Wife," *Premium Times*, August 13, 2014, https://www.premiumtimesng.com/news/166660-ebola-why-patrick-sawyer-travelled-to-nigeria-wife.html.

24. Authors' interview with Luciana Borio (former director for Medical and Biodefense Preparedness, National Security Council), July 31, 2023.

25. "Cetron, Martin (Interview 2)."

26. Manaugh and Twilley, *Until Proven Safe*, 119.

27. Dan Whitcomb, "Americans Say Avoiding International Air Travel over Ebola Outbreak: Reuters/Ipsos Poll," *Reuters*, October 16, 2014, https://www.reuters.com/article/us-health-ebola-poll/americans-say-avoiding-international-air-travel-over-ebola-outbreak-reuters-ipsos-poll-idUSKCN0I51Q920141016.

28. Manaugh and Twilley, *Until Proven Safe*, 119.

29. Gabriel Debenedetti, "Americans Back Travel Ban from Ebola Outbreak Countries: Reuters/Ipsos Poll," *Reuters*, October 21, 2014, https://www.reuters.com/article/health-ebola-travel-idINL2N0SG23O20141021.

30. Jen Christensen and Debra Goldschmidt, "'Out of Control': How the World Reacted as Ebola Spread," *CNN*, https://www.cnn.com/interactive/2014/11/health/ebola-outbreak-timeline; "With Spread of Ebola Outpacing Response, Security Council Adopts Resolution 2177 (2014) Urging immediate Action, End to Isolation of Affected States," United Nations, September 18, 2014, https://press.un.org/en/2014/sc11566.doc.htm; and Wendy Rhymer and Rick Speare, "Countries' Response to WHO's Travel Recommendations during the 2013–2016 Ebola Outbreak," *Bulletin World Health Organization* 95, no. 1 (2017): 10–17, https://www.ncbi.nlm.nih.gov/pmc/articles/PMC5180350/.

31. Whitney Shefte and Jorge Ribas, "Part 2," *Washington Post*, October 27, 2020, https://www.washingtonpost.com/graphics/2020/national/administrations-pandemic-documentary/.

32. "Cetron, Martin (Interview 2)."

33. Authors' interview with Martin Cetron, June 29, 2023.

34. "Public Health Screening to Begin at 3 U.S. Airports for 2019 Novel Coronavirus ('2019-nCoV')," Centers for Disease Control and Protection, 2020, https://archive.cdc.gov/www_cdc_gov/media/releases/2020/p0117-coronavirus-screening.html.

35. Nicole Wetsman, "CDC Expands Health Screenings for Coronavirus to 20 Airports," *The Verge*, January 28, 2020, https://www.theverge.com/2020/1/28/21112053/coronavirus-airports-health-screenings-china.

36. Authors' interview with Martin Cetron, July 20, 2023.

37. "CDC Issues Federal Quarantine Order to Repatriated U.S. Citizens at March Air Reserve Base," Centers for Disease Control and Prevention, 2020, https://archive.cdc.gov/www_cdc_gov/media/releases/2020/s0131-federal-quarantine-march-air-reserve-base.html.

38. Berkeley Lovelace Jr. and Will Feuer, "CDC Issues Mandatory Quarantine for First Time in More than 50 Years to Wuhan Passengers in California," *CNBC*, January 31, 2020, https://www.cnbc.com/2020/01/31/cdc-quarantines-wuhan-passengers-in-california-under-federal-order.html.

39. "DHS Issues Supplemental Instructions for Inbound Flights with Individuals Who Have Been in China," US Department of Homeland Security, 2020, https://www.dhs.gov/news/2020/02/02/dhs-issues-supplemental-instructions-inbound-flights-individuals-who-have-been-china.

40. Danielle Allen et al., *Lessons from the Covid War: An Investigative Report*, The Covid Crisis Group (New York: PublicAffairs, 2023), 77–78.

41. Bandler et al., "Inside the Fall of the CDC."

42. Deb Riechmann, "Trump Disbanded NSC Pandemic Unit That Experts Had Praised," *Associated Press*, March 14, 2020, https://apnews.com/article/donald-trump-ap-top-news-virus-outbreak-barack-obama-public-health-ce014d94b64e98b7203b873e56f80e9a.

43. Allen et al., *Lessons from the Covid War*, 67.

44. Eric Lipton et al., "The CDC Waited 'Its Entire Existence for This Moment.' What Went Wrong?" *New York Times*, June 3, 2020, https://www.nytimes.com/2020/06/03/us/cdc-coronavirus.html.

45. Steve Eder et al., "430,000 People Have Traveled from China to U.S. since Coronavirus Surfaced," *New York Times*, April 4, 2020, https://www.nytimes.com/2020/04/04/us/coronavirus-china-travel-restrictions.html.

46. Jennifer Myers et al., "Identification and Monitoring of International Travelers During the Initial Phase of an Outbreak of COVID-19—California, February 3–March 17, 2020," *Morbidity and Mortality Weekly Report* 69, no. 19 (2020): 599–602, https://www.cdc.gov/mmwr/volumes/69/wr/mm6919e4.htm.

47. Authors' interview with Martin Cetron, July 20, 2023.

48. Authors' interview with Martin Cetron, July 20, 2023.

49. Yasmeen Abutaleb and Damian Paletta, *Nightmare Scenario: Inside the Trump Administration's Response to the Pandemic that Changed History* (New York: Harper, 2021), 121–126; and Deborah Birx, *Silent Invasion: The Untold Story of the Trump Administration, Covid-19, and Preventing the Next Pandemic Before It's Too Late* (New York: Harper, 2022), 110–117.

50. Anne Schuchat, "Public Health Response to the Initiation and Spread of Pandemic COVID-19 in the United States, February 24–April 21, 2020," *Morbidity and Mortality Weekly Report* 69, no. 18 (2020): 551–556, https://www.cdc.gov/mmwr/volumes/69/wr/mm6918e2.htm.

51. Carl Zimmer, "Most New York Coronavirus Cases Came from Europe, Genomes Show," *New York Times*, April 8, 2020, https://stacks.cdc.gov/view/cdc/93351.

52. "Federal Government Adjusts COVID-19 Entry Strategy for International Air Passengers," Centers for Disease Control and Prevention, 2020, https://stacks.cdc.gov/view/cdc/93351.

53. Authors' interview with Martin Cetron, July 20, 2023.

54. "Executive Order on Promoting COVID-19 Safety in Domestic and International Travel," White House, January 21, 2021, https://www.whitehouse.gov/briefing-room/presidential-actions/2021/01/21/executive-order-promoting-covid-19-safety-in-domestic-and-international-travel/.

55. Stephen Bart et al., "Effect of Predeparture Testing on Postarrival SARS-CoV-2-Positive Test Results among International Travelers—CDC Traveler-Based Genomic Surveillance Program, Four U.S. Airports, March–September 2022," *Morbidity and Mortality Weekly Report* 72, no. 8 (2023): 206–209, https://www.cdc.gov/mmwr/volumes/72/wr/pdfs/mm7208a2-h.pdf.

56. Authors' interview with Martin Cetron, July 20, 2023.

57. "Cetron, Martin (Interview 2)."

58. "CDC launches Traveler-based SARS-CoV2-2 Genomic Surveillance Program," Centers for Disease Control and Prevention, 2024, https://www.cdc.gov/advanced-molecular-detection/php/success-stories/airport-genomic-surveillance.html.

59. Authors' interview with Martin Cetron, July 20, 2023.

60. Alice Park, "Want to Predict the Next Big COVID-19 Variant to Hit the U.S.? Look to Airports," *Time*, June 24, 2023, https://time.com/6286825/covid-19-variant-tracking-airports-cdc/; "Pilot Study Outline for Targeted Genomic Surveillance of SARS-CoV-2 in Travellers in Response to a Worsening or Unknown Epidemiological Situation in a Third Country," European Centre for Disease Prevention and Control, January 13, 2023, https://www.ecdc.europa.eu/en/publications-data/covid-19-pilot-study-targeted-genomic-surveillance-sars-cov-2-travellers.

61. Robert Morfino et al., "Notes from the Field: Aircraft Wastewater Surveillance for Early Detection of SARS-CoV-2 Variants—John F. Kennedy International Airport, New York City, August–September 2022," *Morbidity and Mortality Weekly Report* 72, no. 8 (2023): 210–211, https://www.cdc.gov/mmwr/volumes/72/wr/mm7208a3.htm; and Jacqueline Howard and Jeremy Diamond, "SFO Becomes First US Airport to Formally Launch Airplane Wastewater Testing for Emerging Covid-19 Variants," *CNN*, May 9, 2023, https://www.cnn.com/2023/05/09/health/sfo-covid-wastewater/index.html.

62. Park, "Predict the Next Big Covid-19 Variant."

63. Lisa Mascaro et al., "Biden and McCarthy Reach a Final Deal to Avoid US Default and Now Must Sell It to Congress," *Associated Press*, May 28, 2023, https://apnews.com/article/debt-limit-deal-biden-mccarthy-default-01657c829be119850cd65ab9ffb0626a.

64. "CDC Traveler-based Genomic Surveillance Program to Expand to Two New US International Airports in Miami and Chicago," March 12, 2024, https://www.prnewswire.com/news-releases/cdc-traveler-based-genomic-surveillance-program-to-expand-to-two-new-us-international-airports-in-miami-and-chicago-302085869.html.

65. Quoted from a panel discussion at Ginkgo Bioworks 2024 Ferment Conference, Boston, April 11, 2024, https://www.youtube.com/watch?v=wKFmFM7Zdsw.

66. Sylvia Mathews Burwell et al., "Improving Pandemic Preparedness: Lessons from COVID-19," Council on Foreign Relations Independent Task Force Report No. 78 (2020).

67. Authors' interview with Martin Cetron, July 20, 2023.

68. Marco Marani et al., "Intensity and Frequency of Extreme Novel Epidemics," *Proceedings of the National Academy of Sciences* 18, no. 35 (August 23, 2021), https://www.pnas.org/doi/10.1073/pnas.2105482118.

69. Nita K. Madhav et al., "Estimated Future Mortality from Pathogens of Epidemic and Pandemic Potential," *Center for Global Development Working Paper*, November 13, 2023, https://www.cgdev.org/publication/estimated-future-mortality-pathogens-epidemic-and-pandemic-potential.

70. Yanzhong Huang and Rebecca Katz, "Negotiating Global Health Security: Priorities for U.S. and Global Governance of Disease," *Council on Foreign*

Relations Special Report No. 97, September 2023, https://www.cfr.org/report/negotiating-global-health-security.

71. Michael Peel, "The Next Pandemic Is Coming. Will We Be Ready?" *Financial Times*, April 3, 2024, https://www.ft.com/content/d40a3add-8151-4910-aabd-3f1dafabcc35.

72. Quoted from panel discussion, 2024 Ginkgo Bioworks Ferment Conference.

73. Authors' interview with Martin Cetron, July 20, 2023.

Index

For the benefit of digital users, indexed terms that span two pages (e.g., 52–53) may, on occasion, appear on only one of those pages.